KU-876-297

BRAD NEWSHAM has lived in ten of the United States, visited all fifty, and circled the globe four times. He lives in California with his family, and since 1985 has been a San Francisco taxi driver. His first book, *All the Right Places*, was also a travel memoir.

TAKE ME WITH YOU

'He asks everyone he meets – from a saddhu by the Ganges to a 110-year-old Tanzanian on the flank of Kilamanjaro – what the best and worst times in their lives have been. While Newsham is skilled in drawing each exotic city and village, it is these meetings with strangers-quickly-turned-friends that make *Take Me With You* such an engrossing read ... We have been blessed with a terrific travel memoir which takes us to some fascinating places and shatters plenty of assumptions along the way' *amazon.com*
(Best Ten Travel Books of the Year)

'For everyone who believes that travel is mostly about kindness and an open heart, Newsham is an ideal guide. He travels armed only with curiosity and a friendly trust, and brings back treasures that every wanderer might envy. His journey, at heart, is into humanity'
Pico Iyer, author of *Video Night in Kathmandu*

'Brilliant, sharp, unswerving, humourous travel writing ... a wonderful book'
Herbert Gold, author of *Best Nightmare on Earth*

'What gives this offbeat travelogue its interest is the spirit of innocent generosity that inspires it, and that generally infuses Newsham's experiences of people and places'
Boston Globe

'No travel books can be as satisfying as the journey itself, but this one comes close. *Take Me with You* brims with the very details – wondrous, startling, beautiful, strange – that makes travel so stimulating, so perplexing, and so addictive'
Jamie Zeppa, author of *Beyond the Sky and Earth: A Journey into Bhutan*

www.booksattransworld.co.uk

'In this era of conquests and ego-trips, it's refreshing and unusual to read a travel adventure that begins with a generous impulse. We learn a lot about the world in this book, and we learn a lot about Newsham — and both of them are well worth knowing'
Jeff Greenwald, author of *The Size of the World*

'In surefooted language, rhythm and insight, he tugs at our traveller's heartstrings and greatest impulse. He brings us to places within and without, mirroring perfectly the questions that mesmerize and fascinate us the most'
Steve Zikman, author of *The Power of Travel*

TAKE ME WITH YOU

A Round-the-World

Journey to Invite a Stranger Home

Brad Newsham

BANTAM BOOKS

LONDON · NEW YORK · TORONTO · SYDNEY · AUCKLAND

TAKE ME WITH YOU
A Bantam Book : 0 553 81448 6

First publication in Great Britain

First published in 2000 by Traveler's Tales and in 2002 by Ballantine

PRINTING HISTORY
Bantam edition published 2002

1 3 5 7 9 10 8 6 4 2

Copyright © Brad Newsham 2000
Map copyright Keith Granger

The right of Brad Newsham to be identified as the author of
this work has been asserted in accordance with sections 77 and
78 of the Copyright Designs and Patents Act 1988.

Condition of Sale
This book is sold subject to the condition that it shall not,
by way of trade or otherwise, be lent, re-sold, hired out or otherwise circulated
in any form of binding or cover other than that in which it is published and without
a similar condition including this condition being imposed on the
subsequent purchaser.

Set in Venetian

Bantam Books are published by Transworld Publishers,
61–63 Uxbridge Road, London W5 5SA,
a division of The Random House Group Ltd,
in Australia by Random House Australia (Pty) Ltd,
20 Alfred Street, Milsons Point, Sydney, NSW 2061, Australia,
in New Zealand by Random House New Zealand Ltd,
18 Poland Road, Glenfield, Auckland 10, New Zealand
and in South Africa by Random House (Pty) Ltd,
Endulini, 5a Jubilee Road, Parktown 2193, South Africa.

Printed and bound in Great Britain by
Cox & Wyman Ltd, Reading, Berkshire.

To Rhonda, my wife,
and Sarah, our treasure

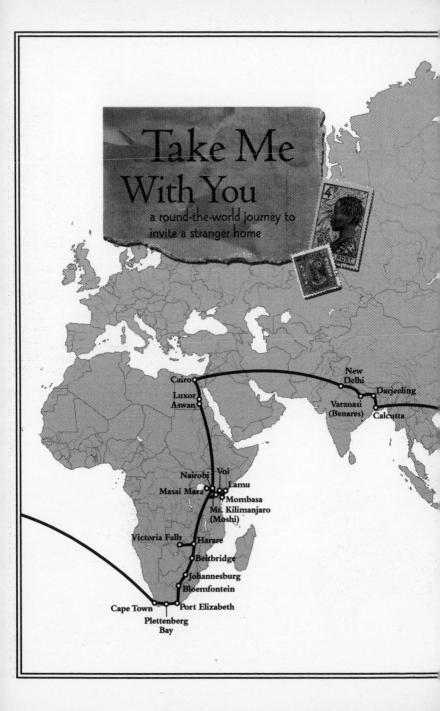

Take Me With You

a round-the-world journey to
invite a stranger home

Cairo
Luxor
Aswan

New
Delhi
Darjeeling
Varanasi
(Benares)
Calcutta

Nairobi Voi
Masai Mara Lamu
Mombasa
Mt. Kilimanjaro
(Moshi)

Victoria Falls Harare
Beitbridge
Johannesburg
Bloemfontein
Cape Town Port Elizabeth
Plettenberg
Bay

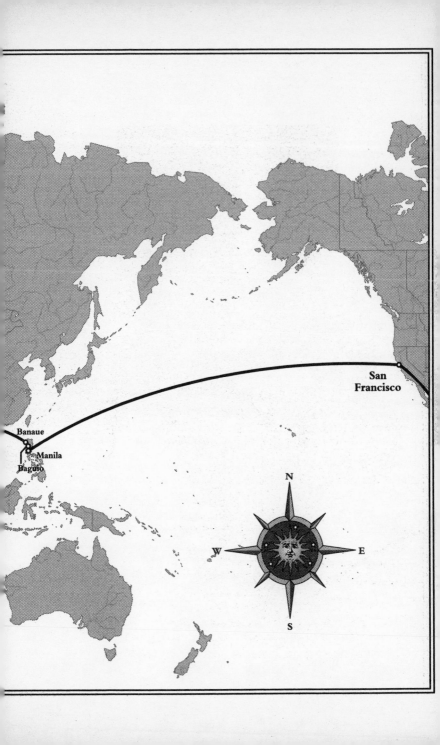

Prologue

The old hunger for voyages fed at his heart.... To go
alone...into strange cities; to meet strange people and to
pass again before they could know him; to wander, like his
own legend, across the earth——it seemed to him there could
be no better thing than that.

——THOMAS WOLFE, *Look Homeward Angel*

In May 1974, toward the end of my first trip away from North America, I traveled into Afghanistan's lofty Hindu Kush mountains—to the valley of Bamian. Bamian had once been a great center of Buddhism, but in the thirteenth century Genghis Khan's army swept through and slaughtered every living thing in the valley. Even the mice, it is said. Now Bamian was home to a small community of farmers, fervent Moslems all, tending crops beneath the image of a 175-foot-tall Buddha carved into the valley's sheer wall fifteen hundred years earlier.

On my second day in Bamian a pair of Australians drove into town and began asking around for directions to the lakes at Band-e-Amir, farther up in the mountains. Their Land Rover was packed solid with gear, but after seeing my wistful look one of them cocked an eyebrow at me and drawled, "You can ride up on the roof."

"What'll it cost me?" I'd been nursing my last $250 since Athens, five weeks earlier.

"If we get stuck, you push."

We spent the afternoon bouncing up a dry riverbed that wound

9

through a narrow canyon. I clung to the roof rack and stared up at the rock walls, at the thin stripe of cobalt sky visible beyond the canyon's rim, and at the many circling hawks. In late afternoon we popped out of the canyon onto a great broad plain surrounded by jagged, white-tipped mountains. A stubble of fresh spring grass was turning the plain from brown to green. I thought: *On the roof of a Land Rover, on the roof of the world.* I was twenty-two years old.

Soon we spotted a series of royal blue lakes in the distance, and then came upon a herder trying to calm his spooked flock. Ours was the first motor he'd heard in...well, he wasn't sure just how long.

We slept curled up on the floor of the herder's hut that cold night, and the next morning stood outside it, scanning the vast and empty landscape. Both Australians had spent the night vomiting (the food? the altitude?—no one knew) and decided to head back to Kabul. While they rested and gathered their strength for the trip back down the mountains, I went for a hike up and over a series of barren, light brown hills, until I came to the edge of a sheer cliff some three hundred feet above one of the lakes.

Far below, golden sparks of sunlight exploded off the lake's blue velvet ripples. Around me, miles of flat, lifeless sand stretched in every direction. The shiny, snow-capped incisors of the Hindu Kush jutted from every point of the horizon. I sat on a boulder, engulfed in a silence so intense it seemed to vibrate, and marveled.

I had left America expecting to spend a month, maybe two months, touring European castles, museums, and bierfests. Instead, the stories told by other travelers lured me first to Morocco, then toward the Middle East, across Turkey and Iran, and, during my seventh month, into Afghanistan. I recall my younger self as a dazed longhair gazing slack-jawed day after day at monuments, ruins, beguiling countrysides, and strange new cultures. From the bazaars of Marrakesh to the mosques of Istanbul and into the Hindu Kush, I could feel history and geography transforming me, and I fell stupidly in love with travel. I met other globe-roamers, and with them shared meals, beaches, and bus seats, and climbed peaks to celebrate sunsets. At night we huddled in cafes or around campfires, swapping tales and swearing that travel was the best thing that had ever happened to us, the best thing that could ever happen to anyone.

From my perch on the boulder, it seemed that for a long time—five minutes, ten minutes, an hour?—nothing in the entire vista moved. And then, in an area of desert that had been empty the last time I scanned it, I noticed a thin black line. It was about a mile away, and from that distance looked like a shoelace laid out in a child's sandbox. I got up off my boulder, moved around for a different angle, shaded my eyes for a better look.

It took awhile, but when I finally identified the lumpy shape at the head of the line as a camel (*Ah*, I thought, *caravan*) the rest of the shapes—dogs, goats, humans—all seemed obvious. As I watched the line glide slowly across the desert and disappear into the foothills, I wondered: *What would these nomads make of my culture? What would they think of New York City? The San Diego Freeway? A Las Vegas casino? Wouldn't the Grand Canyon or a redwood grove or a Safeway store, gleaming and fully-stocked at two o'clock in the morning, amaze them the way their culture and all the other cultures I've stumbled into recently have amazed me?*

When I returned to the herder's hut, the Australians were ready to go. As we lurched back down the canyon, I became lost in thought about the seemingly capricious manner by which each of us is allotted our particular life. What formula had deposited me into a crib in an apartment in the suburbs of post–World War II Washington, D.C., and—almost inevitably—to the top of this jolting Land Rover in central Asia? With one more turn of the cosmic tumblers might I not have swapped destinies, identities, with one of the other young people I'd met on this trip? With the woman, perhaps, who served me couscous every night in the square in Marrakesh, covered completely in robes except for her fiery eyes. Or the Turkish university student, desperate to improve his English, who hid from the conductor in the second-class train car I shared with five other hippies? Or the herder, last night's hospitable herder—he'd been about my own age. What would it feel like to be living one of their lives? What would I be thinking today if I were one of them? What would they be thinking about if they were me?

Halfway down the canyon we stopped to let one of the Australians retch. I used the break to jot down some of these thoughts, plus what at the time seemed like a throwaway line. But back then I had only an immature sense of the staying power of ideas, had no true inkling that this one would rattle around in my psyche until years later, when it would pop to the surface and change not only my life but also the life of an as-yet-unmet stranger. I wrote: *Someday, when I am rich, I am going to invite someone from my travels to visit me in America.*

TAKE ME WITH YOU

1

One Hundred Days

When it is a question of money, everyone is of the same religion.
— VOLTAIRE

The cab driver glanced back at me. "You..." he said. "America?"

It was a Wednesday evening in early November—the pleasant, dry season in the Philippines—and a breeze with the feel of warm coconut milk was pouring through my open window. I'd studied a map on the plane: the blackness beyond the row of palm trees to our left would be Manila Bay. To our right a congregation of burlap lean-tos overflowed onto the sidewalk, and, between two of them, a woman was cooking something over a smoky fire.

"Yes," I said. "America. San Francisco."

"Ah, Cah-lee-for-nee-ah!" said the driver. "California best."

He slowed to acknowledge a red traffic signal, then, reassured, sailed through it. Above the meter were a license and photo identifying the taxi as Golden Cab Number Two (it was painted black) and the driver as Mr. Alfredo Errabo. At the airport Mr. Errabo had agreed to take me to Manila's Ermita district where, according to my guidebook, hotel rooms cost less than $10 a night.

In the past I might have insisted on something cheaper, $5 or less, but this was the best-financed trip I'd ever had. A couple of decades had exhausted themselves since my visit to the Hindu Kush, but I had not yet become rich—by Western standards I had never even been close. But recently I had sold a book, my first, and after paying off all my debts I was left with the biggest stash of my life, $6,800. I thought: *Give up my apartment, put everything in storage, and I can afford a trip.* My editor had asked me to be back for publication in mid-February, and when I sat down with my calendar and counted its squares, I discovered a travel window of exactly 100 days. I studied maps of Africa and Asia and picked out several places I'd always been curious about—the Philippines, Egypt, Kenya, Tanzania, Zimbabwe, and South Africa—and one, India, I was eager to see again. I bought $3,000 worth of plane tickets, set aside $300 for a splurge/emergency fund, and put $1,000 into a savings account—something to come back to. This left $2,500 for expenses: 100 days at $25 a day. In the places I was headed I would be one of the wealthy.

When Mr. Errabo and I had been riding for more than ten minutes the meter read 28 pesos—a sum about equal to the cost of a medium-sized cup of coffee back home. But in San Francisco the twelve-mile trip from the airport to the Transamerica Pyramid downtown cost about $30—without a tip. I knew. Mr. Errabo and I were brothers.

"In San Francisco," I told him, "I am a taxi driver."

He turned to look at me, headlights from behind illuminating his gimme-a-break facial expression. "You," he said, "taxi *owner*?"

"No. Taxi *driver*." I raised my hands to my own imaginary steering wheel. "I drive—like you. Every day, ten hours."

Mr. Errabo snorted. "Ten hours..."

"Yes." I was no slouch. "Ten-hour shift."

"In Manila," he said, "twenty-four hours."

"No! Nobody drives twenty-four hours. When do you sleep?"

"Sleep other day. Today I drive twenty-four hours, no sleep—maybe ten minutes sometimes. Tomorrow another man drive twenty-four hours, I sleep. Next day, I drive twenty-four hours, he sleep." Mr. Errabo jerked the wheel back and forth three times to weave us through a series of beach ball-sized potholes. At the side of the road a group of four men and two women were clustered around a smoking car; the women held babies and waved frantically at us. Mr. Errabo ignored them. "In California, drive ten hours. How many dollars?"

Knowing full well he'd never believe it, I told him the truth: "Average day—$150."

Mr. Errabo looked at me again, his eyes flickering like the digital figures on a calculator. "One hundred and fifty dollars!" he said. "Hah!"

We drove in silence for a while, following the line of palms and the blackness; on our right the blazing lights of the Hyatt Regency appeared, then receded, and were followed by a string of clubs and restaurants whose names—Josephine, Burger Machine—were spelled out in orange and purple neon.

"What is a good day for a Manila taxi driver?" I asked.

Mr. Errabo sighed. "For me, 300 pesos is good day. Five hundred pesos—very good day." Enough to buy a tank of gas at home. We were not brothers, not even distant cousins.

"San Francisco taxi driver money can go Manila," he said. "Japanese taxi driver money can go Manila. Manila taxi driver money..."—he rubbed his fingers together and spat on them—"money no goot. Manila taxi driver stay in Manila."

2

Don't Worry, Be Happy

Good Lord...I don't know the solution of boredom. If I did, I'd be the one philosopher that had the cure for living. But I do know that about ten times as many people find their lives dull, and unnecessarily dull, as ever admit it; and I do believe that if we busted out and admitted it sometimes, instead of being nice and patient and loyal for sixty years, and then nice and patient and dead for the rest of eternity, why, maybe possibly, we might make life more fun.

—SINCLAIR LEWIS, *Babbit*

The next morning I was up with the soft early light, walking. Already the air was warm and muggy—short pants weather—and stepping from my six dollar hotel I caught a whiff of rotting food. Freelance garbage men sifted through the trash in the gutters to salvage empty bottles. The sidewalks were strewn with the curled shapes of unconscious people; most had thin cardboard mattresses, but many slept right on the pavement. Four little boys—five-year-olds, I guessed—slept in a heap in a doorway, arms and legs tossed over each other like ropes; they had no guardian, no mattress, no cardboard, no blankets, and only two of them wore shirts. I could hear one snoring. Two jeepneys crept past bumper to bumper—the names "Wheels of Fortune" and "California Dreamin'" painted on their sides, and the song "Don't Worry, Be Happy" cooing in perfect synchronicity from their radios.

To the traveler arriving in a new place *everything* seems significant: the golden light slanting over rooftops and gilding window panes on the opposite side of the street; the engine noises and garbage stench; the babble of early hawkers; the new pool of unknown lives. I looked around the street and took a deep breath that was strangely gratifying. I'd spent years sitting in my own little part of the globe wondering what this part looked like, and now here it was. The real world. And the real world does not present itself in easily absorbed, seven-minute intervals, broken by sixty-second commercial breaks; nor in groups of five eight-hour work-days separated by weekends. The real world marches at you head-on, in jerky bursts of color and boredom and trauma, reminding you that you are alive and small and not in control of anything at all.

My invite-someone-to-America idea had shaped and reshaped itself many times since that morning in Afghanistan. My present plan: When this trip was over I would sur- prise one of the people I had met along the way, someone who had never been out of his (or possibly her) native country, with an invitation to visit and travel around the United States with me for one month—my treat.

I was uncertain as to just how I would decide whom to invite. Maybe I would meet someone so compelling—so kind, eccentric, or just so much fun—that the choice would be obvious. But if that didn't happen, I would simply, when I got home, drop everyone's name into a hat and draw one out.

As I walked through the Ermita district toward Manila's focal point, Rizal Park, arms shot up from apparently lifeless bundles, palms out- stretched. I gave a peso to a man with no legs, and thought: *In San Francisco a few cents is an insult.*

A young woman, wearing a short skirt and swinging a tiny black purse, caught my eye and slid her tongue across her lips. Even at this hour women in high heels, black net stockings, and frilly red teddies lounged in front of twenty-four-hour bars, and stretched their smooth, peanut butter-colored limbs. Winking at me they cooed, "Hi Joe," while young men leapt up to swing open the barroom doors. "Very nice, Joe. Very nice." Through the front door of one darkened place I saw a searchlight slicing through banks of cigarette smoke to highlight a tiny woman in a white Day-Glo bikini, prancing on a bar top.

In ten minutes I reached Rizal Park, a wide swath of green fronting on Manila Bay. On December 30, 1896, Dr. Jose Rizal—a poet, a genius who spoke more than thirty languages, and the spiritual leader of the Filipino struggle against the Spanish—was executed in the park that now bears his name. Photographs show Rizal standing with his back to the poised firing squad, and a formally dressed mob of thousands—Spaniards and Filipinos alike—crowding around to watch. Today the execution ground is a sprawling green lawn, punctuated by flowerbeds and fountains and statues, open-air amphitheaters, and a roller rink. A sea wall, a promenade, and a row of palms lined the water's edge, and here, hunkered down on benches or spread out on the lawn, hundreds of Filipinos had gathered to watch the mid-morning sun heat up the bay.

I bought a *Manila Bulletin* from a small boy and found a shaded, empty bench. I had barely opened it when four men—each with a camera, a Rizal Park baseball hat, and a badge: OFFICIAL RIZAL PARK PHOTOGRAPHER—lined up in front of my bench.

"Pit-chur? Next to fountain. Only fifty pesos. Very cheap."

They stayed, pleading—"O.K., O.K. For you, forty pesos"—until I showed them my own small camera, and then they chased en masse after a French-speaking couple who had strolled by.

A front-page article described the uproar over Webster's latest dictionary having used the phrase "domestic worker" to define the word "Filipina." Filipinas and Filipinos everywhere were enraged and insulted. The mayor of Ermita had banned the book's sale. The dictionary people were holding firm.

Suddenly a small open hand imposed itself between my eyes and the newspaper. A girl—barefoot, with dirt-stained cheeks, no older than six—stood in front of me, a baby boy cradled in her arms.

"No mama," she croaked. "No papa."

I asked what had happened to them.

"No mama," she croaked. "No papa." The baby gaped at me with stunned brown eyes.

Was this her brother?

"No mama. No papa."

I gave her a peso, but she stared at it as though I'd squashed a turd into her palm. "No mama," she said. "No papa." She left after I forked over a five-peso coin, but immediately a dozen of her peers formed a bleating semicircle around me.

In American terms I was the classic financial dud—the-ne'er-do-well uncle or brother-in-law—but by these people's standards I was a millionaire. My money belt was fat with cash and traveler's checks, and a wad of pesos bulged in my shirt pocket. I passed out pesos, half-pesos, ten-centavo pieces, until all my change was gone, then retreated to a more distant bench and reopened my newspaper.

On the editorial page this caught my eye: "Deepening Poverty in The Philippines: Study confirms 60 to 80 percent of national wealth is controlled by only 2 percent of the population." The article spoke of slums, hunger, unemployment, needed reforms. The Rizal crowd—snoozing, strumming guitars, buying newspapers and bananas and small greasy pastries from barefooted vendors—were obviously from the bottom 98 percent. On this midweek morning no one was in a hurry to go anywhere, certainly not to jobs.

I closed the paper, watched the water and the boats and the lounging people. I had forgotten the Third World's clawing nature, and its rediscovery was a bit unsettling. I had left America looking to add a little magic to the life of someone, anyone, who was untraveled. Now I found myself wanting to add a few conditions: "I will consider only people who are calm." "No one who pleads with or badgers me." "Please, no pushing, no shoving." Loving the entire world was easy; personalizing it might prove tricky.

Several friends to whom I'd explained my plan had said, "Sounds like you're playing God. How do you know you won't just be wrecking some poor guy's life?"

I have what I consider to be a credible response to that line of thought: "O.K. Let's say a flying saucer lands in front of your house. Someone who looks sort of like a human being knocks on your door and says, 'If you come with us, we will fly you around the universe for one month and show you a few things you've never seen before. It'll cost you nothing and you'll be back in this exact spot a month from now. No strings.'

"Do you go," I ask my friends, "or not?"

Most people say, "Yeah, I'd go."

And I ask them: "Would you then hold whoever-it-is responsible for the way the rest of your life turned out?"

No one has ever answered anything but "No" to that question.

I was writing in my notebook when a young man sidled up and settled on the next bench, but from the glance we exchanged I knew that *my* bench was his eventual destination. I scribbled as fast as I could: "Official RP Photographer, French couple, 'No mama, no papa,' guitar music, greasy pastries, barefoot vendors..."

From the corner of one eye I saw him rise, fifteen feet away, and stand absolutely still—eyes lowered, shoulders slumping. On his feet were sandals, and on his sapling-thin frame a polo shirt and corduroys. His arms drooped to a point just below his belt buckle, where his hands were folded together. When I closed my notebook, he raised his head, unclasped his hands, took two steps toward me and stopped. "I may come?" he asked.

"Sure," I said, and patted the spot next to me. He sat, refolded his hands in his lap and stared at them.

I thought, *He'll talk when he's ready*, and looked out across the park. Directly in front of us, teenagers were playing soccer. Even in a pickup match, there's always one who stands out; this one had beautiful legs— V-shaped thighs bulging with tendons, and baseball-sized lumps of muscle high on his calves. He was the best dressed, too—blue shorts and a white shirt, black knee socks and white soccer cleats—and as he dribbled the length of the field, cut through the last two defenders, drew out the goalie and dumped a perfect pass to a wide-open team-mate; he looked like the game's inventor.

As Blue Shorts was mobbed by his friends, my benchmate breathed, "He is best."

I looked over. His eyes were focused on the game; the skin on his face, I noticed, had two tones—as though it was peeling or scarred. "Do you know him?" I asked.

"I only see him play."

"Do you see him often?"

"Every day."

"You are here every day?"

"For one month now," he said, and once more dropped his head.

In front of us the soccer game started up again. Blue Shorts set up another teammate, but this time the shot went wide. My companion laughed, and I turned to look at him. But it had not been a laugh at all. He was staring at his lap, and a tear, a liquid apostrophe, had started down his cheek.

"What's wrong?" I asked.

"I am so sad."

"Why?"

"I am scared."

I put a hand on his shoulder. He was quivering and there was no meat on him. "Scared of what?"

"Manila."

"Oh, Manila's O.K.," I said, but what I meant was: *Don't cry*.

"I don't want to think I am stranded in Manila," he snuffled, "but I *am* stranded."

"Don't you live here?" I asked.

"No."

"Where are you from?"

"Batangas Province."

"How long have you been in Manila?"

"One month."

I asked, "Did you come to Manila to work?"

"No."

"Why, then?"

"To bury my mother."

So...

His name was Ezekiel. He was twenty-six years old. His father had died several years earlier, and his mother, only forty-three, had died suddenly a month ago. Ezekiel wasn't married, but had three younger siblings. As the oldest it was his job to get his mother's body to the family plot in Manila. He'd taken a one-week leave from his job at the Sunkist pineapple farm in Batangas.

"I bury my mother, but on way back to Batangas, someone at bus station picks my wallet. There are many crazy people in Manila." His voice rose for this pronouncement, then faded. For the first time he

Ezekiel —A tragedy followed by a crime had left him stranded in Manila.

looked right at me, his eyes wet. He sobbed, "I have no bus fare. For one month now I am stranded." His chin dropped onto his quaking chest.

Ezekiel had me. Sure, I knew that just about anyone, given a month, should be able, somehow, to come up with bus fare. And, yes, I knew that I could not afford to give money to every unfortunate in Manila who might ask for it. But less than two years had passed since the day that my own father—seventy-one years old, and in apparent good health—had suddenly died. A month, I knew, was nothing. Nothing at all. If Ezekiel's story was true I would put him on the next bus home, but was it?

When his snuffling stopped, I said, "You know, Ezekiel, a lot of people in this park seem to be stranded."

He didn't look up. Fifteen seconds ticked by before he answered: "There are many people in this park who will be bluffing you. I am not bluffing. I am a Christian."

"You could be Moslem, Jew, atheist," I said. "That's not important to me." He seemed to accept this the way I meant it, but the words sounded harsh in my own ear. I asked, "How much is the bus fare?"

In a whisper: "It is very cheap. Only thirty pesos. But I am shy to tell the driver I have no money. And I don't know how to get money."

I said, "I will give you thirty pesos."

When I pulled my wad from my pocket, Ezekiel gulped and said, "Can you maybe give me five pesos more? For my food?"

I gave him fifty pesos, and he let me take his picture. He was no longer the corpse I'd first met. He asked about my trip and described his own small travels—to the islands of Cebu and Mindoro. The waterfalls at Laguna, he said, were his favorite place. I thought: *You wouldn't believe Yosemite.*

"Do you have any dreams, Ezekiel?"

"To see my family," he said. "I have not seen them in a month. They probably think I am dead like my mother. Every day I am hoping someone will help me, but in one day the most I have gotten is five pesos, and I have to eat."

"How far away is Batangas?"

"Three hours on bus." Ridiculously close, impossibly far. "If it is O.K.," he said, "I will go now."

"First, can you please write down your address in my notebook?"

"You want me to pay back?" he asked.

"No, no. It's not that at all. I just..."

And then I couldn't contain myself. I blurted out about my own father's death, about my 100-day trip, and my invitation plan. At the moment Ezekiel "got it" we were facing each other, and I saw his eyes and cheeks and mouth light up as though a fireworks factory had just exploded somewhere over my shoulder.

"America!" he said. "California!"

I thought: *Mistake.* To ignite such hope and then not deliver on it seemed cruel. Two seconds after becoming the first, Ezekiel also became the last potential visitor I would share my plan with.

We exchanged addresses and shook hands.

"It has been a terrible month," Ezekiel said. "Every night I sleep in the park. I have been asking God to help me, but I have been very afraid—I have never slept outside before." He wiped at his eyes, then managed a smile. "Last night when I prayed, God said tomorrow he would help."

He walked across the park, turning several times to look back at me, and finally disappeared among the jeepneys and buses clogging Roxas Boulevard. I studied my map and was relieved to see that he was, in fact, headed in the general direction of the bus station.

3

And Take Me With You

"I am not very rich," a young boy told me as the early morning sun-light flooded the rooftop dining room of the Hotel Eden. "I do not want big job in the U.S. Small job O.K."

— PICO IYER, *Video Night in Kathmandu*

I spent two days walking around sweltering, soot-laden Manila. Jeep-ney after smoking jeepney chugged passed me, with names like "Lady in Red" and "Vice Versa" painted on their sides, and a dozen passengers crammed in back, handkerchiefs pressed to their faces. At seven in the morning, ten in the morning, two in the afternoon, ten at night—where, I wondered, were all these people going? Did the country have a plan?

Groups of teenaged hustlers worked every stoplight, flogging captive motorists with Juicy Fruit gum, Menthol Mints, pens, umbrellas, newspapers, and tobacco. Posters on the sides of public buses read GET HIGH WITH GOD, NOT WITH DRUGS, and a banner in front of the Bible Baptist Church advised PREPARE TO MEET THY GOD. The Philippines is officially 80 percent Roman Catholic, 12 percent Moslem, and 8 percent "other," but Manila's proliferation of huge soft-drink billboards led me to think of the country as 40 percent Coke, 40 percent Pepsi, and 20 percent Sprite.

Half the populace seemed infected with a spirit of benign resigna-tion—laughing, smiling, holding hands as they walked down the street—while the other half seemed bent on escape. Marriage brokers filled magazines catering to Westerners with ads touting the loyalty, devotion, and tirelessness of the Filipina. Country girls fl̶o̶ Manila and wound up in Ermita, working the bars, cruising the stree̶ and hoping to latch onto a ticket out. I did not a get swelled head over the number of women who whistled at me or slid up alongside to coo in my ear; each day, in each block, I saw dozens of Western males— teenagers, middle-aged businessmen, even ghoulish cartoon character types—walking hand-in-hand with young women so scrubbed and beautiful that every one of them could have been a fashion model.

Manila's employment agencies hung signs and ran newspaper ads promising to secure overseas work in Middle Eastern oil fields or on ships. I found it unlikely that the hordes of men and women who spent all day on the downtown sidewalks, beseeching every passing foreigner —"Change traveler's checks, Joe? Best rate!"—could actually be earning a living. Everywhere I went I saw young men smoking, hanging out with nothing to do. Others worked newspaper and tobacco stands (the country's best-selling cigarette was named "Hope") and one-man lottery booths. "Two million, mister," promised a teenager with a clipboard full of tickets. "For one peso, win two million."

The Filipino man who ran my hotel had raised ten children. "I used to think," he told me as we argued family planning one night, "that the only way to be happy was to have as many children as possible. When I was raising my children, that is what I taught them. But my oldest daughter, she got married and moved to Australia. For years she and her husband had no children. They say, 'We are going to work and buy a house first, then have only two children.' I was sad at first, but now I see that she is very happy. So I have changed my mind. There are many ways you can be happy. But I ask you this: If there are three families— one family like mine with ten children, one family like my daughter's with two children, and one family like yours with no children—which family is having the most fun?"

In the Philippines, a family with ten kids and no money might fit right in with the rest of the neighborhood, might in fact be having a grand old time. In America, no way. Nonetheless, the man clearly had a point—more *can* be merrier—and I let the subject drop. Still, as I walked Manila's neighborhoods I became convinced that few of its residents would hesitate if offered an invitation to America. Validation of this suspicion came lumbering down the street one afternoon, in the form of a smoking jeepney sporting a bumper sticker that seemed to have been printed up with me in mind: YANKEE GO HOME, it read, AND TAKE ME WITH YOU.

On the morning of day four I caught a bus to Baguio (BAH-gee-o), the Philippines' summer capital, located high in the pine-forested mountains of northern Luzon. People raved about Baguio's beauty, cooler climate, and, in contrast to smoggy Manila, its lack of air pollution, but it was Baguio's legendary faith healers—its "psychic surgeons"—that caught my attention.

A year before my trip, a mysterious back injury had forced me to retire indefinitely from cab driving. The pain was so excruciating that I had trouble sitting for more than five or ten minutes at a time; but perhaps the most aggravating aspect was that none of my San Francisco doctors could provide a diagnosis, much less a cure. Stomach and stretching exercises were the only treatment that seemed to provide any relief, and it was many months before I started to feel capable of resuming a normal life. My doctors warned that I was nowhere near ready to start driving a cab again, but agreed that I might consider travel.

Nearly a decade earlier, in Idaho, I had met a man named Robert who said he had been cured of stomach cancer by a faith healer in Baguio.

"I was in Vietnam," Robert told me. "Agent Orange. All my stateside doctors said I had three months to live. Then a friend convinced me to go to the Philippines to see this faith healer. He cut me open with his fingertips, pulled out the cancer, and closed me back up. As soon as it was over, I knew I was a lot better. When I got home, my doctors took X-rays—all the cancer was gone. They couldn't believe it. Everyone says these guys are fakes, and maybe they are, but I don't care. I'm alive; I'm healthy. My doctors all promised I'd be dead nine months ago."

In the months before my trip I tried to locate Robert for more details, but he'd disappeared. Or maybe died.

The bus crept through heavy traffic on Manila's outskirts. Japanese cars queued up at Caltex and Petron gas stations along a commercial strip that brought to mind the industrial areas of Los Angeles. And then the traffic thinned, Manila's jumble of apartment buildings and warehouses stopped, and soon we were cruising down a two-lane road through the flat plains beyond the city. Palm trees lined miles of rice paddies and hay fields; groves of magnolias stretched into the distance. Tucked into every nook of greenery were thatch-roofed huts and tin-roofed shacks raised off the ground on poles. Skinny children darted around rows of strung laundry, playing tag, and skinny goats were everywhere, inspecting everything. From horizon to horizon people were pitch-forking hay, wrestling gas-powered tillers through flooded paddies, or raking orange piles of rice husks out to dry.

The realization that a long-awaited trip has actually begun is sometimes slow in coming, but as the bus rolled through rural Luzon, my trip finally seemed a reality. My San Francisco apartment and four years' worth of routines were gone. I was a lone Caucasian on a bus full of Japanese and Filipino tourists, headed to a place I'd never been, where no one was expecting me.

If I could create my own job, I think I would become a census double-checker, responsible for going to out-of-the-way places of my own choosing to make sure that no one has been missed. At the time, the world's population was said to be closing in on 6 billion, but looking out my window, I thought: *Did they count that guy trudging through that rice paddy with the hoe over his shoulder? That man in the mirrored sunglasses casually peeing on the right front tire of his jeep? That grandmother with smoke-colored hair, raking palm fronds into a fire? That woman sitting under the magnolia tree, picking at her throat?*

The plains ended abruptly some two hours from Manila, and we began following a riverbed into the mountains. A fifty-foot waterfall dropped into a clear pool asplash with about fifteen jumping kids. We wound through canyons where men with their trouser legs rolled up were squatting on flat stretches of riverbank, sifting the sand for gold.

Ten-foot sunflowers crowded the road near Baguio, and forests of pine trees climbed up the steep mountainsides. Realty signs sprouted among the sunflowers, advertising subdivisions and building lots, and advising OWN YOUR DREAM. The bus driver dropped everyone off at a Hyatt resort a mile from the center of town. The air here was thinner and cooler than Manila's. I put on a sweater, shouldered my pack, and headed across town, in search of affordable lodging. It was a quiet walk through tall pines oozing smells that recalled the high Sierras, Switzerland, Christmas. Through the boughs I saw the homes of Baguio's 100,000 inhabitants stretching across the ridgetops and spilling down into the valleys. The roofline was low and punctuated with church towers. Bells rang as I walked, and by the time I reached the town center I had forgotten the clamor of Manila.

In Daniel Burnham Park boys knelt under drooping willow branches, launching model boats on a still pond. Youthful soldiers patrolled the paths, the stocks of their machine guns plastered with "Thank You Lord" decals. Pregnant young women—girls actually—herded broods of toddlers. Already 39 percent of the Filipino population was under fifteen years old. How much longer, I wondered, could this country afford a religion that prohibited birth control? But I didn't dwell on the thought; the people all seemed happy, proud of themselves, and I'd come here not to get *them* fixed, but myself.

The tourist information office had already closed for the day, and the window sign said it would not be open the next day, Sunday. I ate a sandwich in a restaurant and asked my waiter if he knew any faith healers. "Sorry," he said. "I am Catholic."

After a fifteen-minute walk from the town center, at the Baguio Village Inn, I rented a cheap room with a firm mattress and a bleeding Jesus nailed high on the wall. The ivy growing around my window framed a view of hillside and pine trees and a pregnant woman hanging laundry. I unpacked and began a course of back exercises. Midway through I found myself smiling. *What am I doing in Baguio?* Since childhood I have fantasized about leaving my life—just walking out the door, taking nothing with me and telling no one, and seeing what kind of life I wound up with ten years down the road. Now, a runaway adult, I lay on my bed, eyes closed, listening to the wind in the pines, and thinking: *I know no one is following me, but if they were, my trail would have just gone ice cold.*

4

Come, My Friend. Sit.

Be careful when a naked person offers you a shirt.

—WEST AFRICAN SAYING

Irma picked me up on a Sunday night.

I was strolling back to my hotel room, spooning down a cup of chocolate chip ice cream I had just bought at the Coney Island Ice Cream stand on Session Road, when she sidled up beside me and said, "Good evening, sir." To me she looked like a typical young Filipina—short and slim, with perfect posture, black hair, and a sense of graceful delicacy. But she looked older than the teenagers with spiked hair and cargo pants who were out cruising the downtown sidewalks. I guessed her to be about thirty.

"Good evening," I said.

"I am cold," she said, the hint of a smile hidden just below the smooth skin of her cheeks, "and you are eating ice cream." Her accent was soft, her voice pleasant—and free, I told myself, of the urgency and sex tones of the women who had stalked me in Ermita.

"Ice cream's good for you." The report card of my life exposes a straight-D flirter.

"Is it better than American ice cream?"

"No," I said, "but a lot cheaper. How can you tell I'm American?"

"Your feet," she said. "They are so big."

"Are you a foot doctor?"

She laughed. "*No-oh*...I teach kindergarten."

31

As Irma and I were exchanging names, three teenaged girls going the other way on the sidewalk smiled at us and let loose with giggles as soon as they passed.

"Do you know them?" I asked.

"No," she said. "They were not looking at me-*eee*. Filipina girls—they like your blond hair."

"Oh," I said, and took another bite of my ice cream.

"Are you married?" Irma asked.

"I *was* married once," I said. "For four years. Now I'm divorced."

"Oh." She frowned. "Maybe here you find right girl. Asian women are very loyal. Maybe you try Filipina girl."

I tried laughing this off. "Gee, I was just hoping to find a faith healer here. Not a wife."

"Faith healer!" Irma laid both her small hands on my forearm. "My brother-in-law is good friends with faith healer. Segundo. That is his name—Segundo. You have some problem?"

"Yes," I told her. "A back problem. For two years now. At home I saw doctor after doctor. They all tried, but no one could help me. Do you think faith healers work?"

"Yes, I think so." She clutched my arm. "But you must believe for them. I think."

I told her I had read stories about fakes—faith healers who claimed they could take out a tumor or cancer, but faked it with chicken blood and chicken parts.

"No." Irma looked concerned. "Maybe there are some bad faith healers. But not Segundo—he is famous. If you want I can talk to my brother-in-law tonight. Maybe he can fix a meeting with Segundo. For you, maybe even discount."

At nine o'clock the next morning I was drinking a glass of mango juice in a restaurant Irma had specified. Not wanting a full stomach to interfere with whatever lay ahead, I abstained from breakfast.

Irma arrived wearing designer blue jeans, a cream-colored sweater, and short heels. Her hair was pinned back. She gave me a shy smile, shook my hand with both of hers, and ordered mango juice.

"I hope you slept well, Brad. How is your back?"

"It's O.K., thanks. Did you talk with your brother-in-law?"

"Yes, but it was late. My brother-in-law, his name is Rene, he could not be sure—maybe Segundo is away from Baguio." Irma tugged at a dangling gold earring. "But if we go to Rene's house this morning, he will know more."

My night had not been very restful—I'd awakened at four in the morning with pins-and-needles in my right leg, and something on my mind. On the floor of my room, in the moonlight, I did stretching exercises and played back my meeting with Irma. The flirtatious undercurrent from the street began to register as a rip tide. Why was she so eager to take time away from her kindergarten to help a stranger she'd known for five minutes? She hadn't seemed grasping or desperate, but what did she want? Never, at home, did women approach me on the street just because they wanted to be friends.

I cradled my mango juice with both hands and looked across the table. "Irma, I need to tell you something."

"What is that?"

"Forgive me, please, if I'm making a fool of myself. I just think it best to be clear. I'm really not looking for a wife."

A wrinkle appeared in her brow and her head tilted to the right, giving her the perplexed look, perhaps, of a chicken listening to an answering machine. "Did I say I was looking for a husband?"

"No, you didn't. But I know Western men come to the Philippines looking for women. That's not why I'm here. I just didn't want to mislead you."

She smiled. "That is Manila only." She reached across and patted my hand. "There are many men in Baguio—Westerner men, Filipinos. If I want a husband, I can have. I like talking to people. That is all."

Now I felt stupid. This trip of mine was all about meeting strangers, and here I was stiff-arming one. "I'm sorry. I talk to strangers, too—all the time. Please forgive me. I just..."

"It's O.K., Brad." She didn't seem upset. "It is good to say what is in your heart."

We took a silent cab ride through town, up one of the nearby hills, and through a glen of jungle foliage and red blossoms. Modest homes lined both sides of a stream. We stopped in front of a house the size of an American one-car garage with an overhead loft.

"This is my brother-in-law's house," Irma said.

I followed her through a gate in the chain fence. There was a banana tree in the overgrown yard, a concrete sidewalk, some strutting chickens.

A tall man, fiftyish, yawning, greeted us at the door, a sleep line slanting across his cheek. He wore black pants and shoes and a white shirt tucked sloppily into his belt.

Irma introduced us.

Rene rubbed his eyes with his left hand as he offered me his right. "So, Mister Brad, you want to see Segundo?"

"If it's not too much trouble."

"No trouble, no trouble. I like to help Irma's friends." He yawned, then apologized. "I am sorry. My job is at Baguio casino. Last night I had to work very late. I am just now waking up."

He led me to the small living room and waved me into a chair. On the wall were a Last Supper painting and a framed needlepoint: GOD BLESS THIS HOME. Jesus was bleeding to death above the door.

Irma spoke in Tagalog to Rene.

Rene asked, "Would you like a beer, Mister Brad?"

"Should I drink beer before seeing a faith healer?"

"Oh, it's fine," he said.

Irma smiled at me and disappeared through a door to the kitchen.

"So tell me," Rene said, "first time to Philippines?"

"Yes. First time."

"How long will you be here?"

"Two weeks altogether. Next week I fly from Manila to India."

"Ah....What part of America?"

"San Francisco."

That woke him up. "I have been there! America is good. Reno, Las Vegas, Lake Tahoe...Frisco is beautiful. If you have seen Frisco you will know that Baguio is a sad place. Come." He stood and led me to the window. The lot next door was vacant, covered with weeds and trash and abandoned washing machines. Six children sat on a mound of dirt, flicking grass at each other.

"They don't go to school," Rene said. "They are poor. That boy on the left, the little one, his brother has leukemia. His father was a mechanic. Last year he is working on a truck and it falls on him. He loses his leg. The company gives him three month's pay and he is finished. He cannot work. You know what leukemia treatments cost. Everything is so expensive."

"Can't Segundo help?"

Rene almost snorted. "Segundo can help with many things. Sometimes he has done great miracles, but he cannot fix everything. And he cannot make food. I can name fifty children like these whose parents cannot feed them. When they are hungry, do you know how they eat? They come to me." He looked sideways at me. "In a moment I will tell you *how* I feed them. In a moment I will tell you *who* pays for that boy's brother's leukemia treatments. But first I want to tell you about a dream I have. May I tell you my dream, Mister Brad?"

"Please."

"You see where that old machine sits? I want to clear that area, make it flat. If I can collect enough money, I will build a tennis court for the children. And a basketball court. Basketball is a big sport here, like in America. Once, Magic Johnson came to Manila and gave clinics for the boys. Now Michael Jordan is most popular. If I can build a basketball court, these boys will have something to do. Maybe someday Michael Jordan will come to Baguio."

"Do you want to build a school?"

"No. A school is too big. That is something for the government...."

Out in the street a car stopped, an old Ford Thunderbird. The horn honked and Rene waved, but I couldn't see the driver.

"No, a school is something for the government, and I am not a government. But I think maybe I can build these two courts."

"Well, I wish you luck," I said.

"*Luck*." He turned away from the window. "I work in the casino—I know all about luck. Luck will not be enough. I have a plan. Come, my friend. Sit. I will tell you."

Irma reappeared from the kitchen carrying a tray with two beers, a bowl of corn chips, and another bowl with chunks of meat afloat in dark juices. She set it on the table next to our chairs, spoke in Tagalog to

Rene, picked up her purse, then came over to me. "My brother is here to drive me to my school. Rene will help you see Segundo. Your back will be better, I hope."

She shook my hand with both of hers. I thanked her several times, and almost before I could assess the implications, she was gone.

"Now I will tell you my plan," Rene was saying.

But this was not how I'd imagined my morning—settling in for a lecture and beer with Irma's not-nearly-so-attractive brother-in-law. I heard the gate clang, a car door slam, and the engine noise fade into the distance. Why hadn't she told me she was going to leave me here? Would I see her again? Why hadn't I asked? I didn't even know her address. And what about this faith healer?

"Rene, what about Segundo?"

"Oh, yes. I tried to reach him just before you arrived. He was not in. Let me try again."

Rene went to a telephone stand in the corner and dialed a number. He spoke Tagalog sprinkled with the words "Segundo" and "Mister Brad," and he laughed several times.

"Segundo's assistant cannot find him right now," he said, settling back into his chair. "He may have gone to Manila. Wait half an hour, we call again. Then we will know."

Rene picked his beer off the table and swigged.

I crunched a corn chip.

"You must have some meat," Rene said.

"Ah, no thanks."

"But this is Baguio specialty—like your sourdough bread."

"What is it?"

"Dog. I know you don't eat dog in Frisco, but here it is a delicacy. You must try it."

He pinched a piece of meat between his thumb and forefinger, let the juice drain off, and dropped it into his mouth. Challenged, I did the same.

Rene watched me chew. "You like it?"

"Not bad," I said, and reached for my beer. "Sort of like pork." *But with a strange kick.*

"Yes," Rene said, "a little. We soak it in vodka to soften it up, and for flavor." He raised the bowl toward me. "Here, have another."

"One's enough, thanks. I had a huge breakfast."

He set the bowl back on the table. "What do you know about casinos?" he asked.

I gulped more beer. "I know a bit. I once had a very brief career as a gambler."

"Tell me," he said.

I told him about being an underground miner in Colorado at the age of twenty-three, and how I'd concluded that there must be some easier way to earn a living. I told him about reading every single book on gambling in the Boulder, Colorado, library; about mining by day, and spending nights in my cabin boning up on the laws of probability, the games of craps, roulette, and twenty-one, and the lives of legendary gamblers. And about how one morning, frenzied by a dazzling new discovery, I hitchhiked to the Denver airport with $800 and a System, and caught the first plane to Las Vegas. Four days later I was back in Colorado, $500 poorer, an ex-gambler in search of a new career.

Rene laughed when I told him the details of my System. "That one will never work," he said. "But there are ways. Casinos are created by humans, so they can be beaten by humans. Especially..."—his eyes drifted toward the window, then swung back at me—"if you have a friend."

He swigged his beer. "You must never tell anyone what I am going to tell you," he said. "I am croupier in the casino. In your country it is a small job. In Baguio it is big job. Not for the pay—for 'the benefits.'" He stared; I made myself not blink, not speak.

"When you work in a casino, you learn to read people," Rene said. "I can read people. I know you are a smart man. I will tell you straight—if you sit with me for half an hour, I will show you how, before you leave the Philippines, you can make a small fortune. You hear my plan. If you don't like it, no problem. If you like it, you can make some money, and you can help me feed those children outside. Help me build them a place to play."

"Rene, I'm not here to gamble. I came to Baguio for the cool air, the pine trees—to see a faith healer...."

"Yes, yes. But are you so rich you can't take one hour to make $5,000, $10,000, maybe $20,000?"

I thought of the $1,000 in my savings account, the single dollar I'd left in checking.

"You hear my plan," Rene said, "then you decide. If you are not interested, no problem—someone else will be interested. Last month I work with a German. In one hour, he makes $11,000."

"How much did he gamble?"

"Very little. It is best if you use your own money, but if you don't want to, you don't have to use even one peso." He smiled again. "It's up to you. Will you hear my plan, Mister Brad?"

I felt a nervous, prelarcenous fluttering in my arms and stomach. How *does* one beat a casino? Aren't they all crooked anyway? Don't they deserve to be cheated? "Rene, I'll listen, but I promise you nothing."

"You see! I knew you were a smart man. You listen—you don't like, no problem." He stood again. "Come."

I followed him to the next room and sat across from him at a picnic table covered with a red-and-white checked tablecloth. Rene pulled a blue tackle box from under the table, opened it, took out a deck of Bicycle playing cards, and spilled a pile of poker chips—reds, whites, and blues—onto the table.

"Do you hate Arab, Brad?"

"No."

"Hate Japanese?"

"I like to think I don't hate anyone." I was thinking: *Eleven thousand*.

"Japanese and Arabs," said Rene. "These I hate. Especially Arab. Filipino hates Arab. In Saudi Arabia gambling is illegal. Drinking is illegal. Having too many women.... But Arab comes to Philippines. He has millions of dollars. He drinks. He gambles. He takes Filipina woman and makes her pregnant." Rene arched his back and poked out his belly. "And Arab won't pay. So when Arab comes to my table, if he loses $20,000, he and I, we are even. He can go back to Mecca now, Mister Achmed...." (Rene's *Ach* sounded as though he were being garroted.) "...Mister Hafooz, Mister Mohammed, and..."—Rene raised his arms like a stick-up victim and bowed three times over the piles of chips—"yes, Allah...yes, Allah...yes, Allah." He straightened and grimaced.

He was priming me, and I could see where it was headed. "Rene, this is criminal."

"Only if you get caught," he said, "and you have to be stupid to get caught. I am not stupid, and I can tell you are not stupid. Think of it as foreign aid. For me it is feeding those boys outside. For that boy's brother it is leukemia treatments. One boy from Los Angeles, he made $6,000 playing with rich Japanese. He said he wasn't stealing; he was just fixing your American trade deficit."

Rene set the deck on the table; I cut. He dealt each of us one card down, one card up. "The game twenty-one," Rene said, "you remember it?"

"Sure." My up card was the ace of hearts. I checked my down card—the jack of spades—and turned it over. "Blackjack."

"Ah," he said. "Very good."

"Very funny," I said.

"You think *I* did that?" he asked, all innocence.

"Yes. Did you?"

"Maybe yes, maybe no."

I took the deck and riffled through it. Nothing out of the ordinary. I shuffled it four times and set it back on the table. Rene cut it once; I reached over and cut it again. I eyed him as he dealt.

My up card was a ten, my down card a queen. This time Rene's up card was the ace of hearts, the very same up card I'd been dealt on the previous hand.

"What do you know," he said, and turned over his bottom card—and there it was, the jack of spades again. "Blackjack," he said.

I took the cards and counted. Fifty-two. I inspected them: only one ace of hearts, only one jack of spades. I shuffled five times, cut the deck and set it on the table.

Rene picked it up and slowly dealt. My up card was a four, my down card a six. Rene's up card was the jack of spades. I watched his hands as he set the deck back on the table.

"Do you have blackjack?" I asked.

"No." He turned over his bottom card—the jack of clubs. "I have two black jacks. Do you think you can beat that?"

His hand added up to twenty. I had ten. "I think that *if you want me to*, I can probably beat it."

"Do you want to win or to lose?"

39

"Win," I said.

"Go ahead. Draw the next card yourself."

I took the top card from the deck. The ace of hearts—twenty-one. "You are very good," I said.

"That is nothing," he said. "In six months a monkey can learn to do that while he is asleep. I have been a dealer for twelve years." He set the cards between us. "Now—you are ready to hear my plan?"

I nodded.

Rene pushed the cards and chips aside. "In Manila it is a ten-minute cab ride from the airport to the casino. When you are ready to leave for India, instead of the usual two hours, you will arrive at the airport three hours before your flight. You will check in for your flight, then go back outside to the taxi drivers. If you are going to use your own money, all you have to do is get into any taxi and say, 'Casino.' If you will not use your own money, a friend of mine will meet you by the taxicabs and will ride with you. When you arrive at the casino, he will give you $1,000 worth of pesos. You will get out of the cab, but he will stay in it and ride away. You understand so far?"

"Yes."

"You walk into the casino," Rene said. "You go to the cashier; you give him the $1,000 in pesos. He will give you chips. You walk over to the high-stakes twenty-one table and sit between Mister Achmed and Mister Yakamoto or whoever else is there that day. On every hand you bet 2,000 pesos—almost $100 per hand. You will watch the dealer's thumbs." Rene had the deck of cards and both hands on the table; he flexed his thumbs. "If ever the dealer's *left* thumb is pointing directly at you"—Rene demonstrated—"you will bet half of your chips. But if ever his *right* thumb is pointing directly at you—this will happen once only—you will bet all of them. This will be your final bet. You will win. You will leave the table and take your chips to the cashier's window. If you are using your own money, the cashier will give you your $1,000 back plus 40 percent of the winnings. If you are using my friend's money, the cashier will give you 20 percent of the winnings. You will go to the airport and fly to India." Rene looked at me with raised eyebrows: *It's that simple.*

But when your conscience works overtime, nothing is that simple.

In 1973 I got a speeding ticket in Nevada, which I didn't think I deserved; I never paid it, and to this day I drive through Nevada with one eye on the speedometer and one on the rearview mirror. And after a series of sleepless nights, I once filed back tax returns—coughing up ridiculously small sums. I could imagine the tossing and turning I'd endure after sucking $5,000 or $10,000 or $20,000 from a Third World casino.

"Rene, I came to look at your country, not to loot it."

"Oh, no. You will not be looting my country. You will be helping it. In America, the casino is also the bank. But our casino cannot afford to be the bank. When you come to the table, the banker will be Mr. Saddam Hezbolah or Mr. Sony Mitsubishi. He will have put up a $20,000 deposit for this privilege, plus a small fee for the casino. You will not be stealing Filipino money, but money from a rich person. And if someone is rich enough to gamble $20,000, you cannot call this stealing."

"Have you ever lost?" I asked.

"Twice. Once when we had just started this, we had a foreigner who was very terrible at gambling. Now we make sure we have good people. I think when I show you everything, you will be good. This foreigner, he was French, and he was very nervous. He bet all the money at the wrong time. But it wasn't his money—it was our money. People are more alert when it is their own money."

"What was the other time?"

"That was different. I know you are thinking, 'These Filipinos—they are going to cheat me.' It is good to think that way, because sometimes in life people do cheat. But it is not only Filipinos. The other time we lost, the foreigner, he cheated us. This was a Canadian man. When he was finished, he had $43,000 worth of chips, but he didn't go to the cashier. He took all the chips and went right out the door and straight to the airport. Before we could figure out what to do, he was on his way back to Canada. We think he gave the chips to some friend to cash for him, because we never see him again. But we are smarter now. We have taken some precautions. I tell you this only because you are a smart man and sooner or later you will think of it yourself. If you are going to cheat us, you should maybe think of some better way."

"Why do you need me? Why doesn't Irma do it?"

"We are watched very carefully, of course. We can let our Filipino friends win only small amounts—if they win too much, our bosses will be suspicious. They will want their share, and they are very greedy. But if a foreigner wins, even if everyone is suspicious, nothing can be done. In two hours you will be out of the Philippines, and even if you want to, we will never again use you. If some day you come back to this dealer's table, I guarantee, you will not win. Once only."

Morals, of course, are like fingerprints: everyone has a different set. Rene's plan did not offend me—there have been times in my life when I'd have leapt at it. But times change, and now the whole thing just felt dirty to me.

A moment of silence passed between us. Rene finally broke it: "You don't have to say anything." He stacked the cards and put them away. "After twelve years in a casino, I know people. You are not going to do it. It is not in your heart. And if it is not in your heart, it is better that you not do it. No problem—someone else will do it." He smiled. "There is always someone else."

5
Disk

We move with eyes shut and ears stopped. We smash walls where doors are waiting to open to the touch; we grope for ladders, forgetting that we have wings; we pray as if God were dead and blind, as if He were in space. No wonder the angels in our midst are unrecognizable.

—HENRY MILLER, *Nexus*

A man wandering down an unfamiliar dirt road on the daylight side of Earth on a random Monday late in the twentieth century does not wonder if his trip has yet begun. The overhead sun was tropical-high, tropical-hot; chickens fluttered through the roadside weeds; chips, beer, and one vodka-laced piece of dog meat clogged my belly. I had just passed up an offer of indoor work at $5,000 an hour. Minimum. *This*, I thought, *is Travel*. One minute you're walking along eating ice cream, minding your own business, and the next you're trying to decide: Is she trying to hustle or help me? Is her brother-in-law a regular hood or a Robin Hood?

A green tennis ball with a slash down its middle lay in the road; I kicked it through Rene's neighborhood, down a hill, across a wooden bridge. Except for the birds singing in the trees, the morning was quiet. The only resident I saw was an older man asleep in a porch chair. Even the dogs were silent, but they had good reason, I knew, not to draw themselves any attention.

I scuffled along for maybe a kilometer before a car rumbled up from behind. I moved aside to give it room; it passed me—a red and yellow...

"TAXI!"

It stopped in a cocoon of dust. I forgot my tennis ball and ran to the cab. I would go back to town, have some real food in a restaurant, start my day all over.

"How long Baguio?" the driver asked as we headed into town.

"Third day. I'm leaving tomorrow morning," I said. "Say, may I ask you a question?"

"Sure."

"Do you know a faith healer named Segundo?"

"Everybody know Segundo. You know Segundo?"

"No," I said. "Someone told me about him."

"You have some problem?"

"My back."

"Long time?"

"Two years."

"Much pain?"

"Sometimes," I said. "Especially when I sit."

"Disk," he said. Show me a cab driver who is not a back expert.

"Do you know if Segundo works on backs?"

"Segundo too old," he said. "I take you to *Casuga*. Brother Ricardo Casuga. He has clinic. He is better."

"Is he good with backs?"

"Casuga good with everything. You want to go Casuga?"

For a decade I'd been curious about these guys—if I left Baguio without seeing one of them I would always wonder. And what if this Casuga really *could* help me? What if this weird day was God's final test: tempt me with Irma, Rene, and thousands of dollars and then, if I passed, send a red and yellow taxi to fetch me to salvation.

"Yeah," I said, "what the hell...."

An instantaneous U-turn pitched me across the back seat. We drove away from town, through the pine grove I'd walked the first day, and stopped at the taxi stand across from the Hyatt resort. A group of men were leaning against a jeepney named "Money Maker." My driver called out and one man separated from the group, came over and spoke Tagalog through the window. He had thick black hair, neatly cut, wore a brand-new yellow windbreaker, and reminded me of the golfer Lee

Trevino. He glanced in at me, then climbed into the front seat. As we pulled away, the driver found my eyes in his rear view mirror. "This Brother Casuga," he told me.

This man! I'd half-expected *my* faith healer to have a rainbow aura. "Oh," I said. "Really?"

"For real," said Brother Casuga. He turned and stretched his hand back across the seat and looked at me with bemused brown eyes. No jolt, no tingling, passed from his body to mine as we shook. "You have some problem, my friend?"

I told him my back story.

"Did you see a doctor?" Casuga asked.

"Many doctors. Three orthopedic surgeons, four chiropractors, four physical therapists." Back sufferers have incredible lists, and this was only my short version. My long one includes an acupuncturist, a hypnotist, a psychologist, two rolfers, a Christian Science practitioner, and a guy who taped crystals to my back and right leg and promised a money-back guarantee.

"What was the diagnosis?"

"They say my right leg has lost a third of its strength, but X-rays show nothing. No one had a diagnosis."

"Are you in pain?"

"Every day."

"Right now?"

The raw sensation in my back and the zinging down my leg seemed to have been there forever. "Yes, right now. It goes away when I'm walking. Also, I do stretching exercises every day—they help, but only for a while."

"I am sorry," said Brother Casuga. He seemed kind, full of compassion, but each of my American healers had also been kind.

"Do you think you can help?"

"We go to my clinic," he said. "We will see."

We drove through Baguio, up Urbano Street, past the Central Baptist Church and Evie's Store. Three boys were exploding cracker balls on the pavement in front of Malinkintal's Bakery. Past Julie's Mix Mart the driver stopped where a muddy footpath led between two houses.

"Is your office *here*?"

"This is my temporary clinic," Casuga said. "New clinic is not yet ready."

Even after our thirty minutes together, the cab driver's meter read only enough for him to afford a small cup of coffee—in America. I gave him enough for a large cup and a couple of donuts and followed Brother Casuga down the path. A piglet squealed and skittered out of our way. Two young boys stopped beating each other with sticks and stared at me; Casuga scolded them in Tagalog and they scampered off. We came to a small one-story house surrounded by a tall iron fence; metal grates covered every window. Inside, a television was blaring. I wondered what I might find under *clinic* in an English-Tagalog dictionary.

Casuga banged on the front door; locks clicked, the door opened—television noise knocked me back. A teenage boy, a vision of the Casuga of thirty years ago, answered the door. Father and son exchanged grunts, and the boy slunk away into the house's interior.

Bloody Jesuses were pinned to the walls at both ends of the living room. Above the huge, blasting TV were two posters: Tom Cruise and Kelly McGillis wrapped in clouds and blue sky; and smudged-faced, rope-veined Arnold Schwartzenager straddling the title *Predator*. On the television screen a woman, bosom tightly wrapped, was prancing around a spaceship in a desert; a video carton atop the console read, *The Day Time Stopped*. Casuga pushed a button; the noise stopped, a cartridge ejected.

"Thank you," I said.

"Sit down. I will get ready." Casuga pulled aside a blanket hung in the doorway of an adjacent room, exposing a jumble of clutter, and disappeared. I heard furniture being pushed across the floor and things being tossed around.

I sat on the sofa across from the blank TV screen. *Am I nuts? Do I really think a Filipino who hangs out at taxi stands is going to do something twenty Western doctors couldn't?*

The thumping from the next room ended. Casuga pulled back his curtain. "You can come now."

I stepped into his room. A blanket was thrown over a desk—concealing who-knows-what disorder—and he'd cleaned off an area around a padded massage table.

"You can take your clothes off," he said. "Leave your underwear on. I'll be back in a minute." And in a moment he returned, carrying a bottle of viscous brown liquid.

"What is that?"

"Oil. Massage oil."

"Are you going to open my body up?"

"We will see," he said. "Please lie down."

I lay on the table on my back. The windows had curtains, and the light seeping through gave the room a golden glow. I thought: *Golden glow or not, if I were still a gambler I'd bet my money belt this man doesn't open me up this afternoon.*

"Before we start, how much do you charge?"

"People give what they can afford."

"I can afford twenty dollars. Will that be O.K.?"

"Whatever you give I will use to distribute among the neighborhood. There are many people here who are very poor. Especially the children. Twenty dollars will make them very happy."

"Thank you." A week before leaving San Francisco, I had visited a specialist at the University of California. He studied my X-rays and MRIs and looked through the dossier of other doctors' reports. He asked me to bend over and touch my toes, to lean this way, lean that way. I lay on his table and he touched me here—"How does that feel?"—and touched me there. He said, "Hold tight on the table," and gave my right leg a sharp yank. Then another. He recommended I see a physical therapist. His bill for our ten minutes together: $232.

I closed my eyes. Casuga pressed out the muscles in my shoulders and rubbed the sides of my neck. He caressed my temples with strong fingers, then placed one hand to my forehead; he became very still. I popped open an eyelid. Casuga was standing over me, his eyes closed, his free hand raised up toward the ceiling, fingers spread. His lips were moving, but no noise escaped. After a moment he dropped his hand. "I will not have to operate," he said.

"How do you know?"

"The spirits say so."

He rubbed oil into his palms, then massaged my scalp. For several minutes he stroked my chest. I relaxed and slid into a rumination on the unpredictability of life; if suddenly someone were to burst through the blanket at the door and demand that I explain and justify my presence in the Philippines and in this man's room, how would I even begin?

He was pressing on my abdomen now, rubbing, probing. He found my liver. Every time someone touches me there I recall another doctor's table, in June 1974, the month I returned yellow-eyed from Afghanistan: *We'll have to run some tests, but I'm pretty sure you've got hepatitis.*

"How did you learn faith healing?" I asked Casuga, my eyes still closed.

"From my grandfather. He lived to be 102. He was still strong right until the day he died."

"How does someone know if they are good at it?"

"You can just tell."

"Will you train your son?"

"We will see." He tipped the bottle into his palm and rubbed his hands together. "Now turn over."

I rolled onto my stomach and laid my cheek on the table's brown vinyl surface. "How often do you have to operate on people?"

"Not very often."

"Is it true you can open someone up with your fingertip?"

"Yes. Sometimes we open skin without a knife."

He worked on my lower back near the trouble spot. I realized what it was I was hoping for: someone with a strong, almost magnetic power in his or her hands, someone who could reach in and pull out whatever mysterious shrapnel or bone chips were tormenting me. Casuga, I realized, was not that person, but he was a fine masseur. And what, really, outranks a good massage?

"Have you seen any miracles?" I asked.

"Yes," he said. "Many."

"What's the best one?"

Casuga was quiet for a moment. "There was a Canadian man who had cancer. I worked with him and worked with him every day. He wanted so badly to be healed. After three months he began to get strong. His cancer disappeared."

I thought: *Cancer!* A sore back should only take about half an hour.

"I will never forget that." Casuga sounded as if even he had been surprised.

"Do many foreigners come to you?"

"Some. Once we had a Russian cosmonaut. He had some problem with his hand. Someone had told him about me. He came with so many police. For days we had Russian police all over Baguio."

"Did you heal him?"

"I think we helped him some, but not completely."

"Do you think you can heal me?"

"After you leave you will get better. A little bit at a time. When I am finished, every night for thirty days you should say three minutes of silent prayers before you go to bed. We will say prayers for you, also. If you say the prayers, and if you have faith, you will get better. It depends on your faith. Faith and healing," Casuga said. "They are the same." He was working my right calf now, rolling the meat of it between his palms, kneading it with his knuckles.

I was drifting into a dreamy state, but not quite ready to let go. "What's the best thing that ever happened to you?" I asked him. It is a question I liked to ask customers in my cab. Many people need time to think it over, but Casuga took only a few seconds.

"I think it was when the Canadian man got better. That was very exciting. We could tell something special was happening."

"Did he send many people to you after that?"

"Yes, a few," he said. "But after a year, the cancer came back."

"Did you heal it again?"

"No. He died."

In my chest, a small ship snapped in two and sank. "Oh. I'm sorry."

"Yes. So am I. We were very good friends. I met his family. He knew my family. When you become close like that with someone, it is hard."

He switched to my left thigh.

"What's the worst thing that ever happened to you?" Few people need time to ponder that question: indeed, many seem to walk through life chanting the answer as a silent mantra.

"That," said Casuga, "was when I wrecked my knee. In an automobile accident."

"Were you driving or someone else?"

"I was."

"Did you go to a faith healer?"

"No. I spent three months in the hospital."

"Why didn't you go to a faith healer?"

I heard him chuckle. "For some things it is best to go to a hospital."

And then talking became too much effort. I shut up and let the spirits have my body. I imagined myself floating up through the ceiling, up above Casuga's roof, then higher to where I could see the town, the surrounding mountain ranges, all of Luzon, and soon the entire Philippine chain. A hundred miles up I stopped and hovered. Across the blue waters of the South China Sea I could see Malaysia and China, and, on the two horizons, bits of Japan and Australia. Straight down below, through a rooftop in Baguio, I could see a man with strong hands working the bottoms of another man's feet. I looked everywhere, closely, but from up there I could see no pain.

6
Sigourney Weaver Slept Here

And what are two thousand years? ... What, indeed, if you look from a mountaintop down the long wastes of the ages? The very stone one kicks with one's boot will outlast Shakespeare.

— VIRGINIA WOOLF, *To the Lighthouse*

At least 2,000 years before Columbus took on the Atlantic, and a good 500 years before Jesus walked on the sea of Galilee, a Malayan tribe called the Ifugao (*Ee-fu-GAY-o*) left their homeland, dipped their canoes into the South China Sea, and paddled to the island we call Luzon. Although the coast was beautiful and inviting, the Ifugao did not settle it; instead, they sought out the most rugged section of the interior, a region of precipitous mountains and jungled valleys, waterfalls, and tumbling rivers. They claimed one of the most spectacular valleys as their own, built thatch-roofed houses on monsoon-defying posts, and, to thank the gods who had guided them to this paradise, fixed the skull of a newly sacrificed pig to the outside of each home.

Then they really went to work. They started by carving small flat fields into the steep mountainsides next to the river. They hauled great boulders from the riverbed and constructed stone walls around their fields. They diverted the river into irrigation channels, flooded their fields, and, finally, planted rice. For the next two millennia Ifugao life ran on a simple formula: more children, more rice terraces. They held periodic pig feasts with plenty of rice wine, and they occasionally launched headhunting expeditions (the hated Ilocanos lived just a few valleys away and required periodic discipline), but the Ifugao obviously spent most of their time working. When in the late 1800s people from the outside world wandered into the Ifugaos' isolated home, they found an area of small scattered villages, dwarfed by the surrounding mountains. But layer after layer of rice terraces, marching like steps right to the valley's rim, more than 4,000 feet high in some places, had tamed these mountains like few others. With a quick bit of figuring, someone calculated that if the Ifugaos' rock walls were laid end to end, they would stretch halfway around the globe, from central Luzon to somewhere deep in the Brazilian Amazon.

To reach the Ifugao region from Baguio requires an all-day, spine-warping jeepney ride along twisting dirt roads (a sign next to the driver said, NO MATTER WHAT DON'T SCREAM).

I took a four-dollar-a-night room in a lodge on the edge of Banaue (*Ba-NAH-way*), a town of several hundred people that is today the Ifugaos' regional center. On the afternoon of day eight I walked from my room along a winding dirt road—a slash cut into one of the steep valley walls—and four kilometers later arrived at a small row of handicraft shops and a concrete viewing platform which overlooked the valley and distant Banaue. The green mountainsides surrounding the platform were stepped with immaculate rice terraces that mirrored the afternoon's thunderheads, making the entire valley shimmer as though God had draped a coat of sequins across it.

I had just managed to identify my lodge among the cluster of structures down in Banaue and was zeroing in on the window of my own room, when a voice behind me said, "Nice view." A Filipino man with the rich brown skin, wide nose, and pleasant smile of the Ifugao had come up behind me. A few moments earlier I had seen him sitting inside the front door of one of the knickknack shops I'd passed.

"Beautiful," I said.

We stood together, quietly admiring the valley, the low clouds, the terraces climbing the mountain walls. On this late afternoon we were the only two gawkers.

"Some people think it looks like a wedding cake," the man said. He was missing a front tooth. "But other people say it is too green—must be *vegetarian* wedding cake." Obviously I was not the first Californian he had met. He was wearing a thick silver wrist watch, stone washed blue jeans, and a baggy white sweatshirt cut off high up on his biceps.

"Do you live near here?" I asked him.

"Down there." He pointed straight over the edge. One hundred feet below us several thatch-roofed homes were perched in a hilltop clearing; rice terrace after rice terrace descended from the clearing all the way down to the river.

Tony — Had left his home in the mountains only once, for a sad trip to Manila.

"That one is my grandfather's house, and there is my father's, then some neighbors', and then in the trees, that last one—can you see?—that's mine."

His name was Tony. He was gentle, well-spoken, and said he had the Christian school in Banaue to thank for his English. He was twenty-two, married, with three children. "There are many other people in the villages,"—he pointed at the jungly mountains toward the north—"who are also my family."

Was life good here?

"Yes, good enough. There are problems sometimes, but mostly it is good. We have electricity now, and cars, and life is a little easier. But also more complicated. Before, there was only the terraces. Now young people don't want to work terraces. They want to go to Manila, or they want to drive tourists around on trikes."

Trikes—I'd seen a dozen young men in the Banaue marketplace sitting with their feet up on the handlebars of their sidecar motorcycles, hoping for fares.

"Who works the terraces?" I asked.

"The people who live here. Me sometimes."

"Do you own one?"

"I own two." He pinpointed two paddies next to the river, hundreds of feet below us. "My father gave them to me."

"Do they feed you all year?"

"Two terraces will feed my family for maybe three months."

"How do you eat for the other nine?"

"Now the government has built this viewpoint, and people sell things here to tourists. I have a little shop." He did not say or insinuate, *Can-I-show-you-a-few-things*? and I liked him for that.

"Do people like the government here?"

"The government is corrupt," he said. "This viewpoint. It was built by the Tourist Board. How many pesos do you think?"

We were leaning on the railing of the viewpoint, a concrete platform supported by concrete pillars anchored into the hillside: some rebar, some gravel, some concrete, a week's labor for a few workers. I thought, *With a decent back and four or five thousand bucks I could build it myself.* I doubled my estimate, did some quick math, and said, "At most, two hundred thousand pesos."

"One point four million pesos," he said, slipping his hand symbolically into his pocket. "The contractor has a big house in the lowlands. Swimming pool."

I asked Tony if people around Banaue resent the famous political corruption of the lowlands.

"People here are not so aware. They think more about the terraces. That is what is important here. Not just for food. For tourists, too."

Nearly all the tourists I'd seen in Banaue had been backpackers who paid a dollar or two a night for rooms and about the same for restaurant meals. Still, their impact on the economy was obvious; most of the prominent buildings in the center of town had recently become cheap hotels.

"The terraces are the only reason anyone comes to Banaue," Tony said. "But now a young person who grows up here, he does not want to work in a rice terrace. He wants to buy a trike or he wants to go to Manila or Bangkok. If he is a big dreamer, America. Someday tourists will come to Banaue and they will see only ruins. Someday the rice terraces will be only a symbol of a lost culture."

Symbol of a lost culture. He reads, or else the educational channel reaches all the way to Banaue.

I asked, "Do you sometimes dream about going to other places?"

"Many times. Especially to America. But I think that will be very difficult. Once some people from Germany bought a wood carving from my shop. It cost 800 pesos. They said they would give me the money or give me a trip to see other places in the Philippines. Then I needed the money, but now I wish I had taken the trip."

Tony seemed thoughtful, bright, not grasping, confident but not puffed up. And he was fluent in English. From our first moment together I'd felt comfortable. I imagined that a month spent with him would be an enjoyable one.

"What's the best thing that ever happened to you?" I asked.

"Oh, I like this question." He thought for a moment. "Maybe when Sigourney Weaver came here to this viewpoint. Have you seen *The Year of Living Dangerously*? They filmed part of it right here, where we are standing. They stayed for many days, but in the movie it is just a few seconds."

"Why was *that* the best thing?"

"For many days they hired extras. Two hundred and eighty pesos a day. Also 280 pesos a day for closing our shops. And 280 a night for being security guards. I did all three. Eight hundred and forty pesos a day." (At the time, less than $50.) "Everyone here was happy."

I scanned Tony's valley. Below us a man and a woman were working a rice terrace, the man patching the rock wall with mud, the woman pulling weeds. Behind us, near the shops, schoolchildren were taking turns throwing their shoes at a tin can—a game children played everywhere in the Philippines.

"I want to change my answer," Tony said. "My family. That is the best thing. Most important."

I asked, "What's the worst thing that ever happened to you?"

No hesitation: "When I lose my eye."

I looked at his face; his eyes looked the same, but now for the first time I noticed that one wandered.

"I have only one eye now," he said, pointing at the right side of his face. "This one is artificial."

"What happened?"

"Someone hit it out with a hammer."

"When?"

"Six months now."

"Is this too personal?"

"No, it's O.K."

"Why'd they do that?"

"I was stupid. Drinking. In Banaue young boys think drinking makes them a man. They drink and they fight. One day I was drinking and I saw two guys fighting. I tried to break them up. Then the brother of one of them, he boxes me." Tony waved his fists through the air. "And of course we fight. Later I go with friends, drinking, and after that, at night, I am walking from Banaue back to the viewpoint"—Tony pointed to the road I had just traveled—"and two of them jump me with a hammer."

"Did you see them coming?"

"No, I don't remember any of it. The first hit broke my eyeball out. The second one breaks my ribs. My jaw was shattered." He pointed to a small wormlike scar on his chin, and to the space where his front tooth was missing. "Some people find me, unconscious, and they get my wife. There are some Christian missionaries down the hill and she went and got them. They put me in their truck and took me to the clinic in Banaue, but the clinic could do nothing for me. People who saw me say they were scared to look at me. They say I am...mess. Is that a word—*mess*?"

"That fits."

"They say I am a mess. All night the missionaries drove me to Manila. My first time to Manila. Last time, too. It was awful. People kept coming in to steal from me. The doctors took my eye out. I was a month and ten days in the government hospital. Twenty-three thousand pesos." Twice his country's per capita income. "The doctors were free, but the medicines were very expensive."

"Who paid for it?"

"I did. I had some money. I was hoping to buy a trike. A second-hand trike is 20,000 pesos, and already I had 12,000 saved. So I used that. Some friends in Banaue, they had a party and collected money and gave it to me. My mother and father helped, and I have almost paid them back. I don't drink anymore."

"Do you know the people who did it?"

"I know. They used to live in Banaue. Now they moved to Baguio."

"They were embarrassed?"

"Yes, I think so."

"Is there anything you can do about it?"

"I am glad to be alive, glad to have one eye still. I don't worry about revenge. Revenge is for when you die. This"—he indicated his face—"not so bad. In Philippines, anyone from first cousin to fourth cousin is close. I have many relatives—even some in Baguio. So someday...somebody from my family...these men will be reminded. Maybe in fifteen or twenty years, but surely it will happen." He grinned, not with glee or malice, but resignation: *That's life around here.*

Smoke curled from a hut down the hillside, bringing with it the smell of roasting meat. I heard children's cries, the river's distant thunder, the calm, reassuring silence of the rice paddies, and thought: *If places can heal, this is certainly one of them.*

"Are you O.K. now? Six months is not so long."

"I think I am O.K. Some days I still have dreams."

"During the night or during the day?"

"During the day. I dream that ghosts chase me."

"Do you have them right now?"

"Yes. Not just now while I am talking to you. But a few minutes ago, and after you leave I think I will have them again. But they are not so strong any more. It is good to be here with my wife, my children, my parents, and my grandparents. I am getting better."

"Do you still want to get a trike?"

"No. I think not. Now I carve wood and I work in my shop. I have almost paid everything back from the hospital, and now I want to make my business strong."

"Is business good?"

"Sometimes yes, sometimes no."

"What do you do when it is slow?"

"Sometimes I take care of my rice terraces. And sometimes I guide people up into the mountains"—he pointed again toward the green peaks looming above us—"to visit the villages where my relatives live."

7
Where the Israeli Man Went

*One of the best paying professions is getting ahold of pieces of country in
your mind, learning their smells and their moods, sorting out the pieces
of a view, deciding what grows there and there and why, how many steps
that hill will take, where this creek winds and where it meets the other
one below...This is the best kind of ownership, and the most permanent.*

—TERRY AND RENNY RUSSELL, *On the Loose*

My backpack and I rode to the viewpoint in a trike at nine o'clock
the next morning. The sound of the motor drew Tony from his
shop.

"Ah, I am glad you come." He pumped my hand like I was family.
"You wait here. I will tell my wife and get some things."

Sitting in a chair in his shop, I was surrounded by carvings of buf-
faloes and headhunters and American eagles.

"The eagle sells the most," Tony had said.

My pack contained: air mattress, sleeping bag, umbrella, poncho;
sweater, trousers, hat, scarf, and gloves; notebook, camera, tape recorder;
water bottle. In five minutes Tony came back, carrying a roll no larger
than a bread loaf. We would be hiking in the mountains for three days.

He padlocked the shop, hooted good-byes to his competitors, and
we started up the dirt road. We would hike up and down mountains all
day to the village of Pula, two valleys over, and spend the night; two
mornings later we would return to Banaue. We had walked barely 100
yards when the thong broke away from the sole of Tony's right flip-flop.

"One minute." He stopped to fix it.

"Are those your only shoes?"

"Yes."

"Let me buy you a new pair before we go." I was wearing ninety dollar hiking shoes.

"No. This is O.K." He dropped it back in the dirt and hooked the thong between his toes. "See?"

We left the road and followed a footpath that skirted the rice paddies and went down steps of stone or dirt to the valley floor. We hopped rock-to-rock across the river and began climbing the opposite side. "When you get tired," Tony said, "I will take your pack."

"I'll be O.K.," I said, hoping it was true.

Ahead lay a jungle-covered mountainside so steep and high I could not see the top. We climbed until we passed the highest terrace, and sat in a clearing, where someone had chopped down a pine recently enough that fresh woodchips still lay in the grass. Tony pointed to the stump, two feet wide. "People are cutting too much."

On the opposite hills we could see logged sections which had been replanted with rows of seedlings. "Planting is good but we are cutting faster than we are planting. And the more we cut, the less animals we see."

"Will we see wild pigs today?" I asked.

"I think not."

The grass we were sitting in was thick and high. "Will we see snakes?"

Quickly: "No."

My brother, Grant, who works for the U.S. State Department, had told me that guerrillas of the New Peoples Army had once roamed these hills, clamoring for land reform and threatening to topple the government.

"Will we see NPA?" I asked Tony.

After a moment—during which he lit a cigarette and I thought: *A month with a smoker!*—Tony said, "No. Not any more. That was long time ago. I knew three NPA. But one was killed and the other two surrendered. Now they have families."

When it was time to go, Tony again offered to take my pack. Again I said no thanks. I didn't tell him, but this would be my first long walk with a pack since my back troubles had started, and I wanted to see how I held up. Also, I will never forget the embarrassment I saw clouding the faces of healthy young Westerners trekking unencumbered through Nepal while barefoot Sherpas carried their huge backpacks.

The trail went straight up through the jungle; steps had been fashioned out of tree limbs in places, but there were no switchbacks. Overhead, gray clouds showed through a ceiling of foliage, but trees and vines were tangled so densely on both sides of the path that I could not see five feet into the jungle.

"During World War II the Japanese never reached Pula," Tony said. "They came to Banaue, but they could not make it to Pula. There was no trail here then. My parents still talk about the war. They say it was no good—no matter what, war is worst. Japanese destroyed crops, burned civilians' houses. In the jungle my parents found fruit and bushes to eat. My grandfather used to go up to the sweet potato farm at night, when the Japanese couldn't see, and dig. One day he and three other men saw four Japanese riding on horses. They thought they would get the horses for meat. They tried to kill the soldiers with spears, but they only killed one. The Japanese shot my grandfather and his friends. Everybody dead. We lose four to one."

"What do people around here think of the Japanese now?"

"The Japanese were cruel, but they were honest. After the war, they gathered the Japanese in Banaue, and they ask, 'Who shot civilians? We will kill you.' No one knew, but many Japanese say, 'I shot civilians.' And then they were shot. There is a word for that—"

"Executed?"

"Yes—they were *executed*. But the ones who said they didn't shoot, they were still alive."

"The ones who were executed—did headhunters take their heads?"

"I don't think so. That was around the time headhunting was being stopped. During the war Ifugaos and Ilocanos fought the Japanese only, but when they left, we had one more headhunt war. Then it stopped for good. Now it is just legend."

He stopped and pointed toward where a birdsong came from the bushes. "Hear that? That is *Ijo*. When he makes that noise—*pit-pit-pit* —

real fast, it is good luck. But if he goes slow—*twit...twit...twit*—that is bad luck."

I said, "Do you believe that?"

He grinned. "Maybe. One time I was cutting rosewood and I heard *twit...twit...twit*...and then I cut myself with my machete." He showed a welt on his wrist. "So, I would rather hear *pit-pit-pit*. In America do you have...I know there is a word for that—"

"Superstitions?"

"Yes, *superstitions*. In America do you have that?"

I told him about black cats and walking under ladders.

"See," he said. "It is the same."

Birds peeped; trees creaked; the earth steamed. Sweat rolled into my eyes and drenched my t-shirt. I thought of people at home, wondered if someone new had had already moved into my apartment, tried to remember exactly the brown eyes of my girlfriend Rhonda. Tony wanted to know how much things cost in America, at what age people married, why so many Americans had no children. Were all the men circumcised or only the Jews?

"It's case by case," I said.

"Are you?" he asked.

"No. Are you?"

"Yes, six years ago, when I turned twenty-one."

"Last year! Didn't that hurt?"

"Yes, some. But it is tradition here. Also we make a hole in our skin and put string and some beads through it. The women like it better—they say it is more fun." He smiled proudly.

"A hole in your skin?" Even to my own ear, my voice sounded hopelessly conventional.

"Yes."

"You mean through...through your..."

He laughed. "Yes, through my *dick*."

"Where?"

We stood on the trail and unzipped our pants. *If a tour group came down the trail, who would look embarrassed now?* In the skin on the underside of his member, Tony showed me a puncture mark.

"It only hurts for a while," he said.

I located the corresponding membrane on my own body, tried to imagine the shot of pain involved, and simultaneously discovered and embraced a commitment, previously subconscious, to endure until death the boredom of life with an unperforated penis.

At a fork in the trail Tony led us to the right. I asked what was down the other fork.

"Valleys where no one lives," Tony said. "We call that trail *the place where the Israeli went*. One time an Israeli man comes to the viewpoint. He asks me how to get to Pula. I tell him he will get lost without a guide. He says he has been all over Israel and to Nepal and he does not need a guide. So I tell him the way to Pula. He gets to this fork and he goes that way. Three days later a friend of mine goes out to a far part of the forest. Nobody goes there except to cut rosewood. He finds the Israeli man, all cut up and afraid. He has spent three nights in the jungle. No food, no water. He is completely lost." Tony laughed. "He thinks with no guide he will save some pesos. At the hospital he spends 300."

We sat on a log in a ridgetop clearing, looking out over a valley of dense jungle and a series of ridges trailing beyond. Not a building, not a twist of smoke, not a sign of man anywhere. We had been walking for two and a half hours and I was soaked with sweat, but my back was loose, not complaining, and my knees were holding up.

"Did you bring the tobacco?" Tony asked.

We'd reached terms the day before: Tony's guide fee was $25; I would pay for all our meals in the villages and I would bring five tobacco leafs, two cigarette packs, and a carton of matchboxes from Banaue—his relatives would expect them. I took them from my pack and handed them over.

"You smoke?" He offered me a cigarette.

I said no, and offered him my water bottle, but he declined. "I think maybe you should not drink," he said, lighting up. "It will be two hours before we reach a stream. If you have some now, you just want more."

"That's funny," I said, and took a big swig, "in America, that's what we say about cigarettes."

In the afternoon the sky cleared and the sun made me glad for the jungle's canopy. We started down the back side of the mountain, into a forest of twisted trees whose roots clawed across the damp trail. "Be careful," Tony told me. "Sometimes people slip here. Do you want me to take your pack?"

"I'll be O.K."

Sometimes Tony whistled—"On Top of Old Smoky," "When Johnny Comes Marching Home"—and sometimes we were serenaded by the *pit-pit-pit* of the ijo bird, the sigh of wind and branches, and the chatter of small animals. Once, Tony pointed at a cluster of red and brown droppings: "Wild squirrel." For an hour we descended through a tunnel in the gnarled forest. I slipped once and fell down backwards.

"Don't feel bad," Tony said. I liked that he didn't try to help me up. "You are strongest walker I have guided."

"I'll bet you say that to everyone."

He laughed. "No, not everyone. Maybe half only. Some are strong, but some are very afraid. We start late this morning, but we will make the village before dinner. With some people, we start early, and still we miss dinner. Even when I carry the pack, some people cannot walk."

"Do you like the people you guide?"

"When you are out walking in the mountains with someone, it is hard not to like them. Especially the girls. I remember two Swedish girls. Their names were 'Ah-sah Oh-sah' and 'May-tay.'" They were both very beautiful. Not just regular beautiful, more than that. They could not hear or speak. Neither of them. We could only talk by signs or by writing. On the road I had to touch them to warn them a jeepney was coming. Once I wrote down, *Too bad we can't all speak and hear*. You know what they wrote back? *Too bad we're not all deaf and dumb*."

As I hiked behind him, watching his flip-flops and the cuffs of his blue jeans lead me through the mountains, it occurred to me that at home I don't know many people who seem as thoroughly content as Tony. I considered his ridiculously small bag, his whistling, his whole demeanor, and thought: *I could live here. Carve wood. Walk in the mountains. Grow old with friends like Tony.*

We had been walking in silence for half an hour when a black snake as fat as a fire hose slithered across our path and disappeared into the underbrush. Tony jumped back, scowling. "Filipino hates snake."

"I guess we'll see NPA guerrillas any minute now," I said, deadpan.

He looked at me, no smile, then turned and started walking. A moment later he stopped and looked back again. "Brad, I think you do not trust me."

Where had this come from? I fell all over myself trying to tell him I had just been kidding. "Really, it won't bother me even if we *do* see NPA," I said. "Any friend of yours is a friend of mine."

He half-smiled. "But I think you do not trust me, Brad."

"Are you serious?" We stood facing each other in the trail.

"I think I am serious."

"Tony, I trusted you the moment I met you. If I didn't trust you, I wouldn't be here right now."

"Then why won't you let me carry your pack?"

"Aaaah..."

I told him about my back, the faith healer, my three-minute prayers, how I viewed this hike as a personal test. Fifteen or twenty miles through the hills was something I wouldn't have considered a year ago. If I could do this, well, who knew, maybe I really was getting better.

Tony's face started to lighten.

"And another thing," I said. "if someone's going to come out to the jungle, I think he should only bring what he's willing to carry. What if a friend of mine were to come down the trail and see you carrying my pack? He'd laugh at me for the rest of my life."

This, he understood. His face softened; his smile spread. "We won't see your friends," he said. "Some NPA maybe. Some headhunters maybe. But not your friends."

"Here," I said, and began to slip off my straps. "You want my pack?"

"No way," he said, but we were both laughing now. "Carry your own pack."

Before we resumed hiking I said, "Tony, thanks for telling me what you were thinking."

"It is best to say what is in your heart," he replied. "This is something my wife has taught me. Before I am married I never know how to do this. Now I practice. *Practice*—is that a word?"

"Yes. Practice. That's perfect."

We dropped down into a pine forest near the valley floor, and crossed a meadow of light green grasses, five and six and ten feet tall. "CAH-ree-bow grass," Tony said.

"Oh, we have CAH-ree-bow grass in America," I said. "We say it a little different—*care-ih-BOO*."

Tony thought this over. "Brad," he said, "what is the word for someone who speaks only one language?"

"Hmmm. I don't know if there is one."

"Yes, I'm sure. I've heard it before."

"*Monolingual?*" I guessed.

"No, there is another word."

"Well, I don't know it...."

"Oh, yes," Tony said, "now I remember. The word for someone who speaks only one language—it is...," he had practiced his pause, "*American*."

A little while later he wiped his eyes. "Joke only," he said.

Around Any Corner

"Aama, how would you like to go to America with us?" My words sounded strangely clear, but reckless, and I alarmed myself at the level of commitment I was extending—more than I had offered before to anyone.

—BROUGHTON COBURN, *Aama in America*

The trail dropped straight down the walls of the valley. Tony went on ahead, trusting me to handle the terrain and my pack. When I reached the bottom, he was gulping handfuls of water from a crystalline stream. I sat next to him, pulled off my shoes and socks, filled my water bottle and dropped in an iodine tablet. Tony took a clean handkerchief from his blue jeans and patted his right eye, where white liquid was oozing from around the edges. During the day I had noticed his eye—the way it wandered, the emissions, the attention it required. I asked, "Does it bother you much?"

"Sometimes."

We were sitting on a huge, smooth rock at the side of the pool; curtains of foliage and the gurgling of the stream sealed us from the world. Our feet dangled in water up to our knees. After their daylong imprisonment, my toes were singing freedom songs.

"Is it O.K. if I ask about it?"

"It's O.K.," he said.

"What did you think about in the hospital?"

He tapped out a cigarette and lit it. "The hospital was awful. I had no family there. When I sleep people steal my medicines. Every time I wake up I check to see if maybe I can see again. I pray for God or maybe

Jesus—but I never seen them. The doctors say they want to take my eye out. For three days I said no—maybe if we wait it will get better. But they say maybe it will get infected and spread to the other one. I got afraid and I said, 'O.K., take it out.' Now I have *this* eye." He tapped it with his finger and it resonated like a Ping-Pong ball. "Plastic."

"Does it feel weird?"

"It feels O.K. The worst is that my face is not the same. My teeth..." He pointed to the gap in his teeth and the scar on his upper lip. "It's not me anymore. I took all the pictures of my old eye and locked them away. This changes my life forever. But sometimes I try to think what it would be like with no eyes, and I think maybe I am lucky."

Tony may have lost an eye and a tooth, may have suffered broken ribs, but his spirit seemed intact. He struck me as far more cheerful than the average Westerner, also more grounded, more at home in the world than I might judge myself. And as we tramped through his stunning homeland, I kept smiling at the thought of inviting him to America.

A part of me ached to stop my search right in that brook-fed valley in the green heart of Luzon, tell him about my free ticket, and ask him to use it. Sure he smoked, and, yes, he had three small children, but I liked him. I wanted to take him to the top of the Fairmont Hotel on a perfect day and show him the Golden Gate Bridge, Alcatraz, the sailboats in the Bay. Drive him down the coast to Big Sur, Disneyland, then over to the Grand Canyon. I knew hikes we could take, hot springs to stop and soak in.

But my trip was still young and I was sure to meet others, and it just wouldn't be right to tell Tony about my plan and then not choose him. I remembered the look on Ezekiel's face when I spilled my story in Rizal Park.

The sculptor Ed Kienholz once inserted a live bullet into a rifle, rigged a timing device to the rifle's trigger, and spun the timer so that the rifle would fire at some random moment during the next hundred years. Viewers of his creation were invited (if they were willing to sign a release form) to sit in a chair fifteen feet from Kienholz's work/weapon, so that the viewer looked directly down the rifle's barrel. Kienholz said his intention was to give the viewer not just a sense of danger, but the *real thing*. Those who sat in the chair—and there were many—said that along with the danger came an exhilaration.

And while traveling is, almost always, a far different thing than staring down the barrel of a gun, this ten-day-old trip of mine had an extraordinary dimension—an immediacy—that my previous trips often lacked. I felt I'd moved a notch or two up the scale of involvement—from observer toward participant. Around any corner I might bump into someone whose life, and my own too, would be forever changed by our meeting. This was not everyday stuff. Now when I encountered a stranger, someone next to me on a bus or on a diner stool, someone selling newspapers or passing me in the street, something magical was present. Possibility itself sat like an imp on my shoulder, whispering, "This could be the one."

During other trips and during my "normal life" I've kept protective walls around myself—to keep out that vast faceless sea of people who want to do me harm. But shifting my stance—from *What do they want from me?* to *What miracle might our meeting produce?*—made me feel light, pleasantly tickled. Sometimes at night in my hotel rooms, writing notes about someone I'd met, I would get almost giddy imagining him opening the letter with my invitation and the plane ticket.

By late afternoon Tony and I crested a ridge and looked down. Behind us were the green ridges we'd spent the day tramping; ahead, the trail led down a mountainside terraced by the first rice paddies we'd seen since early morning. Hundreds of feet below, twenty thatch-roofed homes filled a small riverside clearing. "That is Pula," Tony said, pointing. We were so high, and the mountains so vast, that the little village looked tiny—like second base seen from the top row of an empty baseball stadium. We heard only the river's gurgle and the "*whump... whump ...whump!*" of someone pounding grain in a mortar.

Under a white sky full of beanbag clouds, we hiked through rice terraces, groves of green bamboo, and clumps of shrubs as red as stop signs. "*Dongla* plant," Tony said. "For making war paint in headhunting days."

Our trail was nothing but a series of small rocks pressed into the top lips of the mud walls holding in the paddies—rocks that were often no wider than my shoe and placed two or three feet apart. Were I to stumble or slip, my instant penalty would be a splash into the mud and water of the paddy we were skirting or, worse, a seven-, ten-, or even fifteen-foot drop to the paddy below.

"Does anyone ever fall?"

"A German fell once," Tony said. "He broke his arm and cut his head, but no one has died. Filipinos only fall if they are drunk."

It took an hour to reach the river. A flock of white butterflies flitted in and out of the bamboo groves lining its banks, and one batted me in the ear. Upstream, a five-foot-high cascade of water plunged over a bank-to-bank ledge. Tony and I shucked our clothes and waded into an aqua pool so clear I could see my toenails on the stream bottom. I floated on my back and, looking up, saw that while we'd been hiking and I'd been busy watching my steps, an unseen arm had lobbed pink cotton candy streamers from peak to peak.

There comes a moment early in every trip when I think: *This is sufficient. Already I've gotten my money's worth. If the trip is aborted tomorrow, it will have all been worth it.* I spun slow circles across the pool, my ears underwater, monitoring the river's strong pulse, my eyes watching the clouds turn purple, and I thought: *From here on out everything's a bonus.*

9
All Backwards

As a traveler I can achieve a kind of high, a somewhat altered state of consciousness. I think it must be what athletes feel. I am transported out of myself, into another dimension in time and space. While the journey is on buses and across land, I begin another journey inside my head, a journey of memory and sensation, of past merging with present, of time growing insignificant.

— MARY MORRIS, *Nothing to Declare: Memoirs of a Woman Traveling Alone*

On morning eleven I was sitting on the front step of Tony's uncle's stilted hut in Pula. Four barefoot boys stood in a semicircle around me, watching, seeming to hope that I would take my tape recorder out of my pack—again. Talking and laughing, Tony and his uncle sat with a group of other men under the eaves of the hut next door. I couldn't understand a word, so I'm not sure which incident they had chosen, but I knew they were laughing about me.

They might have been replaying the way Tony led me by the hand into the village last night. The final rice terrace was a monster, seventy yards long, and the wall holding it in was twenty feet high. Years ago, while working construction, I had learned to tightrope my way across four-inch beams, ten and twelve feet off the ground—but not twenty—and never with a thirty-pound pack. A peasant woman, calf-deep in water and leaning on her hoe, found the sight of Tony towing me across the paddy's muddy rim unbelievably hilarious; her cackle alerted the entire village. They laughed, but I would trade dozens of the photos I have of myself for the one that no one took: me, backpack-laden, holding hands with a one-eyed Ifugao, the sun's last rays slanting down on us like a spotlight, and the heads of Pula's curious villagers poking from nearby huts, grins spreading across their faces.

The group of men might also have been laughing about the tube I pulled from my pack upon arrival and inflated into a six-foot-long bed; about the tiny sips I took from their communal bottle; or the few words of Ifugao I tried to pronounce: *ar-co* (sun), *fu-len* (moon), and *wheeskey* (rotgut).

Then again, they might have been laughing about the big joke they played on me at dawn, when they emasculated a pig in the four-foot crawl space beneath the hut where I slept. The pig had complained appropriately, frantically, loud and long, and was supported by several babies and at least a hundred roosters; but when I went out to see what was happening, I found only a mob of chickens, pecking at a red trail of blood.

"They cut off two muscles," Tony told me later. "Balls. Yes, castrate. They stuff some grass inside the wound and then pig runs off. If cut, in one year pig will be very big. If not cut, in two years still very small."

I hardly begrudged them their amusement. Tony said I was the first tourist to visit in a month, and tourists are a welcome diversion in a valley with no newspapers, no TV, no electricity. No toilets, either. "Pig is toilet here," Tony told me shortly after we arrived and I began looking for a toilet. "You don't believe? Go in bushes. Take down your pants. Pig comes running. Some tourists think he will bite, but he won't. He waits for you to finish."

The memory of this slow village would stick with me, I knew. I would remember Tony's uncle's solemn bow toward me when Tony gave him two tobacco leaves; the kids surrounding me, and their wide-eyed, sideways looks at each other when they heard their voices echoing from my tape recorder; the pregnant woman pounding grain and pretending not to watch me write; the mist and the rumble climbing out of the gorge.

Sitting there, looking at the mountains yesterday, it struck me that we go about this travel thing all backwards. A few weeks prior to my trip, my ex-wife Beverly had jumped from an airplane 12,000 feet above Northern California while a man with a parachute was strapped to her back. "Tandem jumping," it was called—the latest way of introducing novices to the sport of skydiving. Now I imagined that the "adventure travel" wave of the future would be tandem jumping into the Third World. Forget dumping the traveler at the airport on the capital's outskirts, where the new country's first introduction would be the inevitable pollution-traffic-noise-hookers-beggars. Instead, strap him (or her) to a native skydiver/guide, and drop him at sundown into an unspoiled paradise—a place like Pula.

Let him marvel at the countryside, the waterfalls, the ancient rice terraces, the pulsing silence, and the efficient pig-toilets. Let everyone gather round to stare at him. Feed him a sweet potato (make him peel it with a stick) and a bowl of rice, then inform him that that was dinner. Make him drink the local moonshine, then sleep on the floor of a hut. Surprise him in the morning with a pig mutilation. Feed him another sweet potato and bowl of rice and call that breakfast. Allow him fifteen minutes to jot in his journal, then start him walking over the mountains to catch the bus to the capital, to the airport; put him on another plane and drop him cold into some other unsuspecting village in some other country. He would remember it forever.

10

Baksheesh!

India! the land of dreams and romance, of fabulous wealth and fabulous poverty, of splendor and rags, of palaces and hovels, of famine and pestilence, of genii and giants and Aladdin lamps...the one land that all men desire to see, and having seen once, by even a glimpse, would not give that glimpse for the shows of all the rest of the world combined.

—MARK TWAIN, *Following the Equator*

Six years earlier I had spent three months in India, and had come away thinking of the country as a vast amusement park that combined elements of the grotesque and the magnificent. "India is amazing," I told people. "India is my favorite place. There is no way to prepare for it except to go there. And you *must* go there. It will shock you, delight you, spin your head around. You will hate it. You will love it."

I was married during the earlier trip, and on our first day in the country, Beverly and I stood for twenty minutes and watched a man levitate six feet off the ground. It wasn't until several hours later that we figured out his trick (or so we told ourselves).

On our third evening we watched a full moon, as shiny as a silver dollar, rise at dusk from among the gardens and minarets of the Taj Mahal. Around midnight I wandered inside the dome for twenty sacred minutes, alone—no guards, no other tourists, Beverly asleep on the front lawn—and thought: *Can this really be happening?*

During our third week, in the city of Ahmedabad, a boy in a crowd whipped a fat snake at me from behind—it was an expert throw; I never saw it coming—and suddenly it had wrapped itself around my neck three times—*whoop-whoop-whoop!*—transforming me from a human being into a thrashing tangle of limbs. I clawed the slimy, quivering thing from my throat and kicked it aside. It was freshly dead I found out, and so would that boy have been if he hadn't outrun me.

In another crowd, at the bus station in the city of Jammu, something reached out and grabbed Beverly's ankle. She looked down and discovered, at her feet, a laughing man who stood (if *stand* is what he did) only twelve or fourteen inches high. His head was normal-sized, but his arms and legs had never developed. His hobby, it seemed, was hanging out at the bus station and scaring tourists.

India put us into the present moment in a way we'd not experienced before, never giving us a clue about what to expect next, while confronting us daily, almost hourly, with novel or horrifying or heart-wrenching situations, whose resolutions required that we instantly reinvent ourselves, find some new, non-Western way of thinking. We finally left, shaking our heads and thinking: *There can be no place as mind-scrambling, as tragic, as magic, as India.* And when planning my 100-day trip, I scheduled three weeks in India—several days each in Calcutta, mountainous Darjeeling, the holy city of Varanasi, and finally New Delhi.

The subcontinent greeted my return not with its infamous heat and dust, but with cool and dripping skies. A tropical disturbance in the Bay of Bengal was moving toward Calcutta, and my plane spent half an hour encased in heavy gray clouds before, suddenly, we dropped from their bottoms and slid across a puddled runway.

Three mustachioed guards stood beneath the terminal eaves, clutching antique rifles and watching our plane disgorge its load of delirious looters. This was not the usual group of bored airline passengers, but a gluttonous victory celebration. Return of the fleet. Everyone had scored big in Hong Kong or Bangkok. The overhead bins were stuffed with booty—VCRs, televisions, stereos. The teenagers wore Walkmans, "U.S. ARMY" jackets, and the latest in multi-zippered fashions.

Inside the terminal I was approached by a man wearing a baggy blue uniform—a customs official I supposed. I was expecting a greeting or an immigration question, but instead he whispered, "Zelling zumzing?"

"No," I said, selling nothing.

"Camaduh?"

"No, no camera."

"Vutch?"

"No watch."

He shrugged and walked away.

I had not visited Calcutta on my first trip to India. The two Scandinavians behind me in the customs line were also first timers; Jari, a doctor, and Tiina, a nurse, were both from Finland. They were lugging backpacks and heading to the same part of town as I, a place named Sudder Street. We had just finished piling our backpacks into the trunk of one of the fixed-price taxis in front of the terminal, when a man suddenly materialized, seemingly out of the wet asphalt at our feet. He was barefooted and barechested, and wore nothing but a stained turban and loincloth that looked like they'd been made from a drapery my mother once threw out during a redecoration. He slammed the trunk closed and sang India's one-word national anthem/demand: "*Baksheesh!*"

Tiina and Jari and I snorted—the new arrival's nervous response toward India—and moved toward the cab doors. They climbed into the back; I went to the front. The trunk-slammer leaped ahead and blocked my door, his palm out, eyes bulging, screaming, "*Baksheesh!*" I reached around him, opened the door, got in and closed it. A young Indian man was seated next to the driver, and now the two of them looked at me: *Well?*

I shook my head—no *baksheesh.*

The driver started his engine.

"Wait," said Jari. He rolled his window down and held out a coin. The beggar took it, looked at it, cursed immediately, and hurled it back through Jari's window. It pinged off the ashtray. Jari said, "I guess he only likes folding *baksheesh.*"

We left the airport, driving too fast, and headed into the outskirts of Calcutta. The rain, falling harder now, had mixed the city's dust into an orange grime that glazed the road. Cows ambled through the streets, lazily swatting tails at their rib-lined flanks. We splashed through potholes and came up fast behind a truck with a HORN PLEASE! sign on its rear; our driver gave a vicious salvo, pulled out, and roared past. I turned to look back at the pedestrians scattered in our wake.

In the rear seat, Tiina and Jari wore thin, anxious smiles. "Maybe we die in Calcutta," Tiina said.

"Not me," I joked. "I've got a doctor and nurse with me."

"Ah," said Jari, "but we have no Calcutta license."

"And no instruments," said Tiina. "No medicines."

Nor were there pharmacies nearby in which to find any, no stores at all, just hundreds of drapery-clad ragamuffins picking at the litter and sludge filling the streets, as they wandered through the wasteland. The road was blocked by six bony men pushing a wooden cart stacked high with bricks; our driver braked and reached down to an auxiliary horn—a Harpo Marx honker positioned by his knee—and trumpeted two-toned insults. Tired-eyed squatters stared out from cardboard shacks erected on the median strip of a wide avenue; others had taken up open-air residence in collapsed brick buildings. Two men, riding a decrepit black bicycle, wobbled into our path, a row of four live chickens dangling upside down from the handlebars. Our driver screamed something in Hindi and blasted his horn, but never slowed. The bicyclists shied and skidded into a woman balancing a basket of cow dung on her head.

Present moment, I thought, *here I am!*

11

Calcutta

I am a man who habitually doles out spare change to winos, I suppose because I see the possibility that I might, one day, total my karma and find myself sitting in an alley behind a tattoo parlor, swigging muscatel from a bottle in a paper bag. But this idea of sins in the previous life resulting in the mutilation of children by beggar-masters and misery pimps—I would not, I decided, perpetuate this system. I would not, as a matter of principle, give money to beggars...I thought: It would be like standing on the brink of hell and tossing in a wet sponge.

— TIM CAHILL, *A Wolverine Is Eating My Leg*

From the moment of arrival, the visitor to Calcutta is a moving target. Even a hotel room is no guarantee of privacy. Cries of misery and commerce floated through the walls and windows of my room, and to open the door (it was visible from the street) was to ignite a barrage of frantic hollering:

"Alooo Meester!"

"Reekshah, Sahib—Reekshah?"

"Umbrella, Babu! Nice umbrella!"

On my first night a cyclone hit Calcutta, bringing gale force winds, blankets of rain, and a power outage. I spent the evening writing in my notebook by candlelight. Toward midnight, when I heard the rain stop and the wind ease, I cracked my door open. Outside I saw not only Sudder Street, under a foot of water but, also, one umbrella salesman, two rickshaw-pullers, and a gaggle of beggars—all whooping for my business. *"Alooo Meester!"* Closing my door on their flooded opera, I felt like Scrooge.

Sudder Street was only two blocks long and was located in one of Calcutta's less forlorn areas; but one night, after the street had drained, I counted more than seventy people, sleeping on its sidewalks and in its doorways, curled up under dirty gray sheets and scraps of burlap: ancient men and women, teenagers, young mothers with infant children. I was struck repeatedly by how small, how thin, they seemed.

The sense of appreciation for self and country that one gains by visiting the Third World is mainly a function of comparison. Every day, I walked miles through Calcutta's slums and parks and plazas, held my breath down alleys knee-deep in garbage, dodged cows, streetcars, and the ranks of cripples and beggars and men pissing against walls, and thought: *Thank God I'm not him. Thank God I'm not her. Oh, geezus, look at that—thank God that's not me.*

At least a dozen times during my stay, I joined the hordes walking across the Howrah Bridge. I watched bathers dip themselves in the brown-sugar waters below, and thought: *Thank God my hotel has a shower.* I watched the vendors lining the bridge sidewalks, and thought: *Thank God I'm not fully grown at four and a half feet like that man selling keyrings, or three feet, like the old woman with the brooms. Thank God I'm not trotting with a twenty-kilo basket of bananas balanced atop my head—imagine his back problems!* I surveyed the unrelenting traffic and thought: *Thank God I'm not the third guy hanging onto the back of that motor scooter, or one of those clinging, like starfish, to the side of that bus.*

Refugees who pour into Calcutta by train stick so close to the Howrah Station that its permanent population is said to be in the thousands. The outside looks like a government office building, the inside like a war zone. Walking through the cavernous interior, through the mobs of people with crutches or withered or missing limbs, I thought: *Thank God I've got all my arms and legs. Thank God I'm not that eight-year-old boy in front of the concession stand, down on my knees with the dogs, sifting through empty Four Square cigarette packs and torn newspapers (headline:* DECAPITATIONS IN DARJEELING), *trying to find something to sell or eat. Thank God I'm not that four-year-old, asleep on the gritty floor without a blanket or pillow, or that blind eighty-year-old, tottering with a stick and a tin cup from platform to platform.*

In America the plea of a rail-thin street person dressed in rags sends my hand creeping toward my pocket. But if I'd allowed that instinct in Calcutta, my wad would've lasted about half an hour. I always kept some coins in my pants, but—the jingle of change in Calcutta being as conspicuous as the crackle, in church, of a candy wrapper—I tried to be discreet about doling them out.

The morning after my arrival I plunked one rupee—a few cents—into the cup of a man with no hands who sat on the ground in front of my hotel, and was immediately pursued down Sudder Street by a posse of hustlers, half of them crippled.

"Sahib! Sahib!"

"Hah-sh, good hah-sh? No? You vunt grahss?"

"Dullas? Change dullas?"

"You vunt gill? Boy-ee?"

"Zelling zumzing?"

"Babu! Oooo, Ba-booo!"

I said: "Sorry...sorry...No, not this morning...No, sorry...Sorry...no..." But I thought: *What if I just took off my money belt and handed it to one of these people?* With per capita income in India being $270 a year, the $2,500 around my waist represented nearly ten years of income. My credit cards and passport would fetch another decade's worth on the black market. And for me, it was all replaceable. But that would be a gesture—a micro swipe at a macro problem. And what difference would it make? The voices of the friends who had called my invite-someone-home plan poorly designed echoed quite loudly in Calcutta.

The Blue Sky Cafe, a Sudder Street backpackers' hangout, served coffee, curd, omelets, sandwiches, and temporary refuge. Getting in was easy, but a troop of beggar women was on permanent guard at the door, waiting to flog their anguish and their naked babies on anyone leaving. One needn't know a syllable of Hindi or Bengali to get their message: "Don't you dare stiff us on a full stomach!"

One morning a woman with a baby boy and an empty metal bowl danced down the street beside me, as though attached to my elbow.

"Hungry," she said.

I dropped a half-rupee coin into her bowl.

"Very hungry."

I added a whole rupee, but she stayed right with me.

"Very, very hungry."

I turned and fixed her with a look—*Enough, woman!*—but she was ready.

"God gave you much money," she said. "I need a kilo of rice."

The truth put simply is simply disarming. When I gave her two more rupees, she smiled and left me, but every day after that, I was hers.

Calcutta had once been a British showpiece of dignified government office buildings, two state-of-the-Empire train stations, and a mile-long park, the *maidan*, stretching through the center of town. Until India's partition in 1947, the city and the entire Bengal region had prospered. But when the British created East Pakistan (now Bangladesh), the government drew the new border just to Calcutta's east, depriving the city's jute mills from access to the surrounding jute fields, and vice versa. The economies of both new countries were, in the Indian beggars' tradition, effectively crippled at birth. This blunder, combined with the region's infamous droughts and famines and exploding population, sent refugees pouring into Calcutta—a stream that has continued, unabated, ever since.

What, I wondered, would a time-traveling British colonialist make of the place now? The dress of the natives hadn't changed, the caste system remained intact, and the human-drawn rickshaws—although outlawed as inhumane in the rest of India—were everywhere in Calcutta. But what would a time-traveler think of the decrepit buildings, the rubbish heaps, the thousands residing at the railroad stations? Would he weep over the *maidan*? What was once a manicured oasis—twelve hundred acres of gardens, pathways and flowerbeds—was now a grazing area for goats and a bathroom for humans. One morning I stopped for sixty seconds on the *maidan* and counted the number of people I could see urinating or defecating: nineteen standing pissers, five squatting dumpers. All men. Where, I wondered, did the women go?

But if India's squalor had remained constant during the six years I'd been away, there had also been some modernization. Sudder Street had two video rental stores, and Calcutta had India's first subway, a gleaming new marvel from which beggars were banned. Upgraded satellite connections allowed me to call San Francisco to wish Rhonda a happy birthday without a trace of static. Color TVs were mounted in Howrah Station so train passengers could keep up with cricket matches and soap operas. And when I bought my train ticket to Darjeeling, the booking office handled the whole transaction, from reservation to typed receipt, on a brand new computer system. But Calcutta's biggest surprise, perhaps, was the few signs discreetly advertising abortions.

The changes, however, appeared to be the trickle-down sort, and seemed bizarre in contrast with all that had not changed. The newspapers talked of India's nuclear program and plans for a space program, but in the General Post Office the public still bought glueless stamps in one line, then moved to another line, where they dipped them in a common pot of stickum. The bureau for permits to travel to Darjeeling was housed deep in a red-brick turn-of-the-century British secretariat; inside I found sheaves of faded documents stacked floor-to-ceiling, with tea-sipping civil servants stationed between stacks—their function, apparently, being to ensure that nothing toppled. Residents of my hotel ate breakfast on a rooftop patio, and each day followed the progress of a building under construction across the alley; one worker's job was to move a pile of sand from ground level to the top floor, carrying it up five flights of ladders one basketful at a time. In five days the pile appeared undiminished. There was a bettors' pool on the job's completion date, but only long-term guests were bothering with it.

In the six years I'd been away, India's population had increased by 103 million—nearly half the population of the United States. That computes to roughly 16 million people a year, 1.5 million people a month, 45,000 people a day, 2,000 people an hour, 31 people a minute. If San Francisco were to be emptied of people and then repopulated at the same rate by which India was growing—a new arrival every two seconds—the city would be filled again in sixteen days. A San Francisco-sized population every *sixteen days!* What group can be more frustrated than India's league of city planners?

One afternoon I was seated, jotting notes, on a low, shaded wall near yet another riverside slum, the Chandipahl Ghat, as I jotted notes, when an older gentleman sat next to me and said: "I see you are a writer." It was a sweltering afternoon, but he was wearing a heavy gray suit and a snuggly-knotted tie. "So tell me, how do you find Calcutta?"

Below was a view of slum-dwellers bathing in the muck of the Hooghly: naked boys splashing each other, squatting women filling tall jars with the river's greasy water. The banks were a paste of mud, banana leaves, coconut husks, broken pottery, and the charred ashes of campfires. Side by side a cow and a man were nosing through the riverside flotsam, and now the man raised something black and stringy, and cried to a friend to come and inspect it. A gang of overhead crows shrieked, laughing at all of us.

"A bit of a mess," I said.

"You will excuse me," the man said, "but you are being too polite. India is a *filthy* mess. India can break your heart. Nobody can explain India, and nobody can do anything about it. I am in the economic development ministry for the Bengali state government. I did my schooling in the States, in Boston, and I came back very much excited. We were going to do such great things. Calcutta had not yet fallen into ruin. It was almost a model city—does it not remind you of your Washington, D.C.?"

Below us an abandoned tugboat was beached ten yards from shore, and at least thirty people were calling it home. While a woman spread laundry on the railings, a man fried something in a huge, smoky pan on the cabin roof. Three boys were teasing a monkey chained to a nearby tree. The air stank of urine.

"Washington D.C.?"

"You have the Mall," the man said, "we have the *maidan*. You have your monuments to Jefferson and Washington and Lincoln; we have our Queen Victoria Memorial. You have grand old office buildings, so did we. You have the Potomac; we have the Hooghly."

"I see," I said.

"Now imagine that thousands of people arrived at your Union Station every day, refugees from Kentucky or Oklahoma or somewhere. Every day, all year long, for nearly fifty years. Imagine that they were starving and homeless, illiterate, that they came from families that had been peasant farmers for dozens of centuries. Imagine that they occupied your benches and your lounges and your restaurants and built their hovels on your platforms. That they cooked and bathed and went to the bathroom wherever they could manage. Would your police arrest them? They could not—where would they keep them all? Would your army kill them? I think not. Could your Red Cross find food and shelter and clothing for all of them? Not even in America would this be possible. Imagine that during a drought or a famine one hundred thousand arrived in a single week. Do you know what your Washington would look like? It would, I think, look much like Calcutta." He stopped and looked at me, but I offered no rebuttal.

"You should thank your God," he told me, "that you don't have to live here."

12

Dee-Troit?

*"It is the old story: the darker-skinned people against the lighter-skinned
people."*

—V. S. NAIPAUL, *Time* Interview

On my last night in Calcutta I visited a Sudder Street snack stand
to drink a bottle of Limca—India's answer to Sprite. From my
table just inside the door I could see and hear two men—one a legless
beggar, the other dark as an African—arguing loudly and pointing fingers in each other's faces. Engrossed in recording the day in my notebook, I paid them little mind until I heard a voice call from the street:
"Say brutha! Wuss 'appenin'?"

It was the dark man. The argument had ended and now he was
alone, standing in the street ten feet away, looking straight at me, smiling. He had silver hair, wore a dark blue sarong, a white t-shirt, and no
shoes. "Where you from, man? Australia?"

I shook my head.

"States?"

I nodded.

"Baltimore? Dee-troit? New Orleans...?"

Maybe the first Hindi phrase a tourist learns is *"Chell-OH...Chell-
OH"* ("Get lost"—always said loudly), and now the owner of the snack
stand walked out into the street and started hollering this, and some
other things, too, at the man. For a couple of moments the man answered back in Hindi, then turned and moved down the street, giving a
final glance back at me.

"Kdezy bleck," the owner said. "Oolweez buthering."

I finished my Limca then hustled down the street. The black man was seated in a doorway two buildings down, waiting for me. "'At man a baaad muthafucka," he said, scooting over to make room. "Where you from man? Portlan'?"

I sat beside him and told him where I was from.

"Frisco, baby! All right, brutha."

"You're not American," I said. "Are you?"

"No man, look ut me!" He was very dark and had extra curly hair, but his facial features were not African.

I guessed, "Fiji?"

"No, man! South India."

"I've been to south India. No one there talks like you do."

"'At's right, Jack. I speak American black language." He raised his right palm. "I speak your language, brutha!"

"That's not my language," I said, but gave him a palm to slap anyway. "Are you a sailor?"

"Aah brutha! How you know that?"

"All those ports you mentioned."

"Oh man. You too hip, brutha!" He raised his hand again, and when I'd slapped it he almost absentmindedly gripped my right biceps. "I'm so happy to see an American. So many American friends I have. But I won't lie to you, man. I ain't no sailor. But I work on American ships."

"In India?"

"Here—in Calcutta. Loading, unloading, helping U.S. Navy. During 'Nam all sorts of Navy ships comin' to Calcutta. That's where I learned to speak black, man. Now sometimes I speak to Africa blacks. They afraid of me, say, 'Why you talk like that? You a nigger?' But I'm a black man. I'm no nigger. I'm talkin' your language now, right Jack?"

"My name is Brad. What's yours?"

"Kah-seem," he said.

"Kasim, I understand American blacks, but I sound pretty foolish when I try to speak like them."

"But you can dig it, man. I can tell," he said. "You know John Kennedy?"

"The president? Sure."

"You like John Kennedy?"

"Sure," I said. "I was only twelve years old when he was killed. My father took me to his funeral parade through Washington D.C. We were all sad. Everyone."

"Kennedy a righteous man, brutha. First president to say, 'These people were born here. We are all the same.' Jack Kennedy—righteous man, brutha. 'We are all the same.'" He released my arm to slap me five again.

"America's the best," Kasim said. "I almost went there. I was best worker in the port. Captain say, 'Kasim, I take you to America.' But my mother cries. She say, 'You can't take my last son.' I have three brothers, but I'm the last one. Captain says he'll send her a hundred dollars a month while I'm gone—man, a hundred dollars, American money!—but she cries. 'My last son.' So I don't go nowhere, man. I'da seen all them places, man, but I didn't."

A young man, wearing a turban and a heavy coat, stopped directly in front of us and started screaming at Kasim, evidently a popular pastime on this street. This newcomer was very loud and angry, and I supposed it was about money. Kasim didn't challenge him, just sat next to me as he spoke in quiet shushing tones, brushing the air with the back of his hand to shoo this man away.

When he had exhausted himself on Kasim, the man turned to me, smiled, and said: "This man is junkie. He is always cheating tourists. He will tell you he is sailor, but he is junkie. He has no job. If you give him money, he will spend it, I promise you, on fix." He turned and walked down the street.

Kasim said, "Sheee-it," and clutched my arm.

"Kasim, are you a junkie?"

"I'm no lyin' muthafucka," he said. "I take fix every day, but I don't cheat people. I just talk. I'm just so happy to see an American."

"Do you have a job, Kasim?"

"I'm no lyin' muthafucka. I did have a job. Good job. My mother, she's got a big ol' stack of my salary papers. If I'm lyin' you can kick my ass, Jack. But I lose my job. Too much fix. Before I meet American boys I never use fix. I was the best worker. Most Calcutta Indians, they're not Kasim's color. I more black like American boys. Kasim is their favorite. They teach me to talk black. They tell me if I go to America, American women—black women, white women—will dig me. They tell me about Dee-troit, Baltimore...Sometimes one ship goes out, new ship comes in, an' these new boys, they already know about Kasim. They say other boys always talking about me, say 'Kasim, he's Indian, but he's hip.' They hear me talk black, they slap me five—they think I'm cool. Then one day, one boy, he say, 'Kasim, you know shit?' So I take needle. But I like it too good, man. I lose my job. Now I take fix every day." He stopped for a moment, and when he spoke again it was in a lower voice. "Kasim tell you the truth, brutha. I'm a junkie, but I ain't no lyin' muthafucka."

We sat there quietly, me trying to figure out a way to avoid what was coming. I wondered briefly how Kasim would do in America, and quickly dismissed the thought: he was much more than I wanted to deal with for a month.

After a couple of moments I rustled my daypack in my lap, "Well, thanks Kasim," I said and started to stand.

He wrapped his fingers around my arm. "Brutha, you got ten rupees for Kasim?"

I pulled free and stood up. "Sorry. I don't think so. I'll buy you a Limca back there if you want. Or dinner."

He let me off easy. "It's O.K.," he said. He raised his hand and we slapped a final five. "Be cool."

13

What I Know About Dying

We help the poor die with God....It is between them and God alone.
Nobody else. Nobody has the right to come in at that time.

—MOTHER TERESA,
Mother Teresa: Her People and Her Work

Calcutta will never be a tourist attraction. It is famous not for food, but a lack of it; not for sights, but for squalor. There were so few foreigners in town that whenever two of us passed in the streets, each with our own personal escort of beggars, we always exchanged nods. My guess was that in the half-dozen cheap hotels around Sudder Street no more than fifty to seventy-five people were registered. Like myself, most had come to see if Calcutta was as bad as they'd heard, but some were there to try and help.

Deborah was one of several from my hotel who had come specifically to work at the Missionaries of Charity Home for Dying Destitutes, commonly known as Mother Teresa's. On my last day in Calcutta—before heading on to the Himalayas, the holy city of Varanasi, and eventually New Delhi—I accepted Deborah's invitation to spend a morning as a volunteer. Deborah, thirty-five, was a small, attractive woman with short dark hair—and a self-described "serious student of Buddhism." Originally from Seattle, she was enrolled at the time in a nursing school in Alabama that had partially sponsored her trip. Single rooms in our hotel cost us US$2.50, but Deborah— "I'm on a real tight budget"—was saving a dollar a night by staying in the dorm.

That morning we each saved another rupee by taking the bus instead of the subway. An Indian man rose from his spot in the "Women Only" seats at the front so that Deborah could sit. I stood next to her, asking questions about what to expect.

"You've seen the streets," she said. "It's a lot like that, but worse, because these people really are on their last legs. You only wind up at Mother Teresa's if you're dying. Some people make it in on their own; others get here because someone finds them dying on the streets and calls Mother Teresa's ambulance. We feed and clean them and do what we can medically. Mainly, we just try to treat everyone, even the poorest of the poor who won't survive the day, with a little dignity. About half of them get strong enough to go back out on the street and half of them die."

"Do you often actually see people...*expire?*"

"Pretty much every day. Not that I'm always there at the exact moment, but when I arrive each morning, I usually hear that someone I worked with yesterday died. Or I'll come back after lunch, and someone I fed that morning is gone."

"Is that hard to get used to?"

"I can think of more fun things," she said, "but it's part of life. I've learned a lot. The meaning of *service*, for one. And humility. Someday I'm going to die, and I'm getting a clearer sense of what that might be like. I hope to do it as well as some of these people. They have nothing, nobody, and they die with a dignity that amazes me."

At our bus stop Deborah led the way through a marketplace packed with vendors, cows, and holy men. There was a commotion ahead, a tumult of shuffling feet, shrieking children, cackling women. Deborah said, "Must be Darryl." Above the congregation I saw the head and shoulders of a tall black man. "They can't get enough of him here."

I've grown accustomed during my travels to getting a fair amount of attention. When I'm not slouching, I'm on the tall side, and my hair, when I spend time outside, takes on the color of the sun; in places where people are short or dark or both, I am often stared at. My theory on attention is that it's a nice thing but it does have limits, and I do not think I would have wanted to be Darryl in India.

"Neee-gro, Neee-gro," the children were screaming. "America Nee-gro!"

Darryl was six-feet-five, 220 pounds, had an athlete's wide sloping shoulders, and was moving so slowly that we quickly overtook him. Small filthy children clung to him like koalas to the world's last eucalyptus—three or four per leg, two per arm. I saw one urchin hurtle through the crowd and launch himself at Darryl's massive back, hit, grab, scramble right up onto Darryl's shoulders, and steady himself with a grip on Darryl's hair. Another boy cried, "Micah Jasson!" and broke into a herky-jerky moonwalk, clearing Darryl a path through the crowd.

"Neee-gro, Neee-gro," screamed the rabble. "America Nee-gro."

Darryl had a high-pitched chuckle unexpected from a man so big—it was almost a tee-hee—and a happy nature to go along with it. He was holding two of the small muggers by their ankles, upside down. "MISTER Negro," I heard him correct them, but he was laughing. He saw us and called, "Hey Deborah, I'm cleaning this place up, but I can't find any dumpsters. Where's that Black Hole?"

Deborah just waved at him. "Come on," she said to me. "He always makes it in eventually."

We came to a whitewashed building which, except for the cow lumbering across the front steps and the ancient white ambulance parked out front, looked like a villa one might find in the Greek Islands. A Western man was down on his knees in the entranceway, scrubbing its concrete floor with a rag and bucket of water, which gave the place a soapy smell. We passed him and entered a large, whitewashed room with high ceilings propped up by wide plastered pillars. Fifty low, narrow cots were arranged in rows, each supporting an emaciated man, who was lying or sitting. A chalkboard on the wall had the date, December 3, and these headings: "MEN" "WOMEN" "ADMITTED" "DISCHARGED" and "DEATHS." A "4" was chalked into the last column.

Next to the door, a man lay on a cot; an I.V. drip tube hung from a hat rack beside him and disappeared beneath his blankets. His skull, no larger than a cantaloupe, was wrinkled and hairless, and his eyes were so deeply sunken that each socket might have held a half-cup of water. His head was thrust back onto his pillow and every three or four seconds he would gasp.

"He won't last the day," Deborah said; she'd seen me watching him. "The night at most. The way he's breathing, that's a sure sign."

"Deborah, Brad, good morning." I turned to see Patrick Petrowski, a young man I had met a few days earlier on Sudder Street. He had the tall, blond look that one associates with California beaches, but was actually a Canadian, who had graduated from university the previous spring and had been traveling ever since. In order to stretch his money and his trip, he was staying in a Sudder Street dorm for Indians where he paid only one rupee a night. Over dinner the night we met, he had told me, "India is by far the most challenging and interesting place I've seen, and working at Mother Teresa's easily the most vital experience of my life. Living in North America..." He shook his head. "I can't believe how much I didn't know."

A month at Mother Teresa's had made Patrick the senior volunteer, responsible for organizing the other male volunteers. Now, in Mother Teresa's doorway, he said, "Glad you decided to come, Brad. Come on, I'll show you around."

There were no doctors in the building, no life support systems. Patrick led me to a room with fifty more cots. I saw a Western woman whom I had noticed in the Blue Sky Cafe one morning. At the time, she had struck me as aloof, hard-looking; I had wondered what was on her mind, but hadn't asked. Now she was sitting on the side of a cot, cradling in her arms the head and torso of a shriveled Indian woman, who was violently sobbing. A circle of workers surrounded them, and from a high window, a dusty beam of light filtered down on all of them. I read terror in the Indian woman's face, compassion in the Western woman's, and concern and helplessness on the faces of the others. I thought: *We should DO something.* I looked at Patrick, but he'd seen it all before. "This is the women's room," he said. "Come on, I'll show you the roof."

We climbed a flight of stairs. A horseshoe of rooms surrounded a rooftop courtyard where laundry hung from lines. "The sisters live up here," Patrick said. In the distance a blue morning sky stretched over Calcutta's low skyline; in the street below were carts, cows, hawkers, fruit stands, and a mob of delinquents waiting for Darryl to reappear.

A woman in nun's robes stepped from one of the rooms. "Sister Rose!" Patrick called. "I'd like you to meet Brad. He's a new volunteer."

In the presence of people who are actually *doing some good* in the world, I feel a sense of inadequacy, that my life is a string of trivialities. As I looked into Sister Rose's gray eyes, I wondered how many one-morning volunteers she had seen, and what she thought of them. I tried to imagine committing my life to this work in Calcutta, to the noise and filth, to a room over a place where people came to die, but I could not. Sister Rose said, "Thank you for coming, Brad," and went downstairs.

In the kitchen Patrick handed me a green volunteer's smock. Breakfast was being served, and together we brought dishes of oatmeal from the kitchen to bedsides in the men's room and cleared away the dirty ones. Some of the men could sit up, but some were too weak; some nodded thank you; others were oblivious. I checked on the man in the entranceway—still gasping.

The many quiet struggles going on in the building had created a kind of group altered-consciousness. One could almost hear the members of the order wrestling with their faith and lifetime commitments; each patient dueling death; each volunteer, the meaning of life. I felt like a shirker: when the morning came to an end, I would return to my hotel for a shower and a nap, and then leave to catch the train to Darjeeling. This, for me, was no more than morning twenty-five on a jaunt around the world, and any significance I had attached to the trip melted in the glare of the fact that half of the people in this building would die before I even got home.

One man was smiling at me. He was perched, birdlike, on the edge of his bed, knees pulled up alongside his ears, butt resting on the backs of his ankles, arms tucked to his sides like wings. He was so small and folded so neatly that he might have flown to America under my airline seat. But when I picked up his plate, I saw he was drooling down his front, and his smile was the frozen kind. He was never going to see America. He would be lucky to see the streets of Calcutta once more—and that seemed like no luck at all.

After breakfast I helped Patrick prop up a few of the weakest men so we could give them fat, yellow vitamin pills and gulps of water. All were pathetically light, fragile as papier mache art projects, their bodies lacking, I thought, the minimum mass needed to support a spirit.

I visited the man by the door—the one with the I.V. hookup and the labored breath. His shrunken brown skull reminded me of head-hunter trophies Tony had shown me in the Philippines. I bent over and brushed his forehead with the backs of my fingers, ever so lightly, and then again, and then some more; his eyes adjusted to absorb me, then lost their focus and closed. Under his blankets, his chest heaved up and heaved down, was still for a few seconds, and then repeated the cycle. And again. And again. It seemed he was working too hard, but I imagined that he liked the gentle way I was touching him. If I was alone in the world and dying, wouldn't I appreciate a stranger's touch? I had spent a few minutes alone with my father's body just before it was cremated; I had stroked his chest and his cold cheeks and kissed his forehead, and sensed that somewhere, somehow, it had been appreciated. This man in front of me had patches of white hair above his ears, and I expanded my stroke to include them. For two or three minutes I kept up a soft steady circuit—stroking cheeks-forehead-hair, cheeks-forehead-hair—and was thinking how nice it was that the two of us could share this moment, when suddenly the dying man gathered his strength and gave his head a violent shake, the way a man buried neck deep in sand would shake a fly off his nose. *Buzz off, kid!*

I looked around to see if anyone had witnessed my rebuke, but everyone was absorbed in other things. I whispered "Sorry" and backed away. What did I know about dying, anyway?

14

Some Blood, Some Vomit, Some Feces

At first, when she started treating the lepers who lived in the train station, the Indian government just ignored her. But then there were rumors that she was converting people to Christianity, and they threatened to deport her. Finally they figured it was better to have her doing her work here than in the train station. The day they told her they were giving her this building, word got around, and within half an hour all of Calcutta's rickshaw drivers descended on Howrah Station and moved every one of the lepers here for free. Now, that would have been a parade to see.

—PATRICK PETROWSKI,
Volunteer Coordinator at Mother Teresa's

A circle of volunteers were squatting Indian style around the wash basins and stacks of dirty dishes on the cement floor of Mother Teresa's kitchen. I knelt down between Deborah and Darryl and pulled a clump of straw from a sheaf on the floor. Like everyone else, I dipped it into the bucket of fine gray ashes serving as our detergent, picked up a plate, and began scrubbing away the traces of oatmeal.

Darryl looked at me and said, "I haven't seen you around." He wore granny glasses on his kind face, and spoke with a "mainstream" accent. I wondered what he'd make of Kasim, Sudder Street's jiving junkie. "Your first day?"

Darryl was from Connecticut, and seven days earlier had flown from New York to London, then Bombay, and finally Calcutta. "This," he said, "is my first time out of the U.S."

"Most people warm up for the Third World with a European trip or something," I said. "Why the cold plunge?"

"I'm a physical therapist," Darryl said, "and I've been working the same job for six straight years. I was starting to feel like I should break up my routine. So I'm going to spend three months here. And from the way things are going..."—he laughed his almost tee-hee—"I'd say this is about as different as you can get."

"Isn't this—tending to dying people—similar to physical therapy?"

"Well, I can see why someone might think that," he said, "but I sure don't. It's a whole different thing. I really like the physical contact here. You don't have to be so...cautious. It's not like I've spent all morning worrying about a lawsuit." The laugh again. "At home I work a lot with old people who have nothing but complaints: 'My food's cold,' 'Channel Five's coming in fuzzy.' So no—I'd say this place is nothing like that place. And when you take Calcutta into account, hey—I'm on another planet. This place is an *experience*. I came here thinking that the sisters would find me a place to stay, but when I got here they just said, 'Here's a list of places—good luck.' So here I am my first day in Calcutta, walking around with this little piece of paper, stepping over beggars and all. They wanted 180 rupees a night at the YMCA, and that's only $15 at home, so I said O.K. It includes breakfast and dinner, too. It's clean there, real quiet, and big, too. Now I know you can find places a lot cheaper"—he looked around the circle—"guys like Patrick staying in a dorm for a rupee a night..."

On the other side of the buckets Patrick just shook his head and kept scrubbing.

"...but I never thought," Darryl continued, "there was anywhere in the world you could stay for six cents a night! How's someone supposed to know that? They didn't teach that in any school I went to. And shoot, if you'd told me, I'd have thought there's no way you could survive a night someplace that cheap. There's places in New York where you might pay thirty dollars a night, but you wouldn't be safe in there without a gun. Or *with* one either. That's something I've noticed here—

96

as many poor people as there are, you can still walk around feeling perfectly safe. I'm big and black, but there's places at home I don't even think about going. We're really losing it in America, you know? I've only been away a week, but already I can see that."

One of the missionaries, a Japanese man named Yuki, came by the circle and asked Darryl and me to wash blankets. He pointed to the side of the room, where a masonry tub was filled with clear water. Beside it was a mound of blankets, some new, some well worn, most a dingy army-green.

Darryl and I moved to opposite ends of the tub. He had done this job before: "We take one blanket at a time," he said, "and we dip it." We each took an end and lowered the first blanket into the water. "Now we swish it around real good..."—Darryl reached his arms in up to his elbows and swished the blanket back and forth—"and lift it up..."—it was heavy now—"and we look for dirty spots."

On my end there was a dark purplish stain. "Is this blood?"

"Oh, we're gonna see some blood on these things," Darryl said. "Some vomit, some feces—maybe some stuff we aren't going to recognize, too. What you do is put that part back in the water and rub it against a clean spot until it goes away...Yeah, that's it. That one came out easy. Looks good. Now we lift it out...and wring it...as dry as we can....There! At Mother Teresa's we call that *clean*. Just drop it down on the floor. Someone'll come by to take it and hang it up on the roof." He peered over the top of his glasses at me. "Still think this is just like home?"

We spent an hour dipping, rubbing, and wringing. To avoid thinking about the stains—red, brown, puke orange—and the fact that we were dipping our arms into increasingly murky water, we talked. I asked Darryl why he'd come to Calcutta.

"Well, I guess I could blame it all on Bruce Lee."

"The *kung fu* Bruce Lee?"

"Yeah. I was just a teenager trying to figure the world out, when I saw 'Enter The Dragon.' Well, I took one look at Bruce Lee and I said, 'How'd this man get that perfect body?' And I started wondering about my own body and what kind of things were possible if I took care of it and trained it. I read a couple Bruce Lee magazines and they said he was into Chinese philosophy—that what you did with your mind was at least as important as what you did with your body. So I started reading Confucianism, Taoism, all the stuff I could find, and that took me to yoga and meditation. I started living my life differently. I started taking my body seriously. I worked out a lot. I wanted to see what my limits were. In the end I went to Boston University on a basketball scholarship."

Dip-slosh-rub-wring. Dip-slosh-rub-wring.

"One day I was watching TV in the dorm, and I saw a show on Mother Teresa in Haiti. I thought, 'This is fantastic.' I didn't know how there could be someone like that, someone who'd take care of these miserable poor people every day of her life when she didn't have to. It made a big impression on me. I told myself that someday I'd like to do something like she was doing. But I forgot about it until a couple of years ago. By then I was really into yoga and meditation and chanting. I had a guru for a while—guess I still do...."

"What guru?" I asked.

"Do you know Gurumayi? She used to be Swami Muktananda's assistant."

I said, "I saw her once a few years ago. I stayed at Muktananda's ashram near Bombay for three days about a month before he died."

"*Wow!* Did you see Muktananda?"

"Every day," I said. "Once he touched me. On the hand."

"*Really?*" Darryl seemed impressed.

"Really," I said. "You want to touch me?"

"No way," he said. "I see where you been dippin' that hand."

The people finishing up the dishes had been eavesdropping on our conversation, and now in Mother Teresa's kitchen there was audible laughter. Yuki poked his head into the kitchen to see what was up, but all he saw were post-joke smiles. He carried away our pile of wet blankets.

"So anyway," said Darryl, "just a couple of years ago I started feeling like I wanted to do something to get outside myself. I remembered a talk I'd had with a priest once. He'd said, 'Oh, yes. All your yoga and meditation and Eastern philosophy will make you strong like a fortress, but after a while you will need to find a way to use your strength.' At the time I said, 'Yeah, yeah,' but now I see the truth in what he said."

Now Yuki and Patrick appeared, dropped a pile of more dirty blankets at our feet, stepped past us and through a door next to the tub, a door I hadn't noticed earlier. Behind it I glimpsed shelves, a linen closet of some sort.

Darryl and I dipped a blanket. "So when I realized I'd reached a plateau with meditation and chanting, I started to look for a way to do something practical. And I remembered that show I'd seen on Mother Teresa in Haiti, and how I'd felt. She had a mission in New York, so I called them up and someone says, 'Hello.' I asked for Sister Agnes because I'd heard she was in charge, and when Sister Agnes comes to the phone she says, 'Do you know who that was? It was *Mother*!' That's what everyone calls Mother Teresa—'Mother.' Now that really killed me! Here's this woman—a living saint, Nobel prize—and I call up her place in New York and she picks up the phone and says 'Hello.' It was about the last thing I expected. Talk about humble. I started doing volunteer work there on weekends. I saw her once. She came for a weekend. Everyone else there was Catholic and they were all going up to kiss her hand, so I did too. I remember tasting salt and thinking, 'salt of the earth. That woman is the salt of the earth!' And, you know, when I got to Calcutta I realized that the taste of that kiss is the same taste you get in your mouth here. It's the taste of Calcutta's air. I'm keeping a journal and that's something I wrote in it."

There was a stubborn fecal stain on the blanket we were working on, and I bent over to rub it out. "It'll come," Darryl said. "Just take your time."

Yuki and Patrick emerged from the closet while I was bent over, grinding two parts of the blanket together. From the corner of my eye I saw Yuki in the lead, carrying the front end of a cot covered with a white bed sheet, Patrick at the rear. And suddenly the face of a dead man passed almost under my nose. That was no linen closet, but the building's morgue. And this was no embalmed man they were carrying, no father with an angelic smile arranged on closed lips. His head was thrown back, throat seemingly frozen during a yell, mouth twisted sideways, eyes wide open and rolled upward as though he died trying to warn the world of something terrible he'd seen.

"Yeah," Darryl said, seeing my flinch. "That's part of the trip. They take the old ones out to the ambulance every morning. You get used to it, but it sure does give you something to think about, doesn't it?"

15

Ooohs and Ahs

Out in the country in India, the day begins early. One sees a plain, perfectly flat, dust-colored and brick-yardy, stretching limitlessly away on every side in the dim gray light.... There is an enchantment about it.... You cannot tell just what it is that makes the spell, perhaps, but you feel it and confess it, nevertheless. Of course, at bottom, you know in a vague way that it is history...a haunting sense of the myriads of human lives that have blossomed, and withered, and perished here, repeating and repeating and repeating, century after century, and age after age, the barren and meaningless process....

——MARK TWAIN, *Following the Equator*

On morning twenty-six, somewhere in the plains stretching north from Calcutta to the Himalayan foothills, I was startled from sleep by a gang of tea vendors who stampeded through my train car, screaming, "CHAI! CHAI! CHAI!" Then: "CO-FEE! CO-FEE! CO-FEE!" And again: "CHAI! CHAI! CHAI!"

A while later I raised to one elbow and opened my window a crack; fresh air snapped inside, raising goose bumps on my bare arms. Outside, a metallic blue dawn was yawning at the state of Bihar. Shawl-wrapped silhouettes slid in and out of a mist that rose over a flat landscape of rice paddies, banana trees, plots of potatoes and radishes, and tall, long-armed banyan trees. It was good to have the subway and buses and video stores of Calcutta behind me, and to once again be chugging through a timeless scenery. A train ride through any portion of rural India is a living history lesson, a time capsule without the capsule.

A barefoot boy padded down a dirt track, a rope trailing over his shoulder to the nose ring of a bullock lumbering five yards behind. Next to a field of mustard seed eleven men squatted for morning bowel movements, their garments hiked up around their haunches as they stared blankly at our train. Women with babies at their shoulders stood in the doorways of huts and watched us fly by. This, the endless countryside, home to three-fourths of the population, was the India of one's imagination.

Midmorning we reached the end of the line, New Jaipalghuri (*Jai-pal-Goo-ree*). In this region, several million years ago, the Indian subcontinental plate collided with the greater Asian landmass. Before impact, both plates had been flat, but now the southern end of the Asian plate crumpled (in geologic terms) like a speeding Toyota meeting a bridge abutment. New Jaipalghuri lies in the plains near sea level, but five kilometers north of town the Himalayas begin their steep tilt, jutting to 28,000 feet within 35 air miles. Imagine Manhattan with the Himalayas towering just across the Hudson River in New Jersey.

The famous "toy railroad" that climbs to Darjeeling, 7,000 feet in the Himalayas, was out of operation that week, but I caught a rickety jalopy just pulling out of the New Jaipalghuri bus station. Minutes later we began switchbacking ladder-steep hills. Stands of pine and fir trees lined the road, and the smell of jasmine poured through the open windows. Our driver slowed to let three monkeys that loped out of the woods cross the road; we could hear them gibbering; they heard *oohs* and *ahs*. Out one side of the bus I could see the flat brown plains stretching back toward Calcutta with pre-collision flatness, and out the other, forested green slopes splashed with pink bougainvillea vines and bright red poinsettias.

The physical characteristics of the inhabitants changed with the geography. The Aryan features of the plains people disappeared, and now young Ghurka boys with oversized heads, burr haircuts, and big square faces stood by the road and watched our bus with wide Oriental eyes. Crews of women, wearing red scarves and trailing thick black braids down their backs, crushed rocks with sledgehammers. Brown teenage boys soaped themselves in small waterfalls.

The road was a series of hairpin turns wedged between jagged drop-offs. In one place a construction crew—five men with picks, shovels, and one wheelbarrow—was repairing a stretch where the mountainside had given way and plunged 500 feet, sweeping away the roadbed and 200 yards of railroad track. It would be months, maybe years, before the train ran again. Now there was an improvised dirt lane just wide enough for one vehicle; we held our breaths and everyone—not just me—laughed nervously when we were safely past.

Two postcards were taped to the bus windshield—one of Lord Shiva, and another of a skull with flames gushing from its ears and the legend, KILL 'EM ALL, LET GOD SORT 'EM OUT. As we traveled down the narrow highway, I surmised that orientation classes for Himalayan bus drivers were probably brief: *"Drive the middle of the road—fast as possible —mash the horn for curves—Any questions?"* Whenever our bus approached another, the two drivers would maintain full speed, swerving to miss by inches only at the very last instant.

In mid-afternoon we came upon a traffic jam—buses and cars backed up in both directions. Two trucks equipped with winches had blocked the road and had lowered wire cables down the mountainside. Everyone piled out to look. A bus exactly like our own was off the road, upside down, smashed on rocks in a ravine 100 feet below. Scuff marks and twisted metal showed where it had plunged through the guard wall. I asked a local man what had happened.

"Driver takes the curve too closely. Goes right over." With his hands he traced a long downward arc. "Twenty people die."

When was this?

"Last week."

I had seen no mention in the Calcutta papers.

"Is not news," he explained. "Only if tourists die. No tourists here. Indians only."

The winches turned; the cables tightened; the bus scraped across the rocks an inch at a time, with loud groans and the shriek of metal being tortured. After twenty minutes it had moved three feet. The truckers anchored their cables to the guard wall, unhooked them, and moved aside to let the traffic clear.

When we'd departed New Jaipalghuri, the bus's aisle had been empty, and each of the thirty-two cramped seats had held a single passenger. But along the way we had stopped in every little village to take on riders; now the aisles were full and many people had doubled up on seats. As we climbed, the carry-on luggage became more interesting: gunnysacks of rice; a television set missing its picture tube; three trussed chickens who had adopted a Buddhist calm. A teenager clutched to his chest a black-and-white soccer ball from which he had yet to remove the plastic wrapping.

The air had cooled; people were closing windows and pulling on extra clothes. The higher villages featured quaint gingerbread houses with window boxes brimming with marigolds, daffodils, geraniums, peonies. I saw, hanging in front of shops, black and yellow clusters that I mistook for strings of tropical fish but later identified as small bananas.

We made a pit stop in the town of Sagada at 6,500 feet, where clouds smothered the mountains and the locals were wrapped in thick sweaters. Wizened old men tottered down the main track, the flaps of their fur caps flopping over their ears. Shacks tilted at wild angles on the hillsides and the smell of coal smoke filled the air, giving Sagada the feel of an Appalachian mining town. But even here the world had intruded. Stores sold posters of Sylvester Stallone and soccer star Diego Maradona; shoppers carried their rice and vegetables home in RAMBO plastic bags. Teenagers seemed to be the most affected: hair drooped in their bored eyes, cigarettes dangled from their slack mouths, and "Black Leopard" tags marked their designer blue jeans.

We took on a large contingent of newcomers for the last leg into Darjeeling; I counted sixty-two passengers, including seven who huddled around the driver as though he were a cold night's campfire. A woman standing in the aisle took the liberty of setting her burlap bundle on my knees, and for the last hour of the ride that's where it stayed.

Even if you've seen them before, a fresh glimpse of the high Himalayas can still stop you short. They exist in a part of the sky that the rational lowland mind recognizes as the exclusive province of airplanes—floating, shimmering, a vivid suggestion that just about anything can happen. If flat, unremarkable bedrock from the plains can be sculpted into glacier-draped peaks, into canyons gouged by wild rivers, and forests filled with snow leopards, yaks, and yetis, is not *everything* possible?

A few minutes from Darjeeling the clouds lifted, allowing the first sunshine since morning. I could hear passengers on the other side of the bus gasping and sighing, but I was on the wrong side, and the aisle was a solid wall of people. My first view of the peaks did not come until the bus dropped everyone at the edge of Darjeeling. I paused at the bottom step, silent, drinking in the view. The town ran along the western side of a mountaintop and tumbled down into a wide, wooded valley. On the valley's far side was a series of mountain ridges, and above them in the distance (across the Nepalese border) was a line of shimmering white giants—pleated, starched, confident. Twelve peaks topped 20,000 feet, and towering above them all was the sheer and snowy face of 28,208 foot Mt. Kachenjunga, with half-mile ribbons of snow blowing backwards from its top.

One of my most common travel thoughts is this: *I will never again let so much time pass without revisiting these mountains, this ocean/forest/canyon/river/falls/meadow/valley. This Earth speaks a language too profound, too enchanting to ignore. No matter what excuse I must invent, I will return next year. Two years at the most.* And as I stood there tingling, sucking in crisp searing breaths, adjusting my neck to the peaks' impossible angle, I renewed my oft-broken vow.

Someone in Calcutta had recommended a lodge, and I followed my map up steep alleys and down narrow lanes. Strands of mist threaded between houses and in and out of the pine trees. Children kicked a soccer ball around a schoolyard. Boys walked with arms looped over each other's shoulders; grown men walked hand-in-hand.

The woman who answered my knock at the Pagoda Lodge seemed surprised, but happy to see me. She led me down a hall, opened a door, and switched on a bare overhead lightbulb to reveal a windowless, ground floor box that reeked with the scorched smell smokers leave behind. "Only twenty rupees," she said. Not even two dollars.

"I was hoping for a view."

She led me down more halls and up some stairs to a wood-paneled corner room, smelling of pine. There was a desk, a double bed with a firm mattress, and windows facing north and west. Strung out in front of me, over Darjeeling's rooftops, was the entire eastern end of the Himalayan chain. It was nearly dusk, and the setting sun seemed to be slanting its last beams of daylight *upward* from the plains, making the cloud bottoms and glazed peaks glow pink and purple. In the valley, lights were popping on and stars were starting to appear overhead.

"How much?" I asked.

"I am sorry," she said. "For this room I must ask thirty rupees."

The previous morning I'd been stroking the head of a dying man at Mother Teresa's. Now I was being offered a two-dollar room with a million-dollar view. I dropped my pack on the bed, pulled out my money, and thought: *I do, with all my heart, love India.*

16

The Purpose of Life

I was told by a [Darjeeling] resident that the summit of Kachenjunga is often hidden in the clouds, and that sometimes a tourist has waited twenty-two days and then been obliged to go away without a sight of it. And yet went not disappointed; for when he got his hotel bill he recognized that he was now seeing the highest thing in the Himalayas. But this is probably a lie.

—MARK TWAIN, *Following the Equator*

In the morning there was an icy layer of my own condensed breaths covering the inside of the windows. I scraped them clean with my American Express card, but this barely changed the view. Outside, a thick fog obscured everything but the construction workers adding another floor to the building across the alley.

The hotel owner brought a bucket of hot water to my door, and I washed in the bathroom down the hall—skipping my hair: it would never dry in this cold.

I walked through Darjeeling that morning with the odd sense that I was one of the loafing employees of a huge refrigerated warehouse. People appeared and disappeared in the fog luffing up the hillsides, or huddled around small fires and rubbed their arms. The hunks of meat hanging in front of butcher shops were bothered by only one or two torpid flies.

The latest paper at the newsstand was one I'd read in Calcutta four days earlier, but videos had arrived in a big way. Any room large enough to hold a few chairs and a television set had been converted into a theater. Chalkboards advertised the day's features. "Western Video" was showing *Rocky IV* and *I Spit On Your Grave*. In front of "Video King," a boy—wearing a denim jacket with upturned collar, and oversized camouflage pants tucked into the tops of his unlaced, oversized Nikes—was scribbling: *Eat Your Heart Out—2:15*.

At the tiny, four-table Himalayan Cafe I took a window seat. Six years earlier, unseasonable clouds around Kathmandu had aborted my attempts to glimpse Everest, and on this trip I was hoping to see it from Darjeeling.

A small Tibetan man, wearing a rainbow colored cap, set a coal stove next to my feet, and gave me an English menu and a shy smile. He said that sometimes the fog stayed thick like this all day, sometimes all week.

A group of other travelers came in and sat down at my table to gather around the foot stove. They'd climbed Tiger Hill outside town the previous afternoon, and once, when the clouds parted for five minutes, they'd seen Everest. "It was way far off in the distance," one of them told me, "but it was Everest."

After a breakfast of Tibetan bread with jam, muesli and curd, and hot lemon water, I set out walking on the one-lane road circling Darjeeling's mountaintop. In five minutes I was on the edge of town, strolling through pine trees with fog racing through their tops. Mountain people heading in toward Darjeeling's markets gave me surprised glances.

The Himalayan Mountaineering Institute and museum lay a mile from town. On a relief map in the main room I located the 29,028 foot tip of Mt. Everest—only a few folds of the map, but 140 air miles, from Darjeeling. In the spring of 1978, twenty-five years after the first ascent by Sir Edmund Hillary and Tenzing Norgay, German climber Reinhold Messner and another man, Peter Habeler, rewrote the mountaineering book by scaling Everest without the aid of bottled oxygen—something previously considered impossible. Two years later Messner returned and repeated the feat, this time climbing alone.

I lingered over the museum's exhibits, including a photograph of a huge scalp and the bones of a huge hand that local lamas say are relics of *yeti*, the abominable snowman. And in the small zoo, just a pine cone's toss downhill from the museum, I watched two Bengal tigers pace their cages, massive paw pads scuffing the concrete floors with each awesome step.

Back on the road I passed tea plantations and a team of women repairing a roadside wall. They were small women, bent almost to the ground by enormous sacks of rocks, straps around their foreheads taking some of the weight. There was a striking young beauty among them, a tall Tibetan with long silky hair and smooth skin. In New York a rich man would be plying her with favors; fashion photographers would be lining up to book her mornings and afternoons. But here she was lugging a boulder the size of a basketball.

On the north side of the mountain I came to a gondola that dropped several thousand feet to the valley floor. Standing here on a clear day, I would have an incomparable view of the Himalayas, but today the gondola's few riders, all locals, disappeared into clouds fifty yards from the tow house.

Walking in the fog, I overtook a man shuffling along with a cane. When I said good afternoon, he turned and looked at me through powerful glasses that distorted his brown eyes.

"Why thank you, young man!" His voice was husky, rasping. "I was just talking with God and telling him how much I appreciated his silences, but that I would be grateful if he were to send me some company."

His name was Ram Ashray Prashad. He wore a fur cap pulled down low on his forehead, and had the features of a plainsman. "My ancestors were Bengalis," he said. "Food merchants living in Bihar. When the British began developing Darjeeling, my family saw the opportunity here. My people go back 150 years in this village."

We passed a rock painted with slogans of the Gurkha party, which had recently been clamoring for Darjeeling's secession from India. I asked Mr. Prashad what he thought.

"It is a good thing. You see, these Gurkha people came many years ago from Nepal and Sikkim to work the tea plantations. Now the British are gone, and these people have many children, and the plantations can hire only a few. They are very low economically and they are neglected by the government. Now some of them have gotten themselves educated and the whole population wants to upgrade itself. This is why I say it is a good thing: When one man is uplifted, mankind is uplifted; when mankind is uplifted, one man is uplifted."

We were walking up a steep path through the woods now, and I took Mr. Prashad's arm to guide him past a slick spot.

"I am sixty-six years old," he said, "and I intend to live to be one hundred."

"So far, has yours been a good life?"

"I will answer that," he said, "but first let me ask you one thing. What is the purpose of life?"

I froze the moment: fog crowding so thick around us that we could see the trunks, but not the tops, of the nearby pine trees; below, in the whiteness off to our left, someone banging two pots together; in the distance, a dog barking; all else silent. *Tell me son, what is the purpose of life?*

Mr. Prashad didn't wait for my answer. "To know God," he said, his lens-distorted eyes seeming to widen. "That is the purpose of life. And to know God there are four stages in life. The first is student life, up to age twenty-five. This is when you should be getting your Ph.D. Then, until fifty, there is the householder stage. This is when you make money—not cheating now. I was once a bookmaker, and I have made *lahks* (hundreds of thousands) of rupees in seconds, and I have lost as much. And I have learned that that which is earned by the sweat of your brow is what you will remember.

"Until fifty you are fit. Then comes the retiring time. And after seventy-five, as you near your death, you begin to know the God who has been with you all along. Earlier in my life I suffered from mental depression. I worried needlessly about stupid things—money, my family. But then I went into deep meditation. In meditation I had to tell the truth to myself, and I saw that my worries were all rubbish. There is nothing one can do about one's family, or about one's money. All worrying about these things will do is make the self crazy. After I saw that, I was O.K. The most difficult thing in life is to tell the truth." He stared through his glasses at me. "You must do one thing," he said. "You must read Gandhi's book, *My Experiment With Truth*. In it he says that the truth is more powerful than your atom bomb. You must always tell the truth. Now, to answer your question, my life has been a good one, and it is getting better the more I tell the truth."

We reached a flat spot where the trail forked. Mr. Prashad stopped. "You were kind to walk with me and to listen," he said. "And now the truth is that you must leave me. I would like to talk with you further, but my thoughts have gone elsewhere."

17

This Damned Country

Within an hour the dysentery appeared in acute form. I asked for a commode to be placed in the adjoining room. I was ashamed to have to ask for this, but there was no escape. I must have had thirty to forty motions in twenty-four hours. My body had now become a lump of clay. The motions continued, leaving me completely exhausted. The exhaustion brought on a delirious fever....

—Mohandas Gandhi,
The Story of My Experiments with Truth

I awoke in the middle of that night feeling like someone was flossing my intestines with barbed wire. The room was black. I sat up and groped the floor with my feet, found my shoes, shoved my toes into them, stood, wrapped a towel around my waist, and shuffled down the hall—debating as I went whether this emergency called for bending over or sitting down. Both, it turned out. First I vomited into the toilet, then sat on it in the dark, shivering, muttering curses while my breaths flapped like tattered curtains around me.

I made at least a dozen more trips down the hall that night, concluding each with the thought: *That's it. I've got to be empty.* But always there was more. I ate stomach tablets that had no noticeable effect; dozed; awoke alarmed; lurched down the hall; returned frozen; lit a candle; read Salman Rushdie's *Midnight's Children* until I was sure the symptoms had passed; and then repeated the whole procedure. By the time morning light started seeping through the ice on the windows I was three times as tired as when I'd gone to bed.

I lay staring at the slats of wood in the ceiling, and taking stock. I had planned a two-day trek to the Nepalese border and back: canceled. Today I would be lying low.

The owner arrived with a bucket of hot water. "Hiking today?" she asked, happily.

I raised to an elbow to tell her the news.

"Oh," she said. "Is not from our water. Our water is very boiled. You take cautions where you are eating." She wished me a speedy recovery.

I scraped a portal in the ice on the window. The fog was even thicker this morning. I heard cries and bangings from the roof across the alley, but could not see the workers.

Fully dressed, I crept back into my sleeping bag, spread extra blankets over myself, and spent the entire day, and then the next, in the Pagoda Lodge, managing waves of diarrhea and nausea that came in forty-five minute intervals. I spoke with no one but my concerned innkeeper, who visited me in the morning and at dusk. She brought water for drinking, but no longer water for washing; I was too chilled, and the air too frigid, to consider shedding my clothes. My breaths billowed out and sailed toward the ice-coated windows I no longer bothered to scrape. The existence of mountains was now purely academic; except during the hour of my arrival, the fog in Darjeeling had been as thick as shaving cream, and I had begun to wonder if I would ever again release a breath I could not see. My one consolation, a small one, was that if I'd gone trekking, I'd have been able to see nothing but the trailbed.

The common wisdom is that the visitor to India goes through three stages: the "Everything Indian is absolutely wonderful" stage; then, "Well...maybe not so wonderful after all," and finally, the inevitable: "*GET ME OUTA HERE!*"

Perhaps I had used up all my Stage One karma during my first trip to India. Since arriving in Calcutta, I had spent most of my time in Stage Two. Oh, I'd had flashes of Stage One—ogling Kachenjunga, strolling in the fog with Ram Ashray Prashad—but there was no doubt about which stage I was in now. *This damned country. Five thousand years and it can't even serve a visitor clean food and water.*

At home several months earlier, I had suffered an evening of fever and chills. Rhonda filled her tub with hot water and soap bubbles for me, placed candles around her bathroom, brought in a chair and sat by the tub stroking my forehead with a cold washcloth. When I had sweated to exhaustion, she helped me to bed and tucked me in; the next thing I knew it was morning and I was cured. Now I missed her. I lay there feeling like a gutshot deer, and recalled, all too vividly, other viruses I'd battled in other cheap hotel rooms: Marrakech '74, Kathmandu '82, Beijing '84. I began inventing excuses to give people for why I cut this trip off after only thirty days.

I read more of *Midnight's Children*, Rushdie's brilliant fable of two children, one fabulously rich, the other fabulously poor, both born at the very instant of India's independence—the stroke of midnight on August 15, 1947. At the hospital, a nurse with an Indian sense of irony switched the two and sent them home with the wrong parents. Rushdie weaves the threads of these improbable lives into the impossible tapestry of India—the caste system, riots, crowds, religions, cows, filth—creating a hilarious, sprawling India that was a welcome escape from the restricted one I was experiencing.

In the middle of the second day, thinking myself better, I ate some crackers, and fifteen minutes later threw them up. I ate more stomach tablets and rode out the night, and on the third afternoon finally did feel that I'd emptied myself. Three hours passed without a trip to the toilet, and shortly after sunset I actually began to feel hungry.

In my walks around Darjeeling I had noticed a restaurant advertising a roaring fireplace every evening. Now I roused myself, cinched my belt around what was left of my waist, and hobbled down the stairs. The night was already as black as the coal dust I could smell in Darjeeling's air—no moon, no stars, hardly any lights coming from the houses. I bent forward as I walked, my stomach feeling as raw and overworked as if I'd done a thousand sit-ups. And it came as no small comfort, and no small surprise, to hear a voice from the darkness call my name.

"Brad!" It was Will Russell, an American I'd met four days earlier in the trekking permit office. Somehow he had recognized my shoes in the pool of torchlight at my feet. "How was your walk?"

"It never happened," I said, and unloaded the story of my last three days. "I'm on a trip that's supposed to last a hundred days. This is day thirty, but if it was day one hundred that would be fine with me."

"Being sick," Will said, "that's the absolute worst part of travel. But it happens to everyone. I had *giardia* a couple of months ago, but I'm fine now. You'll get over it. Promise."

Will had just come from the restaurant advertising the fireplace. "But they're closed tonight," he said.

"Well then, if you're going somewhere else to eat, I'm inviting myself along. God, just talking to someone makes me feel better."

I followed him to the Rumza Bar and Restaurant. There was no front door, just a cloth flap hanging in the entrance. The waiter brought a foot stove and two candles that gave our booth a hint of warmth, but still our breaths hung like wavering kites above us. Will ordered vegetables and rice and I ordered egg drop soup. Even if I couldn't eat it, I wanted something steamy under my nose.

Will was from Connecticut, but had lived in San Francisco during the seventies. He'd left the States three years ago, spent a year in Europe—picking fruit in Greece to support himself—and a year ago had come to Nepal. He liked Kathmandu so much that he'd chosen to live there and teach English.

I asked, "What's the best thing that ever happened to you?"

He thought a moment. "Going to San Francisco when I was twenty. I'd been down and out—kind of suicidal. I'm gay..."—his pause was barely perceptible—"and growing up in Hamden, Connecticut was a real strain. Always having to be someone else. I've always been a gentle person, but all through high school I had to act tough. A couple of years after I graduated, I finally hitched out to San Francisco. My first evening there I was walking around with my backpack, and a woman cooking in a restaurant window on Van Ness Avenue waved me in. I told her I'd just arrived, and had ten dollars to my name. She fed me meatloaf and gave me her address. There were a bunch of people crashing on her floor, but they squeezed me in. This was the first person I met in the city! I felt so good I went and spent my last traveler's check on beer.

"Right off I loved San Francisco. I found work waiting tables and made lots of friends. And finally I could be open about being gay. That was when soldiers were coming back from Vietnam, where they'd been killing women and children—and *they* were heroes. But if two men loved each other that was a crime. Everywhere but San Francisco."

I told him that only in the last ten years had I unlearned my fear of gays. Living in San Francisco, and especially driving a cab in San Francisco, had reversed a lot of my attitudes. The gays I met were typically polite, funny, interesting (and *interested*—several had kissed my hand and one man leaned over the backseat to plant a kiss on my cheek), and they were, by far, the most generous tippers. A third of my income, I figured, came from gays and lesbians.

"We're just people," Will said. "It's like before you go traveling— you think of Arabs as being a certain way. Or Russians. Or Indians. Then you travel and you see they're just people. It's almost impossible for a human being to see another human being without wanting to immediately slap on a label. It's the way of the world. Gays have prejudices about straight people they have to get over, too."

"What's the worst thing?"

"Probably being gay. I think my life would have been easier if I were straight. So much less to fight. Straight people have things to fight, too, but having your sexuality condemned every hour of every day is a little extraordinary."

Our food came, and we talked about different things—our trips, Will's life in Kathmandu. He was thirty-two now, and didn't know what he was going to do when he got back home. He had no apartment, no car, and really didn't want to go back to waiting tables.

We talked about San Francisco—the hills, the bay, the ocean, the people. Will told restaurant stories; I told about the cab fare who put a gun to my head and asked for my wallet. He shared his secret camp spot on the Big Sur coast, and I shared mine at Point Reyes. When Will couldn't finish his rice and vegetables, I polished them off. By the time the evening was over I was feeling half-human again.

18

Porterage Charge

*To understand the real India, the Indians say, you must go to the vil-
lages. But that is not strictly true, because the Indians have carried their
villages to the railway stations.*

—PAUL THEROUX, *The Great Railway Bazaar*

On my fourth morning in Darjeeling the clouds were stacked in heaps on the northern horizon, above Sikkim and Tibet, but there were none over Darjeeling. Outside my ice-free window the Himalayas stood brightly, like a tip-anxious hotel staff lined up to wish me good-bye. They offered no apology for their disappearance during my stay, but I saluted them anyway, tugging once at the crown of my wool cap, which in five days had not once been off my head.

In the central marketplace taxi drivers were cramming passengers into their cabs for the four-hour trip down to New Jaipalghuri. I wanted a front window seat—the window in case I got sick, the front for the extra leg room—and went from driver to driver until I found one who, for five extra rupees, agreed.

We drove through green valleys dotted with tea plantations and past hills topped by Buddhist monasteries; in the far distance were the lime colored-plains, behind us the peaks, looking smug, impervious.

I neither attempted nor encouraged conversation with the other passengers. Past Sagada I looked for the bus wreck I'd seen five days earlier, but I nodded off, my head knocking against the window, and never saw it. How different it was to imagine a trip than to actually take one. At home I'd fantasized wondrous things for this part of the journey, but here I was, slinking from the mountains, brain-dead. *Travel*, I thought, *is like chemotherapy. You just go through it, endure it, hoping that the right things get through to your bones, bring about some beneficial change, inspire some wisdom, and that all the others don't kill you.* Ten weeks still lay ahead, but already I felt the way I usually feel at trip's end—like I needed a nice long vacation.

When I awoke, we were well down the mountains. Everyone in the taxi was shedding coats, but I still felt chilled. I kept my clothes on and sweated, hoping that I didn't stink, and knowing that under all the layers I must. In Varanasi, a day and a half distant, I could bathe and wash my hair.

At three in the afternoon the taxi deposited its passengers at the New Jaipalghuri bus station. My train didn't leave until ten o'clock—seven hours away. At a hotel-restaurant across from the station I ordered half a chicken and a bottle of soda water. Outside, men in sandals and loose robes shuffled down the dusty road. Cycle-rickshaw drivers attacked the arriving buses and tussled over fares. Hindi music screeched from radios. Taxi horns blared at oblivious cows. *Cows again.* I couldn't recall seeing cows in Darjeeling, but what I most remembered about Darjeeling was hurrying up and down the hallway of my hotel. I thought: This *is India. No wonder the Gurkhas want to secede.*

The setting sun was purpling a spider web of clouds above the southwestern plains. For five rupees I hired a rickshaw driver to pedal me the two miles to the train station. We followed crowded streets barely wide enough for two rickshaws or five skinny cows. Women tending bubbling pots squatted over fires in front of mud-brick homes.

I was still wearing my hat, scarf, and layers of clothes, but the air passing across my cheeks started me shivering. It is hard to remember a time when I have felt such a vague connection to my own body. I imagined myself an amorphous observer, hidden somewhere behind my eyes, watching with little interest in the outcome. When wiping my runny nose, I had the odd sensation that I was reaching around from behind some absolute and pathetic stranger to do it for him. And I'm sure I saw boys on the streets pointing at me, laughing, while adults stared.

The train station was, in reality, a sprawling community, temporary home to a few, permanent home to many more. People washed at a common tap. A man was pissing from the platform down onto the tracks. Whole families of Indians had taken over the first class waiting room; a fat man, snoring, lay across one of the tables. I went back out to the platform, found an unoccupied spot next to a support column, and laid my backpack on the cement to sit on. I looked around for other backpackers, but there were none. I thought of Will, of Rhonda, of my editor in New York, and of how surprised they would all be when they learned of my demise in New Jaipalghuri.

There was an electronic message screen mounted above the platform. Red digital figures paraded across: "6:12 P.M. WELCOME TO NEW JAIPALGHURI RAILROAD STATION. PLEASE PURCHASE YOUR JOURNEY TICKET OR PLATFORM TICKETS BEFORE ENTERING THE PLATFORM. PORTERAGE CHARGE." This message repeated automatically, dragging itself in front of my eyes twice or thrice each minute. My bank in San Francisco had a similar sign announcing news headlines, and I had found that one intrusive; here, with cows sauntering up and down the platform, with cripples and beggars clustered around every column, this one seemed ridiculous.

I tried jotting notes but had no energy for it. For that night I have this entry: "When I get home I will volunteer at Travelers Aid." And, without explanation, this: "When I get home I'm going to start a club open only to people born on my exact birthday, September 15, 1951."

I tried reading *Midnight's Children*, but now it irritated me. It seemed so wordy, and I wondered if Mr. Rushdie ever edited his pages. Clearly he had a brilliant mind and a thesauristic vocabulary, but why was he flaunting it? When he tried to slip the word *tergiversatory* by me, I put the book away.

"7:20 P.M. WELCOME TO NEW JAIPALGHURI RAILROAD STATION. PLEASE PURCHASE YOUR JOURNEY TICKET OR PLATFORM TICKETS BEFORE ENTERING THE PLATFORM. PORTERAGE CHARGE....7:21 P.M. WELCOME TO..." Two and a half more hours.

I strolled the platform. Three fast-handed boys at the snack counter were slapping out vegetable-filled crepes—*masala dosa*. I paid twelve cents each for two of them and bought a banana from a vendor.

Must keep my strength up. Bold signs announced REMEMBER THE TRASH YOU THROW ON THE PLATFORM IS PICKED UP BY ANOTHER HUMAN BEING JUST LIKE YOU. But I walked the entire platform without encountering a single trash can, and finally dropped my banana peel into one of the many rubbish piles.

In front of the station, fifty resting drivers sprawled in the seats of their rickshaws. A dozen leaped up when I walked out of the station, but settled back down when they realized I was just looking around, killing time. Under the station's eaves, people were bedding down for the night.

Three thin old women—wearing rags, their faces as brown and wrinkled as old wallets—seemed to have banded together to form a family. They doused the fire on which they had cooked their dinner and then lay down, with nothing but cardboard between themselves and the cold concrete, and pulled burlap blankets over themselves. An old man sorted through a rubbish pile. A scarecrow of a boy—with no shoes, no possessions, and no family in sight—was claiming a spot in the protective light beneath a street lamp. His face was darker than Darjeeling tea, his head a mop of black curls as thick and shiny as wet seaweed. He stared at me with big rupee-sized eyes, then covered himself with newspapers, quivered twice, and was still.

In more grandiose moments I had viewed my trip as a glimmer of hope in a grim world: if I couldn't fix all the world's problems, or even my own, I could at least add some small joy or surprise or delight to someone else's life. But the need I saw in the New Jaipalghuri station overwhelmed my vision, reduced my plan to a frivolity—a lotto. The aspirations of these people were far more immediate and practical than a trip to America. A five-rupee rickshaw fare, a *masala dosa*, a lumpy bedroll, thank you.

I like to think that every human life is significant, each equally valid. But I could see no rebuttal to the nagging suggestion that these desperate lives were, like my own, quite pointless. What on Earth was I doing in the New Jaipalghuri train station? And wasn't it grossly unfair that I had a first class ticket out, while these people were condemned to stay and rest up for another day dominated by the struggle for food? Surely they were human the same way that I was. Surely each of them had some niggling physical problem. Surely each hurt and felt and braced against life the same way that I and everyone I knew in America did. Maybe they had some Indian philosophy, some matrix of beliefs on immortality, afterlife, karma, luck, that allowed them to make sense of it all. But there was no way I could imbue the scene in front of me with higher meaning. In my own intellectual matrix, hunger trumps philosophy every time.

Back at the platform: "8:01 P.M. WELCOME TO NEW JAIPAL-GHURI RAILROAD STATION...." I thought: *What does* "PORTERAGE CHARGE" *mean*? I took my rain poncho from my pack and spread it on the ground. When I unrolled and began inflating my air mattress, a man stopped to watch. Another joined him. Then another. I fluffed up my sleeping bag and slid inside it, made a pillow by cramming my sweater into my stuff sack, snugged up my money belt, and padlocked my back-pack to the zipper on my sleeping bag. By now there was a semi-circle, a silent press conference, gathered around me. I set my alarm clock for 9:45, smiled and said good-night to everyone, pulled the bag up over my head, and fell sound asleep.

19

Ashes and Silk

Archeologists....believe that Jesus Christ during his absence from the Bible between the ages of twelve and thirty, was in fact traveling in India. In India Jesus found a guru who taught him much about mysticism, fasting and levitation...Sixteen years of training enabled Christ to spend forty days in the wilderness without food or drink... to remain in the tomb for three days and nights after his crucifixion... and finally...to levitate on Easter Sunday...

Convinced that Jesus levitated his way back to India, and spent the last years of his life in the Himalayas, the archeologists are now fanning through the mountains looking for his tomb. If the tomb is conclusively proved to hold the body of Christ, it will be interesting to see if the faithful fall by the wayside. Or whether they will return to the source of the teachings, the Eastern gurus.

—GITA MEHTA, *Karma Cola*

My train arrived in Varanasi at night, and I protested only mildly when my taxi driver delivered me not to the ancient two-dollar lodge I had specified, but to a newer six-dollar hotel. His unapologetic explanation: "Iss better."

And he was right. The Hotel Pradeep was clean and recently renovated. Orange neon lettering shone in the front window, marble floors graced the high-ceilinged lobby. When the desk clerk persuaded me to allow my pack to be carried upstairs, three turbaned teenagers sprang to the task.

In my room I closed the door, sat on the bed's firm foam mattress, and for the first time in nearly a week removed my wool hat. In the mirror I saw an accident victim; my hair was rutted and greasy and stuck to one side of my head like a flung casserole. Since my second day in Darjeeling, I had not exercised, and now I spent a half hour on the rug stretching grateful muscles. With the bathroom door closed I took a long hot shower and, when finished, stood in steam so thick I could have lain down and slept on it. I wiped a porthole in the mirror, ran a comb across my head, and trimmed my beard.

At ten o'clock there was a knock on the door. I opened it and was soon surrendering my entire wardrobe—except sweater and bicycle shorts—to the "laundry boy" (actually a man my own age) and three of his six sons.

I wrapped a towel around my damp hair like a turban, and wore my shorts, sweater, and flip-flops down to the restaurant. The staff fluttered around me, their lone customer, sahibing like I was an aging maharaja. I ate a bowl of bright-red cream of tomato soup, sprinkled with orange croutons, and devoured half a tandoori chicken.

My room overlooked the street in front of the hotel and an alley alongside. Around midnight the sounds of an approaching...*carnival?*... drew me from my bedside prayers to the window. A marriage procession that included two bejeweled elephants and the Indian version, perhaps, of a ten-man *mariachi* band sashayed into view and came to a halt at the Pradeep's front steps. For fifteen minutes the revelers tossed tiny streamers up to guests watching from windows, squirted drinks from goatskin bags into each other's opened mouths, and whirled through feverish dance steps—men only, dancing in pairs. When finally they toodled off down the street, I fell into a deep sleep between stiff clean sheets, bothered only slightly by the persistent yap of a dog.

On day thirty-two I awoke late and slowly, smiling at the blank ceiling of my hotel room, savoring the luxury of linens and blankets. This was the first morning since San Francisco that my sleeping bag was still stored in my backpack. I felt rested, and sensed that I had outlasted my illness. If it turned out to be the only bug this trip would throw at me, well, I would consider it a fair, even modest price for the drug of travel.

A boy knocked at the door, my clean, folded clothes in his arms. "Good morning, Sahib!"

Crisscrossing currents of cycle rickshaws, pedestrians, and cows flowed beneath my window. Sunburned German tourists looking baffled wandered among them. A man led a camel past. Under the red blossoms of a jacaranda tree, veiled women displayed flowers and dusty vegetables. Spreading in the distance, basking under a stainless blue sky, was Varanasi—a pinkish biblical city with a three-story skyline and one million residents. Mark Twain, visiting Varanasi in 1897, said the city was "older than history, older than tradition, older even than legend, and looks twice as old as all of them put together."

In fact, Varanasi's recorded past stretches back more than three thousand years. In ancient times, fair-skinned Aryans from Western Asia invaded the Gangetic plain, bringing with them a variety of beliefs and gods, which in time merged with those of India's indigenous people to form the tapestry of Hinduism.

The Varanasi of 1000 B.C. is reported to have been a place of uncommon beauty, famous for its gardens and a "Forest of Bliss." Sanskrit scholars sat beside Varanasi's ponds and lakes and debated the meaning of the ancient Vedic texts. In the sixth century B.C., when Gautama Buddha experienced enlightenment under the Bo tree, he went immediately to Varanasi to share his new wisdom. And it is widely accepted in India that Jesus of Nazareth spent some of his "missing years" studying with Varanasi's masters. Today's residents boast of having seen the Beatles, Allen Ginsburg, and Baba Ram Das wandering their streets.

In the center of town, near the stone steps that line the Ganges, pilgrims line up, as they have for centuries, to dip and purify themselves in a well that is said to have been simultaneously dug by and filled with the sweat of Shiva. And it is the aspiration of all Hindus to, at least once in this lifetime, walk the fifty-mile road that rings Varanasi. But for a pilgrim visiting Varanasi, the very best thing that might happen is that he or she might die there, thus escaping the wheel of life, the endless cycle of death and rebirth: all who die in Varanasi are immediately transported to Shiva's side in his mountain paradise.

But if history and religion have put Varanasi on the map, today's populace depends on ashes and silk for sustenance. Each year thirty thousand adults are cremated at the river's edge. (Children's bodies, deemed too innocent to need purification by flame, are weighted with stones and dropped midriver.) The funeral pyres are manned day and night by a subcaste of cremation attendants, the Doms, who adapt their fees to the wealth of the deceased's family.

While the Doms monopolize the cremation business, the entire town gets in on the silk trade. No matter where you stay in Varanasi, the manager of your hotel will happen to know *the* shop with the finest silk and fairest prices in the entire city—not to mention (he will anyway) the special discount waiting for you, his good friend. Your waiter will admire your fine rugged daypack; but oh, in his brother's shop are the finest handbags in all of India—are you free after lunch? And on the street, the man who materializes at your elbow (in India people do not so much *approach* as materialize at one's elbow), this man with the welcoming smile, matching his gait to your own, will just so happen, no matter where you are headed, to be going your way. He will also know and be willing to show you a shortcut, and soon you will find yourself seated cross-legged, sipping tea and admiring rugs and saris that you don't need, on the floor of his uncle's silk emporium.

20

All-Star Rickshaw Man

*Any American can, I suppose, imagine my pity for Ramon. It was
grounded in the contemplation of an intelligent and ambitious youth
chained by circumstances to crushing and lifelong poverty in a poor
country that offered no future to its ineptly educated citizens.*

—MORITZ THOMSEN,
The Farm on the River of Emeralds

On a very good day a Varanasi rickshaw driver earns thirty to forty
rupees, less than three dollars. But the rickshaw driver who de-
livers a tourist through the door of a silk shop wins a commission, a
commission that balloons with every purchase the tourist makes. Every
factory and shop has its own network of rickshaw drivers willing to try
any subterfuge—sympathy pleas, would-you-like-a-cup-of-tea?, even
thinly veiled kidnappings—to dump the tourist through the door of
an "emporium." Varanasi's rickshaw drivers are clairvoyant when it
comes to knowing what a tourist needs and wants—in a word: silk.

But Shubash (*Shoo-BAHSH*) was different. He said so himself.

He was waiting in front of the Hotel Pradeep at noon, dusting the
seat of his cycle rickshaw as though expecting me. He was a dark young
Indian with black curls falling to his brow, and an outlaw's droopy
mustache highlighting his grin.

"Ah," he called when I approached him, "you are first customer
today."

"How many rupees to the General Post Office?" I asked.

Shubash —Perhaps the hippest cycle-rickshaw driver in Varanasi.

"Is Sunday. GPO closed." His chirping, high-on-helium voice gave him a comic aura.

"Sunday," I said. "That's a Christian holiday. I thought this was a Hindu town."

"Ah," he croaked. "But the British..." and never completed the sentence.

I mentioned a bookstore recommended by my guidebook.

"Is finish," Shubash said. "Business no good. Now is fruit store."

"I suppose we will find only silk shops open today."

Shubash's voice cranked up to a falsetto: "I no like other rickshaw men, only taking you for silk shop. I take where you want. You want GPO I take you—even Sunday. Bookstore is finish, but if you want I take you."

"I was only teasing."

"As you like," he said, and bobbled his head. "I take where you want. If you want go New Delhi, I will take—but first I must tell my wife."

I laughed. New Delhi was 400 miles away.

"But if you want silk shop," Shubash said, "we can go. As you like."

"How about the Ganges?" I said. "Is it open today?"

"Ah, Ganga. Ganga always open, but burning best at night."

"How many rupees to the Ganga?" I pronounced it his way.

"Ganga? As you like."

"I like three rupees," I said—my hotel manager's suggestion.

"As you like."

Not since Calcutta had I been outdoors without my cap and sweater. Air was again sailing up my sinuses according to design, and the sun warmed my cheeks and forearms. As I climbed up onto the padded bench of Shubash's rickshaw, I felt like a condemned man granted clemency.

Shubash mounted the bicycle seat, stood and strained on the pedals, and eased us into the rickshaw gulfstream. A few buses lumbered and squeezed through the narrow streets, and there was a sprinkling of taxis and private automobiles, but Varanasi was clearly the province of the cycle rickshaw. Hundreds of rattletraps just like Shubash's swept in both directions down every dusty street. The passengers, almost all of them Indian, seemed an overweight and angry lot for the most part; it was the rickshaw drivers, lean and wiry like Shubash, who seemed to be having all the fun—nodding and calling out to one another, ringing their bells like cruising teenagers.

Barefooted men lugged cans of paint and boxes of oranges through the streets; barefooted children pushed old tires into a VULCANIZATION SHOP—open on Sunday I noticed. Pedestrians balanced flying saucers of bananas or rice or onions atop their heads, and as we wove among them, I might easily have picked a meal from the air. The noise of the rickshaws was a leathery creaking, punctuated by zinging bells and curses hurled at the wandering cattle. A huge brown cow with a tiny blackbird perched on its back sat in a traffic circle, chewing up the last blades of grass; behind it a young girl scooped up a fresh dung patty and placed it into the half-filled basket on her head. A team of workers hauled baskets of bricks on their heads from one ruined building to a site twenty feet away, where masons were slapping up the walls of a new home. On its first day of occupancy it would already look centuries old, and, possibly—who knew?—contain bricks that once upon a time sheltered Jesus.

We passed a rickshaw carrying two women, swathed head-to-toe in black cloth. Shubash called back over his shoulder, "Here too many Moos-leem."

"You are Hindu?"

"Yes," he said.

"How old are you?"

"Me? Twenty-five."

"Children?"

"One daughter."

Then it was his turn.

"Married?" he asked. *Do you have a wife to shop for?*

"How long Varanasi?" *How many days do I have to work on you?*

"First time?" *Do you know the silk game?*

"What's your favorite thing in life?" I asked him.

"Daughter," he said.

"Do you have dreams, wishes?"

"Maybe son."

He seemed a happy, confident man, with a vague air of hipness—he wore blue jeans with a lot of life left in them and a "Lee" label on the seat. I thought: *If I were a Varanasi rickshaw driver, Shubash would be someone I'd want to know.* Calcutta had been so confronting, and Darjeeling so debilitating, that I'd sometimes almost forgotten my invite-someone-to-America plan. On those few occasions when I did think of it, it seemed merely the pretext to take a trip. But now I was feeling my old self again, and thought: *Is Shubash the one?* The thought had a pleasing symmetry: San Francisco cab driver, Varanasi rickshaw driver.

"You want see my book?" he called.

"Your *book*?" This was *too* perfect. "You're a writer?"

"My book. I show you."

From a pouch behind his seat Shubash pulled a tattered loose-leaf notebook and passed it back to me. As I opened it, a page blew loose and flapped away. "Stop!" I yelled, and Shubash pulled over. I jumped down and ran back through the tide of rickshaws and scooped the page from the dust.

Underway again, I read:

> "Shubash is an all-star rickshaw man. Probably the fastest rickshaw man in town."
> Those Canadian dudes—C. WALTERS, D. SHAY

Oh, that *kind of book.*

> "Everyone else wanted to get me into a silk shop. Shubash took me where I wanted to go."
> —PETER MARTIN, Seattle

"Shubash has been very friendly and reasonable. He took us to the doctor and then to the hospital when my wife was sick. He is not a rip off artist, and I recommend him highly."

—PHIL LEHMAN, Huntington Beach, California

"...a true friend in the land of *baksheesh*."

—ALLEN AND SANDRA SMALLWOOD,
San Diego, California

I wondered: What would Shubash make of the 300 gleaming, eight-cylinder taxis in the Yellow Cab lot? The twin two-mile long cables supporting the Golden Gate Bridge? And what sort of reception would we get if some morning he and I were to knock on the door of the Smallwoods or Phil Lehman, just down the California coast?

"See?" he was calling. A large, red-brick building stood in front of us. "GPO closed."

A few minutes later he stopped in front of a store where women pawed through bins of apples and tomatoes. "Was bookstore," he said—and the guidebook's map bore him out.

When he pedaled me to the river, I gave him ten rupees.

"Want rickshaw tomorrow?" he asked.

A thought came to me. If he was coming to America, shouldn't I meet his wife, see where he slept, went to the toilet? "Tell me if I'm asking too much, Shubash, but I'd really like to see your house."

"See *my* house!" He seemed flattered. "As you like."

"You're sure I'm not asking too much?"

"No problem."

"Thank you," I said. "I would really appreciate that."

"Tomorrow I meet you at noon," he said. "Front of Hotel Pradeep. That my spot. I start noon every day."

"Noon tomorrow—same place. You're sure this is O.K.?"

"No problem."

21

The Second Century

*India...where almost any interaction with another person, no matter
how casual or seemingly benign, sooner or later reveals itself as having
been carefully designed to facilitate the transfer of money from my
pocket to his.*

—LANCE FREE, "The Art of Tripping"

Hindu lore holds that the river Ganges, mother of all life, dropped
from heaven to earth, and that Lord Shiva softened its landing
by straining the falling waters through his hair. When Shiva took up
residence on the banks of the holy river, Varanasi grew up around him,
the holiest of cities.

The world's ancient cities were often built with tight, twisting
streets designed to thwart the cavalry, elephants, and camels of invad-
ing armies; most were nevertheless razed a time or two, but Varanasi
never. Its narrow alleys are hemmed in by timeless buildings as dreamy
and whimsically constructed as sand castles, so that any parachuting
adventure-traveler dropped here might well think he or she has landed
in the second century. Varanasi's skyline is punctuated by the minarets
of mosques, the ramparts of maharajas' palaces, and the domes of
ashrams. The bluff above the Ganges is crowded with red-and-gold-
domed temples dedicated to a bewildering array of gods and goddesses:
Hanuman, the monkey God; Ganesh, the elephant-headed god of wisdom; Lakshmi, the goddess of fortune; Indra, the patron god of travelers. But none outrank Shiva, and one of Varanasi's most important

shrines is the Golden Temple, home to a black, phallic-shaped stone representing the god's legendary regenerative powers.

A series of stone steps, the ghats, extend for a mile along the river. Each dawn, pilgrims and locals alike crowd the water's edge to perform morning ablutions. During the day the central section of ghats, the Dasasswamadah Ghat, functions as a combination marketplace/entertainment/devotional center. And twenty-four hours a day, funeral fires burn on the northern Manikarnika Ghat.

Shubash had left me at the southern end of the ghats, and as I looked north, I imagined I was seeing something similar to what Jesus might have seen. The walls of the buildings atop the bluff tilted at odd angles. Aged row boats ferried passengers across the river's wide, gray waters. People in loose robes wandered along the ghats, hauling water in buckets; cattle and dogs foraged among them. Men sat in circles, discussing, I presumed, the philosophical questions of the day. One man stood alone beside the river, arms spread, beseeching the sky in a language I did not recognize.

Those unable to afford formal cremation fees often do the job themselves, and now I noticed a group of ten people gathered around a small pile of still-smoking embers; one woman was down on her knees, wailing.

I walked north, carefully dodging cow flops (in India one does not so much *walk* as step over things), picnicking families, and kite fliers. A herd of goats, driven by a young girl, clattered past. On a flat section several boys played cricket with a broom handle and tennis ball; the left fielder stood a foot deep in the Ganges, his trousers rolled to his knees.

The Dasasswamadah Ghat, the busiest and most central, was filled with low wooden platforms where barbers, bone setters, herb sellers, soothsayers, and competing masseurs plied their trades. Vendors hawked food. A holy man led his open air congregation through Hindi chants, the drone of *Hare Krishna, Hare Krishna, Hare Rama, Hare Rama* blending with the peeping flutes, clanking cymbals, and thumping *tablas* of musicians camped in every corner. Teenagers peddled beads—"Fine gemstones, Sahib!"—and necklaces made of shiny brown nuts. Fire eaters swallowed great flaming marshmallows. Magicians shuffled shells—guess where the pea is? Men squatted in card-playing circles.

I spent the afternoon sitting in shade near the Dasasswamadah Ghat, alternately reading Rushdie and watching the crowd. I saw a cow slide up behind the chanters and nose at a bag hanging from one man's shoulder. The man turned, startled, and swatted the beast's sacred nose. The cow held her ground, loosed an indignant, crowd-redistributing piss, then moved on.

I had noticed that the Indian version of childhood is both shorter and longer than the American version. Instead of being coddled for two or three decades, Indian children, as young as five or six years old, are put to work in factories or sent to hustle the streets for a few rupees a day. The silver lining is that Indians tend to spread their innocence and unsullied glee out over a lifetime, instead of blowing them all at once. It is no more unusual to see an eight-year-old running a tea stall, than to see an eighty-year-old with mirthful eyes, laughing with a youthful delight seldom seen in older Americans.

Under a tattered awning, a young boy—six years old, maybe seven —with a brazier, a kettle, and four cups, offered tea for sale. I watched him run his stall: attracting customers with an urgent "*Chai! Chai! Chai!*"; collecting money and making change; buying dried dung cakes from a dung-girl; slipping an occasional coin to a passing beggar; rinsing his cups in a small basin; running down the steps to fill his kettle from the river. I cringed each time I saw this. It was, it seemed to me, nothing short of miraculous that his customers were not dropping dead one by one. Sure, he was boiling the river water (or at least heating it up a bit), but how much difference could that make? Humans, dogs, and cattle used this river as a garbage dump, bathtub, toilet. Varanasi's untreated sewage and the charred remains of thirty thousand people a year were dumped straight into the river.

But Hindus maintain that an object or person sprinkled with a few drops of Ganges water—or better, dipped in the river—is miraculously purified. They also believe that the Ganges at Varanasi has a purity unmatched in the universe. What Shiva has touched is holy. The Hindu bathes, brushes his teeth, drinks heartily from the river, and likes to tell scoffing stories about Western scholars who arrive in Varanasi armed with test tubes, notebooks, and years of Western training, and who leave several days later scratching their heads. Maybe Jesus learned his water-into-wine trick in Varanasi? (Mark Twain: "At the Kedar Ghat you will find a long flight of stone steps leading down to the river. Half way down is a tank filled with sewage. Drink as much of it as you want. It is for fever.")

Near me, a man seated cross-legged beneath a bamboo umbrella read tales from the *Ramayana* aloud to an enraptured crowd. Crows cawed overhead. A man leaned up against the wall several feet away from me, lit a pipe, and blew clouds of hashish smoke in my direction. An ascetic, a naked man whose skin and long matted hair were smeared with ashes, stopped and stared at me. I feigned absorption in my Rushdie. Another man, clothed, sat down nearby and twanged a sitar. A series of women stopped and extended their palms: "Babu...*Baksheesh*, Babu!"

My first clue that I was in the twentieth century came when a man with a live cobra wrapped around him appeared at my elbow and knelt beside me. For a few rupees, he said, he was willing to transfer the fat snake from his neck to mine and record the event with a Polaroid camera.

When I walked out of the Hotel Pradeep at noon the next day, I had a bag of sesame candies in my daypack and a bouquet of marigolds in my hand. Shubash was not around, so I waited near the front steps. The roar of a power generator competed with the bleating taxis, quacking scooters, burping buses, and Varanasi's entire rickshaw symphony. Roosters screamed, babies cried, the marigold-seller yodeled for more customers. An angry cow stood on the hotel's front steps, looing loudly until one of the hotel's boys emerged and chased it into the street. *When*, I wondered, *was the last time I'd spent five conscious minutes without unwanted noise? Hiking with Tony*, I thought. *Tony. My trip was more than a third over and he was still my favorite.*

At twelve-thirty Shubash showed up, pushing his rickshaw out of the alley next to the Pradeep.

"Today you want silk shop?"

"I thought we were going to your house today."

"Maybe after silk shop."

I looked down at the flowers in my hand. "Yesterday I thought you said you would show me your house."

"No problem," he said. "After see my house, silk shop?"

"Well, O.K.," I said.

"No problem. Come." He started down the dirt alley next to the Pradeep. "Is just here. We walk." We had walked thirty paces when he stopped and pointed at a wooden door in the wall, but made no move toward it. "That my house," he said. Over the top of the wall I could see the branches of a tree and the upper floors of a mud-colored structure.

"Your house is *through* that door?"

"My house," he said, but he wasn't looking at me.

From my second-floor room at the Pradeep I'd already seen over this wall. On its other side was a mud-brick complex with people straggling in and out—it looked like more than one family lived there.

The previous day, when Shubash had said, "No Problem," I had imagined us sitting—cross-legged, perhaps—around a low table in his living room. His wife would serve tea and arrange the flowers I'd brought her. We would all eat sesame candies.

"Your house," I said, up on my tiptoes, as though to peer over the wall. "It's *through* this wall, on the *other* side of that door?"

"Yes. That my house. You see." His gaze was focused toward the mouth of the alley, back where we'd left his rickshaw. Maybe his wife had said, "No Visitors!" Maybe he lived with her family and was not at liberty to entertain. Maybe he was just embarrassed.

"Thanks for showing me," I said.

"No problem."

As we walked down the alley, I thought about the gap between us, the incredible chasm separating our cultures and our lives. Here I was with a pocket full of money, cut loose from my past and unconcerned about my future. Shubash had a family to worry about, an income to consider. If there wasn't a chance of getting something from me, would he even be wasting his time with me? And if India wasn't so relatively cheap, if it were as expensive as, say, Japan, would I even have come here? Maybe money was God's way of getting people to mingle.

"Now silk shop?" Shubash asked.

"Wait here," I said, and walked up the steps of the Pradeep, through the front doors, and into the restaurant. One of the waiters promised to put my marigolds into a vase.

"O.K., Shubash," I said, settling into the back seat of his rickshaw. "Take me where you will."

"Yes, Sahib!"

I spent $200 on silk scarves that afternoon.

22

Anything That Might Be True

One afternoon in the Himalayas I sensed something behind me and turned to find that a sadhu—one of India's wandering, impoverished holy men—had overtaken me. He was a skinny old man wearing tattered rags, no shoes, and carrying only a tiny cloth bag. I tried talking to him, but he spoke no English and he didn't smile. His expression said, "What are you looking at?" When we reached a steep and rocky area I tried to outpace him and several times thought I'd done so, but each time I looked back he was right there, literally two feet behind me. We were at 8,000 feet, but I never heard him pant for breath or miss a step. Finally we came to an inn. I bought him a cup of tea and snuck off while he and the innkeeper were debating Krishna's sexual appetites.

—LANCE FREE, "The Art of Tripping"

That evening I went to the Dasasswamadah ghats, and from a spot in the shadows watched them empty out. One by one, the entrepreneurs packed their wares and disappeared. The beggar women went wherever it is they go at night. The boy at the tea stall lit a lantern to attract the last stragglers, and then he too folded his awning and left, his cups clanking in a sack that bounced against his back.

It was December but still warm out, and mosquitoes whined at my earlobes. Over the Ganges a new moon was rising—a luminous crack in an unclouded purple sky. As I stared at its reflection on the river, a fat fish leaped a foot above the water's surface and fell back with a plop. A challenge to my belief in the laws of pollution, or a cry for help?

As darkness fell, I noticed the glow of coals coming from a small, mushroom-shaped gazebo near the river. I walked toward it, and heard a weak voice call, "Come, my frenn. Sit." Under the gazebo's roof a wizened Indian man was squatting next to the fire, his knees pulled up to his ears like the drooler at Mother Teresa's.

He had a nice spot just above the waterline, with a view north and south on the river. I ducked inside and sat on a low wall opposite him. A turban was wrapped around his head. Shadows danced across his nose and eyes and white beard.

"Everyone call me 'Kerala Baba'," he said. "I always talking with tourists. Have many friends—America, Germany, Australia."

I told him I was American, and asked where he called home.

"*Pfft...*" he laughed. "I am *sadhu*. For twenty-four years, no address. Sometimes Srinagar. Sometimes Himalayas. I travel many."

"What happened twenty-four years ago?" I asked.

"I come from Kerala."

"Did you walk?" Kerala was nearly a thousand miles away.

"*Pfft...* I take tren."

"Did you have a job in Kerala?" I pictured him as a clean-shaven bank teller, ripping off his tie one day, discarding his suit, and heading for Varanasi.

"Kerala life finish."

"Did you have a family?"

"*Pfft...*Twenty-four years. No family, no sister, no brother, no mother, no father."

"Do you ever get letters?"

"Oh, yes. People always writing me. Have many friends—America, Germany, Australia."

"What address do they use?"

"Kerala Baba, Mir Ghat, Rama Kumar Hotel."

"You live in a *hotel*?"

He pointed behind us to the sheer front wall of a massive, unlit building that rose fifty, sixty feet into the Indian night. "That is hotel.

Closed. No guests. Only rats. Sometimes I sleep there. The postal—he know me."

He pulled a pipe from his robes, lit it from a smoldering stick, and stared at the fire. I smelled marijuana.

"What happened to your family?" I asked.

"*Pfft...*" he said, and passed me the pipe. I took a puff—it was weak, cheap marijuana—headache dope—and passed it back.

Below us the Ganges slapped against the lowest step of the ghats. Reflections from campfires on the eastern sandbar quivered on the river. In the darkness upriver the burning ghats flared—a new corpse being lit. The sky above had a dusting of stars and the thin smile of the new moon, tilted like a picture in need of straightening.

We'd been sitting for some time when I asked, "Baba, do you believe that people really went to the moon?"

"I beleeb," he said, "in any ting dat *might* be true."

"I like that," I said. *Anything that might be true.*

He said nothing.

"Do you ever wonder about America?" I asked him.

"*Pfft...*" he said. "No ever."

Another lengthy silence followed, and was broken finally by a small splash from the river.

"Baba, do you think this water is holy?"

"Ganga? Yes, holy."

"Is it pure?"

"I have walk all of India. All of Himalayas. Nowhere is water pure but like Varanasi."

"Even more pure than where the snows melt?"

"*Pfft...*" he said.

Since I'd arrived, he had not once looked at me, but sat staring into the fire, and now it was starting to annoy me. Why had he invited me over—to see how many *Pffts* it would take to drive me away?

And then I laughed at myself. What did I want out of this man? Why did I half-expect him to impart to me the secret of the universe? Why did I find myself regarding him as holier than me, regarding his beliefs and experiences as somehow more valid and worthwhile than my own?

My mother had an undiscriminating admiration for almost everyone she met. The woman who came to sew our drapes, and who had once been a seamstress at the White House, would, according to my mother, have made a fine president. Our mail deliverers might all have been bankers; the man who mowed our lawn, Secretary of the Interior; our plumber, a rocket scientist. My mother rarely met anyone who was not an undiscovered genius or overlooked saint, and I grew up expecting to find dignity and wisdom in the most unlikely places.

And now here I was again, probing for some special knowledge from a man with no shoes. A man who spent his nights smoking hemp with tourists and sleeping in a rat hotel on the banks of the Ganges. There is a West African saying, "The beginning of knowledge is the getting of a roof."

"Baba," I said, laughing. "Tell me the secret of life."

"What?"

"The secret of life, Baba. If you know it, tell me."

Kerala Baba laughed—laughed so hard he had to reach down in his robes and grab his side. "*Pfft*. This is crazy question. No one can answer. Birds, sky, trees, animals, river, man. This is life."

Except for the occasional swooshing bat, the night was quiet. Rats rummaged through the empty hotel. Somewhere in the darkness, dogs silently gnawed bones. The river rolled by, shimmering. The sky twinkled; trees trembled.

"Baba, in your life, what is the very best thing that ever happened to you."

"*Ahhh! Pfft.*" He flicked something into the fire, and made it hiss. "You ask no good questions. So many good tings in my life. How to choose? Say dis ting is best—dat ting is best?"

"How about the *worst* thing?"

He cried out, put his hands to his face, and rocked. I couldn't read him. Was he reliving an old painful memory—some woman in Kerala, perhaps? Trying to think which example of man's cruelty to man he should relate? Or just hiding from me?

On my first trip to India I was married, traveling with my wife, and would periodically indulge in the married man's fantasy: I would sneak away some morning, ride the train to some distant city, Varanasi perhaps, and spend the rest of my life like a *sadhu*, begging food and money from people. Would such a life be any less valid than the other possible lives that lay ahead of me? Might I not find a life like Kerala Baba's liberating?

When more minutes had passed, I asked again—"the worst thing?"

Kerala Baba took his hands from his face. "Baba," he said to me, "you are kdazy man."

"Nothing bad has happened in your life, Baba?"

"Many tings in life are bad. Some people have no enough food. Some people have too much. Many people eat too much. Drink too much. Many people smoke too much. And, Baba, many people talk too much. These are all bad tings, Baba."

The fire shifted and began to smoke heavily. I said, "Baba, I am going now."

He shrugged.

I stood. "Should I give you money?"

"*Pfft.* Twenty-four years. No home, no address. Money I care not. You give me money, you don't give—I care not. Sometimes people give me money, food. I care not. This life is long. I die, care not. Live, care not. You give me money, you no give, I care not."

"Well, thank you," I said. I had to give him, if not cash, at least a great deal of credit. He was the first self-proclaimed teacher or holy man I'd ever met who, when it came right down to it, didn't want my money. "Very nice to meet you, Kerala Baba. I hope my questions didn't upset you."

"*Pfft!*" Kerala Baba put his hand to his forehead and waggled his fingers. His eyes glowed like the tiny coals of the fire.

"I'll write you a letter," I said, and turned on my heel.

"*Baba!*"

I turned back around.

"You no give money, Baba?"

"I'm confused, Baba. Do you *want* money?"

"I no care," he said.

"If you want money, I'll give you money. If you don't care, I won't."

"Baba, I hungry. No eat today."

His hand reached out across the fire.

I stuck ten rupees in it.

23

The Burning Place

*This shop is two minutes from the burning place. We go outside, we find
dead bodies passing through. So if a man is a real thinker he will realize
he might have won so much from his life, but what he takes with him?
Nothing! He comes with open hand and he goes with open hand. So why
worry and fight about materialistic things, and get the problems on your
own head, if you realize you are not going to take it with you? These
things are Indian philosophy, which, if a man is a real thinker, he will
understand.*

Now! I show you silk?

—ARUN KUMAR, Varanasi Merchant

The Doms, the cremation attendants, discourage tours and cameras but don't mind an occasional quiet Anglo at the funeral
pyres. I walked the dark half-mile along the river, stepping carefully,
trying to avoid the invisible mushy spots. The ghats glowed like a
burger drive-in on the edge of a Midwestern town. Drawing near, I
heard low singing and chanting—*Rama nama satya hai*, the name of God
is truth. Nine fires—nine bodies in various stages of immolation—
were arranged in a tic-tac-toe grid just a few steps from the river. Some
one hundred people were gathered around. Scraps of orange and yellow
ash twitched like excited butterflies escaping into the night sky.

A man in a white robe, the eldest son of someone whose body was
about to be cremated, knelt on the outer edges of the crowd, having his

head shaved by another man. Several people looked at me, noting my arrival, but none seemed to object; a few nodded smiles at me. For a while I stayed at the back, listening to the chanted moans, then slowly worked my way to the front, maybe ten feet from the flames. Several of the bodies still retained recognizable shapes. The faces had all been rendered featureless, the heads now nothing but blackened bulbs. Here I saw a brittle-looking arm-and-elbow assembly, biceps charred, and there a foot, toes smoking. The smell was not unpleasant and not much different, I thought, than the smell of roast goat.

The Doms poked at the fires with long poles, keeping the bodies centered in the flames. I had been there some time when I heard a sharp pop from one of the fires—the brain juices heating up and exploding the skull like a can of spray paint. Hindus believe that this is the moment when the soul wins final release from the body. Behind me a woman shrieked. Her man. For centuries the tradition of *suttee* required a Hindu widow to throw herself on her husband's funeral pyre—to be with him in the afterlife, some said; to save the family from having to feed her, said others. The British ended the debate, outlawing the practice in 1830.

Three dogs waded belly-deep in the river, their teeth and eyes gleaming in the firelight. One of the fires had burned down, and now the workers shoved the coals and ashes a few feet to the water's edge. A dozen other dogs plunged in to join the waiting trio, snarling, snapping, throwing their haunches around like basketball players jostling for position. The coals hissed as they slid in, and immediately triggered an alligatoresque thrashing and hideous growling racket; shortly the biggest dog pulled free with what looked like a length of thigh bone, leaving the others to fight over forearms and fingers. An ungracious end to the ceremony, but one that left no illusions. In the morning light the Doms would sift the riverside silt for jewelry or other valuables.

I sensed no air of sadness about the scene, but instead an overriding sense of inevitability. I scanned the lit up faces around the fires. Most appeared satisfied, relieved, or even ecstatic. We come; we go, they seemed to say. We are all born; we shall all die. Why mourn, why weep over these bodies? Their souls are with Shiva now. It is over; they are free. It is we living who must go on, toiling to unravel our own little lives.

From a building atop the ghats four men were bringing a new litter. Tiny flags fluttered at each corner. In the middle was a body wrapped in saffron cloth and strewn with orange and red flowers. The head seemed small and was tightly bound; between the eye hollows, the nose protruded, pressing almost defiantly against the cloth.

Relatives escorted the litter, surrounding it, heads lowered, singing in soft voices. The man with the newly-shaved head sprinkled the body with Ganges water. A framework of branches and logs had been quickly constructed in the vacated spot; the new body was laid down, more wood heaped on top, and a torch applied to the base. The flame caught instantly and leaped into a wavering ball of oranges and blues, snatching at the linen and singeing it. Excited cries, emotional wails, rose from the crowd; but soon the onlookers quieted down to await the next skull pop.

The heat drove me from the front row. A man appeared at my elbow and attempted to start a conversation—"Excuse me, what is your native country?"—but left me alone when I said I did not feel like talking. I retreated, propelling my mortal body down the river, moving quickly, not really caring what it was I stepped in.

24

The Familiar Hunch

*Midnight, or thereabouts. A man carrying a folded black umbrella
walks toward my window from the direction of the railway tracks,
stops, squats, shits. Then sees me silhouetted against light and, instead of
taking offence at my voyeurism, calls: "Watch this!" and proceeds to ex-
trude the longest turd I have ever seen. "Fifteen inches!" he calls. "How
long can you make yours?*

—SALMAN RUSHDIE, *Midnight's Children*

If any Indian city ever had a chance, it would have been New Delhi.
Instead of tinkering with old Delhi's hodgepodge of alleys and temples, the British built a new city from scratch on its outskirts. Connaught Place, a splendid, circular lawn and garden, was installed as New
Delhi's heart, with wide boulevards radiating outward across the city
like the spokes of a wheel. Originally these boulevards were flanked by
spanking-new, stone secretariats, elegant colonial homes, and flowering
parks and *maidans*, but since independence the Indians have been slowly
making New Delhi over.

My night train from Varanasi pulled in just before dawn on day
thirty-seven. On the avenue outside the train station three men had a
fire going and were boiling tea water in a scorched tin can. Cow pies
covered the pavement. Piles of rubbish lined the curb. On both sides
of the road the bundles of rags, which in India signify a human being's
nighttime resting place, were beginning to stir. Hooded figures
crouched in the shadows, defecating. Men with bowed heads and the

familiar hunch of the pisser stood facing a brick wall running for several hundred yards along one side of the road. For its entire length, from approximately penis height on down, the wall was discolored, the mortar corroding away. *Oh, India!* I thought. But I wondered: *Will I forget all of this as soon as I leave, and simply remember the country as magical and mysterious, the way I'd remembered it after my first trip?*

Near Connaught Place, two businessmen, thirtyish, walked out of a restaurant and fell into step on the sidewalk directly ahead of me. They appeared fit and well-fed, and were strikingly handsome. Their dark suits were tailored, their expensive briefcases looked like they had been polished by one of the sidewalk shoeshine men, and their accents sounded decidedly British.

"The P.M. is handling the Sikh thing quite well."

"Yes, but he must get off the pot with the economy. Since the day we went pooblic, the rupee has lost eight percent to the dulla..."

I took in their starched white collars and gleaming shoes, their immaculate haircuts, their confident, young Turk strides, and was starting to soften—a place that produced specimens like these must have loads of redeeming features—when the pair suddenly veered down an alley next to the Rivoli Theatre, stopped, unzipped, and, still side-by-side and chatting amiably, had themselves a fraternal piss against the theatre wall.

My flight to Cairo was scheduled for the next day. I stopped on the sidewalk and watched these two men, and thought: *I am ready.*

I remembered a restaurant located on the top floor of a shopping emporium near Connaught Place. To reach it I had to climb five flights of stairs and step over or around the sleepers balled up on the landings. Halfway up I approached a landing where three rag bundles lay. One man was just beginning to stand up and stretch. He wore a hooded robe and had his back to me, but as I reached his landing he turned and looked back over one shoulder.

He was not the Indian I had expected, but—and this was no small shock—an Anglo about my own age. I was completely unprepared for the pale blue eyes that stared out from under his hood, no more than a foot away; and he, apparently, found the sight of me equally unnerving.

The moment our eyes caught we jerked away from each other as though we'd smacked foreheads. We were the exact same height, and our hair and beards were the same shade of blond. I thought: *Give him a shower and do something about the red sores on his cheeks (or sentence me to a month on New Delhi's streets), and we might pass for twins.*

"Excuse me," I said.

He wheezed, broke off eye contact, and bent to gather his grimy blanket.

I climbed another flight, and on the next landing stopped and looked back. He was staring up at me with a look of vacant wonder. I began to say something, but a flicker of embarrassment crossed his spotted face, and he turned his back.

I ordered breakfast and sat staring across New Delhi's treetops and rooftops, thinking about my dirty twin and feeling shaken. Were we not each mirrors of what the other might have been? Obviously this man had some time ago chosen to do what I had once contemplated—fading away and disappearing between India's cracks. Now I imagined his life: visa long expired, passport sold to a black marketeer, drifting from ashram to ashram or drug to drug; sleeping on stairways and cadging occasional dollars from tourists. A valid life—no more nor less significant than my own—but one I'd rather observe than experience, thank you.

I went out to invite him to join me for breakfast, but he was gone. Alone, I ate my eggs and toast and sipped my coffee. The sun was leering cautiously over the city's rooftops. I wondered: *What was he doing this minute? Squatting in one of those filthy alleys, his gown pulled up, imagining the life I was leading? Wondering how it all might have turned out if he'd gone back to Europe or America or wherever home was? Wondering what he might look like with a haircut and a beard trim? Or if a healthy diet might not clear up those sores?*

Maybe it's just plain wrong to go back to a place. I came home starry-eyed after my first trip to India and told friends that India was my most favorite place of all. Now I wondered what it was I had found to like. Maybe my earlier enthusiasm was a function of having spent four months, enough time to become inured to the hideous poverty. Given another four months might I not again begin to accept and see beyond it, to rediscover and relish the gentle playfulness of the people, their sweetness and ability to laugh at themselves? In my notebook I wrote: *The last three weeks have been long enough to impress upon me only one truth about this country: India is a shithole. I imagine that every page of this notebook has some reference to the desperate filth.*

I flipped back to my first page from Calcutta, began skimming forward, and on a fresh page listed the words that leaped out at me.

> Baksheesh, cows, wasteland, sludge, squatters, shacks, hustlers, anguish, beggars, rags, rubbish heaps, pissers, dumpers, rats, garbage, flotsam, starving, hovels, homeless, illiterate, lepers, blood, vomit, feces, corpse, stench, urine, babies, flies, diarrhea, GET ME OUTA HERE, fever, nausea, dysentery, greasy, bleat, quack, burp, whine, skull pop, snarling, snapping, thrashing, rag bundles, sores, shithole...

Is it possible that war has been declared on India and that somehow I never heard?

25

Mohammed Ali

I have come across planners at the (Indian) Planning Commission who have convinced themselves that even within fifteen years it is not possible to put the willing labor power of India to work...They have ascertained that in order to put a man to work you need on average so much electricity, so much cement, and so much steel. This is absurd...The Taj Mahal was built without electricity, cement and steel and...all the cathedrals of Europe were built without them...

If we can recover the sense that it is the most natural thing for every person born into this world to use his hands in a productive way and that it is not beyond the wit of man to make this possible, then I think the problem of unemployment will disappear and we shall soon be asking ourselves how we can get all the work done that needs to be done.

— E. F. SCHUMACHER, *Small is Beautiful*

My plan was to spend my last Indian afternoon in the sun on the lawn of Connaught Circle. I would write in my notebook and finish the last few pages of *Midnight's Children*. But the instant I moved my foot from the sidewalk to the lawn I felt scores of eyes lock onto me. When I chose a spot and sat, I saw in my peripheral view a dozen bodies rise from the shade of the park's trees and begin moving toward me. Beggars, shoe shine boys, massage men, fortune tellers. Surrounded, I let a boy named Jungi scrub my shoes. A man named Dasgupta massaged my neck and shoulders. Another, who said his

Mohammed Ali —The Q-tip-like swabs tucked under the lip
of his turban revealed his trade—ear cleaner.

name was Ali Baba, read my palm: *"You have been sick with stomach, but now
you are well. You are missing a woman. You will soon be rich."* The combined
talents of these men cost me two dollars.

They drifted off until only a single man remained. Earlier I had
noticed him at the back of the mob, smiling patiently but saying nothing. Now he sat on the grass, two arm lengths away, grinning shyly—
as though he had some unbearably good secret.

"Hello, Baba." He had long eyelashes, teeth as bright and straight
as piano ivories, and, etched along his upper lip, the world's narrowest
mustache. His smile was so sweet it might have graced India's tourist
posters. His name, too, was a classic: Mohammed Ali. He was not
young—he had three sons—but if playfulness was something barter-
able, I'd have traded my money belt for a dose of his.

The Q-tip-like swabs tucked under the lip of his turban revealed
his trade—ear cleaner. It's a common sight in India: an Indian man
wielding cotton swabs and long forceps, and bent like a lab technician

over the cocked head of a kneeling European. Indian people rarely submit to this quackery; it's a tourist phenomenon. I'd known travelers who had allowed it and swore they could hear better for days afterwards, but I had always regarded them as suspect. Imagine, in India of all places, letting a stranger—some man in a park, on a beach, in a train station—stick something in your ear!

When Mohammed Ali said, "Ears cleaning, Baba?" I only snorted.

"Oh, but it is nice, Baba," he said. "See my book?"

I looked to see what sort of idiots had risked their eardrums:

> We New Yorkers have seen all the scams. I laughed when Mohammed said he would make me hear better, but he wore me down. He is such a nice man. Now my ears are vibrating with noises I haven't heard since I was a child, and I'm recommending that you go ahead and do what I wouldn't have dreamed of doing half an hour ago.
>
> — LINDA, Brooklyn

> A year ago I went to an ear-nose-and-throat guy at home. He charged me $95 to do what Mohammed Ali just did for twenty rupees. And was nowhere near as personable.
>
> — J.T. ROBBINS, Dallas, Texas

> I'm a sixties child, and I thought I'd done it all. But ears—Momma never told me ears could feel so good. Or be so dirty. Sure, I use Q-tips, but Mohammed pulled stuff out of me I couldn't believe. A little tiny stone—now where did that come from?
>
> — PAULA SPITZ, Santa Cruz, CA

"Pretty happy customers," I said.

"Yes, Baba. Everyone happy. Have you ever..."

"No," I said. "I clean my own ears." I pointed at the swabs sticking out from under his turban. "I have those, too."

"But dirt is hard," he said. He opened his pouch and pulled out a small vial. From the moment he sat down his smile had not left him. "I put some drops in your ear, wait some minutes, then I can clean. Sometimes people have things in ears for many years, and they don't know."

But he might as well have been offering to tattoo Krishna's portrait onto my forehead. "I can hear just fine," I said.

He folded his hands and sat there, smiling, as though content to wait for sunset and then dawn and then sunset again if necessary.

"What's the best thing that ever happened to you?" I asked him.

He considered for a moment. "People." He nodded at his book. "So many people. From all over the world. People from every country come to Connaught."

"What's the worst thing?"

He mulled it over. With that smile of his, if he were to answer that nothing bad had ever happened to him, I was prepared to believe him.

Finally his smile faded a notch. Uncertainly: "I cannot read or write."

Since childhood my entire life has been a blur of words: daily newspapers, overdue books, half-finished stories. Subtract the written word from my life and what remains? What use would it be? Yet here was Mohammed Ali, illiterate father of three, radiating a serenity I have rarely known.

"Can you read numbers?" I asked.

"Some numbers."

"Does your wife read and write?"

"No."

"Do your children?"

"They are too young," he said. "Baba, you read and write, yes?"

"Yes."

"Maybe you can help me." Mohammed Ali pulled an aerogram from his bag and handed it to me. "Baba, maybe you can read to me?"

It was from a Japanese woman and was written in English. Kiyoko had vacationed in New Delhi a month earlier, and Mohammed Ali had cleaned her ears. Now she was back in Tokyo, wishing that her trip had been longer and wishing health and happiness to Mohammed Ali, his wife and children, and to all of Mohammed Ali's Connaught Circle colleagues.

He sighed when I was done reading, and put his hand to his chest. "Oh, I miss her so much. She was so kind person. Every day she sits here in the park with all of us. We would talk, oh, of so many things."

I asked for his book and turned back several pages:

> Meeting Mr. Mohammed Ali is the best part of my journey. I thought he would open my ears, but also he opens my heart. This is a very special man.
> — KIYOKO OHKUBO, Tokyo

I imagined Kiyoko, sitting in an office building in downtown Tokyo, staring out the window and daydreaming of her all-too-short holiday. What traveler does not know the post-trip letdown, the clutching rhythms of job and home claiming their due? Often I have sat at home, recalling the kindness and simplicity of people in foreign places, and ached to be back with them again, sitting in their park or rickshaw or silk shop, and soaking in their presence.

Mohammed Ali took a fresh, blank aerogram from his pouch. "Baba, maybe you will write for me? To her."

I took the aerogram, wrote *Dear Kiyoko*, and poised my pen. "What do you want me to tell her?"

He was smiling. "You write."

"But I don't know her," I said. "You spent many days with her."

"You write many letters, yes?"

"Yes," I said.

"I never write, Baba. You write."

> Dear Kiyoko,
> It is a beautiful afternoon here. The only way it could be better would be if you were here. Since you left, the sun seems not so bright in New Delhi. There are no clouds in the sky today, only some airplanes, and everyone here in the park wishes that one of them was bringing you back to us. Since you have gone back to Japan, we talk about you every day and wonder when you will return. We miss you very badly. There

are cows wandering nearby. Most days they make a sound like 'Mooo,' but today it is different. Today they are saying, 'We miss Kiyoko. We miss Kiyoko.' Yes, even the cows miss you.

I was so excited today when I received your letter. The post man told me it was from Japan, and a man from America read it to me. You write so beautifully—your words are like Indian rubies. Thank you for your kind thoughts for my family. Yes, everyone is doing well, everyone except me and all your friends here in the park—we miss you so much. Me most of all. I hope that your parents and your brothers and sisters are all healthy and that you are not working your lovely head too very hard. If you cannot come soon, I hope you will write again.

Your friend, Mohammed Ali

"*Oh, Baba!*" Mohammed Ali pressed his palms together and bowed his head. "Oh, Baba! Thank you. That is beautiful."

"It's nothing," I said. But actually it was one of the most satisfying things I've ever done. Mohammed Ali's first letter. *Japan!*—he would be known now in Japan. There were whole days when this trip of mine seemed devoid of purpose: *I'm here, but why?* Moments like this reminded me: *The being needs travel—new sights, new people, new experience— the way the body needs food, touch, an occasional soak in a backwoods hot spring.* I was a collector. The Mohammed Alis, Tonys, Shubashes, and Ram Ashray Prashads of the world would come home with me in my heart, the same way others had come home with me from China and Afghanistan and Russia. Time would airbrush away the shitty streets, foul water, and the fact that all these cultures were drowning in babies. Someday soon I would, I knew, be sitting in my taxi or in some office like Kiyoko's, fretting about the present and idealizing my past. *I should go back*, the thought would surely come. *I should go SOMEWHERE.*

"Baba," said Mohammed Ali. "Now you *must* let me do something for you."

I sat up straight and tipped my head to the right. Mohammed Ali uncorked a small vial and eye-dropped a fizzing seltzer into my left ear. We sat and let it soak in. The press conference reconvened around us.

"Please be careful," I said, when Mohammed Ali took out his forceps.

"Very careful, Baba."

For a moment I felt nothing, just a tickling in the ear canal. Then, with forceps and the softest of tugs, Mohammed Ali lifted out of my ear something incredible—a brown scrap curled in the shape of my eardrum—and held it in front of my eyes. I opened my hand and he set it in my palm. It was as thin and crisp as a flake of onion skin; longer than my thumbnail, wider than the toothpick on my Swiss Army Knife. Had he extracted and presented to me my liver I would have been only slightly more dumbfounded.

"Yes," he said. "Many are surprised."

The crowd of men were laughing.

"Do you clean *their* ears?" I asked Mohammed Ali.

"No, but they always like to watch."

He fizzed and cleaned the other ear—no trophies there—and then toweled my neck dry. The press conference disbanded, people scattering away.

Mohammed Ali and I sat quietly for a few moments in an intense, symphonic silence. It seemed as though someone had clamped conch shells over my ears. I could hear *everything*: the cows munching the lawn; men from one side of New Delhi to the other pissing on walls; boys at the train station screaming "*Chai! Chai! Chai!*"; the shriek of airplane tires nicking down on the runway out at the airport; even trickles of snowmelt on the glaciers up in Kashmir. Never before, and not since, have my ears felt so good, so new.

I gave Mohammed Ali some money, wrote something nice in his book, and tried to imagine him sitting in the New Delhi air terminal, his ear-cleaning pouch clutched between his knees, waiting for a flight to America. Would he still be smiling then?

26

Domes, Minarets, and Date Palms

"Let me warn you. They are stealing tonight."

—CAUTION WHISPERED INTO V. S. NAIPAUL'S EAR
UPON ARRIVAL IN EGYPT, *An Area of Darkness*

An Air Kuwait jetliner whisked me out of New Delhi before day-break, toward Egypt, where I would spend the next two weeks. The Arab sheiks and businessmen seated around me wore immaculate, pressed robes and white headdresses, and nodded in sleep. Among the grasping hordes of India I had begun to fancy myself wealthy, but here I felt scruffy and underprivileged.

In the pool of light from the overhead bulb, I counted the contents of my money belt and felt my disenchantment with India soften by about half a notch. Whatever my complaints about the country, I could hardly gripe about its cost. Three weeks of hotels, meals, trains, rick-shaws, taxis, newspapers, beggars, and phone calls to America had cost me (not including scarf money) an average of only $16.50 a day. Now I was under-budget for the entire trip—at $22.50 a day.

Dawn revealed the rumpled brown mountains of Pakistan passing under my window, then Iranian deserts as flat and pale as piecrusts, and toward noon the robin's egg blue of the Persian Gulf. A picket line of fleecy clouds cast a chain of splotchy shadows across the water's still surface.

For half an hour I watched the plane's shadow silently glide across the sands of Saudi Arabia, and then lost it over the steel-blue Red Sea.

The sun bounced off waves, which, patterned by an afternoon breeze, looked as clean, shiny, and neatly laid out as the tiled floor of a mosque. The coast of Egypt met the Red Sea in a line of sharp, symmetrical curves and barbs resembling a line of Arabic script. Inland, the Egyptian countryside appeared deserted, barren, and brown. Until we neared Cairo, where bright green vegetation bordered both sides of the muddy, meandering Nile, all of Egypt resembled an empty beach.

Many of my memories of the Islamic world were troublesome, a few downright awful. Years earlier on my first morning in Morocco, at a deserted roadblock ten miles inside the border, a soldier came to the window of my Volkswagen bus, inspected my passport, snarled "Stupid Americans," and disappeared around back. There followed the cracking sound of machine gun stock meeting taillight plastic, and then he was back at my window, writing out a faulty-equipment ticket—payable on the spot, of course.

Later, on a train across Iran, a muscular Iranian Air Force pilot shoved me twice (for no reason I could perceive) and challenged me to a fistfight (I begged off). And on my second morning in Teheran a Khomeini lookalike, a *mullah*, who passed me on the street, grabbed a fistful of my beard and tried to yank it off.

Now, arriving in Egypt, I was braced for more of the same. The *intifada* was raging, and I presumed that in front of the U.S. Embassy I would find furious mobs of *kafiyeh*-wearing men roasting dummies of Uncle Sam and plotting airplane hijacks. Egypt and Israel and Jordan were all inching toward peace, but the zealots who feared it staged impressive eruptions. Tourism in the entire Middle East was considered dicey, as bombs periodically ripped apart cafes, buses, and trash bins, while a steady stream of travel advisories flowed from the U.S. State Department.

Many years had passed since Egypt had launched planes and tanks east across the Sinai Peninsula, but the travelers' grapevine still hummed with stories of lesser Egyptian threats: dirty water, exotic diseases, daggers flashing in dark alleys. Fortunately, however, the crashing noise, which is the soundtrack to all travel, is the noise of assumptions being shattered, and my Egypt was absolutely none of that, thank you.

The night I arrived at the airport, a taxi driver, instead of hustling me into his cab for the ride downtown (six dollars), led me to the correct bus (five cents) and refused to be tipped. In Arabic he gave my destination to the bus conductor, who—after forty-five minutes of highways, concrete apartment blocks, and finally the traffic-choked center of the city—signaled me to get off. The boy who showed me to my hotel room pumped my hand and said, "America is very best!"

As I walked the streets the next morning, central Cairo exhibited a European sensibility. It was a Friday, the Islamic holy day; the traffic I'd seen the previous evening was gone, and only a few small businesses were open. The man arranging fruit in storefront bins across the street from my hotel was the same man one sees arranging fruit in storefront bins in Marseilles or Barcelona, or around the corner from my old Haight-Ashbury apartment in San Francisco. The few people passing on the sidewalk, almost all of them men, returned every one of my guidebook hellos ("*Salaam Alekum*"), and as often as not initiated their own. They struck me as secretly tickled about something, and I took it as a sign of confidence that they allowed me to pass among them without staring. They looked, I thought hopefully, like people who might just be as exhausted by the whole Middle East hullabaloo as the rest of us.

A cold, stiff, mid-December sandstorm was sweeping the city. Palm trees gyrated above the street, tangled laundry flapped on rooftops; but I was quick to notice that there was not even a scrap of airborne litter. Perhaps one's reaction to a place is dictated by one's route of arrival. That morning, two young Canadian men, whose hotel room was across from mine, and who had spent the past six months in Europe and Israel, had asked me: "Can you believe how dirty Cairo is?" But having just had my head held under the greasy surface of India for three weeks, I could hardly have agreed with them less. A week ago I'd seen bodies being dumped into the Ganges and had discovered that my notebook was mostly a thesaurus for the word filth. No, Cairo struck me that first day as being particularly well-tended.

A block from my hotel I ducked into a cafe where rows of pastries were displayed inside fly-proof cases (technology I didn't recall seeing in India), and drank a cup of coffee. At the surrounding tables, men in white caps and ankle-lenth smocks sucked on ornate hookahs as tall and gangly as ostriches. Soldiers leaned over backgammon boards, engrossed, their rifles propped against nearby walls.

At noon a yodeling call from the muezzin, the Islamic clergy, was answered by the city-wide honking of horns. Up and down the street men filed from cafes and trooped toward the mosques. Soon the sidewalks and boulevards overflowed with worshipers, who unrolled prayer mats and knelt in rows to roar their unified prayers. "Alla-hu akbar..." *Allah is great. There is no God but Allah, and Mohammed is his Prophet...*

Needles of fine sand from Qadaffhi's Libya were whipping across the asphalted expanse of Tahrir (Liberation) Square, the heart of Cairo. A customerless shoe shine boy was wrapped so completely in white cloth that he belonged, I thought, across the square with the mummies in the Egyptian Museum. A shoe repair man was busy chasing two dozen rubber insoles down the sidewalk. A newspaperman piled bricks atop fluttering stacks of the *Arab Times, Le Monde, International Herald Tribune*, and—surprise!—the *Jerusalem Post*.

Rifle-toting soldiers patrolled the square, but even they looked like people one might reason with. At the nearby U.S. Embassy the wind had knotted the flag to its pole. No flaming Uncle Sams, no mobs, and only two policemen—holding hands and grinning at each other, the muzzles of their machine guns pointed groundward. I stood and watched them and felt the bulk of my reservations about Egypt sweeping away. A culture which reads the enemy's newspaper, and whose cops hold hands—how totally...*disarming*.

Just beyond Tahrir Square was the Nile, a quarter mile wide, hemmed in by concrete banks lined with date palms and tall hotels. Its silted waters were the light brown color of over-creamed coffee and dotted with empty barges, floating downstream toward Alexandria. I spent the day wandering the quiet neighborhoods and tree-lined streets on the Nile's west bank; at dusk, from the east bank, I watched the sun dip behind Cairo's skyline of domes, minarets, and date palms. A yellow neon light—"CASINO"—popped on across the river. An exact half-moon appeared overhead. The river was now a rippling carpet of blue velvet, and a pink puff of cloud created the illusion of a vapored genie escaping the bottle-shaped Cairo Tower.

I rode Cairo's modern subway back toward my hotel. On the downtown streets cone-shaped shanks of lamb rotated on vertical spits outside restaurants, spicing the air with a juicy roast smell. I stopped into the Cafe Riche—where Gamal Abdel Nasser and his friends met to plot the king-toppling coup of 1952—tipped a sleeping cat off a chair, sat, ordered salad, beer, and lamb kebab, and studied sober portraits of the revolution's philosophers and statesmen hanging on the walls.

At the next table an old man held a magnifying glass to the small print of a fat, leatherbound *Koran*. Nearby two Sudanese exchange students engaged in political debate, savoring thimble-sized cups of coffee and waving cigarettes. I heard a woman's voice tut-tutting in beautiful French, and turned to see a hip young Egyptian couple—he wearing a bombardier's jacket, she, purple leather pants, both with the latest advertising pouts stitched across their lips. They were the first mixed-gender couple I remembered seeing, and, as with the policemen, it was somehow comforting to see them holding hands.

All day long I had had no more than a cursory conversation with anyone, but now, as I looked around my cafe—at strangers dipping bread in bowls of tahini, wiping lamb gravy off their chins—I felt an agreeable warmth. It is, I know, no great feat to climb on an airplane and to go buy a meal in a foreign restaurant; but it is certainly one of the world's most agreeable addictions. One good day on the road easily redeems three weeks of dirt and aggravation.

After dinner I ate an ice cream cone, laid out seven bucks for *The Beginning and the End*—a novel by Egypt's Nobel laureate, Naghib Mahfouz—and went to bed early. A month had now passed since Baguio, since Brother Casuga had instructed me to say nightly prayers. Ever since his treatment, my attention had been less and less on my back. It wasn't healed, but it didn't pain me the way it once had. Now, as I knelt beside my bed a thirtieth and final time, I felt a low level euphoria and wondered: *With good health and a guaranteed income, how long would I be content to live like this, a global appraiser of cheap hotels and restaurants? Not forever, but surely much longer than my allotted hundred days.*

27

A Walkman, Clothes, Maybe a Car

We Egyptians have funny ideas about America. I myself used to run fruit store in L.A., so I know how it is, but most people in Cairo, they think money is everywhere in America. There was one Egyptian man who comes to L.A. His plane lands at LAX and outside on sidewalk he sees a wallet. He can see there is money sticking out from it, but he does not even bend down to pick it up. You know why? He says it is only his first day and he is not yet ready to start working.

—MOHAMMED KAMEL
("YOU PLEASE CALL ME 'MIKE'"), an Egyptian

On Saturday, Cairo resumed the throbbing din for which it is famous. At the taxi stand in front of the Nile Hilton I asked one of the drivers (his yellow sweatshirt said WALK LIKE AN EGYPTIAN) for a ride to the Kenyan Embassy. When we had rolled about fifty yards, I mentioned that I too was a taxi driver. He stopped, backed up, and called to his friends, who swarmed around my window to shake hands and exchange cab driver camaraderie.

As I reached the Kenyan Embassy, the staff was locking the front gate and heading home for the day. Instead of a come-back-tomorrow, one of the secretaries unlocked the gate, escorted me inside, and patiently read a *Paris Match* while I filled out the paperwork.

Later, as I walked along the Nile, a voice said, "Peanuts, my friend?"—and a paper bag was extended toward me. My benefactor was a large, square-faced man of about twenty, wearing trousers and a baggy white shirt. His name was Hashim, but he wanted me to call him "H."

"Thank you for talking to me," H said. "I am going to Europe next week, and I need to practice my English."

"What will you do in Europe?"

"I will look for some possession."

"*Possession*?" He was going shopping?

"Yes," he said. "A job. Work."

"Ah, *position*!"

"Yes. Now you see why I must practice my English."

I pointed to the river, then toward our feet. "If languages were bodies of water," I said, "your English would be the Nile, and my Arabic would be this mud puddle."

H thought this was very funny and offered me more peanuts. "If you would like, I'll show you Old Cairo. My home is there."

He led me two blocks from the river, down a flight of stairs, and through a sunken archway. "New Cairo is built on all the sand that blows in from the desert," H said. "Old Cairo is down low." Indeed, the streets of Old Cairo were nearly ten feet lower than the streets of modern Cairo: here *sands of time* was a phrase deep with meaning.

H steered me down narrow alleys paved with bricks. Some of the buildings had signs identifying them as art galleries or curio shops, but most looked abandoned and seemed as old and tentative as the buildings of Varanasi. "This church is seven hundred and fifty years old," H would say. "That one is fifteen hundred." He pointed to a particularly ancient structure, the church of St. Sergius. "Inside is a cave where the baby Jesus and the Holy Family hid from Herod."

H was one of Egypt's six million Coptic Christians, and he wanted me to know that his ancestors had been here for centuries before Mohammed came along and started all the trouble. He stopped at an open area, littered with bricks.

"Last month there were Christian houses here, but the authorities condemn them and knock them down. They say they are old and dangerous—but these were only five hundred years. Really I think the Moosleems would like to knock down all Christian buildings."

Christmas was just a couple of weeks away, but I saw no sign of festivities.

"Christmas cannot be so big a thing here," H said. "We do not want to make angry the Moosleems. Already it is difficult. On Christmas Eve the boy Coptics, since we are young and strong, have to stand outside the church and protect it. Moosleem boys come to throw stones. They think we have a girl in there, and that at midnight we will all be...you know...kissing her."

Four big dogs, a Doberman in the lead, came running from an alley, growling, showing teeth. "Let us go this other way," H said, and led me down a different alley. "Very strong dogs."

"Probably Moosleem dogs," I said. H found this extra funny, and gave me the last of his peanuts.

We sat on a wall outside the low mud and brick dwelling that was his home, just down the alley from the Church of St. Barbara. (When the possibly-mythical Barbara tried to convert her father to Christianity, he is said to have beaten her to death.) H talked about the waiter's position he hoped to find in Paris or Amsterdam or London and the things he wanted to buy: a Walkman, some clothes, maybe a car.

H's sister opened the door and called to him in Arabic. "It is my time for dinner," he said. "I would invite you in, but today my mother is sick. Come. I'll show you back to the street. We don't want those Moosleem dogs to eat a good Christian boy."

I had read news articles about Cairo's slums, about the thousands who lived in cemeteries on its outskirts, but India had given me my fill of slums. During my few days in Cairo I stuck close to the city center (except for the day I visited the pyramids), to stroll through museums and bazaars, and sit in cafes.

Holiday shoppers cruised in and out of downtown stores aglitter with New Year's decorations. I took in the shapely dresses and high heeled shoes of the mannequins in store windows, and wondered: *Who buys them?* Almost every woman I saw wore the traditional billowy, black robes, with only her face showing—and was usually shepherding a flock of children. As I wandered the city I grew accustomed to seeing mostly males.

Each evening swarms of young men lined up at the movie theatres on Tarlat Haarb Street. Many were big linebacker types, with thick necks, muscular jaws, and what looked like shoulder pads under their clothes. A bunch of toughs, I might have thought, were they not so preoccupied with themselves—bussing each other on both cheeks, loitering hand in hand or with elbows linked.

The Mahfouz book, *The Beginning and the End*, was a bleak portrait of life for Egypt's middle class—and especially bleak for its women. A family might struggle to get its sons educated or placed in good jobs, but the daughters were held back—kept out of sight at home, and veiled in public—while the parents tried to arrange a suitable marriage.

At the start of my trip I had planned to consider anyone—male or female—for my invitation to visit America. But since the Philippines, where I'd met Irma, I had come no closer to meeting a Third World female than I had come to meeting H's sister.

Nor was I drawn to invite any of the men I met in Cairo. The city's citizenry did not strike me as being either in awe or in ignorance of the West—the way people in Asia had seemed. From Cairo, America no longer seemed so unattainably far, but seemed, instead, like one of the city's privileged, outlying suburbs; with a bus map and a pocket full of piastres one might reach America in an hour and a half. Several Cairoites I met—H, for instance—had concrete plans to go West, and others had already been.

Near the Egyptian Museum I met a shop owner, Ehab, who used to live in Phoenix. "I was married to an American woman then," he told me. "Oh, we had lots of troubles."

"Cultural differences?" I asked, knowingly.

"No—money differences. I didn't have much trouble with the culture." Ehab had pale skin, pale eyes, and sun-lightened blond hair; when he had greeted me in near-perfect English, I had at first taken him for an American.

"Before she met me, my wife made one hundred thousand dollars a year as a broker. Real estate. That was in Wisconsin. When I came to the States, she was sick of the snow, so we moved to Phoenix. I got a job in a machine bolt factory, working fifteen hours a day. My wife couldn't find work in real estate—the market was very bad then—so she took a job as a secretary. She did not even make eight hundred a month. But still she spent like she was making one hundred thousand.

We fought. Over everything. I didn't know women could be so angry. I would say, 'The sky is blue.' She would say, 'The sky is red.' I would say, 'We are going to get into trouble if you keep spending.' But she would say, 'I *need* all these things.' Finally we had to declare bankruptcy—we were forty thousand dollars in debt. Even after that, we had fights. Mostly we had arguments, but the last one was a *fight*. We lived on the second floor and she was throwing all my things out the window."

"Did it get physical?"

Ehab shook his head vehemently. "No, sometimes she would hit me, but Egyptian men are very proud. We would not hit a woman. Women are weaker."

One day, as I waited at the Tahrir Square bus terminal for a bus to the Pyramids, I met a man named Ettu, who was celebrating his graduation from management school a week earlier. "Today I am waiting here to meet a friend," he told me. "We will go to a cafe to meet another friend, and then we will all go around together." The hot fashion label that season was "Octopus," and Ettu's sweatshirt proclaimed EGYPTIANS GOT THAT OCTOPUS CONFIDENCE. "Tonight we will go to the movies."

"I saw long lines at all the theatres last night."

"Oh, but you should have seen the crowds for *Sweetheart*. During the Cairo Film Festival it was shown twenty-three times. It," he said, excited as a soccer fanatic, "had many sex."

"Is there no sex in Egyptian movies?"

"No, that would be very unusual. That is why everyone likes the foreign films. Especially Norwegian. Twenty-three showings."

"Did Egyptian women go to see *Sweetheart*?"

"Oh no. Only men."

I thought of the Mahfouz character, Hassanein—a young Egyptian Army officer who was pledged to marry the daughter of his family's neighbor. After two full years of chaste betrothal, Hassanein finally maneuvers his fiancée into a movie house:

> "My heart tells me," he whispered, "that tonight I'll get the kiss I've long desired."

She threw him a threatening glance, then looked straight ahead. In the dark he tried to touch her with his elbow or foot, but she did not encourage him. Finally, under his persistent pressure, she allowed him to take the palm of her hand into his, both resting on the chair arm separating their two seats. Time passed in total happiness.

But that had been written in 1949. I recalled the hip-looking couple I'd seen pouting in the café my first night and suggested to Ettu, "Surely *some* men and women go to the movies together?"

"Usually only men go together," he said. "Women may go together, but usually only during the day. At night, if a movie begins at six, it won't be finished until nine, and that is too late for an Egyptian woman to be out. She will be at home."

Ettu told me about meeting some foreign women, students at the German Institute. "At first I thought they were bad girls because they would be seen in public with boys—talking with boys, laughing with boys. If an Egyptian girl did this, everyone would know she was bad. A prostitute. But when I got to know these German girls, I found they were not prostitutes. They were this way because their culture allows them to be free. Our Muslim culture has different rules. Not so free. When young people like me look at her culture, at your culture, we think you are very fortunate. For an Egyptian girl to go to Germany and travel around—this would be impossible. And even for a man, unless he is very rich, it is too expensive."

Ninety-Nine Names for Allah

Whoever built the Great Pyramid, it is now quite clear, knew the precise circumference of the planet, and the length of the year to several decimals. Its architects may well have known the mean length of the Earth's orbit round the sun, the specific density of the planet, the 26,000-year cycle of the equinoxes, the acceleration of gravity and the speed of light.

—Peter Tompkins, *Secrets of the Great Pyramid*

"Alloooo, meester!"

The cry, floating over the sand, was clearly aimed my way. I kept walking, but stole a look back. Across two football fields of sand a man with a camel was waving wildly at me. Towering behind, and completely dwarfing him, was the Great Pyramid of the Pharaoh Cheops, nearly five hundred feet high and equally long—the lone survivor of the Seven Wonders of the Ancient World. Behind it, to the west, stood the slightly smaller pyramids of Cephron and Mikerinos. Several hundred yards to the east the backside of the Sphinx's deteriorating head protruded from the sand; and, ten miles farther, beneath a faint brown haze, miniature Cairo spread out along the Nile.

"Meeester! Aloooo, Meeester!" The man, seemingly encouraged by my glance, tugged at his camel's reins. I turned and tried to wave him off, but already he was scurrying toward me. I stopped and waited.

Upon arrival that morning I had been relieved to find that the pyramids were not surrounded by slums or a theme park—just one souvenir shop, set at a tasteful distance, and several dozen men offering camel rides. Beyond the pyramids miles of lifeless sand dunes rolled away under a porcelain blue sky. The morning air was crisp—late December in the Middle East as cool as late December in San Francisco. Today the wind was stilled, the sand staying put instead of swirling around, and the cloudless sky promised later warmth—a perfect day to walk in the Sahara. During the past hour, while circling and gawking at the monuments, I had somehow managed to elude or rebuff all the camel men, and was now trudging across the sand, on the verge of escaping into the open desert toward Libya. I wanted nothing more than to tromp off and hide in the distant dunes, and peer back at the wondrous pyramids from a different perspective. Alone.

Finally the camel man arrived, huffing, and planted himself in front of me. "Aloo," he said, twitching his head and firing me a look that said I owed him big for his trip across the sand. Over his shoulder the camel mashed his lips together and glared at me, silently promising to nip off my ear or kick my head in if given the chance.

"Where are you going?" the man asked.

I pointed south toward the horizon's highest sand ridge.

"Ah, yes, view is very best from there. You can see all three pyramids in a line; you can see the Sphinx, the Nile, and all of Cairo. But no walk," he said. "Is too far. You need camel." He turned to look admiringly at his beast. It is said that the *Koran* contains ninety-nine names for Allah, and that the camel looks so smug because he alone knows the one hundredth.

"Do you read Arabic?" I asked the man. Some of his colleagues had not.

"Yes, of course."

I showed him the note that I had, on a sudden inspiration, asked my hotel manager to write in Arabic at the back of my notebook earlier that morning: I HAVE VERY BAD HEMORRHOIDS. I CANNOT POSSIBLY SIT ON A CAMEL.

The man laughed and laughed.

His name was Hassan. He was thirty-four years old, born and raised in Giza, just a short camel spit from the Pyramids. He had a wife and three children, the youngest but twenty days old. "No," he corrected himself, "twenty-one days."

"Congratulations."

"Thank you, sir. Now, let me tell you some things about the pyramids. This first one, the Great Pyramid of Cheops, is same on your one dollar bill. I show you. Give me one dollar bill."

I told him a small lie.

"O.K., O.K.," said Hassan. "When you go home you will get some more. Now I will tell you some things about ancient Egypt. America is how many years—two hundred? But we Egyptians have had a civilization for five thousand years. This Great Pyramid of Cheops—it was built forty-five hundred years ago—in what you would call the year twenty-five hundred Bee-Cee..."

I let Hassan continue, but I wanted to get away from him. Chill, dry air was streaming through my nostrils, cleansing my brain, and the gaping desert was calling.

"...the Cheops pyramid, by itself, contains 2.5 million blocks of limestone and granite. Each single one weighs between 2 to 70 tons apiece. And, no, my ancestors did not find these just lying around here in the desert. They were all *quarried*—you know this word?—between 20 and 500 miles away from here, and brought down the Nile on barges. And when the first Europeans came and started to make their measurements, they were astonished. It is written that 'neither needle nor hair' could be inserted into the joints between these blocks..."

Hassan's monologue was suddenly drowned out by the sound of rushing liquid. His camel—haunches spread, weight shifted backward—was staring at me with a defiant, evil grin, while jetting out onto the sand quart after quart of urine, clear as the desert sunshine. I thought: *If camels were human, Giza would be swarmed by Hell's Angels recruiters.*

"Mister, do you want camel?" Hassan sensed he was losing me. "If you want camel, I can talk with you. No want camel, I must find other tourist."

"Thank you," I said. "But today I will be my own camel."

"You," he assured me, "are a donkey."

I strode into the desert as quickly as possible. At first the dunes were scarred with Jeep tracks, but soon these disappeared. On a knob in the western distance, maybe a mile from me, nomads were stopped for a tea break, the lumpy shapes of their not-for-hire camels silhouetted against the sky. I veered away into the deserted part of the desert and half an hour later stopped in a spot where no one could see me and where I could see no one. A gentle breeze rabbled in my ears, bringing with it the tiny honk of a distant horn and, moments later, the noontime cries of Giza's muezzin. Too noisy.

I walked for another half hour, and in a low, silent spot, surrounded by sand hills, I lay down, using my daypack for a pillow. Behind me, toward the southwest, was an eternity of desert. Directly ahead of me the tops of the pyramids showed over a ridge—the same color as the sand I lay in, as the camel I'd refused to ride.

While researching my trip, I had discovered two shelves of pyramid books in the San Francisco library. I was struck by the technical accomplishment the pyramids represented: the Great Pyramid alone covered an area the size of seven blocks in midtown Manhattan. In comparison, the stone terraces of the Ifugao seemed like the product of a six-year-old, a plastic pail, and a summer day by the seashore.

It had taken me a while to truly grasp the pharoahs' time frame. The pyramid age ended around 2,500 B.C. While the people of Europe were still hunting, gathering, and fighting bears over cave occupancy rights, the Egyptians were building libraries. Four thousand years before Columbus proved to the satisfaction of Europe that the world was not flat, the Egyptians not only knew its shape, but its precise dimensions. And much more.

The nugget of pyramid lore that I found most captivating, perhaps because I'd never encountered it before, was the fact that the Great Pyramid's present appearance—the weathered tiers of tan and crumbling rock that grace posters in every travel agency—is a relatively recent one. Originally, and for millennia after its construction, the Great Pyramid was finished with a polished casing of white limestone eight feet thick. The ancient farmer in his flooded Nileside field, the Roman administrator, the Bedouin herder—all beheld a smooth, gleaming block, brilliantly reflecting the desert sun. *What*, I wondered, *did the cara-*

van traders wandering east from Algeria or the Ivory Coast two thousand years ago feel upon that first shimmering glimpse? Did they slide from their jolting camels and fall to their knees in fright? Awe? Ecstasy? No wonder some people explained the pyramids as the work of extraterrestrials.

During the thirteenth century a series of earthquakes devastated large parts of northern Egypt, and, to rebuild Cairo, workers began removing the Great Pyramid's white casing. Within a few generations it was entirely stripped, leaving the coarser underlying limestone exposed to the elements.

Scholars have never explained how the body of knowledge represented by the Great Pyramid (and the lesser ones, too) could be developed, tested, and codified, and could then disappear from the face of the planet for thousands of years. Shortly after completion and closure of the Great Pyramid, agriculture eclipsed science and building in the Egyptian order of things. Pyramid technology seems to have simply evaporated. No later record, no user's manual detailing the pyramids' function or construction has ever been found.

Now I lay in the sand and wondered: *Have the pyramids taken a toll on the collective Egyptian psyche? After sitting cracked, looted, and unmaintained for dozens of centuries, a daily reminder that theirs had once been the world's superior civilization, had the pyramids not started to mock the Egyptians? Did the Hassans of modern Egypt, scrambling in the dust for their daily few pounds and piastres, resent the constant allusion to just how far they had fallen?*

And what lay in store for my own country? If we lost another war or another industry, suffered another banking collapse, what might our future hold? Would Americans of the twenty-first century huddle in the ruins of the Washington Monument or the St. Louis Arch, peddling key chains or riverboat rides, pointing at the moon—"We went there once. No, really!"—while our leaders begged aid in foreign capitals?

I sipped from my water bottle, thinking about these and many other things, until the sun began to lose its warmth. As I gathered my belongings, I saw a woman galloping on horseback along the spine of a ridge 200 yards away. The horse's tail and the woman's long streamer of hair—both the same rich chestnut color—flew behind them, parallel to the ridgetop. As they sliced through my view of the tips of the pyramids, I found the sight of them achingly surreal. I willed them to turn and gallop across the sand, to come thundering to a halt in front of me, and for the woman to say: "Hop on." But she gave no sign of having seen me. She coaxed her horse into a full sprint to the top of a dune, reined him in, and sat their for several minutes, straddling him, gaping out toward the pyramids, a breeze lifting the hair off her face. I'd had nowhere near my fill of watching them, when suddenly they fled down the far hillside, splashing up puffs of the timeless sand.

29

Horse Beans

It is not easy to move through the world alone, and it is never easy for a woman....Keep money you can get to, an exit behind you, and some language at your fingertips....know how to strike a proud pose, curse like a sailor, kick like a mule, and scream out your brother's name, though he may be three thousand miles away....

At times I wonder that I am still alive.

—MARY MORRIS, *Nothing to Declare:*
Memoirs of a Woman Traveling Alone

The express train to Luxor pulled out of Cairo's Ramses station at dawn and crossed the Nile. On the river's far side I saw my first real Cairo slums; makeshift homes lined the tracks, and trash lay deep in the streets and vacant lots. But my first class car (tickets: $4) was clean and comfortable; I tilted my cushioned seat as far back as it would go and quickly fell asleep. When I awoke, we were in a green landscape that might have been lifted from artwork of the pharaohs' time; lush wet fields lined with date palms spread for miles. On the bank of the wide, sluggish Nile, a forlorn donkey staggered beneath a load of green grass twice its size; atop the grass sat a white-robed man with a brilliant red scarf wrapped around his head. Beside the river a woman scolded a water buffalo; another, squatting, rubbed clothes together in a plastic, orange basin; a third dipped an aluminum jug into the brown water. High bare ridges rose to the east, the start of the mountainous plateau stretching toward the Red Sea; dunes paraded west toward Libya.

Seated across the aisle from me was a young American named Carla, who was traveling to see the dam and the antiquities near Aswan. For the past three months she had been living in Cairo, studying Arabic on a year-long fellowship, and for the most part enjoying the experience. "But lately," she told me, "the men have been making me crazy."

Carla wore layers of loose, shape-obliterating clothes. Dull brown hair hung in her face, and thick glasses distorted her eyes. "How do you mean?" I asked.

"Well, there is hardly any street crime in Cairo. My first few weeks I walked everywhere, day and night—something I wouldn't dream of doing back in Philadelphia. Men were always smiling at me and saying hello, but I thought nothing of it. I wrote letters home about how free I felt.

"Then, about three weeks ago, a friend of mine, a French woman, invited me to something called a *millad*. An Egyptian man had invited her, and said it was O.K. to bring friends. So she invited me and another American woman, and we all went in the man's car out into the desert. There was nothing there. It was not at all like *this* scenery."

Outside we were passing vineyards and fields of bamboo and rice. A yoked bullock lumbered in circles, powering a wooden machine that lifted buckets of water out of a lower ditch and emptied them into a higher one.

"A *millad*," said Carla, "is a dance celebration the Egyptians have one week after a baby is born, so we assumed there would be other women. But when we arrived, we found out we were it—we three women and fifty Egyptian men. Still, we weren't particularly worried. Egyptian men had all been very kind to us so far, and these men seemed no different. And at first it was really fun. We were all twirling around together, and I was thinking what a great thing this was and wishing everyone at home could see it. But it got wilder and wilder. We danced ourselves into a frenzy..."

Her calm, flat monotone made it difficult to imagine her doing anything in a frenzy.

"...and before long these men really lost it. All of a sudden they just attacked. Our dance pretty much turned into a rugby game. Thank God the man we came with and one or two of the others stayed sane. They pulled the loonies off us like they were unloading a truckload of watermelons and stuffed us into a taxi. Without them, I think we'd have been ripped apart.

"Then, just a few days later, I went into a perfume shop in Cairo, and the owner invited me into the back to see a special perfume. As soon as we went behind his curtain, he grabbed me and tried to kiss me. And that very night a man on the subway grabbed my breast. When I first got here, I guess I was sort of wide-eyed and trusting. But not any more. Now I'm jumpy. When I go out, I dress so I won't be noticed. I see the men entirely differently now. They *really do* think women are property here. Any woman walking around unprotected is up for grabs. It must have been my naivete that let me go two months before seeing that."

I told her about Ettu, how he had first thought the German women he met were prostitutes, how he'd said it was unusual for a man and woman to go to a movie together.

"Did you see the lines at the movies?" Carla asked. "Only men. I felt sorry for them. If they're not allowed to date or even to *see* their own women; well, of course they're going to go nuts over a Westerner. I don't want to criticize their religion, but I don't see that it works very well."

Every few minutes our train sailed through towns that looked Indian in their levels of deterioration. Minarets were surrounded by mud or brick huts with chickens and goats grazing in the yards. The countryside between towns presented mile after mile of bucolic scenes, infinitely repeated: cattails ten feet tall lining canals and riverbanks; vineyards and fields of bamboo, rice, and sugar cane stretching into the distance; men scooping mud from irrigation ditches; boys feeding weeds into smoky fires; women bundling up sheaves of green grass and loading them onto donkeys. Fifty-five percent of Egypt's population lived in the countryside, most of them not more than a ten-minute donkey ride from the Nile, and I found the sight of them passing by my window both hypnotic and reassuring. On any given day, even during this age of the computer, a majority of the Earth's population rises at dawn and goes forth to nurse crops. This minute they are out there by the stooped hundreds of millions: weeding, reaping, sowing—proof for the gawking tourist that the past is indeed still with us, and suggesting that a very similar tomorrow will surely come.

In midmorning we stopped in the town of Bani Suef. Boys on the platform peddled newspapers, none in English, and men sold newspaper cones stuffed with nuts. Leaving the train, I heard a commotion and looked down the platform. A large man speaking loudly in Arabic, stood at the center of a circle of some forty others wearing white robes and gowns, but this man wore a blue uniform, and I recognized him as the conductor of my train. Moving closer, I noticed that his shirt was torn at the shoulder and a trickle of blood oozed from a two-inch slice on his cheek. He was a commanding figure—tall, uniformed, grandfatherly, his arm raised like a prophet, his index finger pointing straight upward—and although I could not understand even one of his angry words, I believed them all.

Standing opposite him in the circle was another Egyptian man, quite upset, and between them was a policeman, listening intently. When the conductor had had his say, the second man started in—speaking loudly, waving his arms, pointing his finger skyward in an obvious imitation of the conductor. But his mustache had a sinister curl, and no posture he could assume would speak as loudly as the conductor's bloodied cheek. When this second man stopped speaking, the conductor hissed something at him, the two lunged at each other, and suddenly, like the barroom crowd in every cheap western movie, the circle of onlookers began indiscriminately grappling and shoving one another. In front of me, two men who had until now been intently watching the debate, glanced at each other and began throwing elbows at each other's faces. At last, the raucous Egypt I had always imagined.

I moved quickly to the train and went to my seat. Scant seconds had passed by the time I looked out my window, but already the crowd had calmed. The policeman had been joined by another, and they had separated the two central characters. The onlookers, seemingly mollified, were straightening their robes and ambling back onto the train.

When we were again in motion, I was drawn by the sound of a ruckus coming from the small nook between cars. The conductor was standing at the sink in the restroom, the door wide open, dabbing at his face with a handkerchief, and again telling his side of the story to a circle of onlookers. When finally he had fixed himself up and departed, I asked around and found a man who spoke English.

"What happened?" I asked.

"There was a...confusion."

"A fight?"

"No, not a fight," he said. "A disagreement. The passenger had lost his ticket. He said he had bought one, but now he could not find it. And in the confusion the conductor...you saw his face. In the end the passenger, he apologized, and the conductor accepted." The man laughed. "But what else could he do?"

We were alone in the vestibule now. I thanked the man, a short, kindly looking gentleman. His curly black hair was shot with gray, and his bulging paunch strained the buttons of his blue shirt. His name was Adil. He lived in Cairo and worked as a translator. I asked if he could identify the crop I had seen out the window—the one the women were bundling and the donkeys carrying.

"Pleasure," he said, and now began ticking off every single thing we saw. "Rice, donkey, tomatoes, lemon grove, tomatoes, buffalo, cactus—this cactus plant needs no water...Over there is some sugar cane...And over there, that is horse beans..."

It was the crop I'd been wondering about—tall, dark-green grass, the area's main crop. "*Horse beans?*"

"Yes, horse beans."

"Is it for animals to eat or humans?"

"Yes, for human beings or for animals. It is very important. All Egyptians used to take it for breakfast. It is rich in protein..." And then he was back to his play-by-play. "Ahh, there is cow, donkey, bamboo, horse beans, palm tree...*date* palm tree. And here, cabbage, big cabbage ...corn, little cabbage, horse beans...egrets—those white birds, egrets..."

We blew through another small town: "Village...train station, mosque, mosque...factory, see the new buildings? And those others, those are old buildings...soccer game—there is no school today. Friday..." And back to the countryside: "Banana trees...cows...cows... horse beans...rice, onion, orange trees. Those are *casorina* trees—two kinds: that one is for wood, that other one is for shade. Wheat! There was wheat—did you see?"

This monologue quickly became annoying. I could tell a mosque from a train station, and a soccer game from a palm tree. Trying to change the subject, I asked Adil what things he translated.

"Newspaper stories. From Arabic into English, and from English into Arabic. Date palms, cabbage, small cabbage, horse beans...railroad tracks. This railroad and the highway follow alongside the Nile from Alexandria all the way to Aswan..."

I asked Adil how old he was.

"Fifty-one years. Canal, women planting rice, horse beans, army trucks..."

The best thing that ever happened to him?

Adil turned from the window and smiled. "Oh, that is when I am with my family. Every one of my kids, they love me. I have six kids. My oldest girl is seventeen. She is at Cairo University. My baby, my four-year-old, he hangs me all the time..."

"He *hangs* you?"

Adil wrapped his arms around his torso, and tilted his head over until it lay on his shoulder, giving me new insight into every garbled newspaper article I have ever read. "He hangs me all the time. Even when I am asleep, he comes in and gets on top of me to give me a hang. Oh, yes, my family. That is the best." Adil smiled and turned back to the window. A convoy of trucks were lined up at a railroad crossing. "Army," he said. "Many jeeps. Horse beans, cabbage..." We passed a construction site—twenty men carrying baskets of sand from ground level up to the second story: "New house..." Adil pointed at the riverbank: "Cattails..."

I asked what was the worst thing.

"Once I fell in a canal," he said. "I almost died, but I am a survivor. You see, this is one thing about Egyptians. When things are good, we live well. But when things are bad, we can also live...bamboo...not so well, but we live."

I asked: "When you are going about your daily life in Cairo, do you ever think about the pyramids out there on the edge of town?"

"I think often about the past glories of our ancient civilization. Now there are other, much stronger cultures, but we look at our pyramids and we know that we made a great contribution. Plato wrote about us. He came upon a group of his people one day...buffalo...arguing about some point of philosophy, and he told them: 'The Egyptians already solved that thing thousands of years ago.'"

Was Adil's life easier today, or had it been easier in the past?

"It is more difficult now. Maybe ten, fifteen years ago...donkey... you could get lunch for one piastre. In Nile Hilton you could get lunch for forty-five piastres. Now it is unthinkable. What do you pay for your hotel?"

"Thirteen pounds, fifty piastres." (Less than six dollars.)

He turned toward me. "Thirteen pounds! That must be first class!"

I laughed. "You flatter me. First class would be two hundred pounds. The Nile Hilton costs at least two hundred pounds." (Eighty-five dollars.)

"Tcht, tcht, tcht," Adil said. "An official in government, a high official, after twenty years...camel...he will make two hundred pounds salary every month. Many things are changing in Egypt. Not everything, but many things. See these aerials?"

On the edge of a small town we saw a group of three new white-washed homes with orange shutters at the windows and tall antennas atop the roofs.

"Now there are TV's," said Adil. "Videos. People go to work in the Gulf States, come back with money, build nice houses. It is not the same any more. Now we have movie stars. Many things are crumbling. Now some people are even having divorces sometimes."

I told him I was divorced.

He turned from his window and cocked his head at me. "But why?"

I tried to shrug it off: "It is popular in America."

Adil shook his head. "It is still quite rare in Egypt. It is very difficult to get divorced. Very difficult to get married, so very difficult to

178

get divorced. My wife is my uncle's daughter. We had known each other since we were small. When I was twenty-eight, I went to my uncle and asked him, and he agreed to ask her, and she agreed. But even after you ask a girl and even after she has said yes, everyone in her whole family will investigate you. They will ask all your friends about you. 'Is he a good person? Does he have problems?' And everyone from your family will be asking the same questions about her. So later, if a husband and wife start to talk about divorce, all the relatives come around. To the husband they will say, 'She is a good wife.' To the wife they will say, 'He is a good husband; you have children.' Brothers, uncles, cousins, sisters, everyone will try to prevent divorce. In both families it is the same. Is it not like this in America? How did you find a wife?"

"We met in college," I said. "Afterwards we lived together..."

"In *same house*?"

"Yes."

"Did her parents agree to this?"

I said, "It's different in America."

"Did she consult them, ask their permission?"

"I think not."

"And did *you* consult *your* parents?"

"No," I said. "I told them as soon as we moved in together."

"What did they say?"

"They were not happy, but they got used to it."

"In America, if you move in together, does that mean you are married?"

"Sometimes, but not always. After several years we were talking one day and we decided to find out what being married was like. A few days later we went and got married."

"Did your family come?"

"No. We went by ourselves."

Adil said, "You see!"

"Maybe now I do."

"And was it harder to divorce?" he asked.

"Emotionally it was...*very* difficult, but legally it was even easier than getting married. We had only been married for four years. In California, if you have been married less than five years, and if you have no

179

children, and if you own very little property, it is easy. You can pick up the telephone and order some papers to be mailed to your house. If you are in a hurry, for $1,000 you can get divorced in one week. If you have not so much money, you can do it in two weeks for $500. And if you have very little money, and if you are willing to wait for six months, you can do it for $65. We chose the six-month plan."

"*Then* did you have to consult your parents?"

"No. They were aware we were having problems, but it was a shock to them when we actually did it."

"How did you tell them? Did you go and see them?"

"No, they lived 3,000 miles away."

"You live 3,000 *miles* from your parents?"

"Yes."

"How did you tell them?"

"I called them on the telephone. Only my father was home."

"Was he angry?"

"He was sad. He really liked my wife. We cried together."

"Didn't the law say you had to consult *someone*?"

"No. We weren't required to consult anyone. We did it all through the mail. We didn't even have to leave our house. No—once we did. We had to go to the bank..."

"The *bank*! In America you get divorce at a bank?"

"No, there is an official at the bank, a notary public, who can witness your signature. We signed the papers in front of him and dropped them in the mail and waited six months, and they sent us back a paper saying, 'You are divorced.'"

"And you say this is popular?"

"Not this method so much. But yes, many people are divorced."

We were quiet for many miles, watching the donkeys and horse beans and miles and miles of sugar cane, eight and ten and twelve feet tall, pass by our window. Without apparent consideration Adil had fathered six children, while I was looking down the barrel of my fortieth year, still wondering if conditions would ever be right for me to have even one. And here I was, unemployed, wandering, spending in the course of my 100-day trip more money than Adil would earn in five years. Adil said he could live when times were bad. Could I? I wondered.

And what, exactly, constituted bad times? From Adil's frame of reference I probably had never known even bad minutes. From the point of view of the people out the window, those slaving over their horse beans, my entire life had been a cruise aboard a luxury liner.

"Let me ask you this," Adil finally said. "Now that you are divorced, which way of getting married do you think is the better one? Yours or the Egyptian's?"

"But my answer," I said, "will be slanted by the way I was raised."

"That is O.K. But I want to know, if you were going to get married again, would you do it your same American way or the Egyptian way?"

It occurred to me that someone who likes to consider himself halfway intelligent, someone like myself, should be learning from all this travel. Wouldn't a semi-wise person adopt a few of the superior customs observed in other cultures? Clearly, I thought, there was merit in the Egyptian way. Maybe I should pay attention here.

And then I remembered Hassenein, the Naghib Mafouz character, waiting two years to hold his sweetheart's hand.

"The American way," I said.

"Agghh!" cried Adil.

30

Seven Hundred Gods

*It was rare for an Arab visitor (or an Egyptian for that matter)
to explore the ancient monuments or gaze in wonder at the great
Pyramids. Instead the Arab tourists shopped or watched movies on
video recorders by day and spent the nights in outdoor tea gardens or
in nightclubs dense with cigarette smoke, where the children and wives
would nod off by midnight and their fathers and husbands would share
two-hundred-dollar bottles of whiskey and cheer the plump, gyrating
dancers until dawn.*

—DAVID LAMB, *The Arabs*

Luxor may be the world's most "wellcoming" city (the many signs
greeting the visitor are invariably spelled with the emphatic dou-
ble-ell). No fewer than fifty times a day some passerby, his robes
scuffing along the dusty streets, fixed me with a bemused grin and
wished me *Well-come* (invariably pronouncing it in an emphatic, two-
part manner). The man selling flowers outside the train station smiled
at me, flourished his hand at the town in the background, and said
only *Well-come*. The teller in the Bank of Egypt said *Well-come*, asked if
my trip from Cairo had been comfortable, was I enjoying Luxor, and
only then began the business of cashing my traveler's checks. On the
night of my arrival, I found, in the lobby of the Hotel Sinai, a group
of Egyptian teenagers seated around a man of about fifty years, who
upon my entrance immediately called out, "*Well-come*, my friend. Sit,
have a cup of tea."

It had been a long train ride. "Do you have any rooms available?" I asked.

"Yes, yes, my friend," he said, not moving from his sofa. "But first you must sit down and have a cup of tea."

"Are you the manager?" I asked.

"No," he said, "I am Ra—god of the sun."

The young men around him laughed like he was the god of comedy.

"How much," I asked, "are your rooms?"

"You sound like French," the manager said. "'*Ow maach*? *Ow maach*?' This the French people say first thing when they walk in door—'*Ow maach*?'" More uproar. "Sit, my friend! Have a cup of tea. If we must, *we* will pay *you* to stay here."

I dropped my pack and joined their circle. The manager's name was Adly, but he told me—without further explanation—that I should call him "Magic Man." He had a happy glint in his eyes, and was, apparently, adored by the thin, slightly anxious-looking young men surrounding him. "Please," he told me, "tell these boys about your travels. How did you find Cairo? What did you think of the Pyramids?"

Everyone leaned forward. At first I thought they were putting me on. Would they really be so interested in a hit-and-run tourist's observations about their own country? But as Magic Man interviewed me, it came out that only two of the seven young men had ever made the twelve-hour, seven-dollar train ride to Cairo. They listened to me as intently as I would listen to a returned astronaut.

In the middle of my second cup of tea, a young man in an Egyptian army uniform entered from the street. As one, the group cheered his arrival: "Ahmed!" One young man leapt up and rushed to him; the two hugged fiercely for a long moment and then strolled out through the front door. I saw them wandering off in the light of a streetlamp, cheeks touching, arms draped over each other's shoulders.

"Those two are brothers," Magic Man told me.

"How long have they been apart?" I imagined the soldier having just returned from a long assignment on the Libyan frontier, or prolonged duty in the Sinai.

"Since Sunday," said Magic Man. This was now Friday night. "Every week the soldier goes away on Sunday and comes back on Friday.

We Egyptians, we have no money, so for us there is nothing like our families."

When finally he showed me to a large, clean room with a firm mattress, Magic Man asked, "Can you afford twelve pounds?" A few dollars. "If not, I can make it less."

In Egypt I found that my mission—to find a person to whom I might repay, in one lump, with accrued interest, all the drops of hospitality that had been rained on me during my years of travel—was beginning to fade from my mind. I had collected no name to drop into my hat in Cairo, and now I was letting the trip wash over me, nudge me this way and that.

At first this realization bothered me, caused some knee-jerk guilt. Then I relaxed. Seventy-five percent of my conscious moments at home are spent wishing I was somewhere else in the world, somewhere with fewer cares and responsibilities. And now, in Egypt, I decided to embrace this wish-come-true. It also occurred to me that this feeling of drift was a predictable, almost mandatory, stage of a long trip. The euphoria and wonder that seize a trip's beginning eventually fade, and not until they do can the meat, the bones, the real heart of a trip be revealed.

Furthermore, I told myself, it would be wise for me to anticipate, even to plan for, a similar awkward stage during my visitor's trip to America. Even in one month his wonder and excitement might wear off, and if they did, I should not blame myself, should not blame him, should not try to fix or jumpstart things. I should let them be.

Luxor occupies the site of ancient Thebes, which in the year 2000 B.C. was a city of one million. Today 100,000 people live in Luxor, most of them squeezed onto a half-mile-wide strip between the Nile and the railroad tracks. Mosques and minarets nudge up against bazaars, taxi stands, and the occasional toppled column. *Faluccas*, small boats with thin, white, impossibly tall sails, skate on the river at the town's edge.

The Hotel Sinai was located on Television Street, named for the 100-foot communications tower sprouting from the street's center. In contrast to this special measure taken to ensure access to American reruns, the automobile seemed almost superfluous in Luxor: tourists walked or pedaled rented bicycles or rode in gaudy horsedrawn carriages down avenues named Karnak, Mohammed, and Nefertiti.

Luxor's history reads like a menu of the famous—Tutankhamen, Ramses, Alexander, Ptolemy, Cleopatra, Antony—but the modern ruler is clearly the lowly tourist. Millions arrive here each year, eager to traipse the ruins, ogle the fallen columns and bewildering artwork, all the while spewing trails of yen, francs, and dollars. It is an invasion with which the town's populace seems to have made an easy peace.

One day, as I ate breakfast in an open-air restaurant near the train station, a funeral procession—men only, shouldering a casket draped with a gold cloth—marched down the main street and across Luxor's central square. There was a loud scraping of chairs as the clientele of every establishment rose to their feet. Only when the marchers had disappeared—when the waiters again began to circulate and a buzz of conversation gradually returned to the square—did I recognize just how well and how automatically everyone—tourists and locals alike—had performed.

All day and well into the night, the cafes and restaurants around the square remain crowded. Local men clustered here, philosophizing, sucking tobacco smoke from communal hookahs, and keeping one eye on the tourist women and the other on the entrance of the station. The arrival of any train immediately transformed this bunch into an army of touts, offering every new arrival a choice of hotels, flowers, jewelry, or bits of statue and painted rocks. For every Luxorian who bade me *Well-come*, another furtively pulled some dubious treasure from beneath his robes and whispered: *Antiquity?*

The city is built atop and surrounded by a true wealth of ruins —the remains of great, sprawling stone temples, dedicated to an encyclopedic array of gods and pharaohs. The Smithsonian Museum in Washington D.C. contains an exhibit of obsolete space hardware—space stations, booster rockets as big as grain silos—that dwarfs and boggles the mind of the afternoon visitor. But in Luxor, one can spend days or weeks—or, in the case of an Egyptologist, a lifetime—wandering through forests of countless towering columns, larger and taller than the Smithsonian rockets, through time-ravaged halls and courtyards, and the weedy gardens of once-immaculate palaces.

On the riverbank in midcity—across from the tourist bazaar, and surrounded by rows of souvenir vendors—lay the Luxor Temple. At night the sun set behind this monument to Amun, the god of creation, and Ra, the sun god, silhouetting ancient pillars and date palms, and turning the Nile into a shimmering velvet highway. A mile downstream lay the immense complex of Karnak, large enough to hold about ten of Europe's grandest cathedrals. Developed and refined over a period of fifteen hundred years, this site was named Ipet-Isut, literally "the most perfect of places," its innermost areas off limits to all but the priests and pharaohs. Today it is a fabulous expanse of broken down stonework and once-sacred lakes drained of water and filled with rubble. Huge statues of gods and rulers, who in their times had inspired dread and awe, lay strewn randomly, their faces hacked away. Admission was $1 (50¢ for students).

The more I wandered these sights, the more convinced I became that the locals were ambivalent about them. In California, the natives swarm out to make love to their state each weekend, but never did I see Egyptians strolling the ruins or admiring their countryside. The typical resident of Luxor certainly did appear to value the economic bonanza of the antiquities, but seemed otherwise to revere them no more than a Beijing pig farmer reveres China's Great Wall. It occurred to me that this was only logical: Why worship something from which your ancestors were excluded? And furthermore, what people who rose at dawn to eke out $700 a year and raise four or five kids had time leftover to become fluent in forty centuries of history? Or the patience and interest to sort out the seven hundred gods and goddesses worshiped by the ancient Thebans? The entire region, I thought, must have breathed a sigh of relief when Mohammed emerged, wiped the slate clean, and revealed the one and true God, Allah.

31

Baksheeshkebab Bonboni

After months of tropical travel I had become accustomed to...child
beggars and hawkers, to...feeling their hands tugging on my pants...
In a crowded market, I can sometimes trick myself into believing that
the children who sell flowers, lottery chances, and Chiclets are out of an
Our Gang movie, dirty and unruly but having great fun. But this
was too obviously unpleasant work...

— THURSTON CLARKE, *Equator*

During the heyday of Thebes the west bank of the Nile was the site of a massive industry dedicated to preserving the memories, bodies, and earthly belongings of the pharaohs and other lesser nobility. Skilled craftsmen fashioned booby-trapped tombs, embalmers refined the art of mummification, and guards did their best to thwart the inevitable grave robbers.

The morning that I chose to pay my respects to this fallen capital was a warm one (southern Egypt being notably hotter than Cairo), and as I pushed my rented bicycle onto the ferryboat *Sinbad* for the short ride across the Nile, I wore only shorts and a t-shirt. Smock-wearing locals crowded the *Sinbad,* giving it the air of a hospital barge full of lab technicians, orderlies, interns, surgeons, and patients. A very dark man wearing pants and a rainbow-hued *dashiki* approached me and asked if we might talk. He was, he said, a refugee from the Sudan. When he learned that I was from San Francisco, he told me that he was close friends with Manute Bol, the seven-foot-seven-inch tall Sudanese who, at the time, played American professional basketball. Although this man stood but about five and a half feet tall, he assured me that everyone in the Sudan was so tall that even an average Sudanese bed would fit Manute. Playing American basketball was no big deal for Mr. Bol: having to push two beds together each night in order to sleep had been his most challenging American adjustment.

The crossing was short, and soon I was pedaling away from the river along a road lined by date palms and bordered by fields of sugar cane—dark green and taller even than Manute Bol. All around lay the ruins of ancient tombs and mortuary temples. Until the advent of the modern tourist era, these sites had been inhabited by ruin-dwellers, but recently the antiquity authorities had chased them off, and now their small ramshackle homes lined the road. Women in the front yards tended chickens or emptied buckets of dirty water. The veil was not mandatory here, and often these women answered my *Salaam*s with cheery *Well-come*s, while their children ran at me with outstretched palms, crying for sweets: *"Bon-boni! Bon-boni!"*

I stopped in the shade of a date palm and bought a bottle of soda water from a vendor. Children surrounded me, pleading, *"Bon-boni, bon-boni!"*—and, when I said I had no *bon-bons*, quickly generalized their demands: *"Baksheesh, baksheesh!"*

An older man shooed them away, but his concern was not decorum, as I at first imagined, but territory. From beneath his robes he pulled a cloth bundle, and, while glancing over both shoulders, unwrapped it to reveal a small rock painted with a picture of a pharaoh lounging distractedly under a date palm. "Antiquity," he said. "From King Tut's tomb." But the paint was shiny, still moist-looking.

When he left, a teenager strutted toward me: "Hey Moos-tahsh! You want guide?"

"My name," I told him, "is not Moos-tahsh."

"Your name—what?" he said.

To say "Brad" to a non-native English speaker is to induce a look of befuddlement. "Buhd?" he will say, haltingly. "Bart?" "Bird?"

I looked at this young man, and suddenly a new name popped from my mouth. "Baksheeshkebab!"

Slowly a grin spread across his face. "No!"

"Yes," I said, "Baksheeshkebab." And I did like the ring of it.

"This is a name?" He started to laugh and signaled two friends to come over. "Mister, tell them this name."

"Baksheeshkebab," I said, straightening my back. "Baksheeshkebab Bonboni!"

They looked at each other, once, twice, and then, chortling, reached out one after another to shake my hand. *Well-come, Well-come, Well-come.*

"But in my country," I told them, "to laugh at a person's name is not polite. What are your names?"

They looked uncertainly at each other.

"Come on," I said. "I told you mine."

"Mohammed," said the first one.

"Mohammed," said the second.

And, like the tumblers of a slot machine lining up a row of cherries, the third, somewhat sheepishly, mumbled, "Mohammed."

But what did I expect? Even President Mubarak, known in the West as Hosni, was in Egypt universally referred to as Mohammed.

I spent the day bicycling from ruin to ruin, and by mid-afternoon had reached the western edge of the Theban valley. A steep trail wound up the barren cliff behind Queen Hatshepsut's temple—a colossal, three-tiered, rose-colored ruin the size of Washington's Pentagon. I locked my bike and climbed half an hour to the clifftop. Spread below were miles of Theban ruins, sugar cane fields along the Nile, and, near Luxor, the white sails of *feluccas* drifting over the river like windblown feathers. The ridgetop was empty except for one Egyptian man, sitting on a boulder beside the trail. As I neared him, he flashed a rock painted with a pharaoh lolling under a date palm, and I sped quickly onward. Behind me I heard, and ignored, his cryptic cry, "You will be back, my friend. I know what you want."

Ahead and below was the Valley of the Kings—not the grand vista suggested by its name, but a narrow box canyon of yellow cliffs reminiscent of, say, Utah, its floor and walls honeycombed with the tombs of sixty-two pharaohs. The trail brought me almost to the entrance of the tomb of Tutankhamun. Historians consider Tutankhamun's rule almost inconsequential (he held the throne for nine years and died suddenly at the age of eighteen), but the discovery, in 1922, of his treasure-filled tomb, untouched for over three thousand years, was a find of unmatched importance.

The crypts were all empty now, their wealth having been moved to the Egyptian Museum in Cairo, and to museums and private collections around the world. In Seattle I once queued up before dawn to file through an exhibit of Tutankhamun relics—golden masks and jewel-studded ornaments.

But in comparison to its magnificent treasure, Tut's tomb had not stood the test of time. Paintings on its walls had faded to near invisibility. The burial rooms reminded me of the drab tunnels in the molybdenum mine where I once toiled, but these rooms were certainly more crowded: I found myself one of a tourist horde traipsing in all our if-this-is-Tuesday glory through passageways and tombs once considered sacred, leaving behind candy wrappers and the butts of Cleopatra cigarettes.

I tried to shut the others out, to imagine myself back three or four thousand years; to conjure up the craftsmen, slaves, overseers, and donkeys pulling carts of rubble; and, perhaps centuries later, quiet, moonless nights marred only by the whisper of looters. I wondered what I might see and hear if I fast-forwarded this scene another century or another millennium. A deserted canyon? Endless quiet? But my reveries and the last vestiges of mystique evaporated when I overheard an elderly American couple ask a tour guide two urgent questions. He: "Do they take American Express at the snack bar?" And she: "Do they have Diet Pepsi?"

Late in the day I climbed back over the ridge. The Egyptian man was still sitting at the top of the pass. "I am right," he cried. "You are back." Again he offered his painted rock. No matter how spectacular the view, I found it extraordinary that he would spend all day sitting on this barren ridge, hoping to sell something like that to someone like me.

"Thirty pounds," he said.

"No thanks. I have very little room in my pack."

He twitched his eyebrows at me and gave a look I believe he thought was seductive. "For you, twenty."

"I'm sorry. I just don't want it."

He fluttered his eyelids.

He was wearing one of the thick cotton smocks common to men throughout Egypt. This one was white with red stripes, and hung loose and shapeless all the way to his ankles. "This thing you are wearing...," I began, thinking to change the subject.

"*Galabia*!" he said. "You want *galabia*!" He began to tug it up over his head and dance his way out of it.

"No, no—its name. *Galabia*. I just wanted to know its name."

"*Galabia*, thirty-five pounds. I give you for twenty."

"No," I said.

He stopped undressing, but he looked confused. "You come to my house to drink tea?"

His offers were too quick, too desperate. "No thanks," I said.

He waved vaguely at the valley. "My house down there. You come to my house; I give you what you want. I know what you want." He leered. "We Egyptians, we know these things."

I tried a new direction. "What's your name?"

"Jamal."

"Are you married?"

"No. Just finish Army. Two years. Is expensive to get marry." Reminded of his purpose, he hoisted his rock. "Fifteen pounds."

"In the valley," I said, slowly, "there were many shops. I came up here to see the view. And to be quiet."

The demented, overeager look passed from his eyes. "Hokay," he said, "hokay." And then he was silent.

We looked out over the valley, at the sun now headed toward the mountains behind us, at the shadows lengthening behind every statue and temple below. The mountains for miles around were absolutely barren; only in the distance did we see colors—the patchwork fields of sugar cane, corn, and horse beans on either side of the river. Noises from the valley drifted easily up to us: someone pounding a rock with a sledgehammer, the whine of a motorbike, a vendor in the parking lot below slamming the shutter of his stall.

"I want to go your country."

Jamal's statement cut like a sharpened scimitar through my trance.

In the last few days I had become a full-fledged, monument-hopping tourist, concerned mainly with my accommodations, food, the cost of tickets.

"My country?" I said. "How do you know where I am from?"

"America," said Jamal. "We Egyptians know these things. My dream is to go to America. Not to work. Just to visit. New York ...Michigan..."

"Michigan? What do you know about Michigan?"

"Is very beautiful country. The day Sadat is killed, I am in Aswan. There I meet some people. I am walking on the street and I see them crying. They are Americans—two men, one woman. I ask why they are crying. They tell me Sadat is just now shot. I did not know yet. We went into a bar and drank three bottles of whiskey. I do not like alcohol, but that day I took it. I was very sad, but then my friends started telling me about Michigan. They tell me about how green it is, and surrounded by water. It has hills and cows, and lakes that are one hundred times bigger than Lake Nasser. The more I think about Michigan the more I know I will love it. I think it must be the opposite of Egypt. In Egypt we have sand everywhere but the Nile. Look at these mountains—all brown. No tree anywhere—only by Nile. My friends say in Michigan they keep sand only at the beach. When they need sand for golfing course, they must bring it in trucks, because everywhere else is green. Oh, how I would like to see this green everywhere."

His words were like the *beep-beep-beep* of an airliner's navigational system, alerting the pilot that the ship is off course. I had left home in search of people with Jamal's very attitude, but had been lulled to sleep by the day to day parade of places and faces.

Jamal stood. "You come walk with me. I show you very quiet place. Best view. Is just near."

I followed him along a chalky path for a hundred yards. As we rounded a corner, we saw a group of thirty-five tourists with backpacks outlined on a higher ridge. They were being led up into the mountains by two men wearing *galabias*. Parachuting adventure-travelers? I wondered. Nervous chatter and the sound of feet slipping on loose rock carried down the barren mountainside.

From up above someone screamed Jamal's name. "Today not quiet," he said to me, and then screamed back in Arabic.

"My brother," he explained, when the yelling had stopped. "Some-one wants to see my rock. You want to climb hill with me?"

And thirty-five backpackers? "No."

"You want *galabia*? Last price—fifteen pounds."

"No thanks."

"Ten?"

"No."

"You come to my house tonight?

"No."

"Tomorrow maybe you come?"

"Who knows?" I said, and then slapped him with the cultural checkmate of "*Inshallah*." God willing.

"Ah, *Inshallah*," Jamal gushed, and clasped my hand in both of his. "You come back. I know what you want. You come back and I tell you what you want. *Inshallah*." He turned and sprinted up the hill, raising a plume of dust as he ran.

Light slanted from the mountains to the west—putting the fore-ground in shadow but giving a pink sheen to the peaks on the far side of the river. Below, Queen Hatshepsut's parking lot had emptied of buses and taxis; only my bicycle remained, chained to the bike rack. The distant wail of a muezzin drifted to my ears. Sparrows flitted around me. Descending the moonscape, I heard a racking cough from below and spotted a young boy sitting on a rock beside the trail at the bottom of the cliff. I followed his cough like a beacon, and ten minutes later stood only a few feet from him.

"Hello Mister." He held up a painted rock, familiar looking, and knocked it against the boulder he sat on. *No cheap stuff here*. "You need antiquity? Only five pound."

He was about eight years old and wore a filthy *galabia*. He would not meet my eyes.

"No," I said, truly sorry. "I need nothing." I asked: "How old are you?"

He looked confused. "So-dee," he said, "*Eh-rah-beek*."

"Sorry," I said. "English."

"English price, four pound. O.K. For you, three pound."

"I am sorry." I turned and walked away. But something was swimming around in my stomach.

Behind me the boy begged. "Two pound."

I wondered: *Where will he be in twenty years? What is his biggest dream in life—dinner?*

His last offer was half cry, half cough—"One pound..."—and more than I could take. I turned and scanned the trail and the mountain above. They were covered in shadow now, and totally deserted. The backpackers had long since vanished. I was this boy's final chance today. When I rode back to my hotel and a hearty meal, where would he go? I walked back, gave him five pounds and put the rock in my daypack. A mere gesture, I knew, but a gesture that might help us each make it through the night.

32

Yamma Yamma Yamma

When technology advances enough that the hero no longer gets wind in his face, he stops being heroic...Astronauts, for example...Everyone recognizes they're just well-trained businessmen. Why? No wind in the face.

—ED BURYN, *Vagabonding in the USA*

Five minutes into my bike ride home I met Mahmoud. He was a young boy wearing a mischievous smile and a *galabia*, and waiting astride a miniature donkey at the side of the road. The treeless plain around us was the site of a group of crypts known as the Tombs of the Nobles; teenage boys liked to stake out these smaller, untended monuments in hopes of extorting "admission fees" from, or selling painted rocks to, stray tourists. And at first I assumed this was Mahmoud's mission. But today, at least, it was not.

"Hallo," he called. "We race?" And without waiting for an answer, he turned his donkey, kicked his heels into its ribs, and darted ahead of me, grinning back over his shoulder.

"O.K.," I said, and stood on my bike pedals. I caught him and for a few moments we stayed even—I could hear him giggling next to me—but Mahmoud's donkey wasn't into it the same way Mahmoud was. As I pulled in front, and as the gap between us began to widen, Mahmoud cried, "Come to my house for tea!"

His voice was playful, with none of Jamal's desperation or the pathos of the boy with the rock. I slowed and looked back at him. "O.K."

He reined his donkey and pulled up next to me. "Yes?" He seemed to not believe it.

"Yes," I said. "Let's go."

"This way," he said, elation showing on his chubby face, and spun his donkey in the opposite direction. I turned my bike around and rode beside him.

"What's your name?" I asked.

"Mahmoud," he said. "Your name?"

"Baksheeskebab Bonboni."

He looked across at me and laughed. "Say again."

"Baksheeskebab Bonboni."

"This is good name."

We rode for a couple hundred yards and turned down a rocky, unpaved road, past an uninhabited half-ruin—a pile of bricks and beams with a collapsed roof. We stopped next to it, at a newer, whitewashed building with thick masonry walls and double doors of dark wood. Obviously Mahmoud's family had scavenged the original house to build a taller, neater one next to it—Egyptian history in microcosm. Mahmoud slid to the ground and slapped his donkey's rump; the animal clattered away across the old bricks.

Mahmoud's knock on the front door was answered by a tall female. Later, when I was familiar with his family, I thought myself foolish for having quickly wondered whether this was Mahmoud's sister or his mother; but, then, I'd hardly seen any Egyptian women at all. "My sister," Mahmoud told me. "Sabah." (*Sah-BAH*)

The two of them spoke briefly in Arabic, and when Mahmoud said the words, "Baksheeskebab Bonboni," they both laughed.

Sabah swung the door open and ushered me into the front room, which was screened from the rest of the house by a gauze curtain. It was dark here, light entering only through the open door; but, when Mahmoud slipped past the curtain and disappeared, I saw a tall white refrigerator standing in the otherwise bare next room. I heard Mahmoud holding a muffled conversation in Arabic with someone unseen.

"Tea?" asked Sabah, and then she too disappeared and added her voice to the whispers.

There were three sofa beds in the front room, and I sat on one, across from a large Sanyo TV. On the wall was a poster of a smiling Egyptian soccer player in a MANSOUR CHEVROLET jersey.

In a moment Mahmoud returned with his rakish older brother, Mohammed. Mohammed was sixteen, taller and thinner than Mahmoud, and seemed enchanted by my unexpected arrival.

"Baksheeshkebab Bonboni?" he asked. "Is very unusual name."

"Well," I said, "it's really my name just for today."

"Oh, but it is a very...very *perfect* name."

Mohammed said he had learned his English, which was stronger than Mahmoud's, in school. He sent Mahmoud to fetch his school books and then showed them to me—science, mathematics, and geography, all in English. He opened the geog-

Mahmoud —Astride a miniature donkey, he sized up a tourist on a bicycle. "Hallo!" he called. "We race?"

raphy book to a map of the world and asked me to point out where I lived and which places I had been to. Mohammed said that he had not yet been to Cairo, but that he and Mahmoud were both hoping to go soon. They had an older brother, Ahmed, studying geography in a college in Alexandria, and they were planning to visit him.

Soon we were joined by another sister, Nefisa, a ten-year-old sprite with a direct and fearless gaze. Bemused, she looked me up and down—the first time in Egypt that I'd been studied so unabashedly by a female. She shrieked when Mahmoud told her my name for today.

Sabah returned with my tea, followed by the youngest member of the family, two year-old Hameed. Hameed was frightened of me and hid behind the curtain, peeking around when he thought I wasn't looking, and then ducking away whenever I did.

"It is first time he sees someone not Egyptian," said Mohammed. "You are first in our house."

Darling Nefisa, 10 years old

Mohammed said that the father of this family—another Mohammed: Mohammed Hamid —worked at Queen Hatshepsut's Temple selling rock paintings to the tourists, and was not yet home from work. This was one of the busy times of the year. "Many tourists," Mohammed said. "Many tourists in summertime, too, but we like winter better. Summertime is much too hot, even for Egyptians."

Mohammed struck me as an earnest sort. He said that he considered his studies "very important," and that he regarded my arrival as "quite some honor." Mahmoud sat beside him, trying to follow our conversation, the smug look on his face saying how pleased he was with having brought home a find like me. Nefisa sat next to Mahmoud, staring at my face, my shoes, my daypack, while Sabah kept refilling my cup and offering more sugar cubes. Hameed stayed wrapped in his curtain, his tiny slippers protruding from its bottom.

Outside, the donkey's wheezing hee-haw announced the approach of Fatmah, lady of the house. Nefisa said, "Shh!" to me, and we all sat there, saying nothing, the children stifling giggles, until the door opened. Fatmah entered, a long black tent of a gown covering everything but her face; at the sight of me her expression went completely blank. All her children began to howl, delighted at having caught her by surprise.

Fatmah fired a look at Mohammed, who quickly translated me into Arabic ("yamma yamma yamma Baksheeskebab Bonboni yamma yamma yamma") until finally his mother smiled. She turned her face to me and said, "Well-come." She sat down next to the television and a giggly family conversation ensued, in Arabic. At the end of it Mohammed said they would all be honored if I might stay for dinner.

"Oh, no-no," I began.

"No, no, no..." imitated Nefisa, and everyone laughed.

Little Hameed popped from behind his curtain to cry, "Naw, naw, naw," and then hid again when everyone, laughing, looked over at him.

I explained that I really had just a short while to chat—the last ferry back to Luxor left at dusk—and reluctantly they accepted this.

There was a silence, then Sabah asked how old I was. With Mohammed translating, we went through all the children's ages: Sabah was 17, Mohammed 16, Mahmoud 14, Nefisa 10, Hamid 3. The absent older brother, Ahmed, was 19. Fatmah refused to reveal her age.

Using Mohammed as interpreter, the family interviewed me. Nefisa asked if I owned a car in America.

"Yes," I said.

"We do not," said Mohammed, "only the donkey. But in Luxor that is enough."

Fatmah asked if I owned a house.

"No," I said. "To buy even a small house in San Francisco would cost 500,000 Egyptian pounds."

There was much clucking around the room. Fatmah seemed the most disbelieving. She questioned Mohammed, who turned to me: "Is this right—five hundred thousand pounds? For one house?"

"Yes," I said. "At least. A house big enough for seven people would cost a million."

The donkey snorted again, loudly, and I did an imitation that seemed to go over quite well. Hameed, emboldened by his siblings' laughter, unfurled from his curtain long enough to cough out his own imitation (was he mimicking the donkey or me?) and then retreated.

"*Horab*," said Mahmoud. "For you this animal is donkey, but for us *horab*." We compared the Arabic and English words for camel, television, ear, nose, and shoe, and ran through the names for tea in Brazil, China, England, India....

As we talked I silently wondered which of these people I might invite to America. Mahmoud had found me—he should have first claim.

But Mohammed spoke better English—and I liked his confidence, politeness, and his curiosity about the world. If I invited one of them, would not the other be jealous? And would not their absent older brother, Ahmed, be forever resentful?

The one I would really have liked to invite was Nefisa—she would melt every heart she encountered—but I knew it would never happen. No poor, rural Moslem family was going to entrust their ten-year-old daughter to a divorced American. And wouldn't the older Sabah feel slighted? Mine, I saw, was a gift that might possibly rip the Hamid clan apart.

But my reservations were overridden as I basked in the warmth they so easily shared with me; at least one of them would wind up a name in my hat. And I particularly liked the balance of the idea: tourists streamed through their lives every day—shouldn't at least one member of the family have a chance on the other side?

When they saw me to the door, Fatmah pulled Mohammed aside and, although I could not have understood her words, whispered to him. He disappeared into the house and returned with a painted rock —one I had seen many times that day. I protested. They insisted. And finally I slipped it into my pack—making sure not to let it clink against its cousin. As I rode up their dirt and rock driveway, the six of them stood waving in the doorway, and called *Bye-bye* and *Salaam Alekum*. (Peace be on you.)

The road back to the ferry was slightly inclined, and I flew down it feeling renewed, even ecstatic. My trip had meaning and purpose once more. I had one or more names for my hat. Realistically, I thought, it would have to be Mahmoud or Mohammed. But nothing else was particularly realistic about this plan of mine—maybe I could find a way to bring both of them. Why limit my thoughts? Who knew what was possible? Maybe my soon-to-be-published book would sell a million copies. I would buy a bus and invite *everyone* to spend a summer driving around America: Ezekiel from Rizal Park; one-eyed Tony from Banaue; Shubash the rickshaw man and Kerala Baba from Varanasi; Mohammed Ali, the New Delhi ear cleaner; plus Mahmoud, Mohammed, *and* Nefisa —no, the entire Hamid family. Oh, what the heck—maybe even Jamal and his *galabia*.

As I sped past the tourist office, several voices called, "Baksheesh," but I ignored them.

And then: "Baksheesh*kebab!*"

It took a few seconds to recognize my own name; but when I did, and turned and looked back, I saw the three Mohammeds I'd met that morning, standing, waving, pointing me out to some more of their friends. "Baksheeshkebab Bonboni! Halloooo..."

"Hallooo!" I answered and waved my arm over my head until the cries faded behind me. With gnats and mosquitoes nicking and dying against my forearms, I sped along the darkening road, past cane fields and date palms and colossal, defaced statues. I flew through an intersection where a portly policeman was leaning down to chat and hold hands with the driver of a car stopped in the middle of the road. Over my shoulder the sun sat on the horizon—a fat, ripe peach being sliced through by a shimmering blade of horizontal cloud. As I neared the river, one of the ferry workers spotted my final, frantic approach and held the boat as I sped down the last hill and coasted aboard. He pulled the loading ramp behind me, smiled, and said simply, *"Well-come."*

33

Uhuru

The woman sitting next to me (on the airplane)...was a pioneer of Kenya, she explained. With her parents she had trekked onto the highlands in an ox wagon. She remembered the thatched hut which was their first home, the mornings when they found that elephants had trampled the shamba and the nights when lions slept on the veranda. She paused for a second to look out into the night through the porthole...Somewhere to the right of the wing tip was her old farm. "It was sold last week," she explained. "This country no longer belongs to white people like you and me. I'm not bitter that the black man has finally come into his own but I know that there is no place left for me out here."

—JOHN HEMINWAY, *The Imminent Rains*

At the Nairobi airport a black customs agent offered me a hearty "*Jambo*"—the Swahili hello—and stamped my passport. A black man, driving an orange taxi, whisked me across a plain of green-gold grasses, and dropped me among the tall office buildings at Nairobi's core. It was 7:30 A.M. and the capital was just waking up. I caught a whiff of what smelled like orchids, and sniffed soft equatorial air. Six weeks of travel still lay ahead of me—three here in East Africa, three more in southern Africa—and I would, happily, be spending much of that time wearing shorts and t-shirts.

Nairobi still had a colonial feel: wide, tree-shaded boulevards, government office buildings entwined in red bougainvillea, and parks canopied by flame trees the color of marmalade. But the lamp poles were festooned with signs cheering the anniversary of *uhuru*—freedom from British rule—and as I looked around I saw only black faces: black boys and girls in blue and white school uniforms; black newspaper vendors sorting bundles at curbside; black women in red and yellow sarongs congregating at bus stops; black men with smart suits and shiny briefcases, striding confidently down Moi Avenue—a street named after the country's black president.

Like most white Americans, I am not unfamiliar with blacks: I have studied and worked with many, and have blacks as neighbors and friends. My pale body has integrated more than a few basketball games, and while living in Dallas, Texas, I frequented a gym where I never saw another white person.

But I had never been to a place like Kenya—a country of black people, for black people, and run almost entirely by black people. President Moi, his cabinet, the army, the police—all black people. Haile Selassie Avenue, Jomo Kenyatta Avenue, Ralph Bunche Road—all named for black people.

Towering over the tourist office was a giant flame tree, its orange-leaved branches shading an entire plaza. Several black teenagers were seated on benches. Spotting me, they rose and hurried over, calling, "*Jambo! Jambo!*" They filled my hands with the fliers of competing safari companies. One young man wearing a coat and tie gave me an earnest look and, in impeccable, lilting, British-accented English, said, "Will you please read this one at your earliest *cone-vee-nee-ence*?"

I walked toward the northwest side of town, toward the YMCA. A young woman with a lime and purple scarf wrapped around her head and a baby cradled in either arm smiled as I passed her bus stop. A man whose hair and short beard were streaked with gray—the first person I had seen who was clearly my senior—nodded, and said, "*Jambo.*" In the median strips of the city's boulevards, barefoot women weeded rows of corn; one woman watered the stalks with buckets of water scooped from a rain puddle.

Streams of students walked down University Avenue toward the schools on State House Road. At a small stall in the shade of a eucalyptus tree, a teenage boy sold candy, Juicy Fruit gum, and ears of corn that he was roasting over a small brazier. A dozen gangly young people carrying school books were lined up, awaiting their turns. Kenya's university graduates were guaranteed jobs with the government, but there were thousands of graduates each year, and few jobs, and now the job waiting list was five-years long. I thought: *By the time these students earn degrees and find jobs, this corn roaster will be driving a Mercedes.*

The YMCA was a large, well-kept building, surrounded by a lawn, flower beds, and clipped hedges. A framed, two-foot-by-three-foot portrait of President Moi hung in the lobby. The black man behind the counter said *"Jambo,"* and gave me the key to a clean room—ten dollars a night with three meals included.

As I unpacked, birds chirped in the bushes outside my window. A Kenyan woman sang a lullaby while sweeping the walkway. I showered down the hall, with treetops and bright blue sky visible through the bathroom transom, and took the edge off my jet lag by napping—under a sheet—the first time since Varanasi that I had slept without my sleeping bag.

That afternoon I walked back downtown beneath galleons of white clouds sailing across the sky, and visited several safari companies. One had a van leaving the next morning for Masai Mara National Game Park. I signed on for three days and two nights of camping and, I hoped, elephant, hippo, and giraffe.

By evening I was back at the YMCA, sitting on the veranda, looking out toward the lawn, jacaranda and banana trees, and swimming pool. The veranda was crowded with mixed groups—blacks and whites, men and women—drinking sodas, smoking Sportsman cigarettes, and bantering in British-accented English. The clouds that had been gathering all day were now fused together, darkening the sky. The air had a rich, fertile, pre-rain smell. *Africa*, I thought. The cold Middle East—indeed, the entire rest of the world—seemed distant and inconsequential.

In the pool's shallow end, a white boy with his eyes squeezed shut was lunging around, bleating "Marco," while a half dozen black friends shrieked "Polo" and leapt from his path. Above the deep end a boy of about ten, his loose, bright pink swim trunks threatening to slip from his bony black body, was trying to summon the nerve to leap from the high dive. Several times he put his toes to the edge of the board and joined his hands over his head, but each time a chorus of taunts rose from his friends in the water below. And each time he backed away, flustered. The spectators on the veranda started to hoot.

"It will nawt be coming up to you."

"You must jomp before night comes."

The teasing went on for several minutes, until the wind picked up and the treetops began doing the Watusi. The sky darkened three shades, and the last thing I saw before the clouds opened was the pink-suited boy scrambling down from his perch. For five minutes rain fell furiously, rattling the building, and pouring off the roof in a translucent sheet. Swimmers leapt from the pool, sprinted across the lawn, and huddled in groups on the veranda, laughing, and shaking themselves dry.

I watched how confident they looked, how free. One of them saw me watching, and flashed an electric, full-mouthed grin that took me by surprise. Neither this boy nor his ancestors had ever known slavery. And even during the seventy-year colonial blip in Kenyan history, the Masai, Nandi, Kipsigi, Luo, Baluia, Kalingen, and Kikuyu tribes had always greatly outnumbered the British. This, I thought, is *uhuru* smiling at me. I smiled back.

The rain stopped as abruptly as if we'd just ridden through a car wash. The dark clouds slid off toward the coast. Rays of light flashed over the pool and glinted off the yard's shiny banana leaves and becalmed palm trees. The boy in the pink trunks began walking across the lawn toward the high dive. "Oh, no!" someone called, and the jeering started up again. I watched the boy climb the ladder, and thought: *I'm going to like this place.*

34
Wazungu

*This was Africa as it used to be and soon will be no longer, lonely,
magnificent and alive with secrets....Some movement catches your eye
—a herd of impala grazing on a patch of green; across to your left
hurries a white-tusked warthog, her four piglets trotting behind in single
file; over there something tawny slips into a grove of thorn-trees—
an oryx, a waterbuck, a lion? You think you are alone, but eyes are
watching every movement; you think you are hidden, but nostrils quiver
on the alert; you think all is silent, but a baboon barks from the rocks,
a francolin calls, a reedbuck gives his shrill long whistle.*

—ELSPETH HUXLEY, *The Sorcerer's Apprentice*

Two friends of mine once lived for a while in Kenya and came
home with stories of snow-tipped mountains, game-filled plains,
and exotic peoples. I listened to the reverential tone of their voices,
noted the faraway look in their eyes, and envisioned myself behind the
wheel of a topless Jeep at sunset, careening over red dirt hills, zipping
past herds of gawking giraffe, veering around dumbfounded hippo and
charging rhino. Near the villages, sinewy black men and bare-breasted
women would wave at me and cry *"Jambo!"*

But I never did drive my topless Jeep. Early on my second day in the
country a poptop safari van, loaded with tents, cooking equipment, and
sleeping bags, stopped at the YMCA. The driver/expedition leader was a
Kenyan named Michael, who wore blue flip-flops, khaki trousers, and,

next to his chocolate skin, a cheap white sport shirt. He had an excited look on his face—as though this were his first safari instead of mine.

Three English tourists and the expedition's factotum, a Kenyan named Mnene (Um-NAY-NAY), were already in the van. Michael performed a quick round of introductions and stowed my pack. We gassed up at a Kobil Oil station tucked in a pine forest at the edge of town, then headed west through groves of banana, eucalyptus, and acacia trees. Rows of tin-roofed shacks were hidden among the foliage. Three bored-looking African boys peered at our van through the strands of a barbed wire fence. At the center of a group of girls, a would-be

Michael —"Sometimes I wish I was rich," said the safari guide, "so I could visit everywhere. But I meet tourists who have seen Russia and China and America, and they are not happy. I can read faces. Maybe these people have money, but they are afraid of everything. Some look like they do not enjoy life."

ballerina twirled on her toes, crumpled to the dust, and then arose, laughing, to twirl again.

Mnene, a small, taciturn man, whose furrowed brow made him look like he was harboring a pain too deep to share, sat in the front passenger seat. At first I thought he was in his fifties, but later—on the afternoon of the second day, when he saved all of us from the lions—he moved like a man in his twenties.

Two of the British, a married couple named Nigel and Grace, sat huddled together in the center seat. This was their first time away from England, and during the next few days I would rarely see them more than a few feet apart.

I shared the rear seat with a Coleman ice chest and Nigel's brother, Rupert. Rupert wasn't a tourist the way the rest of us were.

He was employed by the VSO, Britain's Peace Corps equivalent, and taught English across the border in Tanzania. He was spending his Christmas holiday in Kenya with Nigel and Grace.

"Kenya is heaven compared to Tanzania," Rupert told me. "Every development worker in East Africa counts the days until he can visit Nairobi: movies, Chinese restaurants, bookstores, other foreigners. By African standards Kenya is a First World country."

The forests broke, and for a while we had views of rolling hills with neat stone walls sectioning off squared fields. Michael called from the front seat, "When the settlers came, this area was called the 'White Highlands.' Now many of the farms have been broken up and given back to the Africans."

Later Michael stopped the van and pointed into the roadside scrub. "Can you see the thorns on these trees?" They were unmissable, three and four inches long. "We call these the wait-a-bit. If you get caught in these thorns, you will have to wait-a-bit, until you can think of a way to get yourself loose."

An hour from Nairobi, we stopped at a lookout over a sprawling valley that just might have been big enough to hold the entire San Francisco Bay Area. January was normally dry season, but this year there had been rains, and the valley floor was golf-course green. Cutting across it was a brownish-red dirt road, our route west toward Masai Mara.

This area of East Africa has the best-documented claim to the title "Birthplace of Man." In 1976, near Tanzania's Olduvai Gorge—just a hundred miles south of us—a team of anthropologists led by Dr. Mary Leakey discovered an astonishing set of tracks. These were the footprints of a party of hominids, two adults and one child, forerunners of us *homo sapiens*, who walked through an area of soft volcanic ash one day nearly four million years ago. The larger adult, probably a male, walked ahead; the other walked behind, placing her or his feet in the tracks made by the leader. The youngster skipped alongside them, and at one point turned and looked at something to the left. It might have been most anything, as the tracks of elephant, pig, rhinoceros, hyena, baboon, and one sabre-tooth tiger were also found in the same dried ash.

"The most remarkable find I have made in my entire career," Dr. Leakey said. "They are the earliest prints of man's ancestors, and they show us that hominids three-and three-quarter million years ago walked upright with a free-striding gait, just as we do today."

As the afternoon wore on and we neared the park, our van's occupants were all silent—all, if I was typical, lost in ruminations on our ancestry and entranced by the scenery. The plains rolled by—flat stretches of savanna, mostly treeless, stretching to the smoky outlines of mountains on the far horizon.

In mid-afternoon we began to see Masai: men in ponchos and capes, squatting under thorn trees, talking; women with shiny bald heads and shiny bare breasts gathering wood beside the road. In the distance we saw their *bomas*, circled huts of mud and wattle that blended almost invisibly into the rest of the countryside.

Beneath a roadside tree a group of seven young boys pogoed up and down as though engaged in rebounding drills. When they saw our van they stopped and ran along the roadside—sprinting barefoot across the thorniest, rockiest ground imaginable—kissing their fingers and calling, "Sweet! Sweet!" All of them carried spears; all of them were smiling. One of them was absolutely naked.

Suddenly Rupert yelled, "Antelope!"

We four tourists had been scouting the horizons, each silently hoping to be the first to spot wild game. Now Rupert, who wore thick eyeglasses, had seen a herd near a distant circle of *bomas*. His brother Nigel said what the rest of us couldn't: "Those are cows, you numbskull! You're embarrassing the family name. If you see a lion bringing down an elephant, please just whisper to me."

"Zebra," Michael called. Rupert had jumped the gun by a mere thirty seconds. Browsing at roadside were six convict ponies oblivious to our presence, their tails twitching. I had the sudden awareness that for untold miles we had not seen a fence.

Michael again: "Giraffe."

And there were half a dozen of the tilted giants, surrounding an acacia tree—like hook and ladder trucks at a six-alarm blaze—devouring its highest leaves.

"Wildebeest." Moving among the flame trees were fifty sad-sack cousins of the American buffalo: dirty brown coats, humped backs, scraggly blond beards, and Rastafarian manes. In an open area we saw fifty more. Then a hundred.

It soon seemed we'd stumbled upon a mass zoo break: three Thompson's gazelle with thin, black racing stripes along their sides, a dozen more zebra, five giraffe loping through the scrub in seeming slow motion, and just twenty feet from the road, a herd of thin, deer-like animals with startled eyes and Mickey Mouse ears.

"Impala," Michael said. "And there—topis. See their markings?" At first glance topis looked like small horses—but at second glance I noticed their twin horns, the small humps on their backs, and the markings that spread like oil stains across their light brown haunches.

Michael said, "Bushbuck," and pointed out a hundred small, horned antelope, lazing under a shade tree.

It went on for another hour and a half—each herd larger, each pasture more lush and crowded than the last—until a checkpoint marked the entrance to Masai Mara. The park was hilly, covered with meadows and scrub forests, cut by streams, and filled with animals.

By late afternoon we were pitching our tents in a wide valley, at a bend of a small clear-flowing river. A landmark baobab tree, three times the height of any other tree in our valley, dominated our campsite. "This one might be three or four hundred years old," Michael said. Its branches spread beyond our tents and the van, and reached across the river. On the opposite bank was a grove of "sausage trees"—trees that would have been unremarkable had not seed pods the size and color of ten-pound salamis dangled from their lower limbs. Browsing in the grove, undisturbed by our presence, was a herd of antelope, their French-toast-colored coats dotted, apparently, with sugar.

Michael came over to me. "For one minute," he said, "I want you to look at that hillside."

He stood at my elbow, watching my face while I stared at a forested slope two hundred yards distant. At first I didn't get it. A hillside, a few trees, clumps of brush...

"There you are," Michael said. He had read the flicker in my eyes at the very instant I saw, finally, what he had wanted me to see: that the hillside was covered not with shrubs, but with wandering wildebeest, topis, antelope, gazelle, giraffe—hundreds of them calmly browsing, giving the hillside the pulsating look of a bee hive on a hot summer day.

While Mnene fixed spaghetti, the rest of us went on a firewood search. The area near camp had been picked over, and to find a productive spot we had to drive a couple of miles and cross a meadow filled with topis.

On the return Michael said he knew a spot favored by lions at sunset. He drove our log-filled van to the top of a grassy hill and there, under a pink sky, a dozen lion cubs lay in a heap, nipping at each other's heads. Two adult females lounged nearby, batting lazily at any cub that wandered into range, sending it rolling. Michael pulled to within fifteen feet, but the pride, already accustomed to safari vans, paid us scant attention.

When we were again within sight of camp, but still several hundred yards away, I asked Michael if it would be safe for me to walk the rest of the way. His demeanor all day had been that of pleasant host, but now he turned to me with irritated disbelief. "You can put that silly thought out of your head. If I go back to Nairobi with but three tourists, I will be unemployed tomorrow. And who would hire someone so stupid? 'You took a tourist to the Mara and fed him to the animals! Oh, sir, I am sorry. We have no jobs.'"

I could see the big baobab and our tents straight ahead. The grass on both sides of the road was short; no animals visible. "It's really that dangerous?"

"Yes, it is. You know nothing about the bush. This is a *wild* place. I see you always writing, so you must read, too. There is a book—*The Man Eaters of Tsavo*. You read this book, then you come back and tell me if you want to walk the bush by yourself."

That night, after the others had gone to bed, Michael and I lingered at the fire. Beams from a half moon etched a pattern of branches onto the silvered ground beneath the baobab, but then clouds moved in, leaving us in smoky darkness, with the light of the fire flickering on our faces.

After a while, Michael said, "I saw one bottle left in the cooler."

Sitting on a log, we poked the fire, took swigs from the expedition's last Tusker beer, talked quietly and listened to the occasional howl ("Jackal," said Michael) or muffled thump coming from the darkness.

Michael was thirty-eight years old, married, and had three children. Nine years earlier he had quit a desk job at a Nairobi insurance company and hired on with a safari outfit. "I think sitting at a desk can kill you," he said. "Certainly, it will kill parts of you. Sometimes this safari life can also be difficult—safari after safari, not seeing my family for maybe a month or six weeks—but I think it is better than working inside. The salary is not as good, but sometimes people give fantastic tips—when that happens this job is a pleasure."

"I imagine I'd be pretty happy if I had your job," I told him.

"I think I am happy," he said. "I worry sometimes—about my wife and my children. Will my children be able to go to university and find jobs? Today the waiting list is five years, but in five years how long will it be? I am glad I have only three children. Sometimes I wish I had the money to start my own company, but then I see what a hassle it is. If I have some vans and hire drivers and guides and cooks, then there are people depending on me. What if there is a coup and the tourists stop coming? What if poachers shoot all the elephant? And what if these crazy rains stop falling? This year is good, best in more than ten years, but we have had a bad drought."

I asked if he'd seen all the animals there were to see, or was he still surprised sometimes?

"The Big Five—hippo, rhino, elephant, lion, water buffalo—I have seen these many times. But whenever I think I have seen everything, then there is something new. Last month, as we are coming around a corner, there is a python in the road, and he is wrapping up a Thompson's gazelle kid. The kid's mother is nearby, but there is nothing she can do. Finally the python wraps it all up and swallows it, yes, swallows it whole, starting with the head first. This is very unusual, a fantastic thing. You do not hear about this one.

"Another time I saw a lion charge a buffalo, and it was gored right here"—Michael touched a finger to the side of his throat. "The lion had a big gaping hole. Air was going in the wrong place. I went and reported it to the rangers. They want to know these things—maybe they can come with a dart gun and fix the lion's throat—but they could not find him."

"Do many Kenyans come on your tours, or only us *wazungu* (foreigners, whites)?"

"Never has a Kenyan come with me. For a foreigner these things are all new, but already most Kenyans live in the bush. So they know all they want to know about the animals. A foreigner sees an elephant herd and he thinks it is a beautiful thing. But a farmer sees the same thing and he worries that maybe now all his crops will be trampled. Or a lion—a Kenyan does not ever want to see a lion."

"Not even a Kenyan who lives in Nairobi?"

"Almost everyone who lives in Nairobi has some family in the bush, and he will visit whenever he can. So he has seen these things. Besides, most Kenyans cannot afford safaris. These three days are costing you the same as what a farmer will earn in five or six months—if his rains are good. He will not pay to see a lion or an elephant. If a farmer has saved some money, he will go to Nairobi and see lights and city people and movies and tall buildings. If someone from Nairobi has saved some money, he will want to go to London or Paris."

"Where would you go?"

"Sometimes I wish I was rich," he said, "so I could visit everywhere. But I meet tourists who have seen Russia and China and America, and they are not happy. I can read faces. Maybe these people have money, but they are afraid of everything. Some look like they do not enjoy life."

"Do *you* still enjoy coming here—seeing the animals, the countryside?"

"I have done this so many times—even if you put a cloth around my eyes, I could drive from here to Nairobi. So it is different. For me it is a job. But I do not mind. It is a *good* job for a Kenyan. I get to know how the foreigners are. I get to talk to many people."

"What is the best thing that ever happened to you?"

"By what standard?" Michael asked.

"Your own standard."

"I guess I would have to say the birth of my son. My first son. The eight-year-old. He is really the only thing I value. When he was born, that was a really special thing."

213

"What's the worst thing?"

"I was put up in jail for three days—for something I did not do. They said I stole something. I had not done it, but I could not prove it. I was all alone in the world, and had no way to get help or to prove that I was innocent. If I had done it I would have had some way to cover myself, but I did not. Yes, they were rough—they beat me. The police here are quite stupid. Then after three days they found this thing, and they found out who stole it. They let me go, but they did not even say they are sorry."

"I'm sorry," I told him.

"Yes, thank you. But this one still hurts."

The fire hissed. The stream sang lullabies. A drop of rain fell on my arm.

"Out of all the tourists you have met, which ones do you remember?"

"I have seen all types," he said, as though we were a subphylum. "Let me think...I remember one black man from America. Before he comes to Africa someone has told him that he must see a cheetah. So he has it in his head—'Michael, I *must* see a cheetah.' I tell him it is chance—I will try, but you never can know. He says, 'No, Michael, I *must* see a cheetah.' All day we look. We see lion and rhino and hippo, and someone tells us a cheetah has been seen across the park, so we go, but it has gone into the bush. 'Michael, I *must* see a cheetah.' The next day it is the same, 'Michael, I must see a cheetah.' And finally the other people, they have to say, 'Look, leave Michael alone. He is trying, but he cannot *make* you a cheetah.' So, finally, he quit."

"And then," I speculated, "you saw a cheetah?"

"No, that man never did see his cheetah, but the very next trip I take we see *three* cheetah."

35

Technicolor Kenya

The woman known on board as The Countess...said she was a travel writer. "I am writing a story for the best and most brilliant newspaper in the world"—and she named a German daily paper. "They respect me so much that in seventeen years they have changed only one sentence of mine."

"What was the sentence?"

"It was very reactionary you will think," The Countess said.

"I'll be the judge of that."

"All right then. 'Three hundred years of colonialism have done less harm to the world than thirty years of tourism.'"

I smiled at her and said, "That's brilliant."

—PAUL THEROUX, *The Happy Isles of Oceania*

My first awareness the next morning was of someone tugging at my foot.

"Brad!" said a stern voice. "You *must* see this one. Come. Right now!" Another sharp yank. "I have been trying to wake you. Everyone else is already up. You will be sorry to miss this one."

And, somehow, five seconds later I was standing outside the tent, buttoning my shorts while cold, wet grass numbed my bare feet. The morning light was pink, shimmering; through cobwebbed eyes I registered the concerned, black face of the man who had awakened me—*Ah yes, Michael.* Beyond him I saw the others, standing under the baobab, their backs to a low, popping fire as they clutched coffee mugs and pointed quietly into the distance. Something rustled behind me. I turned and saw two gray monkeys, resting in the lower branches of the baobab tree, not fifteen feet away: they snickered at me.

"Over that way," Michael whispered. He pointed off to the east, and then walked back to the group at the fire.

The sun, a tangerine eye peering through the morning vapors, had just cleared a range of low mountains. The countryside gleamed from a downpour that had lasted much of the night; a rosy mist hovered over the deep grasses. The river, swollen to its banks, looked as flat and shiny as a polished ballroom floor. On its far bank, antelope grazed beneath the sausage trees.

The entire scene was almost too perfect. I thought: *Subtract the tents and the van; subtract myself and the three other Europeans; subtract the bargain-store nylon shirts and trousers worn by our African hosts, and this could be a Disneyland production ("The Garden of Eden") or a Smithsonian exhibit ("The Dawn of Creation").* I felt a physical hollowness, almost a hunger, which had nothing to do with the smell of Mnene's coffee and frying bacon.

But it was not the smells or the early light that had the group so riveted. Less than a hundred yards upstream a line of elephants, hooked up trunk-to-tail, trunk-to-tail, was crossing the river. The sun hung directly above them, and their backlit silhouettes were sharply defined in the rising mist—some twenty adults with babies interspersed among them, wee trunks grasping mothers' tails.

This vision stopped me short, braked my mind's constant sorting and worrying, and now the rest of my trip slammed into me from behind like an inattentive tailgater. A few days ago I had lain in the sand behind the Pyramids. Further back was India—bodies roasting beside the Ganges, the knee-weakening sight of the Himalayas—and before that the Philippines...and now, technicolor Kenya, amok with animals. Somehow this incredibly rich meal had been jammed into the space of two short months. I thought: *Clearly, I am traveling too fast to absorb so much wonder.*

I watched, aware of my breath and heartbeat, as the linked line of elephants noiselessly crossed the river. I tiptoed over to the silent group, and Michael handed me a cup of coffee. We watched the elephants climb the riverbank, and when the last one had disappeared over a ridge our group gasped a communal "Wow!"

Michael turned to me and said, "Tell me—was that worth a few minutes of sleep?"

I sipped my coffee and thought: *If I invite Michael to America, how do I repay this? Sunrise over the Grand Canyon? Atop Mt. Shasta? A trip to Kauai and a swim with the dolphins? Or might he actually prefer Las Vegas and a pocketful of dollars?*

After breakfast we loaded into the van for a "game drive." Animals were everywhere. A hundred yards down the road we saw two elephants, undoubtedly from the river-fording group, noisily ripping down tree limbs at the edge of an acacia grove. We passed meadows filled with grazing hartebeest, wildebeest, and topis. Strung out along a ridgetop were fifty impala.

In the first half hour we saw no other vans, no tourist cars, no rangers. We had this section of the park, this priceless morsel of Africa, to ourselves—just us, the animals, and the sun, climbing hand-over-hand up its invisible rope, as it burned away the mist and turned the sky a powder blue.

Without speaking, Mnene pointed toward some birds circling in the distance. Michael drove across a meadow and stopped where a mob of vultures, hyena, and silver-backed jackal were tussling over a white rib cage and several scattered bones.

"I think this was a topi," Michael said. "Those lions we saw last night probably killed it. When they kill something, they eat only the good parts—the liver and the heart and the best meats. Jackals eat the rest. Then the vultures pick the bones clean. And at last, the hyena. You know this movie *Jaws*? Hyena is called 'Jaws of the Serengeti.' This one has more powerful jaws than any other animal. More even than a hippo. They crush even the biggest bones and suck out the juice. Nature is very efficient. If you fall down and break your leg, these birds will pick out your eyes, and then clean your bones. And soon not even your bones will be found."

We drove toward the park's tourist lodge, through herds of giraffe and zebra. In the middle of a long green fairway, broken only by a single twisted flame tree, was a lone loping hyena—all head and shoulders, no butt.

"Balloon," said Michael, and there, cresting the northern horizon like a second sun, was the tip of a blood-red hot-air balloon. Against the green hills and pale blue sky it was a spectacular sight, a reminder of the modern world so briefly and happily forgotten. It hung, rose higher, then fell below the horizon, only to bob back into view moments later. Michael frowned. "I do not like these. They change the park too much."

Rupert seemed perplexed. "Wouldn't a balloon be easier on the park than our vans?"

"No!" Michael was vehement. "The rich tourists will not sit in a van for eight or nine hours. They must fly in. So now Masai Mara has an airstrip. And they will not camp, so there must be a new lodge. Soon they will want a swimming pool. And the Minister of Tourism will give them whatever they want. These people will pay anything. Two hours in a balloon—do you know what this costs? Four thousand shillings! That's what a farmer earns in one year." (Per capita income in Egypt and the Philippines was slightly over $500 a year, in India and Kenya slightly under.)

Near the park's lodge we saw a hyena defending a prized mud puddle against the advances of two brilliantly colored birds. The birds' heads, otherwise black, had strips of red at the sides, circles of white around each eye, and were topped by golden mohawk plumes. Red bow ties were painted at their throats, and tuxedo tails of white and gold and black trailed behind them. Nearly a yard tall, they looked like a couple of kids who'd just been given a paint set.

"Crown birds," said Michael.

In a nearby pond thirty huge, hulking birds stood motionless, all facing the pond's center. Their coats were a dirty gray, and the effort of carrying around their mammoth, clublike beaks had left them all hump-shouldered. They exuded the air of a mafioso clan, collars upturned to avoid identification as they watched a confederate's casket being lowered into the ground.

"Marabou stork," said Michael, "is an ugly bird."

We stopped to let three bald-butted baboon pass in front of our van. Michael said: "Pants were designed with baboon in mind."

We passed a water buffalo. Michael said: "Very big, very ugly."

Snuffling, low-slung warthogs: "Herbivorous."

Two zebra, one mounting the other from behind: "Making love."

A pair of thin birds, walking with the chopped, awkward steps of young girls new to high heels, picked their way through the tall grass beneath a sausage tree. Mnene, sitting next to Michael and wearing a yellow t-shirt that read SURVIVOR—SPRING BREAK '89—FT. LAUD-ERDALE, cleared his throat, and said: "Secretary birds."

In our twenty-four hours together, these were the first words Mnene had volunteered. I had observed each of us *wazungu* approach him, fail at attempts to draw him out, and then leave him alone. Now, encouraged by this sudden eruption, we all echoed him—"Secretary birds! Ah, yes, secretary birds!"—and made an exaggerated show of pointing out the window.

"What's in those sausages?" asked Nigel.

"Seeds," said Mnene.

"Ah, seeds!" we all said, exchanging significant glances. "Yes, seeds."

Two baboon sat on the lowest limb of a gnarled tree. As we stopped to watch, one swiped at the other and knocked it five feet to the ground. It landed with an audible thud, looked back up at its mate, looked over to acknowledge our laughter, then climbed to resume its former spot on the limb.

"Watch this," said Michael, and for fifteen seconds we sat silently...staring...wondering...until the first baboon smacked the other to the ground again.

"Some day," said Michael, gasping, wiping his eyes, "I would like to sit from sunup to sundown and watch baboon. They are the most funny."

36

Wait a Bit Grass

I was aroused at dawn one morning by a man who came rushing to my tent to tell me that one of my jemadars (foremen) had been seized during the night and carried off by a huge lion...When we reached the spot where the jemadar's body had been devoured, a dreadful spectacle presented itself. The ground all around was covered with blood, morsels of flesh, and the larger bones, but the unfortunate man's head had been left intact, save for a couple of holes made by the lion's tusks. It lay a short distance away from the other remains, the eyes wide open and staring, with a startled, horrified look in them.

— COLONEL J. H. PATTERSON, *The Man Eaters of Tsavo*

As Michael drove toward the hippo pools on the far side of the park, a blue Land Rover with a shattered windshield passed going the opposite direction. Inside we could see the faces of two dour-looking Africans.

Rupert said, "Those guys didn't look too happy."

"Those are cops," Michael said. "Rangers. Poachers have shot out their windshield. They are angry because the poachers are beating them. In nearly a year I have not seen one rhino. Sometimes I have seen eight vans come to look at one lion, or one cheetah. Now the lions don't care. These are supposed to be wild animals, but they are not wild any more. They are accustomed to the vans. Sometimes on a slow day, just for fun, one of the drivers will start off across the open field, driving very fast, like he has seen something. And five vans will chase after him. We cannot do this too often. The rangers complain because the vans tear up the ground.

"I sometimes wonder how much the parks can take. Every month there are more vans, more balloons, more airplanes. The Minister of Tourism, he wants dollars. Anyone can start a safari company. Today there are a thousand vans in Nairobi. I have taken people on tours and then seen them in Nairobi six months later—starting their own company."

We drove for more than an hour and stopped at a bend of the muddy Njombe River, the border between Kenya and Tanzania. We ate lunch and took dozens of pictures of thirty armor-plated hippos—splashing, nuzzling, mock-fighting, blowing waterspouts into the air, or snoozing on sandbars.

On the way back to camp Michael slowed as we approached a small thicket at the side of the road. "Sometimes lions sleep here in the day time," he said. "Ah, yes. We are in luck."

Michael pulled the van off the road and into a narrow opening in the side of the thicket. One thick-maned king of the jungle and four queens were stretched out on their sides in a central clearing, napping in tall grass only two or three feet from our tires, their tawny hides heaving up and down. Michael switched off the motor, leaving us in a primal, near-total silence.

"Listen," said Michael, "they are snoring."

It was true; we heard the lions wheezing like old drunks. Rupert, Nigel, and Grace stood on the middle seat and poked their heads through the pop-top, cameras poised.

"Not exactly an action picture," Rupert called down. "Make 'em move, Michael."

Michael's door was on the opposite side of the van from the lions, seven or eight feet away. When he opened it and banged it shut, the male and one female raised their heads from the grass. Above us, shutters clicked furiously.

Later, when all the photo opportunities had been exhausted, when Michael started the engine and put it into reverse, we heard the alarming whine of tires spinning, grabbing at nothing.

Michael paused, then tried again.

Nothing.

He tried rocking the van forward a few inches, then slamming it backward, but again we heard the slick whir. In Michael's side mirror I watched the back tire dig six inches into the sod.

Michael shut off the motor.

"This," Nigel suggested, "might be wait-a-bit grass."

Grace said, "Michael's *not* teasing!"

Michael slumped in his seat. To Mnene, he said, "Give me those matches."

"Going to burn them out?" Rupert guessed.

"I'm going to smoke. And think."

Michael smoked.

Mnene smoked.

We all sat, and we all considered.

We had water. We had some food. We had plenty of Sportsman cigarettes. Presuming, as we thought it safe to do, that our van was lion-proof, there was nothing to worry about. True, we were twenty miles from park headquarters, but sooner or later another van would pass our way; sooner or later a ranger would happen by and take command of the situation. Sooner or later.

"Lions don't attack vans, do they?" Grace asked.

Michael studied her. He had something smart in mind—I could tell—but he saw Grace's fear. "No," he told her, "I have never heard of this one." But to me he said, "*Now* would you like to walk in the bush?"

After his cigarette, Michael tried again to drive us out, but only dug us in deeper. Two of the lions, then a third, rose to their feet and looked our way.

"Oh, no!" said Grace.

"Maybe they're leaving," said Rupert.

"Not until tonight," said Michael. "They won't be going out in the sun. They are just moving around a bit. We are too noisy for them." The three lions moved a few feet farther away from the van and lay down again.

At breakfast I had recounted Michael's story about the *mzungu* (single foreigner) who wanted to see a cheetah. Now Rupert said, "O.K., Michael, we've seen enough lions. Now I *must* see a cheetah!"

Michael snorted and lit another cigarette.

Finally it was Mnene who came up with a plan. Several sticks were visible in the brush toward the van's rear, and Mnene thought that if he could gather enough of them and stuff them under the rear tires, we might gain some traction. But the lions were too close to the van's front doors for him to go in and out that way, and the van's rear door only opened from the outside.

While the rest of us kept a sharp watch on the lions, promising to scream if even one of them stirred, Mnene crawled up through the pop-top onto the roof. Watching the lions, he crouched atop the back of the van, and then—in one move—dropped to the ground, opened the back door and leapt inside, pulling the door not-entirely-shut behind him. Had the lions been merely faking, watching for their chance through half-closed eyes, they might have pounced the instant Mnene jumped from the roof, might have feasted on his liver, heart, and whatever other good parts he had. If they had caught him opening the door, they would have had all the heart and all the liver they wanted.

Mnene paused at the back door to make sure the lions were still sedate, then gathered sticks from the "safe" side of the van and shoved them under the tires. But it was futile. Even with Rupert, Nigel, Grace, and myself bouncing our combined weight over the rear axle, and even with Mnene's sticks underneath it, the tires just spun.

In the middle of Michael's third cigarette, Mnene's second, and Rupert's first, a Land Rover putted over the horizon. Michael beeped our horn. The Land Rover stopped. Following a shouted conversation between drivers, Mnene crept from our van to the Land Rover. The other driver handed Mnene a chain with hooks on either end, and—while the lions dozed and the tourists in the other van recorded everything on videotape—Mnene began connecting the two vehicles' bumpers.

One of the lions stood up.

Everyone in our van shrieked, even Michael.

Mnene scrambled back inside—moving so fast that Michael said, "There, Rupert—there was your cheetah." But the lion just moved farther away from us and lay down again.

At last the Land Rover jerked us free. A few minutes later, as we were bouncing down the road again, I heard Grace ask Michael for a cigarette.

37
Enjoy It

I love travel with a passion, the good days and the bad. And I don't care to analyze the reasons too deeply—running to, running from, inner journeys, outer journeys, fear of commitments, fear of dying, fear of missing out on things—all of the above, or none. Who cares?
—DAVID YEADON, *The Back of Beyond*

My friends who had once lived in Kenya had extracted from me a promise to visit Lamu, an island off the northern coast. The beaches were long, white, and empty, they said, the breezes gentle, the people friendly. Lamu had no roads and no cars, electricity was a recent and unreliable phenomenon, and the only way to get there was by boat from the mainland. "Your kind of place," they assured me.

And a few weeks earlier, in Cairo, I had met Dave and Julie Stone, two backpacking Americans who now lived in Moshi, Tanzania. The Stones said their living room window framed a perfect view of Kilimanjaro, and invited me to use their home as a base camp. Dave had climbed the 19,340-foot peak, and predicted that I could do it in five or six days, up and down.

On night sixty-three I boarded the overnight train from Nairobi to Mombasa on the coast. My plan was to ride a bus from Mombasa, north along the Indian Ocean, then ferry across to Lamu. After two or three days I would backtrack to Mombasa, ride buses to the Stones' home in Moshi, climb Kilimanjaro, perhaps swing by for a look at

Ngorongoro Crater, and then dash for Nairobi in time to catch my flight to Zimbabwe—fifteen days away.

Even thinking about it wore me out.

When I awoke the next morning, we were half an hour from Mombasa. The air was cool and smelled of ocean and palm trees. The sun had just risen over a hilly green plain dotted with small round huts that looked like beer barrels hidden under hula skirts.

The aging shed that served as Mombasa's railroad depot lay at the western edge of town, across from a small overgrown park. Several people had spent the night in the park, and now they were sitting in the tall, littered weeds—yawning, stretching, looking around as though surprised and a bit disappointed to still be there.

I walked down Haile Selassie Road, past seedy hotels and old dry goods stores whose wooden awnings reached out to shade the sidewalks. Mombasa struck me as lazy, sleepy, messy—a seductive, peeling version of Key West in the late 1960s. And I was enchanted by its name, now ringing in my head like a mantra. *Mom-BAH-sa. Mom-BAH-sa. Mom-BAH-sa.*

Shops here, as in Nairobi, were protected at night by private security guards; most had departed at sunrise, but one, fast asleep, was still slumped on a stool in front of a grocery store, club gripped loosely in his hand. Toward the center of town I stepped aside to make room for two guffawing black women who staggered past on four-inch heels, their enormous breasts and behinds squeezed into tubes of red and black spandex—sisters of the women who clog San Francisco's Tenderloin district whenever the fleet or a convention comes to town.

At the bus station I bought a ticket for the next morning's bus to Lamu. On Jomo Kenyatta Road I took a $2.50 hotel room with insect screens on the windows and a ceiling fan so lethargic I feared each rotation might be its last.

Toward the middle of every trip, I begin to be nagged by the dawning awareness that sometime in the all-too-foreseeable future—tomorrow, next week, two months from yesterday—I will be going home. The sand in the hourglass, full and trickling so slowly at trip's beginning, is suddenly slipping away like water down an unplugged sink.

While unpacking, I acknowledged with a catch in my heart that I was on the downside of this trip's halfway hump. Having seen quite a few new places, and having compiled a roster of potential invitees (including, of course, Michael), I already rated it a success. But as each passing hour and spent dollar brought me closer to the end, I was developing a wistful, unsettled feeling. The road had become my home again, and the thought of returning to America and gearing back up to rat race speed was distinctly unattractive.

European traders and adventurers have been a presence on the East African coastline for centuries, and during Kenya's colonial era, Mombasa was a favorite retreat for the country's whites. A small number had stayed on after *uhuru*, and others still traveled from abroad—mostly from England, Germany, and Italy—to winter along the coast. Every diner on the covered patio of the Castle Hotel was white, every waiter black. Remove the row of Land Rovers parked out front, and a time-traveling British colonialist might proclaim Nairobi unchanged since 1939.

But things *had* changed. The groceries, small hotels, tea rooms, and bookstores were now all run by blacks or by Asians—descendants of the imported laborers who had stayed on after completion of the railroad. Other than the Castle Hotel congregation, the whites kept to the edge of things, scuttling quietly from shade patch to shade patch. But the heat and intense midmorning sun didn't seem to faze the blacks, who strode confidently down the middle of streets, sprinted after buses, called out exuberant *Jambos* to each other, or talked in animated groups on the sidewalks.

A pair of huge concrete elephant tusks—a salute to the region's lucrative ivory trade—formed an arch over Kilindini Road. Until recently, freighters full of ivory had sailed from Mombasa Harbor in broad daylight. But after some 90 percent of Kenya's elephant herds had been slaughtered, ivory trading had been banned. Tusks still left Kenya in prodigious quantities, but usually in smaller, faster boats that slipped from hidden coves along the coast on moonless nights.

Old fishing boats were docked in the harbor. Muscular black men sat atop wooden barrels along the wharf, beer bottles in hand, gossiping, reliving the morning's sail. Others bent over the catch of the day —silver fishes, four feet long—gutting them and tossing them into waiting carts.

Fort Jesus, built by the Portuguese in 1593, still guarded the harbor mouth. Stubby black cannons poked through the portals of the crumbling walls, aiming impotently at two anchored trawlers. The tide was out, and boys walked barefoot along the harbor's exposed bottoms, searching for shells or things to salvage. Several *dhows* (small Indian Ocean boats), their triangular sails lashed to their masts, were keeled over in the mud, awaiting the tide's return and a spot of wind. Stretching from the harbor's mouth to the distant, curved horizon, was the Indian Ocean—becalmed this morning, and so gray and shiny it looked like a planet-sized ball bearing.

Beside the fort, boys kicked a soccer ball back and forth. Feeling a heat-induced listlessness, I sat in the shade of a mango tree, my back against a wall. A warm breeze blew the hair up off my forehead. I thought of America. In just over a month I would land in New York, where it might be ten degrees below freezing. There would be things to do, people to see. Thank God, I still had five weeks of the road's unpredictability remaining. Each morning I awoke to a day of mystery— saw new landscapes, ate new foods, met only strangers, and rarely knew where I might lay my sleeping bag that night. But a month at home and this adventure would surely fade. Days would pass when I would speak only to the same two or three familiar people, and months during which I would eat in the same two or three predictable restaurants. I might even forget which closet my sleeping bag was stored in. I would gradually come to fear the uncertainty and unsettling freedom of the road, would be able to cite a hundred reasons why I couldn't go traveling this year. Next year, maybe.

Now I closed my eyes, listened to the ocean's hum, the boys' yelps, the shrill complaints of the harbor birds, and the rustle of palms. A two-fifty room. Fresh fish dinners. Fifty cent beers. *Remember all this*, I thought. *Enjoy it. Never take it for granted.*

38

On That Spot

"Six weeks ago I saw a man shot at point-blank range, on a (Nairobi)
street at midday, and he was in police custody...He had grabbed money
from a teller in the Standard Bank. The guards chased him, trapping
him between parked cars. They beat him with clubs...He struggled up,
staggering a few feet before a plainclothes policeman stepped from the
crowd, drawing his revolver. The thief grabbed the barrel, trying to
point it away. He was crying, screaming, begging for his life. Then
another cop just walked up and shot him in the head. He died on the
sidewalk. The police flipped open his coat and retrieved the money. I
read it was nine thousand shillings ($480). They left his body there,
and for an hour people walked around it."

—BILL, an American development worker
quoted in *Equator,* by Thurston Clarke

A dozen long lines stretched across the lobby of Mombasa's cavernous post office: FOREIGN PARCELS, TELEGRAMS, etc. I was
standing about twenty back in the FOREIGN AIR MAIL line, scanning
the room, when I spotted a portly Italian man whose name, I was soon
to learn, was Farina Giacomo. Mr. Giacomo, a rumpled-looking sort in
his late fifties, wore a pink t-shirt, baggy shorts, and sandals. A horseshoe of white hair ringed his otherwise bald head; his walk was a wob-

bly shuffle, and as I watched him work his way through the crowds, I wondered if he weren't just a bit hung over.

Mr. Giacomo had approached to within six or seven feet of me when a lanky African man in his late twenties suddenly darted into his path. The African wore a jungle-green shirt, khaki trousers, and flip-flops, and now, slowed by Mr. Giacomo's lumbering presence, he did a speedy right-left two-step, grimaced, *Oh, these bothersome crowds*, stepped right again, and brushed past.

Had I not been so near, and had I not already been watching Mr. Giacomo, I would never have realized the purpose of this encounter. The African's little shuffle had been designed for and had succeeded at freezing Mr. Giacomo's forward motion for an instant. And in that instant I saw the African's left forearm slide into Giacomo's belly—not too sharply, but just enough to cover for the quick motion of his right hand, which whipped in and out of Giacomo's front pants pocket. I caught a flash of wrinkled brown leather. The African took two more quick steps and then ducked into the FOREIGN PARCELS line, queue-jumping ahead of an old woman fumbling with her purse.

Approach, dance, snatch, and escape—a neat move, like a halfback juking a tackler—all in less than two seconds. Before it even began to register on Giacomo that something had happened, the thief was already standing anonymously in line, the wallet hidden in a newspaper clasped innocently in front of him.

But on some level, Giacomo had sensed it. He took a step, stopped, and, even though there was no pocket there, patted at his breast. He groped at his pants pockets, front and back.

I had observed these seconds as though in a television-watching trance, but now my feet moved, and suddenly I was standing over Mr. Giacomo with my hand on his shoulder. He looked up at me, quizzically, as though I might be a son he hadn't seen in thirty years.

"Is your wallet gone?" I asked, unable to own what I'd seen. I pointed at the picked pocket.

Mr. Giacomo swiveled his head from side to side, befuddled. His face, I noticed, had not felt a razor in three or four days, nor the sun, it appeared, in about a month.

"Your wallet," I said. "You've lost your wallet."

Heads began turning in the silent lines around us. From the corner of my eye I noticed the thief shift his feet, but he kept his back to us and his eyes averted.

"No English," Mr. Giacomo stammered. He pointed across the lobby. "My friend—he English." I turned and saw another white man working his way toward us through the crowds. When I turned back, the thief had disappeared...

There he was! Fifteen feet away now, strolling toward the far doors, feigning an air of nonchalance. Twenty feet away...

And then I was gliding quickly through the lobby of the Mombasa post office, dodging bodies, Mr. Giacomo abandoned. I got an angle on the thief, beat him to the door by two steps, stopped and turned to face him. My hands reached out; my fingertips touched lightly but firmly against his right and left biceps. Our eyes locked onto each other's at the same level, a foot apart.

"That's not yours," I said.

His eyes were filled with a terror I hadn't expected. He said, "It's yours," and thrust the newspaper at me. "Take it."

But I didn't take it. How did I know the wallet was still *in there*? My fingertips stayed put. "You stole the wallet," I said. Were his arms *trembling*?

He pulled the wallet from the newspaper's pages—"It's yours, take it," he repeated, this time pleading—shoved it into my hand, and pushed past me and out the door. I didn't try to stop him. He picked his way through the traffic on Makadara Road, merged with the pedestrians on the far sidewalk, pulled a pair of dark shades from his pocket, slid them on, turned a corner and was gone.

A hundred faces watched me recross the lobby and give Mr. Giacomo back his wallet. With a bewildered smile he offered me money, then insisted on writing his name and address in my notebook. His friend said, "Farina have big house in Torino. Ten rooms. He want you bring all your amigos. Eaten...,"—he tipped an imaginary bottle to his lips—"drinken..."

A black woman came up to us. She stood well over six feet tall. "You are good," she said, looking down at me over the top of her glasses. "That other man is bad. I wish a policeman had seen this one."

And then she said something I hadn't yet considered, the full meaning of which would not sink in until later, when I ran the incident back through my mind.

"We have a way of dealing with these boys," the woman said. "If you would have grabbed him, we would have shot him right there on that spot."

39
Tsst!

How many people is too many? Over time, the debate has spread between two poles. On one side...are the Cassandras, who believe that continued population growth at the current rate will inevitably lead to catastrophe. On the other are the Pollyannas, who believe that humanity faces problems but has a good shot at coming out okay in the end.

Indeed, the two (sides) are barely on speaking terms...Told in an exchange of academic gossip that an eminent (Cassandra) ecologist has had himself sterilized, an equally eminent (Pollyana) demographer says, "That's the best news I've heard all week!"

—CHARLES C. MANN, "How Many is Too Many?" *The Atlantic*

In Nairobi another traveler had assured me that I could get a Tanzanian visa at the border, and that I could reenter Kenya on the visa I already had. But I thought it wise to have this information verified. Following the incident in the post office, I began walking across town toward Mombasa's immigration office.

As I walked, I felt flashes of pure elation. I had done something bold and instinctive, had acted without thinking, and, to Farina Giacomo at least, I was a hero. And I had seen others in the crowd steal admiring looks at me.

But now the words of the black woman began to bother me. What if a policeman *had* been there? I surely did not want to see a pickpocket executed. I had embarked on this trip hoping to infuse some stranger's life with a little magic; how ironic, how sobering—no, how absolutely shattering—it would be to, instead, cause someone's death.

The thief's image kept running through my mind. I remembered the feel of his reedy biceps quivering against my fingertips, saw him sliding on his dark glasses and disappearing around the corner. It seemed, somehow, like a missed opportunity to come away from the trip's most vivid moment ignorant of even the tiniest detail of the life of the person with whom I'd shared it. Who was he? A man desperate, perhaps, for money to buy medicine to save the life of a spouse or child or parent? An illiterate, his country ravaged by colonialism, now hungry and confused in the chaos left behind? Or just a punk who refused to earn his own beer money?

The air in Nairobi, 5,280 feet above sea level, had had a soothing quality, but Mombasa's afternoon air felt like warm tea. Heat waves rose from the asphalt, making the tall roadside weeds seem to dance. Ramshackle stucco houses stewed in roadside groves of trees. Two black men stood talking in the shade of a giant mango tree and, as I passed, one of them made a "Tsst!" noise behind me.

But I was not in a talking mood and pretended not to hear.

He made the noise again, louder, more insistent—"*TSSSST! TSSSST!*"—but I kept walking.

Two minutes later I heard a "Hello" directly behind me. I turned around. It was one of the men from under the mango tree. He was a few years older than me, had a large head, a wide flat nose, yellowed eyes, and was one of the darkest people I've ever seen. He wore a white shirt, black slacks, and black tie shoes.

"You do not remember me?" he asked, staring coldly.

"You were under the tree back there."

"No," he said, "before that. At the bus station just one hour ago you asked me directions to Immigration."

I said, "I think you have me confused with someone else."

"You do not remember me!" Now it was an accusation.

"That was someone else. I have not been at the bus station since early this morning."

233

"Aren't you the Australian?"

"No." I smiled. "It's hard to tell *wazungu* apart, isn't it?"

He seemed greatly offended at my little joke, and scowled openly. "I was coming to show you the way to Immigration," he said.

This was going very awkwardly. I didn't really want to be shown the way to Immigration. And I didn't like that I was so obvious—couldn't a white man walking down this road be headed elsewhere? Also, I didn't particularly like that this man's stony face had not yet revealed any trace of softness.

But even if his manner were stiff, his offer was polite, and now, doing my best to hide my irritation, I said, "Thank you." I extended my hand. "My name is Brad. What's yours?"

He looked at my hand but left it dangling. He made a noise that sounded like "Owner." A title? A name? A pre-attack grunt? "Are you coming?" he said.

He turned and walked ahead. I caught up with him, and without speaking, we walked side by side for two hundred yards. At a large concrete office building set in a field of dry and yellowing weeds, Owner turned in at the driveway. The silence was killing me, and when we reached the front door, I yanked at the handle. Locked.

"Immigration is at the back," Owner said. I followed him along the side of the building. He stopped at a door near the back and pointed inside. "That is the Immigration Office. It does not open until two o'clock."

I tried the door anyway. Locked. Through the glass, over a deserted counter, I saw a sign: VISAS.

Owner took a few steps and stopped at the corner of the building. "Tell me your questions," he said. "I will answer them." And he turned the corner and disappeared.

This was crazy. I looked around and saw three black men asleep under an awning at a construction site fifty yards away. Each, I noticed, was using a gray cinderblock for a pillow. There were no other people in sight.

I walked to the building's corner and peered around it. Owner was sitting on the bottom step of stairs leading to a second story.

"What are your questions?" he said, bored.

I told him.

"Let me see your passport," he said.

I hesitated. "I think I'll just come back at two o'clock."

Now he really did smile, amusement not malice. "You are afraid of me."

"Yes," I admitted.

He pulled a ring of keys from his pocket. "I work in this office. At two o'clock I will open it. You do not need to be afraid of me."

"Let's go inside," I said.

"You do not need to be afraid of me."

"Sometimes," I said, "it is good to be afraid."

"Sometimes."

The watch on Owner's wrist said 1:45. Leaving to come back at two o'clock would be silly. Where would I go; what would I do for fifteen minutes? And my fear of Owner had begun dissolving the instant I'd acknowledged it. I took out my passport, gave it to him and sat on the steps. He studied it, then told me I needed no more visas. I could get a Tanzanian one at the border, and could reenter Kenya on the one I already had. I said, "Oh, good," but I thought: *I'll double-check with whoever appears beneath the VISAS sign at two o'clock.*

Owner closed my passport and handed it back. "So," he said, "you have been here for five days now. What do you think of Kenya?"

"I have not seen enough of it to answer yet."

He looked sideways at me. "You are still afraid of me," he said, tossing his hands. "I have a job. I have a degree. I have no weapon. I am not going to rob you. You are younger and bigger. Why are you afraid?"

"I'm not any more."

"But you were," he said.

"Well, you were so angry."

"I was *not* angry."

"Oh, come on," I said. "You were frowning so hard I thought you might hurt yourself."

He half smiled. "I thought you were ignoring me. I thought you were the Australian I had met and you were ignoring me."

"I *was* ignoring you. I hate that sound you were making."

"*Tsst?*" he said.

"Yeah, that. I hate it. In America that's the sort of noise we make to scare away cats and dogs."

Something clicked in Owner's throat, and then in his whole demeanor. He leaned back on the steps and laughed. *Ho, ho, ho.* He squeezed his eyes shut—*ho, ho, ho*—opened them, and looked at me sideways again, nodding and smiling. "To scare away dogs," he echoed; this was hilarious—*ho, ho, ho.*

Finally, he caught his breath. "To stop someone in America, what do you do?"

"You say 'Excuse me,' or 'Pardon me, Sir,' or even just 'Hello'— like you did later. Never *tsst.*"

This set him off again, and his gentle, prolonged laughter drew two black men, who poked their heads around the corner. They were wearing the black slacks and white shirts of office workers, and when Owner saw them, he waved them over.

"This boy is from America. He was afraid of me...," he tried to control his laughter, "he was afraid because I said 'Tsst!' to him." And off he went again.

The men came over to us, but they seemed mystified. Owner wiped his eyes and sighed. Now more people came around the corner. They each nodded toward Owner and gathered around us, leaning against the building or crowding around our step. These impromptu press conferences, erupting as unexpectedly as surprise birthday parties, are one of the very best parts of Third World travel. No one in the West has time for a stray foreigner, but throughout Asia and Africa foreigners are viewed as cheap amusement. Someone will ask a question—"Excuse me, what is your native country?"—and a dozen others will crowd behind him. I looked at these black faces, fourteen men and one woman, and thought: *What a rich life I have.*

"This boy has been here for five days," Owner explained, "but he will not say what he thinks of Kenya."

"What do *you* think of Kenya?" I said, addressing all of them. "Is it better since *uhuru*?"

"Oh, yes," said a man in the front.

"I am forty-three," said Owner, "so I remember the old days. There are some things the whites used to do better, but soon we will also master them. We have had twenty-five years. We are organized now."

"How are the blacks treated in America?" asked the man in the front.

"Things are difficult for American blacks," I said. "America has not yet gotten over slavery."

"Can a black man get a good job?"

"Oh, yes. There are many rich and middle-class blacks. But most things are run by whites. Kenya is the first place I have seen that is run by black people. In America, if I go to a hotel and see a black man behind the counter, I assume he is working for a white man. Here, maybe he owns the hotel, or maybe he works for another black man. The trucks are all driven by blacks, my train engineer was black, and I imagine the head of all the railroads is black. The president himself is a black man."

"Yes," said Owner. "Here maybe the general manager of a company is a white man. Or maybe the accountant, or some of the key people— but they all have to have work permits, and there is always a black man learning to do their jobs."

The man at the front said, "Do you have a degree?"

"Yes," I said.

"What is your job?"

"I am a taxi driver."

There was a murmur in the crowd.

"You have a degree," said the man at the front, "and you drive a taxi?"

"In America a degree is not a guarantee of anything," I said. "Many cab drivers have degrees."

Someone in the back called, "But do people respect you? In Kenya no one with a degree will be driving a taxi."

"In America," I said, "people with degrees drive cabs, work as carpenters, miners, waiters, dishwashers. I have washed many dishes in my life."

"But to travel is expensive. How many dollars salary for a taxi driver?"

"Guess," I said.

But no one would.

"A hundred and fifty dollars a day," I told them.

A howl arose. The average Kenyan earned three hundred dollars a year. I thought: *How can they imagine America?*

"But," I said, "in my city a one bedroom apartment rents for a thousand dollars a month..." Muttering. "A simple visit to a doctor costs fifty dollars. If you need to spend one night in the hospital—a thousand dollars..."

The woman blurted, "We have *free* hospitals."

Yes, I thought, *and may I never have to visit one.*

"To have a child and give it an education," I said, "costs about $250,000. In America you almost have to be rich to afford a baby."

"In Kenya even poor people can have babies," someone retorted.

I travel with a demographic chart published by the Population Reference Bureau in Washington, D.C. I said: "The average Kenyan woman has 6.3 babies. Do you think," I asked innocently, "that Kenya has a population problem?"

Owner said, "Oh, no! On the train from Nairobi—you saw all that empty land. No, the number one problem is employment. It used to be that with a degree you would at least have a job as a clerk. Now, no." He waved to include the entire group. "We all have degrees, and we are all lucky to have jobs. Many people with degrees have no job."

"Kenya's population is increasing by 3.3 percent per year, "I said. "If that keeps up, your population will double in twenty-one years. If you think you're lucky to have jobs now, what will it be like with that many more people?"

"How do you know these things?" said the man in the front.

I had been hoping for a chance to pull out my chart, and now I did. Everyone gathered around. No one seemed interested in the population and growth figures, but they were all eager to know how Kenya's per capita income compared to that of its neighbors.

The man in front called out the figures.

"Kenya...$300.

"Somalia...$280."

Cheering.

"Ethiopia...$120.

"Tanzania...$240.

"Uganda...There is no figure for Uganda, only a blank spot."

Much chuckling.

"When I look at this chart," I said, "it appears to me that the more children a country has, the less chance it has to provide for them. But when a country stops having so many babies it has a chance."

My suggestion met immediate opposition. "That does not apply in Kenya," said a tall man at the back who had not spoken before. "So what if you have ten children? Cholera wipes out five just like that. Then you have only five."

I thought: *Only five!* I said: "But what about some other family that has *twenty* children and has *no* cholera."

"That is another family. *You* still have only five."

"I have no children," I said. "Am I poor?"

No one said I was poor, but they all seemed to regard me as though I might have cholera. Finally one of the men said, "Oh, you have your many statistics, but statistics only tell 50 percent of the story."

Another said, "No, only 42 percent."

A wave of laughter.

A white man poked his head around the corner to see what the fuss was, and looked surprised to see the entire staff of the Mombasa Immigration Office gathered around a *wazungu* population chart.

Owner looked at his watch. It was ten after two. "Time to go to work," he said, with a foreman's authority. The group began to dissolve, moving toward the front of the building. I folded my chart. "I will let my staff into the office," Owner said. When we exchanged addresses, he jotted "Richard A. Ownor" into my notebook.

I waved goodbye to all the people in the office, and shook their boss's hand. "Sorry I was afraid of you," I told him.

"Oh," he said, "but sometimes it is good to be afraid."

40

Dead-Center Nowhere

Bus travel...

  *When a man puts a sack of potatoes in your lap ("Just for a mo-
ment," he assures you) and then disappears; when a mother hands you a
howling baby and falls asleep for three hours; or when a dog chews a
hole in your shirtsleeve ("He likes you," says the owner), rare is the
man who wouldn't feel a little cross.*

  —ERIC LAWLOR, *In Bolivia*

My bus to Lamu rolled out of Mombasa under a clear sky, the
morning air still sweet and breathable. The bus was the American school bus type—old, but seemingly in good condition. Its two-
person benches were small and closely spaced, but the padding had not
yet entirely petrified and the aisle provided plenty of room to stretch
my legs. We would reach Lamu in five hours, six at most, the driver's
assistant told me. There would be time for a swim in the ocean before
dinner.

  We quickly reached the maize fields on Mombasa's outskirts;
through a line of eucalyptus trees I caught glimpses of the sea, a gun-
metal blue this morning. And then, only twenty minutes into the journey, stinky black clouds of smoke began gushing in through the
windows. The driver pulled to the side of the road, and everyone
trooped off for a look. While the assistant jacked up the bus and removed the right front wheel assembly, other men crowded around and
offered diagnoses.

"The bearings."

"No—it is just needing lubrication."

The driver bent down. "Brakes," he declared. "Two hours."

The assistant flagged down a pickup truck heading back into Mombasa and went in search of parts and a mechanic. The driver announced that everyone was welcome to walk to the next town, Porini, and he would pick us up when things got sorted out; but a nearby "Pepsi New Generation" billboard said that Porini was seven kilometers down the road, and no one took up his offer. Instead, we moved around to the shady side of the bus and settled down in the grass.

Many passengers wore bright new clothes purchased in Mombasa, and now they exchanged compliments and bazaar tales. A baby—just learning to walk, and wearing a too-big baseball cap with holly sprigs and the word X-MAS printed on its bill—lurched from person to person, offering to share a package of "Asante" biscuits. A female voice poured out of a boom box: *Every woman needs a man, to hold her all night long.*

I sat with Kirk, a tall, husky, blond native of Kansas, who was traveling with dark haired, round-faced Ruth, one-quarter Native American. "A Tlingit princess," she said with a pretty smile. Kirk and Ruth had met six months earlier while working at an Alaskan bear lodge, open only during summer and accessible only by water-plane. As we traded stories, the patch of shade provided by the bus grew shorter.

Two hours passed before the driver's assistant returned with a mechanic; by the time the brakes were fixed and we were again rolling across the coastal plain the sun was directly overhead. My ocean swim would have to wait until tomorrow. *In America*, I thought, *people would grumble, glance at their watches and threaten lawsuits for a delay like this, but here no one seemed disturbed.* Nor was I.

The road cut through groves of fern palms and eucalyptus trees, then salt marshes, tall with reeds. The local residents were mostly barefoot, barely clothed, and lived in thatch-roofed huts with walls of sticks and mud. A naked woman stood in front of one hut and shook out a sheet of gray plastic; goats congregated around her, hoping that something edible might be involved.

Around one o'clock in the afternoon we reached the town of Malindi. The Arab influence was pervasive here on the coast, and on this stifling hot day women walked the town's wide dusty streets wearing black Islamic robes. Nearing the bus station I caught sight of a mob of several dozen people who, having spotted our bus, were now rising to their feet, hoisting bundles, surging forward.

Fifteen minutes later we creaked out of Malindi, the overhead racks sagging with bundles and the aisle packed solid with people. The bus reeked of body odor and fresh manure. Several people were traveling with live chickens; one man had tried boarding with a baby goat, but the driver had forbidden it.

Just beyond Malindi the pavement ended and the road became a washboard dirt track, scarred by ruts and potholes. Earlier I had been able to read, but now this was impossible; I closed my book, gripped the vibrating seatback ahead of me, and braced for the periodic craters. One pothole dislodged a pineapple from the overhead racks: I saw it freefall into the heads of the crowd toward the front and heard a child's wail. Dust drifted in from outside, but whenever someone tried to close a window the people squashed in the aisle screamed that they were suffocateing. I soaked my handkerchief, mopped my forehead and neck, and thought: *Thank God I've got a seat.*

And then after half an hour the bus slowed and stopped. In a spot which looked to me like dead-center nowhere, forty people were standing on the roadside. If I'd been asked, I would have said we didn't have room for even one more person, but this was Africa, and we stopped and began loading them on.

I wondered: *How did these people know to be here? What secret schedule had they gotten hold of? Was this the driver's and his assistant's way of supplementing income?* When we'd left Mombasa everything had been orderly—one seat per person, crisp little tickets for all, no live animals. At Malindi the situation had degenerated. Now it was turning surreal.

When twenty people had boarded and twenty more were still waiting, the driver's assistant began yelling and gesturing at those standing to move back. But already the aisle was more tightly packed than a cattle car: roosters were crowing madly, people were screaming and being jostled off their feet. A Kenyan man fell onto my lap, pushed himself back up immediately, and apologized—but it was hardly his fault.

"Polepole," someone cried—*Po-lay-po-lay* (Easy, easy)—and others took up the chant. "Polepole, polepole." But for ten minutes the newcomers bucked and shoved and bulled their way aboard, squeezing those in the aisle, rib cage to rib cage. And as I watched them, I remembered...

At the beginning of each shift in the Colorado mine where I worked, men and women were herded into a huge metal box known as the Cage and lowered by cable 3,000 feet into the mountain. The Cage's capacity was 100 people, but 200 to 300 of us reported for each shift, so there was always considerable shuffling to see who could miss the first trip or two down. In fact, the reluctance to press together was so great that often the Cage appeared full when only 60 or 70 people had boarded.

"Count 'em," a foreman would order.

Some brown-nose, hoping to make crew boss, would do it—"Only 73, boss!"—setting the stage for my favorite part of every day. "Where's Brumbaugh?" the foreman would scream. "Getchurass over here, Moose! Rest a ya stand back."

And then Moose Brumbaugh, a stout, barrel-chested fellow whose name arose during every Strongest-Man-in-the-Mine debate, would set down his lunch bucket and thermos, hitch up the suspenders of his yellow rain suit, and, with a running start and a loony grin, launch himself like a bowling ball at the backs of those crowded at the gate.

Suddenly—and it worked every time—there was plenty of room.

Somehow, all forty people at the side of this red-dirt Kenyan road managed to squeeze into the bus. During the next hour I did a careful census, visually sorting out arms and legs and heads; when finished I had counted no fewer (but possibly more) than one hundred and one people. Not one hundred and one in the entire bus, but one hundred and one *standing in the aisle!*

Then we stopped again and took on seven more. This time the front door was left open and most of them hung outside, with one foot on the bus's step and fingers clutching at the windows. I watched them apprehensively for a while, but they all seemed practiced at this style of yoga and at last I lapsed into a fitful and awkward sleep.

My dozing was broken by an excited cry. Ahead of me Ruth and Kirk were pointing out the window toward an emerald meadow, lined by palm and banana trees. Tall thunderheads billowed from the treetops to the highest heavens. The sun had dropped toward the horizon, and bounding away through the green grasses and the magical late-day light was a herd of at least five hundred zebra and topis. As I looked around the bus I noticed that everyone was smiling; but the foreigners and the locals were amused by different things. While we *wazungu* stared out the window, captivated and charmed by the wildlife stampede, the Kenyans nudged each other in amusement at our excitement over something so ordinary. Ah, I thought, wouldn't it be fun to show them a day in America? Wouldn't they be amazed by a ride on a half-empty BART train zipping under the bay from San Francisco to Oakland? A drive across the Golden Gate Bridge on the opening day of yacht season? A playoff game at Candlestick Park?

In late afternoon we stopped in a one-store, twenty-shack village and deposited more than half our passengers. The heat of the day had passed now, and soon the bus was stopping again, this time for good. The dirt highway had dead-ended beside a wide body of blue-green water where a launch waited for us. As we made the twenty-minute crossing, the sun slipped behind the low, jungle-covered island ahead of us; the sky turned purple, and the foliage on both sides of the channel faded from jade to black. The young African crew slipped about the boat, collecting fares, adjusting cargo, and bumming Sportsman cigarettes from the passengers. The warm wind in my face, the shudder of water across the boat's bottom, the day's last rays of light deifying everyone's countenance—suddenly the extra long, extra crowded bus ride seemed a minor annoyance.

A string of weak lights, Lamu City, came bobbing into view along the right bank. As we cut the motor and drifted to the moorings, I noted palm trees and ancient black cannons; old two-story buildings with candle lamps shining in the windows; wandering dogs and donkeys; and black men in colorful kerchiefs waiting to help unload our boat. I thought: *New Orleans, 1800.*

Just a hundred feet from the town's main dock, I took a four-dollar room with whitewashed walls, a high ceiling, and a pyramid of mosquito netting suspended over the bed. I did some stretches, emptied my backpack (originally a dark blue, it had emerged from the bus's hold a camel color), carried it down the hall and into the shower, and scrubbed the dirt off both of us. I brushed my teeth, placed my toothbrush next to the lineup of seven by the common sink, then dressed in shorts, t-shirt, flip-flops, and went out to the balcony. The sky across the channel showed only the last traces of day—streaks of red and purple and one jagged bolt of orange. No cars, no roads: no traffic hum. Men speaking Swahili walked below, oblivious to my presence fifteen feet above them. From somewhere came a snatch of Tracy Chapman music and the smells of marijuana smoke and roasting meat. I watched the coconut trees along the waterfront stir in a faint warm breeze and thought: *How right of my friends to steer me here.*

I sat at a candlelit table on the front porch of a restaurant adjacent to my lodge. Inside, several young black waiters hovered around the table of two deeply tanned *wazungu* women, who were enjoying plates of lobster. One man spotted me and broke away from the group.

He said, "Welcome to Hapa Hapa. (In Swahili: *Right here.*) My name is Jacob. I have not seen you before. You are new?"

Jacob brought me a coconut shake and later a roast chicken dinner; when I'd finished eating and was paying the tab, he asked how long I was staying.

Two days, I told him. Maybe three.

"Oh," he said, "many tourists come here thinking to stay for only one or two or three days. But it is not so easy. In one day you will fall in love with Lamu. In two days you will change your mind. In three days you will be wanting to marry a Lamu woman and start your family here."

41

Six Tourists and a Good Wind

Those long beaches are enticing to the idle man.
— ROBERT LOUIS STEVENSON

For several centuries Lamu was an important stop on the old Indian Ocean trading routes. *Dhows* loaded with ivory and barrels of palm oil sailed from the island and returned months or years later carrying silks, spices, and gems from India, dates and figs from the Middle East, and, eventually, the ideas of the prophet Mohammed.

But in the 1,000-plus years since the arrival of Islam, the event that most impacted Lamu was the completion of the Uganda Railroad in the early 1900s. After this, goods shipped through Mombasa reached their destinations weeks earlier than goods shipped through Lamu, and the island slipped into obscurity. A few *dhows* still veered off the Dubai-to-Zanzibar route to dock at Lamu, but it was only the smaller *dhows*, and Lamu's shrunken economy was no longer able to absorb so many of their goods.

It must have been a relief to Lamu's residents when Lamu was "discovered" by roaming hippies in the late 1960s and early 1970s. At first there was the usual tension associated with the arrival of strange newcomers, but when several hippies married locals and bought houses near the beach, the town accepted them. Word of Lamu slowly spread along the backpack circuit: "Tropical wonderland: Empty beaches, abundant fruit, plentiful ganja, friendly people. Lamu City looks like a movie setting—narrow alleys, mosques, whitewashed homes. Don't get busted, don't catch malaria, and you'll live like a sheik on five bucks a day."

With adjustments for inflation the description still fit when I discovered Lamu, but the island was no longer a secret. The price of a house near the beach was approaching the price of a house in San Francisco; the rumor spread that Rod Stewart was thinking of buying one. A dredge was at work cleaning the channel, and a group of expats was overseeing construction of a new dock. A crew of Chinese was said to be improving the road from Malindi and planning to pave it eventually. A small airstrip had been installed on the mainland, and now there were irregular connections to Nairobi and Mombasa.

Yet the island had not lost its charm. A dirt promenade—lined with coconut palms, benches, and old cannons with fresh coats of black paint —ran along Lamu City's half-mile waterfront. Men led donkeys, loaded with sacks of grain, through the town's narrow alleys, forcing pedestrians to flatten against the walls to let them pass. Other free-roaming donkeys huddled at intersections like India's cows, trading intelligence reports on potential scavenging spots. Vines of purple, yellow, red, and pink flowers cloaked the arches and grillwork of whitewashed homes and wrapped around the railings of second-story balconies. People gossiped in the shade of enormous, sprawling banyan trees.

Lamu Island is an imperfect square shape, roughly five miles on each side, with Lamu City situated on the leeward side, two miles from the ocean, facing another nearby island and the more distant mainland. A dozen small lodges and restaurants catered to tourists, nearly all of them backpackers, but most of the island remained uninhabited jungle. On a stretch of the southern and eastern shores one could walk for five, six, seven miles, along sand dunes and wide white beaches, lapped by the clear blue waters of the Indian Ocean, and never see a house or another person.

Newspapers reached Lamu late or sometimes not at all. The launch departed to the mainland each morning, and did not return until afternoon or evening. The few government offices and most businesses closed daily from noon until three p.m. Or maybe four. It seemed that every time I passed the police station, an officer was slumped in a chair on the veranda, head fallen forward onto his chest, sound asleep. Men wearing Moslem caps sat on benches outside the town's three mosques and chewed *mirra* leaf, the popular local stimulant.

The end of my first full day found me aboard the *dhow* of a young man named Ali, who had enticed me and five other backpackers to take a short evening cruise. We flew up the channel under pillars of crimson clouds, sails full, boat keeling, salt spray spritzing faces and forearms.

Wearing cutoff blue jeans and a DYLAN-SANTANA t-shirt, Ali sat on the *dhow*'s rim, tiller in one hand, lit joint in the other. He was twenty-five and single, but maybe, he said, not for long. Just a few months earlier he had borrowed roughly US$1,000 to buy and over-haul this boat. Already he had repaid half the loan: if this kept up, soon he could afford marriage.

By this point I had asked hundreds of people what was the best thing that ever happened to them, and was starting to think that maybe I'd heard all possible answers, but Ali had one that was new to me.

"Just this," he said, smiling broadly. "Just this—to be sailing along here in Lamu with six tourists and a good wind."

Languorous Lamu quickly seduced me from my itinerary. The island was the sort of place I dreamed about almost every day at home, and now the idea of finding this jewel and then rushing away after two days in order to embark on yet another boat-bus-taxi-airplane whirlwind seemed blatantly manic, a massive violation of the traveling spirit. I definitely should climb Kilimanjaro and visit Ngorongoro Crater, I told myself, but shouldn't I plan another, lengthier, trip and do them jus-tice? *Besides, what good is a trip with no beach break?*

As I brushed my teeth at the end of my third day on Lamu, the tan, rested-looking fellow peering back from the bathroom mirror clinched the deal. Eleven days remained before my plane left Nairobi for Zim-babwe, and I resolved now to take them one at a time; if I spent all of them here on Lamu, that would be just fine.

My routine quickly became fixed along the lines of least resistance. Each morning I was awakened by light seeping through my window, or by the *scritch-scritch-scritch* sound of the lodgekeeper sweeping the hallway. I would make my way to the second floor balcony and join the six or seven other *wazungu* patrons as they watched the sun's gentle rays ease over the horizon, work their way up the channel, and filter through the palms. Our gathering also had a social purpose—to watch the morning boat leave and note which of our friends were on it. Each day a dozen or so backpackers departed, sacrificed to the mainland gods of careers and schedules. Wearing traveling clothes instead of the shorts and flip-flops standard on Lamu, they looked embarrassed—packed in among crates of empty Tusker beer bottles, and waiting stoically—while the boat's crew paced the waterfront screaming *Moooohm...BAH-saah! Moooohm... BAH-saah!* and the captain struggled to start the engine.

When the launch disappeared up the channel each morning and the sound of its motor faded away, the island seemed to relax a notch. The locals headed to homes or jobs, if they had them, and the *wazungu* went to breakfast.

A waterfront restaurant named Sinbad's—a palm frond roof propped up by two tree-trunk-sized supports—became my morning hangout. Sinbad's stereo played classical music early in the day and I liked letting the harp strings, peeping flutes, and rippling piano keys massage me to life. What I soon came to regard as *my* table had a view of palm-lined waterfront, mangrove swamps on the far side of the channel, and boatmen lounging along the seawall while halfheartedly trying to interest tourists in *dhow* rides.

When my father retired after thirty-three years in the CIA, he joined a group named the Association of Former Intelligence Officers. I had always considered Dad a reticent sort, but I once accompanied him to an AFIO quarterly meeting, held at an Air Force base outside Washington, D.C., and watched in fascination as he waded into the group of four hundred, exchanging handshakes, introductions, opinions, reminiscences. As I watched him I wondered if I, career-less me, would ever have a similar group, a collection of like-minded colleagues with whom I could sit down, light up a memory, and pass it around.

For all of Lamu's authentic charm and balmy breezes, I think I most enjoyed the sense of being among peers. There were roughly a hundred other wanderers on Lamu during my visit, most of them seemingly kindred spirits. Everyone said hello or *Jambo* or nodded or smiled to everyone else, and it was considered acceptable etiquette to pull a chair up to any tableful of people that caught one's fancy. *Wazungu* grouped together for *dhow* rides or hikes around the island, and visited each other's lodges. The island's soundtrack was a mixture of laughter, rustling palms, reggae music, and—always—someone telling a story. Every morning five or ten young or not-so-young travelers would trickle into Sinbad's for a shilling-ante poker game. While arguing politics and philosophy and whether to put on a Vivaldi tape or Dire Straits, we won and lost fortunes in shillings and traded the minutiae of each other's lives. I heard tales of treks in Tibet, bandidos in Bolivia, lovers left in Ladakh. I met travelers fresh from the annual Christmas gathering of backpackers in Goa, India; from a week-long barge trip down the Congo River; Peace Corps workers on leave; and one couple recently stranded for a month in the desert of war-torn Sudan when their train broke down.

Since my meeting with Ezekiel in the park in Manila, I had mentioned my trip's mission to only one or two other travelers. But I'd been thinking about it a lot during the past ten weeks, examining it from every angle, and the more I looked at it the more I liked it. I shared it with my poker mates one morning and they were all delightfully receptive—no one accused me of "playing God." Somewhere along the road each of them had had the same thought: *Wouldn't it be fun to share my own country with a foreigner?*

But what the group most wanted out of me was cab stories, and I anted up as many as I could—the gun held to my head, the fist applied to my forehead, the hookers, the flirters, the gropers, the big tippers, and my sprints down the streets of San Francisco after people who opted to run instead of pay.

An American woman—Kate Lance from Rye, New York (during a Tracy Chapman song Kate had mentioned that she and Tracy and several others had once shared a house in Boston)—asked me, "What's your favorite part of the job?"

Cab drivers spend lots of time debating such questions, and long ago I had reached my conclusion on this one. "My favorite moment," I told her, "is when I'm driving down the street, empty, looking for a fare. I see someone running down the sidewalk, screaming, trying to get the attention of a bus driver up ahead. They bang on the bus's side but it pulls away blowing exhaust all over them. They stop running and their shoulders slump and that's when I pull up alongside. 'Hey! Hop in! We'll catch your bus for free!' Some people just say, 'Oh, thank you!' and jump right in. But most don't trust it—they're sure I'm going to run some scam on them. But I say, 'No, really—this is the absolute best part of my job!' And that usually does it. We chase the bus down and I drop them a bus stop ahead, or if they're not headed halfway across town, I take them wherever they're going. By the time they get out, their whole day looks like a lot more fun—and so does mine."

"That," said Kate, "sounds just like what you're doing with your trip."

"Oh, I like that," I said. I'm sure that my expression was one of surprise and that my fingers started itching for the pen and notebook in the bag at my feet. "I never made the connection before, but I really like that."

42

Bhang

Everyone knows the First Commandment of Travel:
Thou shalt not be caught with ganja!

—TOM SAMPSON, poker player, Lamu

One morning at Sinbad's everyone was trading rumors about a pot bust said to have occurred the previous night.

Nine *wazungu* busted for pot.

No, seven.

No, it was nine arrested for expired visas—one girl dragged out of bed in the nude.

The prisoners were all in the Lamu jail.

No, they were taken to Malindi.

No, to Mombasa.

Someone insisted that no one at all had been arrested, but that the rumors had been sparked by a spot visa check the Lamu police conducted twice a year.

This last scenario seemed the most likely to me. For one thing, no one at the table personally *knew* anyone who'd been arrested. For another, I myself had been visited at one A.M. by a troop of ten Kenya Police who knocked on my door and asked to see my visa. When I asked why they came in the middle of the night, their leader smiled. "If we come in the daytime," he said, "you are all at the beach."

Indeed.

My own daily schedule seemed to be typical. Following breakfast and poker at Sinbad's, my early afternoons were reserved for the beach, for reading, sunning, and swimming in the warm, calm, clear blue water; and my late afternoons for the terrace of Poponi's Lodge. Poponi's—a 45-minute walk down the channel from Lamu City, and the last building before the long run of beaches—was Lamu's lazy nod toward luxury. Rooms started at $135, and the food, said to be excellent, was also pricey; but fifty-cent beers were served on the terrace bar, and a few locals made a living offering, in lowered tones, baggies of *bhang* (local for ganja). Every afternoon the place was packed.

After several days on Lamu I was starting to slow way down, starting, I imagined, to feel the ancient rhythm of Africa. Time here was seamless, each moment and hour and meal flowing effortlessly, naturally to the next, marked only by lengthening shadows or the progress of the moon. Each day seemed to have forty-eight hours and to allow time enough for everything and everyone. I read Beryl Markham's *West With The Night* and Isak Dinesen's *Out of Africa*—two books I'd intended to read for years.

One morning, while Jackson Browne sang about letting disappointments pass and letting laughter fill your glass, I looked away from the happy group at the poker table. Under the eaves of the roof I could see unbroken jungle running along the far side of the channel and a pale African sky stretching above it. *Dhows* floated along the waterfront, sails voluptuous with breeze. Men, gossiping and mending nets, sat on the seawall. A young boy galloped past astride a miniature donkey. I wondered if I could pass the rest of my life this way, trading stories, watching an idyllic scenery reflect the changing slant of tropical rays, and listening to the best music of my formative years. Maybe, maybe not, I concluded, but I could surely understand why the early arriving *wazungu* decided to hang up their backpacks and marry locals.

But paradise is a fragile thing, hard to find, easy to crack. And on my eighth day Lamu began a rapid unraveling.

When I saw Kirk from Kansas at the communal sink that morning, he told me that Ruth, the Tlinget princess, had come down with malaria. Yesterday she had felt woozy; today she had chills and a massive headache. She'd visited the local doctor and taken the malaria-bomb drug Fansidar, but was still fighting a fierce fever. Their room was down the hall from mine, and the fact that we were presumably serviced by the same mosquitoes was more than a little unnerving. I checked the calendar and took my malaria pill a day early.

A bigger shock awaited me at breakfast. A copy of Nairobi's English language newspaper, *The Standard*, was lying face-up on a table at Sinbad's. My eyes were drawn to a front-page article entitled BHANG: SIX TOURISTS JAILED FOR ONE MONTH.

> Six tourists found in possession of 10 kilogrammes of bhang in their lodge in Lamu District, were yesterday sentenced to one month's imprisonment each without the option of a fine, by a Malindi court...

Finally the bust rumors of a few days earlier made sense. At the newsstand I bought a copy of *The Nation*, which had a similar story, but listed the amount of *bhang* as only ten grams (enough to fill one or two film canisters) instead of ten kilogrammes (enough to fill the trunk of a police car). I spent the rest of the morning talking to lodge and restaurant owners and other backpackers, many of whom said they'd been acquainted with the unfortunate six. By day's end I had the story pieced together.

On the day she arrived on Lamu, a New Zealander named Andrea was greeted at the dock by a local tout named Jobert. As he escorted Andrea to an inn, Jobert fell in love.

"Jobert is always hanging around," Andrea's innkeeper told me. "Andrea gets tired of him. But now Jobert thinks she is his girl, and always he is bothering her. 'Would you like *dhow* ride? Would you like to walk on the beach with me?' When the other *wazungu* staying here see what is happening, they stay close to Andrea, protect her. Now Jobert is never alone with her. He gets angry. He says, 'You don't like me.' Andrea says yes she likes him, but she likes many other people also."

On the afternoon of the bust Andrea and three other New Zealanders went to the beach. It was a normal Lamu day: sun shining, palm trees shifting in the breeze, people splayed out in the sand. Around three o'clock the foursome retired to the terrace at Poponi's and ordered a round of beers. A few minutes later Jobert came up to them and said he had seen them smoking *bhang* on the beach, and wanted to search their bags and arrest them. The staff and the other customers at Poponi's laughed at this, and finally several Kenyans shooed Jobert away. But half an hour later he came back with some police. The police said a complaint had been filed and it was their duty to search the bags. They searched, but found nothing. Still, they arrested the four *wazungu* and escorted them back to the inn.

The innkeeper again: "When the police come here they go up to the room. When they come back down, they say they have found some *bhang* hidden in a canopy. They show a tiny plastic bag, enough maybe for two joints—three if you make them small. The tourists say they do not know who it belongs to. Maybe some other tourist left it there from last year. Everybody thinks maybe the police brought it with them. Sometimes things can be put on you, you know. But nobody says this. The police say that since no one will confess, they must arrest everyone. They arrest all four, plus two others who are staying here. None of these people are guilty of anything—this is just politics. A lot of Lamu people are upset. These things are bad for us. Bad for tourism. This is not Lamu people doing this. This is the government. You write that down."

That afternoon I took a long solitary walk. Lamu still looked like paradise, with its palm trees and *dhows* and the small waves still flipping themselves up onto the long empty beaches; but it seemed less innocent now. Poponi's was as subdued as the Yellow Cab lot the day after a cab driver is murdered: people clucking and shaking their heads and asking each other *Did you know him?* and trying to convince themselves that the same thing will never happen to them.

That evening Kirk didn't come down to dinner. "The malaria hit him a few hours ago," said Tom Sampson, an Australian staying in the room next to mine.

And Lamu's magic spell was broken.

I bought tickets for the boat to the mainland and the bus ride to Mombasa, and on morning seventy-five of my trip I boarded the launch for the ride back to reality. While the boat's crew paced the waterfront screaming *Moooohm...BAH-saah! Moooohm...BAH-saah!* and the captain struggled to start the engine, I found a spot among the cases of empty beer bottles. Up on the balcony of the lodge where I had spent the past ten nights, I saw several *wazungu* waving good-bye. It felt awfully peculiar to have hiking shoes on my feet again.

43

The Best Money Can Buy

Applying for a difficult visa turns any traveler into a coward.
—THURSTON CLARKE, *Equator*

A month had passed since I'd met Dave and Julie Stone in Egypt, but their invitation to visit Tanzania (*"When you sit on our living room sofa and look out the window, you see a perfectly framed view of Kilimanjaro."*) had been on my mind ever since. Having lingered in Lamu, I no longer had the five or six days needed to climb the big mountain, only enough to bask briefly in its presence.

I stopped in Mombasa overnight and paid a visit to the six imprisoned *wazungu*. They all swore their innocence, but said they were not being mistreated and that they expected to survive their one-month sentences without too much difficulty.

The next morning—with only three days remaining before my flight from Nairobi to Harare, Zimbabwe—I boarded a bus to the Tanzanian border. After Lamu's bustling camaraderie, I savored the anonymous feeling of being the lone *mzungu* on an old and battered bus headed to a place I'd never been. And, as we were now moving away from the Indian Ocean's coastal malaria zone, I felt I'd accomplished something by escaping with my health.

The road was a narrow blacktop that rolled out engineer-straight for an hour at a time over a gradually rising plain covered with thorn trees, gnarled thickets, and twisted cactus—a living definition of the word *bush*. Through the window I saw red dirt trails leading off into the lacy tangle of scrub. A hawk glided across the road and landed atop a solitary flame tree, bare but for two orange blossoms. Women wearing gaudy green, blue, and purple dresses and even gayer scarves walked beside the road. Men, some of them sporting old rifles, tried to flag us down but our driver stopped for no one.

In Mombasa I had changed some dollars on the black market, and nearing the border I became tense, worrying that a zealous Kenyan customs inspector might gripe about the inconsistencies on my currency declaration. But I was not the only one with things to hide. Other passengers nervously adjusted their bundles, and across the aisle I saw one man stuffing wads of cash into his wife's blouse.

As we filed off the bus at the border, I saw our driver and a male border guard stroll behind a tree and exchange a fat roll of bills. A female border guard harassed one of our female passengers, yelling and gesturing angrily toward the woman's bulging gunny sack; but when the woman pressed something small into the guard's palm, the harangue abruptly ended.

When I stepped into the office marked FOREIGNERS, I found an official who apparently had bigger concerns than low-budget *wazungu*. He was whispering with a man from my bus, and stopped just long enough to glance at my passport and currency declaration, stamp them, and wave me away. As I passed through his doorway the whispers resumed.

But when we had cleared Kenyan customs, changed to a Tanzanian bus, and driven across the two-mile no-man's-land, I found that I had been worrying about the wrong thing. The Tanzanian customs compound was innocuous-looking: two small sheds, a row of simple homes where the inspectors and their families lived, and a flagpole and large baobab tree dominating the center of the compound. But when my turn at the processing counter arrived, the Tanzanian official looked up from my passport and said, "Where is your visa?"

"I am expecting to get it from you," I said. Richard Ownor, chief of Mombasa's Immigration Office, had assured me this was standard.

"Impossible," the official said, and pushed my passport back across the counter. His furrowed brow gave his face a sour expression. "Visas must be procured outside the country."

"But..."

"Next!" he called, and the second person in line stepped forward around me.

Stomach knotting, I moved toward the door. By the bus the driver and a group of men were huddled in a circle, laughing, flashing fistfuls of money at each other. Birds fluttered in and out of the baobab. A blue-green-black-gold flag hung limply against a pole. *Tanzania*, I thought. Was it possible I would be turned back at the border? Possible I would come this close to Kilimanjaro, but never see it?

I needed to do something productive, and fast. The bus would leave when everyone was cleared, and I would be stuck. Sunset was an hour away, and there would be no more buses headed back to Kenya until tomorrow. If I walked the two miles back to the border, I might, with luck, find a truck or car heading back to Mombasa. If each of the known variables and all of the unknown ones worked out in my favor, the absolute best case scenario was that by this time tomorrow I would be back at this same border crossing with a valid visa in hand.

Some situations have *baksheesh* written all over them. Once, in Poland, I had been coerced into "tipping" a train conductor two American dollars before he would give me the sleeping berth I'd already paid for. And a railway official in New Delhi suddenly found open space on a train that had been full until the moment I handed him the Bic pen he'd been admiring. But I had never bribed my way across a border. Was there some proper etiquette?

I stood and watched the official. He was all business, firing questions and scornful looks at the people from my bus, muttering all the while, and angrily flailing his rubber stamp at their passports. I had been watching him for a couple of minutes—mulling strategies and trying to contain an escalating sense of doom—when a young boy came sprinting across the compound, his bare feet kicking up bursts of dust. He brushed past me in the doorway, darted around the counter and touched his little hand to the man's thigh. Immediately the man withdrew his attention from the travelers in front of him and bent down to the boy. They spoke in Swahili, but I understood the tone: the boy had seen an amazing butterfly or patched things up with an enemy or found a half-shilling coin lying in the dirt just now, and simply *had* to tell his father. The father held the boy's hand, listened with a smile that said you-are-the-world's-most-precious-thing, and thanked the boy for his wonderful news. As the boy ran back outside, I moved a five-dollar bill from my money belt to my pants pocket, and felt newly confident about the crime I was about to commit.

When all the other passengers had been processed and were reboarding the bus, I stepped back up to the counter, took off my backpack and set it at my feet.

"How old is your son?" I asked.

"That one?" The man did not look up from his papers. "Oh, he is four, I think."

"How many children do you have?" If he was an average Tanzanian he would, I knew, have seven-point-one.

"A few." *Get to the point, kid.*

"Well, I was just thinking that it's going to cost me some shillings to go back to Mombasa for a visa. And I was thinking that it's a shame I can't just get my visa here. And I thought that maybe, instead, I could contribute my shillings toward your son's education."

"Hmmmn." He looked up at me, not without interest.

"Do you think we might possibly work that out?"

He looked back at his paperwork. "Maybe."

"What would help?" I asked.

"Give me your documents."

I pushed them across the counter. He ignored my passport and went straight for the currency declaration form. "You have dollars," he said.

"A few," I said. "Maybe I could contribute five dollars."

"Twenty."

"Twenty dollars!" Twenty dollars was the average Tanzanian's monthly income and would cover a week in a cheap hotel; on Lamu it would pay for lodging, meals, and drinks at Poponi's for two and a half days. "That's a fortune," I said. "Five is the most I can afford."

The man shrugged.

"Well, thanks anyway," I said. I bent down and, slowly, casually, as though walking all the way back to Mombasa was no big deal to a swashbuckler like me, hoisted my pack. I snapped my waist belt and deliberated over the right snugness for my shoulder straps, conscious all the while of his eyes on me. "I guess I'll be heading back to Kenya now," I said, moving toward the door. I stopped on the threshold. "I'll get a visa in Mombasa. Be back tomorrow. Or maybe the next day."

As I turned away, I heard the magic words. "Just a moment."

I straddled the doorway. The man moved from the counter to his desk, pulled a sheet of paper from a drawer, and with his chin in his palm pretended to study it, as though not he, but this important document determined my fate. He returned to the counter and nodded me over. "Five dollars will be O.K.," he said. I laid the bill on the counter, and he vacuumed it into his trouser pocket with the practiced ease of a casino dealer. "How many days would you like?"

"Three will be plenty," I said.

"I will give you even a week." He banged my passport three times, as though killing a particularly tough scorpion, and smiled easily now. "Tell me," he snorted, "would you really walk back to Kenya?"

"I was surely thinking about it. Twenty dollars is a lot of money."

"To me, yes," he said. "For you, maybe. But I meet many people who think it is nothing. Very few pretend they are going to walk back to Kenya."

"I'm sorry," I said. "I really should have come with a visa."

"Oh, no," he said. "Better this way for both of us. I help you; you help me."

"Well," I said. "I do hope your son gets a good education."

"Oh, he will," said the man. "The best money can buy."

44

Kibo and Mawenzi

In the late 1800s, German and British diplomats were working to establish the border between Tanzania and Kenya when they deadlocked over who should get Kilimanjaro. The story goes that Queen Victoria intervened. "We've already got Mt. Kenya," she said. "And it's King Wilhelm's birthday; give him Kilimanjaro as a birthday present and let's be done with it." And a little zigzag was drawn around Kilimanjaro, and if you look at a map of Africa, you'll see it's still there today.

—DAVE STONE, Moshi, Tanzania

Within a few kilometers of the border a dramatic change of scenery occurred, the scrub giving way to a cornucopian landscape. Stretching away from both sides of the two-lane blacktop were fields of tall green grasses that looked fresh from the Creator's imagination; grab a handful and squeeze, I thought, and surely a quart of clear, sweet water would pour forth. Thousands of bright yellow sunflowers, six, seven, eight feet tall, rose above the grasses like curious, innocent eyes. To the right were the foothills of Kilimanjaro, gentle knolls carpeted by the lush grasses and dotted by groves of brilliant flame trees. In the western distance, sunlight leaked through a seam in the sky and hung like a curtain of gold lace across the countryside. I thought: Now *I can say I've been to Tanzania.*

My map showed we should be bumping into Kilimanjaro any time now, but a haze kept it obscured. I'd been scanning the horizon since early morning, and had begun to empathize with the professional geographers of 1850s Europe, who had sniffed at early explorers' reports of Kilimanjaro. A snowcapped peak, they said, could not possibly exist just three degrees south of the equator.

My fellow passengers were in the midst of their own dramatic transformation, their daylong mood of solemnity turning jocular. The man across the aisle from me was the same man I'd seen whispering with the customs official back on the Kenyan side of the border. Now he leaned over, and asked, "And what are you smuggling, my friend?"

"Nothing," I told him. "I'm just a tourist."

"Yes," he said, smiling broadly. His nose was the wide, squashed nose of an unlucky boxer. "We are all tourists on this bus. This is what it says on our visas: *Tourists*."

He was saying this as much for my benefit as for the benefit of those eavesdropping in the rows around us; they were men mostly, and now they all laughed lustily. *Heh-heh-heh-heh*.

"But we," the man went on, "consider ourselves businessmen. Supply and demand. Free market economy. But let me tell you, we are all smugglers." He was wearing a loose shirt, jade green like the landscape out the window, and covered with images of red and orange flowers. The pockets of his baggy trousers bulged, and he wore his hair in the bushy Afro style popular in America during the 1960s. He had, I thought, hiding places for hundreds of bank notes.

"But whatever you call us," he said, "*we* are what is keeping Tanzania's economy alive. Three years ago our shilling and the Kenyan shilling traded at one to one. There was *no* black market. But let me tell you, the Tanzanian shilling has fallen like it was rolling down the side of Kilimanjaro. Our government still says that our shillings are as valuable as Kenyan shillings, but everyone knows it is not true. On the black market we must give ten Tanzanian shillings to buy just one Kenyan shilling. To put money in the government's bank is the same thing as burning it in your hearth. Everyone worries that soon the Tanzanian shilling will be worth nothing, so they come to us and beg us to take their shillings to Kenya and trade them on the black market. For our service," he said, "we receive a small commission."

Heh-heh-heh, snickered the men behind us. Even the driver looked back and flashed a grin.

I said, "I suppose you must pay off the border guards."

"Some days pay, some days not. But of course we are careful to keep them happy. And *they* are careful to keep *us* happy. And you," he said. "Did you make the inspector happy?"

All the men leaned in to hear me tell the story of my visa. At the end I asked, "What do you think—was five dollars enough?"

"Oh, whatever you agree to is fair," said the lead smuggler. "Supply and demand. Democracy. Even if the inspector pretends to be angry, let me tell you, he is always happy to see a tourist with no visa. If you already have a visa, what will he get? Nothing. We think that maybe he even pays the people in Mombasa to send him tourists with no visas."

"Really?" I thought of Richard Ownor, whom I had come to regard quite fondly. "Do you know the people in Mombasa?"

"No," said the man. "But I know Africa."

As we were talking I glanced outside. The sky had cleared considerably, and now to my surprise and delight Mt. Kilimanjaro's snowy bulk loomed high above us against a background of burnished blue. It startled me that something large enough to blot out half the sky could stay hidden until we were right on it. The haze still clung to the mountain's lower slopes, creating the impression that Kilimanjaro had a detached peak: a base and a top, but no middle.

"Ahh," said the smuggler. "The sisters. They are showing off for you. Usually they cloud up this time of day."

"The sisters?"

"There are two tops. You see? These are the sisters—Kibo and Mawenzi."

Kilimanjaro once had the same classic shape as Japan's Mt. Fuji, but eons ago its volcanic cone collapsed inward, leaving behind two peaks. The western peak—the one to the left, the one to which people refer when they say *I climbed Kilimanjaro*—rose to 19,340 feet, with symmetrical sides and a year round snowcap. The eastern peak was bare, dirty brown, flinty, and, at 16,892 feet, significantly shorter.

"The pretty one is Kibo," said the smuggler. "The ugly one is Mawenzi. Let me tell you a story about them," and by his cadence I knew he had told it many times. "One cold day the fire in ugly Mawenzi's hearth went out, so she set out for the house of her pretty

264

sister Kibo to see if she might borrow a few embers. Kibo asked Mawenzi to come in and please stay for a while. In our country it is considered quite rude not to invite a visitor to come inside, even a stranger or an ugly sister. It is also rude to accept too quickly, so Mawenzi said no. But when Kibo asked again, as she must, Mawenzi said, 'Well, maybe just a little.'

"A pot of food was simmering on Kibo's fire, and again, since she did not want to be rude, Kibo asked if Mawenzi could not eat with them. Mawenzi said no, she had to be going. But when Kibo insisted, she said, 'Well, maybe just a mouthful.'

"Kibo was not only prettier, but also a much better cook than Mawenzi, so she spooned up some of her hot, delicious potage. Mawenzi gulped it all down, collected her fire, and said good-bye, but when she was only halfway home, Mawenzi found that she was still hungry. And she remembered her empty wood pile. She thought also of how she was not a good cook like Kibo. And since it was cold and also raining, she turned around and went back to Kibo's.

"Kibo invited her in of course, and of course Mawenzi ate some more of Kibo's delicious food. Then she left again. But before she arrived home, she remembered all the same things as before, and she turned back to Kibo's house. Now her excuse was that her borrowed embers had gone out. But this time Kibo grabbed the pestle for grinding her maize, and with that she gave Mawenzi a good beating. And that is why this evening you see these dents and bumps on Mawenzi's ugly head."

The bus and my smuggler friends headed on to Arusha after dropping me in the center of small, quiet Moshi. It was the magical hour before dark, and Kilimanjaro hovered over us like an attentive bodyguard. Moshi lay in the plains on the mountain's southern, rainy side—distant enough to avoid Kilimanjaro's daily afternoon showers, but close enough to drink of the runoffs. This was one of the most fertile areas in all of Africa.

I'd already had several enchanting views of Kilimanjaro, but none more so than the view from the Stone's sofa. As promised, the mountain was perfectly centered in their living room window, a vision framed by morning glory vines. In the yard an emerald and tangerine colored bird was perched in a mango tree, and another, vivid black and white, in a banana tree. Even indoors, the honeyed air gave the impression that the world's perfume industry was headquartered in Moshi. Watching the light change Kilimanjaro's snowcap from pink to scarlet to purple, I wondered whether Queen Victoria would have been quite so cavalier about the Crown's real estate if she had come to Moshi, whiffed the jasmine and frangiapani, and watched an imperial sunset.

Dave and Julie were from Oregon, an attractive, tennis-playing couple in their mid-twenties, and had been in Moshi for almost two years. Julie had arrived with a contract to teach music at the local American school; Dave, a newspaper reporter, had arrived planning to spend his time writing freelance articles on Africa. But while they'd both loved being here, Dave had begun to feel increasingly isolated— cut off from editors, uncertain what subjects to write about. Over a dinner of chicken and rice, served by their Tanzanian maid, N'dena, we talked about Dave and Julie's recent decision to return to Oregon.

"Thousands of people would think we're absolutely crazy," Dave said. "Oregon's beautiful, but when we leave here, we'll probably never again live in a place so lush, so stunning. We'll never know this level of luxury—someone to cook and clean for us!"

"Or top the vacations we've had," Julie said.

Early on they had bought a used Land Rover, and, while Julie's school was not in session, had driven several thousand miles exploring Africa. Julie was paid an American salary, and even with their trips, they'd been able to bank 90 percent of it.

But Dave was feeling he'd strayed about as far from his journalism career as was wise, maybe even farther. *This gap in your resume, Mr. Stone, where it says only 'Tanzania'—would you mind explaining that?* In May, a month before Julie's term was up, Dave was going home to look for a job and a place for the two of them to live.

Theirs was a dilemma I could relate to. I think of my traveling self as better, more wide awake, more relaxed and open than the dullard I am familiar with at home. My stay-at-home self, hypnotized and numbed by America's competing distractions, often despairs of hope for the world. But when I buckle on my backpack, lace up my walking shoes, and travel to some distant peaceful place, everything seems fresh and full of promise. Almost nothing seems impossible.

And I've often wondered what would happen to my traveling sensibility if I were to move to one of the dreamy places I've visited—Lamu, for instance, or Moshi. Would I stay relaxed and open forever, or all too soon find myself hypnotized and numbed again, and antsy to go traveling? If living in San Francisco can't boost a person into a state of perpetual ecstasy and optimism, what place on Earth might?

During dessert the lights went out. "Happens once in a while," Julie said, lighting candles. "Would you like a hot bath? Now's the time—before the water in the water heater goes cold."

Julie surrounded the tub with candles, and I took a stack of recent periodicals—*Newsweek, Esquire,* the *Christian Science Monitor*—into the bathroom with me. But as I sat in my first bath in months and leafed through them—catching up on the serial killers and political scandals of a distant home that, from Moshi, seemed bizarre and frightening—my mind was still mulling the Stones' decision to return home.

Certainly I could understand how in Moshi—with fruit bursting from every branch, a wife bringing home bushels of money, a gorgeous mountain sprouting in the picture window, and drunk on the smells of honeysuckle and roses—a career would be an easy thing to misplace. But it was hard for me not to think that in six months Dave and Julie would be sitting on a living room sofa with a view of Interstate 5, watching television sitcoms and kicking themselves.

My night of speaking West Coast American English had been a delight. Throughout my trip, and even on Lamu, I most often found myself lurching through conversations in "backpacker-ese" with English-speakers of every conceivable accent and ability. But the Stones knew every nuance of my English, and I caught every inflection in theirs. The ease and familiarity came as a relief.

And now it occurred to me that I should anticipate a point in my visitor's trip to America where he might yearn for the tastes and sounds of home. I was hardly a rookie traveler, yet I knew the occasional twinge of loneliness. The Stones had each other plus a homey community at the American school, but their compass was still clearly pointed toward America. Whoever came to visit me would be leaving his country, culture, and comfort zone for the first time. It would be unwise of me to expect him to take everything in stride. I should be prepared to deal with a new phenomenon—*someone else's* bout of homesickness.

America had enclaves of immigrants from just about every culture on the globe. San Francisco had a large Filipino community, and at the cab lot I had met hundreds of drivers from India, Egypt, and East Africa. Before my friend arrived I would be smart, I told myself, to visit a few of his culture's restaurants, cultivate a resource or two from his community. Might he want a meal from home on his first evening in America, or would he prefer to share the salad I usually threw together in my kitchen? And what, I wondered, what in the world would he be thinking that first night, bathing in my tub, lying in my spare bed halfway around the world?

45

Honest George

"Write and tell us if you (re)turn. We think you (re)turn. Because why? We think that you shall never forget us. Because why? We think that you remembered still our face and our mother's names."

—KAMANTE, houseboy
quoted by Isak Dinesen in *Out of Africa*

After lunch on day seventy-eight Dave and I drove north from Moshi toward Kilimanjaro's foothills. Just outside town the pavement ended and the road became a collection of red-tinted ruts and potholes. Our goal was a waterfall located some six thousand feet high on the side of Kilimanjaro. Dave had never been to it, but a guide-book printed by a Moshi hiking club gave vague directions, and we thought we'd give it a shot.

As we began gaining altitude, we lost sight of the peak. Thick green jungle appeared on both sides of the road, and cool, damp air enveloped us, taking the edge off the midday heat. We passed fields of banana trees with leaves the size of small aircraft wings, and plots of coffee bushes adroop with beans. Wherever a farmer had cleared the land we saw dark soil so spongy-looking that I imagined if we stopped and jumped on it, it would toss us like a trampoline. Jacarandas and flame trees—purple and red and orange and yellow—challenged my eyes' and my mind's ability to process. I heard an embarrassing series of *Wows* and *This is beautifuls* falling from my mouth, and, after a while, just shut up and stared.

We passed a group of children who stood at the side of the road, gaping wide-eyed at us; a few turned and fled into the forest.

"Shy," I said.

"No," said Dave, "scared. Their parents tell them stories about *wazungu* who will carry them off if they don't do their chores. Also we look pale and sickly to them. *Wazungu* take some getting used to."

There were older Tanzanians walking up the road (Kilimanjaro has no bus service), and the sound of our motor made hitchhikers of them all. Dave picked up as many as could fit into the back. Some had been shopping in Moshi, but most wore laborer's clothes and had spent the day working in the fields. One young man wore a clean white sport shirt, creased gray trousers, shiny black tie shoes, and now, in thickly accented English, he asked my name.

"*Bread?*" he said, when I told him.

"Brad."

"Bread?"

"O.K.," I said. "Bread."

"My name is Oh-ness, Bread."

"*Oh-ness?*"

"No," he said. "Oh-ness."

"*Ernest?*" I tried.

"Oh, O.K.," he said.

Ernest had a wide, open face, an easy smile, and a large head that he carried perfectly upright on his small body. His right thumb was wrapped in a messy, iodine-soaked bandage; that morning, he said, he had cut himself with a knife and headed for the hospital in Moshi to have it treated.

"Does it hurt?"

"Oh, I don't care about it," he said.

The guidebook's directions were sketchy. Eleven kilometers past a certain fork in the road a line of tall fir trees would appear on the right. Immediately past the firs we should turn down an overgrown path just wide enough for one vehicle and follow it until we came to a *shamba*, a farm. We should ask the *shamba*'s inhabitants to guard our vehicle and point us toward the falls.

But the Land Rover's odometer was broken, and soon after we

passed the indicated fork, Dave and I began studying every fir and every overgrown path, wondering how to choose. The guidebook was several years old; the firs might long ago have been chopped down or the path swallowed by jungle.

An hour from Moshi we had picked up and dropped off dozens of passengers, and now only Ernest remained. When Dave asked where he lived, Ernest said Kishimundu, a tiny village already several kilometers behind us. After overhearing us talk, he explained, he had decided to come with us and guide us to the falls. He'd never been to them either; all his life he'd been intending to go but had never gotten around to it. Clearly, he said, this was all meant to be. Just think about it. If he had not cut his thumb this morning, he'd have never gone to town. If he'd never gone to town, he'd have never been walking on the road when we came by. And if he weren't with us, we'd never find the right fir trees; but he knew the very ones we were talking about.

"Sounds good to me," Dave said.

Still, as we passed several groups of firs and several overgrown paths, and as Ernest said *Not these—further* each time, Dave and I began wondering how much faith to put in him. If he'd never *been* to the falls, how was he so sure of himself?

We came to a group of exceptionally tall firs.

"No," said Ernest. "Is further." The road narrowed until it was a path itself—wide enough now for just one vehicle. "Yes, is further," Ernest kept saying from the back seat, and we kept going.

Finally he said, "Next part." And around the bend we came upon a straight line of firs twice the height of any seen so far. Beyond them was an opening in the forest—tall with weeds and barely wide enough for the Land Rover. A cow, standing in the middle of the opening, eyed us with a mixture of interest and terror, and when Dave steered toward it, the cow turned and ambled slowly down the lane. We followed three paces behind, knocking down four-foot weeds that fell under the hood and scraped noisily on the underside of the chassis, until we reached a large vegetable garden, and behind it a small house. A woman and several little children stood in the doorway. When Dave killed the motor the children ran to us and began tracing their fingers gently across the Land Rover's dusty finish.

The house and garden were set on a cleared bluff at the edge of the mountain. While Dave and Ernest traded *Jambo*s with the woman and explained our presence, I moved past the garden to the clearing's edge and studied the view. We were in Kilimanjaro's cloud-forest zone. Thick clouds churned above like cavorting gray whales. A mixture of ferns and fir trees cloaked the nearby slopes, and, wherever possible, farmers had cleared small level plots for coffee and bananas. Moshi's cluster of crossroads, basking in sunshine on the plains, miles away and thousands of feet below us, looked like a caveman's dream: a nirvana with electricity, a hospital, and bathtubs above which the twist of a knob produced instant hot water.

The woman gave Dave a gift of several bananas and assigned two of her young sons to accompany us—down a fir-lined trail that occasionally opened to views of jungle-covered ridges falling away below us and clouds rolling through the forests above. The barefoot kids bolted ahead and Dave went after them, but Ernest's slick-bottomed go-to-town shoes held him back with me, and now he unloaded a barrage of questions. What did my father do? Was I married? In America, at what age will a man marry a woman? How many women? In America did everyone own a Land Rover? Did I know anyone in America who owned a store?

When I had a chance to interview him, I learned that Ernest was twenty years old, the eldest of five children. His father was a subsistence farmer and his family's life a hard one, but Ernest was determined to make it better. Two months ago he had opened a small store, the only store in Kishimundu; if his neighbors wanted things like soap, biscuits, or ballpoint pens, they no longer had to walk down the mountain to another village. They could come to Ernest. But owning a store wasn't as easy as everyone thought, he said. Keeping it stocked was expensive and complicated; the suppliers wanted cash for almost everything, and deliveries often didn't arrive for weeks. But the people of his village expected Ernest to provide credit and were slow to pay; or worse, they expected *zawadi kidogo*—little gifts—for patronizing Ernest's store. It was strange, he said; since he'd become a merchant, they all thought he'd somehow automatically become rich.

English was difficult for Ernest, and I was relieved when Dave fell back to join us and the two of them lapsed into Swahili. As they talked,

I ruminated on Ernest as a visitor to America. He seemed energized from his trip to Moshi. What would he make of a real city? And who more than he would truly appreciate a fully-stocked Safeway?

A few moments later Dave and Ernest fell silent. When Ernest walked out ahead of us, Dave remarked to me: "Having a shop is a big deal up here. George has literally become one of the most important men on this section of the mountain."

"George?"

"That's his name," Dave said.

George —Opening a kiosk-sized store high on the slopes of Kilimanjaro had made him, at twenty, one of the most important men on the mountain.

"He told me it was Ernest. Or Oh-ness, maybe."

"Let's see," Dave said. "*George!*" he called, and up ahead our guide spun around.

"I thought your name was Ernest," I told him.

"*Oh-ness*," he said. "Oh-ness George."

Dave said, "Oh-ness? Is that Swahili?"

"No. English. I write for you."

I produced pen and notebook. "Ernest" wrote *Honest George*. "Is my good business name," he said. "Oh-ness George. So people will know they can trust me."

The falls turned out to be several wispy trickles that dropped thirty feet into a small pool. "It's not Niagara," Dave said, "but I'm glad we saw it."

Honest George seemed particularly enlivened. "Does anything in America compare to Kilimanjaro?" he asked. As we hiked back over the

273

now-muddy trail, he asked if I had a camera. He had a camera, he said, but no batteries. Batteries were the most difficult item to keep in stock—everyone needed them for flashlights and radios. Could I take his picture and send it to him? He would very much like to receive a letter from America.

As we'd been walking, the air had been cooling, and now the clouds thickened and lowered and wind began gusting through the branches. Rain fell furiously for five minutes, drenching everyone, but before we reached the Land Rover, the sun had returned and all our clothes had dried. Dave tipped the woman a few shillings for watching our car and for the use of her sons; she gave us a papaya.

On the way down the mountain, we stopped in the ten-hut village of Kishimundu. Honest George's shop was the size of a newspaper kiosk in downtown San Francisco, but he insisted we squeeze inside, knee-to-knee and shoulder-to-shoulder, and drink warm bottled beers with him. Dave was right: Honest George was now a Kilimanjaro VIP. He barked an order and a young boy ran and fetched a plate of smoked fish for all of us to share. He punched a Bob Marley tape into his boom box, and no one seemed to mind the warbling caused by half-dead batteries.

Arranged on the mostly-empty shelves were stocks of school note-books, ballpoint pens, steel wool, coffee, tea, margarine, tins of sardines, cans of animal fat, packaged biscuits, bars of soap, jars of petroleum jelly, and—even here—bottles of warm Pepsi *and* Coca-Cola. Honest George's biggest seller was Marlboro cigarettes, which he sold mostly one at a time to the teenagers and young boys who hung around the shop gawking at the three of us. In this village, where time meant little, half of them proudly wore wristwatches.

I tried to pay Honest George for his hospitality, but he wouldn't have it. "I am so happy we have met," he told Dave and me. He raised his bandaged thumb. "This is the best bad thing that ever happened to me."

Before we left I took a picture of Honest George sitting on the front bumper of Dave's Land Rover. The teenagers hanging around the shop insisted I take one of them, too. When we climbed into our seats, Honest George thanked Dave in Swahili and then came to my window. He lowered his voice and looked me in the eye. "Do not forget me," he said, "I will be wanting to see the snaps. I will be waiting for your letter."

"I'll send it," I promised, and wondered if it might not contain somewhat more of a surprise than he was counting on.

46

Mzee

All nations lay claim to Africa, but none has wholly possessed her yet. In time she will be taken, yielding neither to Nazi nor to Fascist conquest, but to integrity equal to her own and to wisdom capable of understanding her wisdom and of discerning between wealth and fulfillment. Africa is less a wilderness than a repository of primary and fundamental values, and less a barbaric land than an unfamiliar voice. Barbarism, however bright its trappings, is still alien to her heart.

—BERYL MARKHAM, *West With the Night*

"There's someone I think you should meet," Dave said. We were back on the outskirts of Moshi now. "He lives up another part of the mountain, and it might take some looking before we can find him, but I really think you'll appreciate it."

The truth was that I was hungry, worn out, and by now plenty tired of bouncing around in the Land Rover. A full round of buses and taxis lay ahead of me the next day and my flight to Zimbabwe the next. And for the past several hours I'd been picturing a quiet evening at home: dinner, conversation, another hot bath, another dose of *Esquire*, *Newsweek*, and the *Christian Science Monitor*. "Won't Julie be expecting us for dinner?" I said.

"Oh, she'll understand," Dave said. "It's your one day here. I can't stand the thought of you leaving without meeting this guy." *Trust me. Please.*

We drove across the plain east of Moshi for several kilometers. Past a roadhouse named the "Golden Shower Restaurant" we turned onto a dirt road leading to a dusty little village—two blocks of barrack-like shanties huddled around a grocery store and a bar.

"The guy I eventually want you to meet is one hundred-ten years old," Dave said, stopping in front of the bar. "But right now I'm trying to find his grandson, a guy named Franklin Njombo. Franklin's married, but just about every night he meets a girlfriend at this bar. No one's supposed to know, but everyone does. I'll be right back." Dave disappeared into the bar.

Women with babies slung across their frontsides sauntered down the dirt road, and looked curiously at the stranger sitting in the Land Rover. A pack of screaming children—several furious girls chasing two scared boys—ran across the road and disappeared behind the bar. A rust-colored dog drank from a rust-colored puddle. A cow searched for a lost contact lens in a nearby patch of weeds. And above us, clear again this evening, were Kibo, her snowlined cheeks rouged with the last light of day, and poor Mawenzi, bare and brown.

Dave returned, shaking his head. "Not here," he said, and I hoped he'd call off the expedition and head back toward Moshi, toward dinner and hot water and slick magazines. Instead: "We'll have to head up the mountain."

We started back up the slopes of Kilimanjaro, traveling on a different dirt road than the one we'd traveled in the afternoon. It was dusk now, and groups of people were streaming up toward their homes. Dave again kept the back filled with hitchhikers. As they departed, several came to Dave's window to shake his hand, and I didn't need to know any Swahili to interpret their smiles: Keep this up, and you're going to give *wazungu* a good name.

In the last remnants of twilight we parked high up the mountain in a driveway surrounded by banana trees. Dave shut the engine off and told our passengers that this was the end of the ride. They emptied out, tossing us *thank yous* and *asante sanas*, and disappeared up the road.

"I think this is the right place," Dave said. "You wait. I'll go see if Franklin's wife knows where he is."

Dave walked down the drive to the house, a neat, one-story building of wood and brick, its roof level with the tree line. I thought: *Why not two stories?* From the present windows one would see only leaves and trees and vines: but a second floor would allow a spectacular view over the jungle treetops and the fields toward Moshi, of the plains in the distance, and of Kilimanjaro's higher reaches.

"A view," Dave said, when he returned and I mentioned this to him. "I'll bet no one around here ever thought of building a place for the view: for water, soil, transport—yes, for the view—never."

Franklin Njombo's wife had told Dave she had no idea where Franklin was (I doubted this) but she suggested we try the store Franklin's cousin had recently opened just down the road. We left the car in the driveway and walked, picking our way over the ruts. Already it was dark and stars were poking out one by one. "I should have brought a flashlight," Dave said.

Franklin's cousin's store, like Honest George's, had been open for only two months now. But compared to George's closet, it was a supermarket: concrete floors, cinderblock walls, oil lanterns, and quadruple George's inventory. Franklin's cousin said that no, he had not seen Franklin, but he'd heard he was coming "just now." He brought two chairs out to the front porch. Dave and I sat and cut our hunger, very real now, with a package of biscuits and warm Sprite.

The way it was, Dave said, was this: Franklin Njombo was an accounting clerk in Moshi, and one of the first people the Stones had met on arrival. Once, over a year ago, Franklin had brought Dave and Julie up to see his home on the mountain and meet his grandfather, who lived just a few hundred yards from where we sat. Tanzanian hospitality aside, Dave didn't feel comfortable about returning uninvited with a new friend. He was sure, though, that if we could find Franklin, it would be arranged in an instant. But he also didn't want to spend the whole night waiting here; Franklin might be working late, might be at the bar with his girlfriend, might be any number of places. We looked out at the shadows the store's lanterns cast in the jungle, listened to the chatter of night creatures, and talked about marriage. I said I suspected that Franklin's wife had a pretty good idea about where he was right now, about who it was he saw after work every night. Yeah, Dave agreed, in a small community like Moshi it would be hard not to know; but it was something accepted here. There was a tradition of multiple wives in much of Africa, and it seemed that Franklin and his wife had reached some sort of understanding.

We'd been waiting half an hour when Dave—possibly sensing my weariness, possibly missing Julie—said he thought we should call it quits: Franklin might be gone all night. I didn't try to dissuade him. We said our good-byes to Franklin's distressed cousin—"But I am sure he is coming just now"—and started back to the Land Rover. We had walked fifty yards when we came upon a man walking toward us in the darkness.

"Stone!"

Franklin Njombo was in his late forties, an extremely short man—less than five, maybe less than four-and-a-half feet tall. But even before I'd gotten a good look at him I knew he had a big spirit. He threw his arms up to the dark night:

"Stone, where have you been for all these years? Oh, we have missed you on this mountain!" He grabbed Dave's shoulders and then pumped my hand. Of course, he said, but of course, Stone and any friend of Stone's were always welcome at his grandfather's house. "The *mzee* (revered elder) would be so horribly upset if he knew you were close and had not come. And tonight is perfect—I think they are roasting a pig."

Franklin had been walking in the dark when we'd come upon him, but for our benefit he pulled out a flashlight and led us on a ten-minute walk down the road. Cool air and a moist, decaying smell seeped from the walls of jungle to either side of us. Insects chattered; tree limbs shifted and creaked; things popped in the darkness.

We arrived at a compound of several masonry buildings. A thin layer of smoke and a delicious meat smell spiced the courtyard. It was not a pig being roasted tonight but a goat, a young boy told Franklin. We were led into the central building, into a large front room lit brightly by several lamps and occupied by a half dozen men much older than myself, and by several younger men and boys who seemed to be catering to them. There were handshakes all around, and Dave and I were given cups of homemade beer to drink and handmade wooden chairs to sit in. This was a big night, someone's birthday, and everyone was excited to have strange visitors. There were no women present, but during the evening several came into the room to bring drinks or chairs or to talk briefly with one of the men; and once in a while a pretty teenager poked her head in through the door to stare at Dave and me.

The almost total lack of interaction I'd had with local women on this trip had been gnawing at me lately. They were kept from me, it seemed. Almost never was I left alone with one: for a visitor, the Third World is a universe of men.

"The goat will be done around midnight," Njombo told us. "Stay and wait."

But it was now only eight o'clock. "We can't," Dave said. "We've had a long day, and Julie will be wondering about us."

This news was met with much disappointment as it was translated around the room. "Stone is like a son," Njombo told me, looking soulfully at Dave. "The *mzee* is always asking, 'When is my son coming?' Yes, Stone is like a son!"

Dave, who had met the *mzee* exactly once—and that more than a year earlier—looked sheepish about all this praise. "I've been meaning to come up, but you know how the time goes," he said, and those struck me indeed as the words of a son.

While I was trying to guess which of the old men was the *mzee*, he was led into the room by a young boy. He had a fragile, old-parchment-like aura and was slightly stooped, but didn't appear to really need the boy; rather the boy's assistance seemed like a privilege the *mzee* (or possibly the boy) had earned. Njombo explained to the old man that the long-lost Stone had come and, miracle of miracles, had brought a friend from America. Another writer. Njombo indicated that the *mzee* wanted me to sit beside him, and when I did, he took my nearest hand in his. He did not appear so awfully ancient; his eyes were clouded but alert and there was plenty of life in his grip. But all of the others deferred to him, and when he spoke, Njombo amplified his comments around the room so that all might benefit from them. Njombo offered to translate for me: What would I like to ask the *mzee*?

"How old is he?"

People around the room called out answers in Swahili, and when Njombo translated he said that everyone else thought the *mzee* was one hundred-ten, but the *mzee* himself was calling it one hundred-six. But everyone agreed he'd been born in the 1880s. Electricity in the home was unknown. Man had not yet flown. Cars were still decades away.

I asked if the *mzee* remembered the two world wars. Njombo had to describe them several times before the *mzee* understood, and then he waved his free hand, dismissing them. They had been unimportant. During the first one the German *wazungu* had fought a few battles with the British *wazungu*, but it hadn't amounted to much. He remembered droughts that had killed many more people.

"How many children does he have?" I asked.

The *mzee* wasn't exactly sure, but he knew that currently he had more than a hundred great-grandchildren.

"In his long life, what is the best thing that ever happened?"

The *mzee* thought for a moment, smiling to himself, his head bobbing up and down. Presently he said that there were three best things. The first, the very best, he said, pointing to the cross on the wall, was Christianity; it had given his people a new way to look at their brothers. The second was transportation; the *mzee* still liked to walk—in fact just last week he'd walked ten kilometers to have his hair cut—but it was good to be more mobile, especially during emergencies or when you wanted to visit family in far away villages. And the third best thing was the end of slavery. Slavery, said the *mzee*, was the worst thing. He was ten or twelve old years old when it ended, and vividly remembered the chiefs selling other human beings to the Arabs. (I was relieved that the slavers in this area had been Arab and not European.) This was a bad, terrible, wrong thing—you never knew when the Arabs would come, or who the chief would choose to sell. The Christians wanted this to end, the *mzee* said, and they were right. He pointed to the cross again.

The process of talking to the man was a bit tortuous. When I would ask a question, Njombo would announce it loudly to the rest of the room before putting it to the *mzee*. The room's older men would discuss my question in Swahili, often interrupting their discourse to have Dave clarify a point (invariably reaffirming that Stone was truly like a son, an *mzee* in his own right), and then Njombo would put my edited question to the old man. The old man would give a short, or sometimes a very long rambling answer; this answer would be debated at length in the room in Swahili. There would be more testimony to Stone's *mzee*-ness, and then finally, maybe ten minutes after I'd asked my question, Njombo would deliver an answer in his arabesque brand of English. It seemed that Njombo spoke two forms of English, only one of which I understood. When he spoke only to me, I understood him easily, but when he spoke to the whole room, I had trouble catching even half his words. Dave had the knack, however, and would translate for me.

After an hour Dave said it was time for us to leave. Fifteen minutes of protestations followed (the goat would be ready in just another two or three hours), then handshakes, and finally good-byes. Njombo said the *mzee* wanted me to tell everyone in America to come visit him. They had plenty of goats left and could always brew more beer.

As Njombo walked Dave and me back to the car, I found myself moved by everyone's hospitality. A visitor showing up in a Third World village is an *event*. I have never been terribly comfortable as the center of attention, although a part of me lusts for it. How would my visitor to America feel? I didn't want to overwhelm him, but I did hope he would feel welcomed, honored. A foreigner in San Francisco can go absolutely ignored: *So, you're from Baluchistan—did ya see that ball game today?* But I hoped my friends and family would fuss over my visitor, pamper him a bit, and genuinely find his presence at least fractionally as remarkable as these people on Kilimanjaro seemed to find mine.

When we reached the Land Rover parked in his driveway, Njombo blocked Dave from the driver's door with his body and said, "An hour ago I sent my son to tell my wife to fix a small dinner. Now you must join me."

I laughed when I heard Dave, who had been called *son* and *mzee* too many times this evening to refuse, say, "We can only stay a short while, Njombo. I have a wife at home, too."

"Yes, but Julie would want you to eat with us. And my wife is like the *mzee*—she is always asking me, 'When is *Mzee* Stone coming to visit

282

us? He has not been here in such a long time.' So you must come in and touch one spoon," he said, "and then you can go."

By candlelight, at Njombo's dining room table, we ate a large and tasty meal with two of Franklin's adult sons—tomatoes, onions, potatoes (both fried and mashed), popcorn, mangos, tea, and cow milk. We were served by a woman who looked roughly my own age. I wondered how she fit into this equation—was she a distant relative, the wife of a son, or hired help? But as she tiptoed noiselessly through the ring of darkness surrounding the table, serving and removing platters, no one introduced her, no one even spoke to her. I smiled at her and said thank you a couple of times; she smiled back graciously, but said nothing.

The meal was easily one of the most pleasing of my entire trip. "And every single item," Njombo said proudly, "was produced right here on this homestead."

In his own house, away from the excitement of the *mzee*'s circus, Njombo's English was easily understandable. And he did his best to make sure that I, the writer from America, saw the slopes of Mt. Kilimanjaro as civilized and not as some savage backward place. Sitting erect, the wobbling candlelight dancing on his white shirt and still snuggly-knotted tie, he told me, "I think that people in America, when they think of an African village, they do not even think we have permanent houses. I think sometimes people in the West believe we run around without clothes, blowing darts at each other and eating monkeys. But you have seen, we are not naked here in our villages. Tell people that you sat at dinner with a savage who was educated by the British, that you sat on chairs and ate with silverware. Please, won't you have some more po-tah-tos?"

I was truly touched by the evening—not just by the unexpected meal, but by everything: the torrent of hospitality; the sense of fecundity and magic permeating the mountainside; the act of holding hands for an hour with a contemporary of my grandfathers, both dead more than forty years; and by Njombo: living without electricity, spreading a late night meal grown in his back yard, and concerned that the world should regard him as a modern man.

Sometime around eleven we were standing in the driveway. I believe I was able to hide my surprise when the woman who had wordlessly served our meal sidled up next to Njombo and the two of them slipped their arms around each other's shoulders. "This is my wife," Njombo said proudly. And now three small children crowded in around us and were also introduced.

We made small talk—nice to meet you, delicious meal, lovely kids, great home—but I don't remember much of it. I only remember that I stood there thinking: *She tiptoed around serving our food, filling our glasses, and no one—not her husband, not her sons, not even Stone—acknowledged her!* In America a waiter, a garbage hauler, even the lowly cab driver, is treated with more outward respect.

But Njombo's wife seemed to nurture no grudge. She stood there beaming, looking genuinely at peace with herself, seemingly proud of the way we'd emptied all her platters. Knowing about his girlfriend, I had judged Njombo harshly even before meeting him. Now I looked at the couple's obvious pride and affection for each other, and knew that I knew far too little about them or their culture to be haughtily critical of it. Njombo was wealthy in ways I could not approach: he had a solid profession, a piece of fertile land and his own house, several children and innumerable relatives, apparent health, and an enduring marriage. I might learn a few things from him: how to grow food, raise kids, respect an elder, make a stranger feel welcomed.

"*Bwana,*" Franklin told me, "you are always welcome here. Dave is a great man and he is always welcome here, and you are a *bwana*, and always welcome here. This village will always remember you."

Five minutes later Dave stopped the Land Rover in the middle of the road. We got out to relieve ourselves. "Shut off the lights," I said, "and the engine."

The jungle, the crops, and all the *shambas* between the Indian Ocean and the Atlantic were asleep, gathering strength to attack the next dawn. The air smelled of coffee, honey, sex—as delicious as Mrs. Njombo's meal. The sky, a moonless sieve, leaked precious drops of silver and gold. As I stared upward, I identified a feeling I rarely have at home, but have almost routinely when traveling: the palpable sense that this evening, this morning, this bus ride, this conversation, this silence, this thought, is vitally significant. Thank God, I hadn't skipped Kilimanjaro. I had dallied on Lamu, had almost turned back at the Tanzanian border, and several hours ago, when Dave had suggested this lark, it was all I could do not to whimper in favor of home and hearth, a magazine, and a hot bath.

I heard Dave peeing in the dirt to my left.

"*Mzee*," I said.

Out of the darkness: "Yes, *bwana*?"

"Thanks for bullying me up here."

"Oh, you're welcome," he said, "but you were pretty much a pushover."

"You don't know how badly I wanted to just go back and take it easy tonight."

"Oh, I think I know," he said. "If you want to repay me, you can come to Oregon in about five years and give Julie and me a kick in the butt."

47

Now We Are Here Drinking

Anne had been thinking of a story she knew...of a dying slave who is asked by a priest where he thought he was going after death. The slave answers not to heaven, as expected, but whispers instead, with an ecstatic upward smile, "To—Africa"—and was gone.

—PHILLIPS VERNER BRADFORD AND HARVEY BLUME,
Ota Benga: The Pygmy in the Zoo

It was late in the eightieth day of my trip and thunderstorms were rumbling through southeastern Africa when my plane entered Zimbabwean airspace and began its descent. Lightning flashed on the horizons as we sailed down over lush hills broken by tremendous outcroppings of granite. Huge rivers, appearing silver under the day's gray skies, meandered through misty valleys like spools of film spilled across a cutting room floor. Neat farms checkered the broad expanses of this Montana-sized, fist-shaped country, their fields of grain giving a light yellow hue to all the greenery, and adding a hint of order.

Flying over the Middle East, across the great sandy stretches of Iran and Saudi Arabia and Egypt, I had wondered why people have fought, and so ferociously, over such a barren landscape. But flying over Zimbabwe, above the jungles and rivers and farms and bouldery highlands, as great shafts of light poked through the cloud cover to highlight this tidy homestead, that twist of river, that noble granite peak, I thought: *I see what all the fuss was about.*

In 1890, 500 white settlers financed by the British diamond baron Cecil Rhodes rolled their wagons north from South Africa, looking for new lands to settle. Within five years, following the violent suppression of the native Shona and Matabele peoples, Rhodesia was firmly under white control, a British territory. The Shona and Matabele were assigned to reservations called "Tribal Trust Territories," and required either to work four months each year on the white farms or pay a "hut tax" for the privilege of continuing to live in what had always been their homeland. They were excluded from voting, holding office, and owning land—from the very best parts of what was by all accounts a very good life. By 1950 Rhodesia's 250,000 whites enjoyed, perhaps, the world's highest standard of living, but the country's 1.5 million blacks were beginning to chafe.

In the late 1960s a guerrilla war began to disrupt the countryside. Black fighters, equipped and trained by Russia, China, East Germany, and North Korea, and based in camps in neighboring Zambia and Mozambique, attacked the huge white-owned farms that fed and employed Rhodesia's people and oiled its economy. Any white person was considered a legitimate target.

As the years dragged on, as more and more farms were destroyed and families wiped out, as stories of guerrilla atrocities swept the country, white Rhodesians began to leave. Some were upset by their government's refusal to share power with the country's blacks, whom they viewed as partners or as family. ("But we always had good relations here," was a refrain I would hear daily.) Others were unwilling to see their sons sacrificed to the war. But for many it was strictly an economic decision: if they departed early, they could get their money out and, hopefully, resume a peaceful existence in another country.

Finally, as the result of an agreement brokered in London, British-monitored elections were held in 1980. The result was no surprise: the country's population was 70 percent Shona, and Shona leader Robert Mugabe was elected prime minister in a 70 percent landslide. The country was renamed after an extensive set of eighth-century ruins ("Zimbabwe" is Bantu for "stone dwelling"), and the capital's name was changed from Salisbury to Harare—after a historic chieftain.

When I visited, Zimbabwe's population had swelled to nearly 10 million and was now more than 99 percent black (by most estimates only 50,000 whites remained). Robert Mugabe had long ago established a one-party Marxist state, and effectively appointed himself president-for-life. The once all-white government now had a single white cabinet minister, and no one was permitted to take more than US$250 a year out of the country. The economy was sputtering and prices were soaring.

The airport bus dropped me in the heart of a downtown one might find in any small, prosperous Midwestern American city: five-story office buildings, wide streets with curbs, sidewalks and no litter, and a central park, African Unity Square, that I strolled through in the dark. The people I passed were all black, and seemed to regard me and my backpack with benign curiosity. In ten minutes I reached the quiet, overgrown residential area where my hotel, the Earlside (the cheapest hotel listed in *Africa On a Shoestring*), was located. At the official exchange rate, my windowless cube cost $13.

I spent my first evening at the nearby German Club, a one-story tavern set within a grove of trees. A late model Mercedes and a Land Rover were parked among the rows of beaten sedans in the gravel parking lot. Inside, the walls were covered with posters of hilltop castles and smiling fräuleins in tight ski outfits. It was Friday night, and the customers—evenly divided between whites and blacks—were crowded around tables strewn with bottles of Castle and Lion beer, the air filled with laughter and tiers of cigarette smoke.

At the bar I ordered a Stoney Ginger Beer—a zingy, non-alcoholic drink that I would became nearly addicted to during my time in southern Africa.

"You are German?" the man on the next stool asked me, then introduced himself as Kgosie, and the next man down as his friend Jackson. They both wore fresh blue jeans and sports shirts, unbuttoned to reveal hairy chests, and reminded me of the happy black construction workers one sees celebrating quitting time in American beer commercials. The first few minutes of our conversation were pretty much one-way—them interviewing me. They learned that I had been traveling for

288

eighty days; that I'd just flown in from Nairobi; that I would spend a week in Zimbabwe, including a visit to Victoria Falls, then catch a bus to South Africa; that I was divorced, American, and that my grandmother was Czechoslovakian.

"The most beautiful girl I ever knew," said Jackson, "was Czech. Her name was Helga."

"Last time you said her name was Olga," Kgosie corrected him. "And you said she was Yugoslav."

"O.K.—Olga. And now that you mention it, she was not Yugoslav. She was Russian."

I said, "Where are you from?" Meaning: *What part of Zimbabwe?*

"'*Where are you from?*'" Kgosie snorted. "I do not like this question. It is a white man's question."

"It is not!" I said. "Everyone asks it. When I sat down, you said, 'You are German?' That's the same thing."

"No, it's different," Kgosie said. "In Zimbabwe, if you are white and you say you are Zimbabwean, then everyone knows you are a white Zimbabwean. But if you are black, they say, 'What is your name?' And if you have a South African name, like I do, then they say, 'But that is not a Zimbabwe name. Where are you *from?*' My name betrays me."

"Is it bad to be from South Africa?"

"Not if you are a tourist. If you are just passing through, everyone loves you—but no one trusts an immigrant."

It seemed I had gotten off on the wrong foot. "Let me start over," I said. "I have a different question."

"O.K.," said Kgosie.

I said, "You are German?"

This caught both of them midsip. Beer flew from their glasses. Jackson leapt from his stool to slap foam from his pants.

"*German!*" howled Kgosie. "In all of Germany there are no blacks. One, maybe two. Do you think we are these two?"

"I don't know. In Kenya I met blacks from South Africa. In Russia I met blacks from Ghana. In America I know blacks from Ethiopia. That's why I asked."

"You have been to university?" Kgosie said.

"Yes."

"Then surely you can think of some better question."

I said, "O.K., I've got one for you."

Jackson said, "Wait! Let me put down this beer."

"This one is safe," I said. "What's the best thing that ever happened to you?"

Jackson had no hesitation: "Flying a jet fighter—that was my best thing. Nothing else comes close. During the war I was in a flight training program in Russia—in Rostov, near the Black Sea. There were one hundred blacks there. They called us 'freedom fighters' but they made us sweep our own rooms and the whole hall. At university in America, who sweeps the halls? The students?"

"Once a week," I said, "maids vacuumed my dorm room."

"You see! The Russians did not treat us well. They talk always about solidarity, about blacks and whites being brothers, but when we walked down the street in Rostov, the kids would run from us screaming." 'What happened to that man? Was he burnt?' They were kids, so they did not know better, but even the older people did not know how to talk to us. The only thing they knew was if they found a black man walking drunk in the street, they should take him to the university. My program was for six years, but I quit after three. The hardest part was knowing I would never fly a jet fighter again. That was the *worst* thing that ever happened to me."

Kgosie said, "I can tell you *my* worst thing. I made one mistake in my life. We were not married, but my girlfriend got pregnant because of me. The European way is to screw and only marry if you want to. But I had no contraceptive. How could I not marry her, make her face this life by herself with my child? Now I have three kids—eight, and four, and two. I love them, but I am always wondering what would have happened if I had married someone I wanted instead of someone I had to."

"Are you two happy with the way the revolution turned out?"

Jackson said, "When we were winning the war, we thought we would make a great country out of Zimbabwe. Now we see it is a hard thing to make a great country. Kgosie and I have jobs, so we are luckier than most. Each year Zimbabwe has 200,000 'school leavers' (high school graduates), but they must fight over only 10,000 new jobs." Jackson raised his bottle. "I am happy we can pay for these beers."

"What are your jobs?"

"We work for the Zimbabwe telephone minister," Kgosie said. "I am a 'cable jointer.' Jackson works in the office."

"Is Zimbabwe's telephone system modern?"

"Yes, you can call anywhere in the world," Jackson said. "Anywhere except Zimbabwe. All city-to-city calls are made by satellite, but town-to-home calls all go by cable. So it is easier to call America than to call the train station. I have a friend who, when she wants to tell her neighbor something, will call her mother in London and have her mother call the neighbor. It is the easiest way."

"Were you both soldiers during the war?"

"Probably everyone in here," Jackson waved his arm to take in the entire room, "was a soldier in the war. Whites and blacks. Maybe I shot at some of these same people. Maybe they shot at me. Now we are here drinking."

How Much Maize Can
Twelve Children Eat?

This country, with its institutions, belongs to the people who inhabit it.
Whenever they shall grow weary of the existing government, they can
exercise their constitutional right of amending it, or their revolutionary
right to dismember or overthrow it.

— ABRAHAM LINCOLN, *First Inaugural Address (1861)*

Perhaps like most people who have never witnessed a revolution—a
war, a violent change of government, or some other society-wide
collapse of order—I have often wished that I might, someday, stumble
upon a short one. How else would I ever know if revolution was the
heroic thing philosophers make it out to be, the popular sport it has
become in Latin America, or just a godawful inconvenience?

When Martin Luther King was assassinated, I climbed the hill behind my family's house in northern Virginia and watched columns of
smoke corkscrew up from the burning slums of Washington, D.C. Two
summers later I was among a crowd of 400,000 concertgoers uncere-
moniously teargassed by police on the grounds of the Washington
Monument. And four summers after that, on the day Richard Nixon
resigned, I stood in a hushed crowd across the street from the White
House and watched a helicopter whisk him away. But all of this was
tame by Zimbabwe standards.

During the war's fourteen years some 30,000 Rhodesians were
killed and roughly four times as many were wounded—figures that will

scar everyone in a small country. The war ended with a collective sigh of relief and grand hopes for the future. The musician Paul Simon came to Harare and gave an Independence concert attended by 100,000 people. Pundits rated Zimbabwe's chances for prosperity better than those of any other newly emancipated African country. In the entire Belgian Congo, for instance, there were fewer than a dozen black university graduates at Independence; Zimbabwe had 20,000.

But Independence did not bring Zimbabwe prosperity or even much peace. For several years after taking power, Robert Mugabe's young, brutish government made capricious arrests of both white and black Zimbabweans perceived as threats; confessions were tortured out of some and lengthy prison terms meted out. Food shipments were withheld from the Matabele sections of Zimbabwe. Much of the country's management pool fled. What was left? I wondered.

Saturday morning was warm and dry, the sky a cloudless, paint-store blue showing no trace of the previous evening's storm. I was walking among the immaculate flowerbeds, clipped hedges, and trim lawns of African Unity Square when I was set upon by a black man with yellow eyes.

"Give me money," he demanded angrily, walking beside me, matching me step for step. Most people wore shirtsleeves, but this man wore a heavy brown coat buttoned all the way up to its fur collar.

"For what?" I said.

"Give me money," he repeated through clenched teeth.

Scared of him, I gave him a Zimbabwe dollar. Hoping to loosen him up, I said, "This is my first day in Harare."

"Give me more," he insisted, as though I were fudging on an old debt. But suddenly he veered away from me. And then I saw the reason: directly ahead, two policemen entering the park on brown horses.

From the airplane I had seen only the country's beauty, but on the ground its disappointment was palpable. The government was trying to project to the world an image of calm and solidarity; but in this magnificent land no one seemed particularly happy with the way things had turned out. Black men employed as clerks strolled downtown Harare in ill-fitting sport coats, with cheap ties knotted around their necks, seemingly bewildered by the sight of black politicians zipping around town in stretch limos with police escorts, their sirens screaming. The whites I met wrung their collective hands and wondered aloud whether they shouldn't have joined in the exodus.

A long stretch of First Street had been closed to traffic and paved with red bricks, and now blacks sat confidently at the mall's cafe tables—tables that, not long ago, had been off limits to them. A window sign at Cuthbert's haberdashery suggested that everyone "Make a Date With Fashion." Eric Davis Outfitters was plugging Van Heusen dress shirts, and F. W. Woolworth's was holding a January clearance sale. Shoppers inside Athletes World were browsing shelves of soccer cleats and expensive high-top Bata sneakers. Anyone short of cash was invited to stop at "Founders—For Friendly Finance." Several of the stores were run by white people. In contrast, before Independence almost *everything* had been run by white people. Now the few remaining whites were basically hired help.

I sat on a bench in the shade of a tree, near a crowd that had gathered around a group of street musicians—two guitarists, two men thwapping their palms on hourglass-shaped drums, and a young girl shaking a tambourine. Two women with lilting voices sang *Soldiers...We are soldiers...Fighting for the Lord* (Zimbabwe is 70 percent Christian).

As I scanned the circle of people watching the musicians, I spotted just a few whites: an older man wearing a gray tropical suit, carrying a briefcase, dropping a coin into the tip bowl; and a young woman and young man pushing a baby stroller.

Along the edges of the crowd a black man with a New York Yankees hat jammed tightly on his head pushed a bicycle ice cream cart: *"Dairibord—Nourishes the Nation."* Several men held folded copies of *The Herald*—its headline: MUGABE CALLS FOR NEW POLICY ON THIRD WORLD DEBT. Most of the wrists I could see sported silver watchbands; leather tote bags hung from shoulders; hands clutched plastic shopping bags. But a steady stream of people stopped to rummage through a nearby garbage can.

Harare had a botanical garden to stroll, a small Queen Victoria Museum to browse, and in the nearby countryside a group of balancing rocks to ogle. But for me its greatest attraction was its attention-starved populace—people eager to fill a stranger's ear with opinions on "the situation," as Zimbabwe's long-running predicament was referred to. And instead of the two days I had planned for Harare, I stayed for four, listening to everyone's side of the story.

In front of the Harare train station I met Comede (Co-MAY-day), a fifty-five-year-old taxi driver who sat beside me on a ledge while waiting for a fare. "Before Independence," he said, "you and I could not sit like this. People would think I was stealing something from you." He looked at me as he laughed at this ludicrous suggestion, his vast gut quaking like a swamp. "So it is good that those things have changed. But every day, the economy, it gets a little worse."

That morning's paper had announced an increase in the price of maize. And overnight the price of train tickets had risen 10 percent.

"Why do you think this is happening?" I asked.

"Because after Independence so many white people left," Comede said. "The whites knew how to run things. They had some problems, yes, but they were not corrupt. Now always some crook is coming around, telling me, 'You are in arrears in taxes. You owe me this much.' But they do not know how much I make. Sometimes you make a lot of money, but sometimes you sit for five or six hours and make only five dollars in a day. You are a cab driver—you know how it is. But these tax people, they say, 'You are making lots of money. You have to pay.' They are just crooks. They are robbing us. Sometimes it is hard to feed my family."

"How many children do you have?"

"Twelve," he said, "but that was the old system. Now we are advising the young people that two is a good number. If you have twelve children now, you are asking for trouble. Do you know how much maize twelve children can eat?"

At the American Express Office I fell into conversation with Peter Neville, a Robert Redford look-alike. Born and raised in Rhodesia, a war veteran, Neville was now the local general manager of a business machine company. He spoke to me with extreme warmth, a trait exhibited by all the whites I would meet in Zimbabwe—as though I were a long lost fraternity brother. I told him I'd been in the country less than twenty-four hours, and wondered if he might not fill me in on the place.

"How refreshing! So many people seem to know everything about Zimbabwe before they get here." He said this about as politely as such a statement can be said, laughing, and camouflaging the bitterness of his words. "They know what bad people we whites are, exactly what our mistakes have been, and they're eager to tell us. If you'll forgive me, I must say that most people haven't got a clue what Rhodesia was all about."

And, with that, he swept me into his Land Rover for lunch at his home in the posh northern suburbs. Before Independence these orderly neighborhoods, full of small mansions surrounded by blooming gardens and neat lawns, were occupied solely by white people. But on the drive out I saw families of blacks turning Mercedes down long driveways and closing the iron gates behind them. An Indian family lived next door to the Nevilles.

We sat at the dining room table, looking out over a large back yard, swimming pool, and an enormous avocado tree, while Neville's black butler served us ham and sweet potatoes.

"Most of the world thinks Rhodesia was a horrible, repressive place," Neville told me. "But I've been to Europe and the States, and I think that blacks and whites in Zimbabwe got along better before Independence, and still do, than blacks and whites in the West.

"Things had to change, of course. To think we could go forever without sharing power with the blacks was clearly wrong. And, as fast as we could, we were trying to change that. But there were political problems and we couldn't change fast enough. In the end, we ran out of time. Instead of waiting for a thoughtful solution, we had to settle for a *quick* solution. But I think the changes have made things worse, not just for whites, but for everyone.

"My great-grandfather was one of the pioneers. He built a 5,000-acre farm, but that's all gone now. I've been back twice to visit, and I'll never go again—it was too sad. The blacks who used to work with us were still there, but they were all thinner. Their clothes were ratty. They looked sad, and they told me they were unhappy. And why wouldn't they be? For fifteen years we all fought together to keep the farm—I was using an automatic weapon by the time I was eight years old—and now they work for someone who doesn't treat them as well, who doesn't feed them as well, who doesn't run the farm the way they know it can be run. The place has fallen apart."

When I asked what was the best thing that had ever happened to him, Neville briefly closed his eyes, and smiled as though he were watching a group of children play tag on a beach. When he reopened them, he told me in reverential tones about a six-month, 1,300-mile solo canoe trip he'd taken down the Zambezi River. The trip's purpose was to raise money to help save Zimbabwe's rhinoceros, which had numbered 100,000 thirty years earlier but had been poached down to 1,500 in recent times. He had raised US$45,000.

The worst thing?

"The war," he said. "I saw, actually *saw*, six of my men, my friends, go. Yes, bullets. Or mines. Probably the very worst part was leading 150 men into Mozambique to take out a base of 4,000. We did it—we had air support—but after that, I knew it was just a matter of time. You can't go on against those kinds of numbers forever..."

"After Independence, we had a one-year grace period to get our pensions out. I had been wounded a couple of times and I got $20,000. I went to the States and got my commercial pilot license. For two years I flew for an oil company in Dallas. During the war I didn't think what I was living through was so bad, but in the States I went through several psychologists. When I came back, after several years of living peacefully, I finally realized the enormity of what had happened here. After you've been here a while, you'll realize that most whites of my generation are gone. The old people stayed, or some of them went away and now have come back, but you won't see many people my age. And in another five years I don't intend to be here. I'm married now and I've got two kids, and I want them to grow up some place normal. We're thinking Australia, probably."

On my last day in Harare, at the mouth of an alley near the train station, I saw a hand-lettered, cardboard sign that said SHOE REPAIR AND POLISH—SAME DAY SERVICE. An arrow pointed down the alley, and I

Mshook —"During the war everyone was made promises. 'You fight for us, when we win you will get a farm.' But when we win, the leaders tell the men, 'OK, you are finish. Go home now. Your job is finish.'"

followed it until I came to a small stall where a thin black man was sitting on a crate and applying new half soles to a pair of loafers. A set of wooden shelves beside him held brushes and several cans of polish. I leaned down and pointed to my worn heels. Could he beef them up?

"Yes," he said, and waved at a crate across from him. "You sit, sit."

His name was Mshook; he was thirty-nine years old and had three children. During the war he had stayed in Harare, out of the fighting.

"Soldier is a garbage job," he said, sewing new rubber heels onto my shoes with fishing line. "You go out in bush with rifle; you can get killed. During war everyone was made promises. 'You fight for us, when we win we will give you a white person's house. You fight for us, when we win you will get a farm.' But when we win, the leaders tell the men, 'O.K., you are finish. Go home now. Your job is finish.' If they complain, the leaders give them five hundred dollars and say, 'Now you are finish.' And barely before the man even gets home his five hundred dollars is also finish. No, soldier is garbage job."

A handsome young man wearing a sport coat and tie arrived to pick up a pair of shoes Mshook had resoled. His name was Takesure (the English words *take* and *sure* cobbled together), and he was on a short break from his job as a clerk for a firm that repaired business machines. I asked Takesure if he knew of Peter Neville's company.

"Yes," he said, "it has an excellent reputation. I would like to work there. I have been with my present employer for five years, hoping for a

promotion. But there is no promotion."

Takesure asked where I was
from, and when I answered, a
smile spread across his face. "San
Francisco!" he echoed. "Oh, to
travel is my favorite thing."

"What places have you visited?"

"To Kariba. And to Mas-
vingo." Both places were within
four hours of Harare by car. "I
have never been out of Zimbabwe. I would like to go—I hear
good things about Mozambique
and Zambia and South Africa.
But it is better to see places than
to hear about them. Most of all I
would like to go to America—
Florida, Miami, Texas. These are
all good places, I hear."

Takesure —His longest excursion from
Harare was four hours by car. But meeting
a Californian, a smile spread across his
face: "Oh, to travel is my favorite thing."

Takesure was twenty-three,
married, with one child. "I am
planning to have at most three children," he said. "Everything is too
expensive. Since five years ago, the price of ten kilograms of millie-
meal has went from two to seven dollars. People are angry. Next year
there will be an election. These ministers will have to answer. Every
day there are stories about ministers becoming rich, but the people
are getting angry. People have to go to South Africa or Botswana to
bring things back. If you buy an electrical machine for two hundred
dollars in South Africa—a desktop calculator, maybe—you can sell it
in Zimbabwe for six hundred or seven. Extraordinary profit." He
asked, "Would it be possible, theoretically, to send things from the
United States to Zimbabwe?"

"Like what?"

"A color television."

"It would be possible, theoretically," I said, "but it would also be difficult and very expensive. Color televisions cost a lot of money—even in America. Shipping costs a fortune, and there would be an import duty and probably bribes to pay."

"I would like to have a color television," Takesure said. "Everyone in America has one, yes?"

"Not everyone," I said. "For years I didn't, but last year I bought a small one, black and white, for watching sports."

"Yes, sports," Takesure said. "Those are good. But the best is *MacGyver*."

Before he left, I took his picture and he wrote his address into my notebook.

"Will you promise to send me a letter from America?" he asked.

Conversations in Zimbabwe are so drenched in politics, so thick with recriminations and justifications, so inward, really, that it had come as an enormous relief to find someone expressing an interest in something faraway. And when Takesure was gone I wrote in my notebook: *Gentle, polite, wide-eyed. Reminds me of myself at that age. Maybe I'll ask him to come and pick out his own color TV.*

49
What a Wonderful World

Scenes so lovely must have been gazed upon by angels in their flight.
—DR. DAVID LIVINGSTONE,
Missionary Travels and Researches in Southern Africa

One of the great overlooked bonuses of travel is the chance to reacquaint oneself with the sky. Rarely does a harried city dweller have the time to look upward; but during the past many weeks the sky had again become the dreamy friend I remember from the long summer afternoons of my childhood.

My bus from Harare to Bulawayo rolled through green cornfields spreading under a vast collection of the same clouds that sail over America's Great Plains. Stubby clouds with flat bottoms and ruffled tops crept overhead like floats in a parade. Above them, fat blobby clouds shifted like organisms seen through a microscope. Majestic thunderheads towered into the upper reaches of a deep blue dome.

I wondered: *What would it have been like to grow up under this Zimbabwean sky, with Harare and Johannesburg and possibly distant London as my compass points, instead of Washington and New York and Moscow?* Instead of dreaming about vacations to the Grand Canyon and California, would I have fantasized about Kariba and Cape Town? What would growing up in a home like Peter Neville's have been like? Or growing up black, and having as my highest aspiration a position as gardener or butler for a white family?

In Bulawayo I caught an overnight train for Victoria Falls. The scenery changed quickly, the American Midwest falling behind and Africa reemerging. No crops here, only scrub growing from red dirt.

Cattle wandered in and out of the bush of a wide dry plain aglow with a yellow sunset.

When I awakened in the morning, we were chugging through a narrow valley, green and wooded, and the first thing I saw outside was a warthog grubbing in the tall grass of a meadow. I saw an occasional deer or monkey flash past the window, but the guidebook promised that lion, hyena, antelope, baboon, jackal, elephant, hippo, and hordes of snakes roamed and slithered across this part of the country.

Not long ago the greatest danger to travelers in western Zimbabwe was posed not by wild animals but by humans. In 1982 a truckload of adventure travelers on a Cape Town-to-Cairo run had just departed Victoria Falls when they were attacked by Matabele guerrillas. Four men (two Americans, an Englishman, and an Australian) were marched off into the bush at gunpoint; two Scandinavian women were left behind with a message from the guerrillas indicating that the men would be held until the government released two captive Matabele leaders. For months a massive search was conducted, but the Westerners were never found. (Eventually it was acknowledged that the unfortunate four were killed within twenty-four hours and their bodies dumped into a mine.)

My brother Grant had visited Zimbabwe long before me. Ironically, he was the driver of one of the first vehicles to come upon the bullet-scarred truck and the stunned Scandinavian women. Now I looked out the window and shuddered, as I've often done when thinking: What if Grant had been an hour earlier?

Four hours behind schedule the train pulled into Victoria Falls, a jungle outpost on the crocodile-rich banks of the Zambezi River. The small township's centerpiece is the Victoria Falls Hotel, a lovely colonial relic established in 1905, and still featuring sprawling gardens and lawns and scurrying black butlers. It was surrounded by a grid of modest homes, a gas station, a campground (I shared a cheap cabin with two other backpackers), and a few shops (I ate most of my meals at a Wimpy's restaurant). Of course none of these would have existed if not for the famous cataracts that lay barely a kilometer from the center of town, and whose distant throb I could hear from my bed at night.

The Matabele had named the falls "Water Rising as Smoke," but in 1855 Dr. David Livingstone—on one of his far-flung expeditions to bring "Christianity, civilization, and commerce" to the African interior—renamed them, in the British tradition, after the reigning monarch.

And majestic they are. Victoria Falls' dimensions—over a mile wide, and 320 feet high (Livingstone lowered a long, weighted rope down into the gorge to measure them)—are more than double those of Niagara Falls. Imagine the deck of the Golden Gate Bridge raised to twice its present height, and the water of the mighty Mississippi pouring off in one enormous sheet into San Francisco Bay.

But the river was not running at capacity when I saw it. Rocks were visible at the top of the falls, dark dividers in an immense sweep of white—creating the impression of a mile-long keyboard. I spent large parts of my three days at Victoria Falls marveling at the waters' joyful leap into the cauldron below, and at the rainbow (sometimes multiple rainbows) always visible somewhere in the spectacle.

The clouds of mist rising from the gorge annually dump more than 100 feet of water onto the nearby land, spawning a fantastic rain forest. Pathways looped through a dense variety of trees, among them ebony and fig. A tangle of fat vines and jungle creepers crawled through the tree limbs like so many abandoned fire hoses. Tawny deer, with white spots like the antelope of Masai Mara, wandered calmly through the misty forest, beside regal peacocks with spread tails and fluorescent blue heads. I was entranced by a nearby meadow flourishing with thick grasses—as though a million landscape artists had jabbed their brush handles into the soil, their skyward tips dripping a luminous springtime green.

I was astounded by how few visitors there were. For two consecutive mornings, between the hours of eight and nine I had Victoria Falls National Park completely to myself. On my first day I roamed the falls for hours, the mist soaking me to the skin. At one point I was standing alone on the edge of the canyon, ogling the permanent rainbow down in the gorge, when a gust of wind sneaked around behind me and dumped what seemed like a warm bucketful of Stoney Ginger Beer on my head and shoulders. The effect was exhilarating, but on subsequent trips to the falls I brought an umbrella.

Toward noon of the second day I was wandering through the rain forest, umbrella in hand, when I saw John, one of my cabinmates, and a young woman walking toward me. Both were drenched, their t-shirts clinging to them, but neither seemed to care. John introduced the woman as Lisa, from Connecticut. Lisa had just finished three weeks on her own in Zambia, and wore her blond hair in a grown-out crew cut. She looked at my umbrella with a bemused smile, and teased, "Where's your sense of adventure?"

"That's great," I said. "You come to deepest, darkest Africa, you're in the middle of a rain forest next to a monstrous falls roaring so loud that you have to scream to be heard, and what do you get? 'Where's your sense of adventure?' That's just great."

That afternoon I rented a bicycle and rode away from town along a dirt path through the jungle beside the river. Rounding a bend, I found my way blocked by a dozen monkeys. As they eyed me from fifteen feet away, regarding me with expressions of smirking curiosity, I was suddenly, uncomfortably aware that I'd never before encountered monkeys without iron bars or thick glass between us. The dimwitted expressions that looked goofy in zoos now seemed quite threatening. I noted their size—several of them were almost as big as me—and planned my defense. If they rushed me, I would hurl the bike at the leaders—aim for their knees, maybe take out one or two of them—and swing my daypack at the followers. Hopefully that would keep the rest from following my sprint back toward town.

But suddenly they broke, loping into the bush on all fours, screeching at each other, curlicued tails raised. I rode on into the jungle, senses newly abuzz, past the BEWARE OF CROCODILE notices, thinking: *No sense of adventure!*

Several kilometers from town I pedaled up a potholed asphalt road to the top of Elephant Hill, the area's highest point. A modern luxury hotel once operated here, but during the war a heat-seeking missile fired by guerrillas across the border in Zambia had missed its intended target, a Rhodesian aircraft, and instead honed in on the hotel kitchen's exhaust fans. A fire swept the hotel and left it a charred ruin. I rode my bike through the doorless front entrance and into the cavernous lobby, adjusting my eyes to the darkness and dodging the trash scattered in front of the check-in counter. When I rode out onto the terrace and circled the swimming pool—empty of water, full of garbage—warthogs scattered into the surrounding bush.

The terrace provided a panoramic view of the great Zambezi, curling out of the jungle to the west and flowing lazily around the islands upriver from the falls. Several miles to the east, a low vaporous plume signified the falls. When the river ran high, a cloud of mist often rose to 1,000 feet and was visible from 40 miles away. When the moon was right, this terrace was a popular place for spotting lunar rainbows.

That afternoon, as I pedaled through the thick green jungle and back toward town, I suddenly felt sorry for all Zimbabweans. Wasn't it almost unthinkably dumb that for decades this spectacular country should stagger along like a mortally wounded elephant? How had the whites been so blind and fearful, or simply lethargic, as to not share the land's bounty with the people whom they had displaced? And how had the Mugabe government, inheriting a modern economy and infrastructure, managed in the space of a few years to starve, kill, or alienate vast segments of its population?

The previous evening a thirty-two-year-old man with the enchanting name of Never had sneaked into the campground to try to sell souvenirs. He crouched on the porch of my cabin and, while keeping watch behind him for the guards patrolling the campground, showed me his collection of trinkets and animal carvings. Never said he was the oldest of seven children, and was married with three children of his own. His oldest was nine, the same age as his youngest sister. During the war, Never said, he trained in Zambia and had become expert with an AK-47.

I asked, "Are you happy with the way things have turned out?"

"I am happiest when I have good work," Never said. "The best work is plowing. I like plowing, but it is difficult to find work. During the war we were made promises, so many promises, and here I am selling beads and things. I am not happy. The white man oppressed, but the black man Mugabe does the same thing. But it is not good to talk like this." He sighed and held out a necklace. "You give me twenty-five dollars for this one."

The longer I spent in Zimbabwe, the less eager I was to contemplate politics and war and atrocities. I began to realize that possibly the worst aspect of living through a revolution was that it might grow old long before it produced changes. The children of Victoria Falls had grown up in turmoil: tribal bickering, curfews, funerals. Would they ever see revolution's rewards?

I hadn't particularly liked Never—he was too grim and too aggressive to spend a month with—but I found myself wondering how he or Takesure or most Zimbabweans would react to America. For 135 years, America's wars have all been fought in other countries. Would someone who'd grown up in Zimbabwe find San Francisco's military and political calm, its orderliness, unnatural? I doubted it. I imagined they would find it heavenly. If a windfall were to suddenly remove me from the constant struggle to keep afloat financially, how long would I miss that struggle? Not a minute. Not on your life.

One night I joined John, Lisa, and several other backpackers for the buffet served on the Victoria Falls Hotel patio. All of the waiters were black, all of the diners white—an observation that everyone must have made, but no one mentioned. The brave new world of equality had arrived, was an unquestionable fact of life in Zimbabwe, but in the hotel's colonial ambiance no one seemed eager to challenge the roles of yesterday.

At one end of the candlelit table the men debated whether there were an officially designated "Seven Wonders of the Natural World." If there were, Victoria Falls would surely, it was agreed, be one of them. At the table's other end, the women shared lighthearted complaints about the annoyance of shaving their legs and the ridiculousness of wearing swim suits while sunbathing. I listened—while waiters hustled platters of turkey and roast beef and bowls of fruit across the patio, while black musicians played waltzes, while white couples in formal wear clung to each other on the dance floor—and found it a relief to hear people laughing and discussing such mundane topics. Overhead, through a canopy of acacia and palm trees shone the same stars that had shone before Rhodesia was formed, before the Shona and Matabele ever heard of each other. And when the band stopped, I could hear the distant roar of the Zambezi—750 miles from its source, a thousand miles from its Indian Ocean destiny—oblivious to wars and changes of government, tumbling along on its mindless joy ride.

On my last day I was standing in the meadow near the falls, in tall, thick grass as green as Wisconsin in May, when a family of three Africans slowly passed across my field of view, left to right. They were fashionably dressed and evenly spaced—Dad in the lead, Mom several paces back, and then a young boy, furiously pedaling a red tricycle. Behind them the white curtain of water shimmered and roared, geysers of mist shot up out of the gorge, and above them a rainbow arced, suspended in midair. Overhead, the African sky was unfurled like a bolt of blue silk.

I stood there for some time, admiring the scene and wishing for a camera, when my eyes caught a movement off to the left. Emerging from the rain forest and heading directly toward me was an African teenager with a boom box the size of a suitcase swinging at his hip.

No, I thought. *Not here.*

But when he was near enough for the music to be audible over the roar of the falls, I was startled to recognize the sweet, gravelly voice of Louis Armstrong warbling "What A Wonderful World." Satchmo was going on in his throaty rasp about some things he'd seen "one bright blessed day": trees of green, red roses, too; clouds of white, skies of blue. He'd seen a rainbow glowing, babies growing, friends getting along, and found himself humbled and moved by the simplicity and profundity of it all.

Looking around, I saw black and white butterflies as big as helicopters, fluttering yellow birds, polka-dotted deer, heavy vines drooping from big bushy trees; I saw the falls plummeting, plummeting, and heard their roar—so loud and yet so soothing it was almost a lullaby. At the gorge's edge the strolling father and mother and their excited youngster ambled under the bridge of the rainbow. It struck me that the words Louis Armstrong was singing might well have been written here (or, more likely, up on the dry patio of the hotel) on a day just like this one. Australian Aborigines believe their ancestors literally sang their continent into existence, and at Victoria Falls, at this fortuitous intersection of music, mood, and scenery, that theory seemed eminently sensible.

As the young man passed me, he smiled. "Howzit?"

"Good," I said. "Very good."

He strolled away, barefoot and soaked, the brown skin of his back showing through his white, newly-translucent t-shirt. As the sound of his box faded, I noticed how the drumming of the falls induced a pleasant vibration in my chest, sedated my mind. Nowhere in the panorama did I see soldiers or politicians—and the noise would have tabled any attempted political discussion. Revolutions come, revolutions go. And after a week in Zimbabwe I had decided that it would be all right if I were never to witness a revolution. It would be preferable, by far, to peruse the wonders of the world in peace, singing them into existence, perhaps, and thinking, like Louis Armstrong, *What a wonderful world*.

50

Applause from the Womenfolk

Indeed I tremble for my country when I reflect that God is just, that his justice cannot sleep forever....Nothing is more certainly written in the book of fate than that these people are to be free.

—THOMAS JEFFERSON, Inscription on the
Jefferson Memorial, Washington, D.C.

Dawn was pinkening the bush as the overnight bus from Zimbabwe pulled up to the checkpoint near Beit Bridge. I had spent the night thrashing in my seat, trying to sleep, and as I rubbed my sleepy eyes I saw three white soldiers, smoking and joking in a tight circle next to the customs shed. Each of them wore a bristly brown moustache and uniform of camouflage hat, shirt, pants, and polished black combat boots. Snapped into the holster of his shiny black belt, each had a large black handgun.

Standing just a few feet away from this closed huddle was a fourth soldier—a lean man with a kind, sympathetic face. He wore the same camouflage outfit as the others and the same shiny black boots, but there were two things different about him: he was black, and his belt had no holster, no gun. He appeared uncomfortably self-conscious, clasping his hands behind his back, then holding them stiffly at his sides, then behind his back again. And why wouldn't he? I wondered. Was this some Afrikaner practical joke—putting a weaponless black on display, while the whites, armed and smirking, turned their backs to him: *See there, we're integrated.* As I took my first step onto South African asphalt, I caught the black soldier's eye and squeezed off a quick smile at him. But our eyes had barely met when his darted away, and I was left with a stupid grin on my face, feeling awkward and confused. The grin was a simple thing to get rid of, but the feeling would last for ten days. And then some.

Apartheid still had a couple of years left to run—no one knew exactly how or when the changeover to majority rule (South Africa was 75 percent black) would come, but everyone inside and outside South Africa considered it a matter of time. Still, during my visit, it was obvious that the whites were in full control.

All the inspectors inside the customs shed were big, beefy white men, rocking back on their heels, arms folded across their chests, glowering over the tops of their moustaches at those of us approaching the counter. The person ahead of me in line was a short, elderly black woman, nervously wringing her handbag while an official scanned her Zimbabwean passport. He asked her a question I could not understand, and she gave a reply too soft for me to hear.

"Spik op!" the inspector barked. It would have been easy for him to lean forward a bit, but he held his position, glaring down as though greatly inconvenienced; the terrified-looking woman raised up on tiptoes.

Oh, stop it! I wanted to yell at the man. But of course I didn't. I, too, was intimidated. When our bus finally pulled away from the border I scribbled some notes—"More of a shakedown than a welcome"—and fell into a fitful sleep.

South Africa is dominated by a vast central plateau of varying fertility. In the north, near Beit Bridge, it was a great, brown, shrub-dotted plain, and when I awoke, we were crossing it on a two-lane highway. Ranches bordered by rows of eucalyptus trees and equipped with silver windmills were set back from the road, and often separated by miles. We slowed to enter a small town dominated by a church spire and filled with jacaranda trees and modest homes. It was a Sunday, and a South African Sunday appeared to be the same sort of slow, sleepy event that it is in America. Eight blacks sat outside one cafe and eight more outside another. Through the door of a suburban garage I saw a pleasure boat mounted on a trailer.

Our bus driver, a bull-necked white man in his late twenties, was built like a linebacker. He wore white loafers, a white t-shirt with the sleeves rolled up to expose biceps covered by naked-lady tattoos, and gray slacks so tight I could see his underpants label outlined on his buttocks. I disliked him the moment I set eyes on him. Half the bus's passengers were white, half were black, and nearly all were traveling on Zimbabwean passports. What, I wondered, were they thinking about? Most—like the woman across the aisle from me, the same woman who'd been bullied by the border official—stared straight ahead with blank expressions. A few slept. All were silent. For miles the only noise was the sound of air punching its way through barely opened windows; and then I heard a low murmur toward the front and saw our white driver and his black assistant sharing orange slices. Seeing them talking easily, jovially, I regretted my earlier snap judgment, and all my unspoken others. Who was I to judge these people? And when had I last shared an orange with a black person?

We slowed to enter Pietersburg, another town of quiet streets. A statue of a white man reading a speech dominated a bushy green park. The parking lot of the "Pick N' Pay" on Markstraat was newly asphalted and lined with hundreds of freshly painted spaces—but only one car was parked there. We dropped two passengers at the deserted train station; passed a drive-in movie screen, a junk yard, and a billboard recommending Sunshine Kafee; and soon were back in the countryside, traveling on a four-lane divided highway, toward Pretoria and Johannesburg.

Just a few minutes beyond Pietersburg, the driver beckoned to his assistant, and the two of them huddled alarmedly over the dash panel. We coasted to a stop beside a red dirt field sprouting corn stalks two feet high. The driver and his assistant exited to examine the bus's rear. Outside I saw a dirt driveway leading up to a ranch house identified by a sign as the home of Bas and Thelma Visser Symansdrift. In the trees behind the house were four huts with thatched, conical roofs: *Where the blacks lived?* A series of hills, pointy as upside-down ice cream cones, rose behind the huts, and above them spread a blue-and-white checked tablecloth of a sky.

The assistant returned. "Ladies and gentlemen...We have a water hose that has burst just now, and we will have it fixed shortly in just a few minutes or hours. Does anyone have a knife?"

All the men filed off the bus, and, not wanting to appear unmanly, I joined them. We gathered around the engine compartment, a semi-circle of three whites and five blacks, to watch the driver wrap tape around the offending hose. A Toyota pickup truck pulled off the highway, and a Texas-sized rancher and his equally large son, both white, both wearing straw cowboy hats, stepped out.

"Do you boys have enny wot-uh?" our bus driver asked them, his Afrikaner accent thick and guttural.

The rancher's son lifted a five-gallon water can from the bed of the pickup.

"Ah, gude," said our driver. "Now we need a fun-oo."

"We 'even't enny fun-oo," said the rancher.

A black man in the circle was holding a one-liter Coke bottle. Without speaking, he poured the last couple of inches of cola onto the ground, walked to a nearby fence and converted the bottle into a funnel, western-style, smashing it once against a fence post and knocking the bottom cleanly off.

"Ah," said the rancher, "zumwun widd a plahn."

The black man handed the bottle to our bus driver.

"Thank you, mon," said the driver. "Later I buy you enotha butt-oo."

The driver's assistant held the funnel while the rancher's son filled the radiator with water, then we all piled back aboard the bus to applause from the womenfolk.

It was good to see this small show of humanity. Coming into this country, I had not known what to expect, and the scene at the border had left me wondering if I was not in for ten days of hostilities. But now I'd been part of a group of ten men—five white, five black—faced with a problem, and had seen it settled quickly. It was a little thing, sure, but it made me hopeful.

We drove south, past more small towns, until early afternoon, when we left the freeway and wound through the streets of the capital, Pretoria. Our route to the train station (to drop off more passengers) did not take us past South Africa's parliament buildings, but through an area of older, red-brick apartment blocks. Groups of blacks, dangling their legs and watching our bus, sat on brick walls. Three black policemen patrolled the sidewalk in front of King Burger, and each, I was pleased to see, had a holstered pistol on his hip. On Paul Kruger Street I noted two young white girls standing among a group of blacks, ogling the display windows of Morris Outfitters. I wondered if I was not looking at South Africa through an overly sensitive racial prism. Maybe, I thought, but maybe it was appropriate here; after all, the *Daily Rand* reported not only a person's name but also his or her race—always capitalizing: White, Black, Coloured, Indian.

South of Pretoria the scenery turned gradually from brown to green, putting me in mind of the countryside near St. Louis, Missouri; suburbs of quasi-mansions with golf-course-green lawns, a building under construction—soon to be a Holiday Inn—heavy power lines running three towers abreast and laser-beam straight all the way to the horizon. The highway was six lanes wide now, with elevated overpasses and four-leaf-clover interchanges—and smooth, with none of the wobbles, lurches, or jarring crashes induced by highways in Kenya, India, or the Philippines.

Johannesburg came slowly into view, its core of downtown highrises surrounded by a range of gold-tinted hills rising to 200 and 300 feet on the city's outskirts. Before the discovery of gold in 1886, Johannesburg had been essentially flat; but for the past century miners had been pulling ore from the earth, processing out the wealth, and dumping the residue near the mine openings. Now these bare, sterile mounds gave Johannesburg a raw, unfinished look, and as we drew closer, I wished we would just pass it by. I hadn't been in a big, muscular city since Cairo—Nairobi and Harare had been frontier outposts, in comparison—and now I noticed myself tensing up.

As we took the DOWNTOWN JOHANNESBURG exit, the black woman across the aisle, motionless for most of the trip, suddenly clapped her palms together in the air in front of her face. She flicked a stunned fly to the floor and squashed it with the sole of her shoe, muttering in a tongue I did not understand.

51

The Tip of a Rocket

He stood for a moment in the room...Outside, the stir and movement of people, but behind them, through them, one could hear the roar of a great city. Johannesburg. Johannesburg.

Who could believe it?

— ALAN PATON, *Cry, The Beloved Country*

Of the places I have visited, none has been so difficult to sort out as Johannesburg in the waning days of apartheid. Maybe I had trouble because I arrived lacking any strong mental images of the place. Arriving in Egypt I already knew how the pyramids would look. Prior to Kenya I had mental images of lions stalking zebra on the Serengeti plain. I had preconceived notions of clouds cloaking Kilimanjaro, of spray rising from Victoria Falls. But no such tourist poster cliches of South Africa were imprinted on my imagination. My identification with the country was simple: *apartheid*.

South Africa's races were officially relegated to separate living areas, but lately several white areas throughout the country had been "graying." One of these was Johannesburg's Hillbrow-Berea neighborhood, where wide, clean, tree-lined streets and rows of ivy-covered brick apartment buildings created the stately feel of Washington, D.C.'s embassy district.

Hillbrow-Berea had once been exclusively white, but several years before my arrival blacks had begun trickling in, and the authorities, perhaps weary of playing the heavy, perhaps curious to see how this integration scenario would unfold, had looked the other way. Several white property owners had filed lawsuits attempting to have the government either enforce or scrap the segregation laws, but these cases had bogged down in the court system, and many whites had moved away. Now the area was at least 50 percent black-occupied, and easily 90 percent of the people I passed on the streets were black.

A few apartment buildings had been converted into long-term residence hotels. All had black desk clerks, and most had groups of blacks hanging out by the doorways or in the television lounges. At the first few places I was told, "Sorry, full," and was starting to wonder if I weren't running up against some unwritten code. But finally, at a tidy-looking place with the comfortable name of The Pads, the desk clerk told me that one single room remained.

I took the key and headed toward the stairs, passing the dozen black men and women watching professional wrestling in the lounge. The sounds of a screaming crowd and an announcer's voice ("The key to that takedown was his windmill approach...") came from the television, but those watching it were absolutely quiet, staring silently at me as I walked in front of the screen.

My second floor window looked onto an air shaft, but the room was spacious and high-ceilinged, had a desk, a closet, a radio, a firm mattress, and a reading lamp. I unpacked, stretched, showered, and lay down for a nap, while noticing the periodic cheers and groans from the television lounge. From a room down the hall came the sounds of Elton John reminiscing about a pet crocodile he had owned back when rock was young. A telephone rang in the hallway. I thought: *Not a chance in hell that's for me.* After twenty rings, a man answered it and explained loudly and sternly that he couldn't possibly go out tonight. "Man, it is Monday tomorrow. You know what most people do on Monday—we *work*, brother!"

The guidebook warned of muggings in Hillbrow-Berea, even broad daylight muggings, and that evening as I went out in search of food, the desk clerk warned me to "be smart." But the streets felt safe enough. The air was warm and filled with traffic noises and disco music and the chatter of people cruising the sidewalks. At the corner of Smit and

Twist Streets, at a 24-hour grocery run by a family of Indians, I bought a chicken-mayonnaise sandwich, a bag of chips, and an Appletizer soft drink, then sat on the lip of a trash receptacle out front to eat. Hillbrow-Berea bordered Johannesburg's first-class hotel area, and from my perch I had a view of shimmering highrises looming against the night sky. Black hookers in plastic miniskirts clacked past on high heels. An old drunk black man came by to ask for my empty bottle. A drunk white man with his shirt sleeves rolled up to his shoulders stopped to ask me the time, and, apparently in reaction to my accent, volunteered that he had a son in Los Angeles and another in San Francisco. He was Yugoslavian, but he'd lived most of his life in Johannesburg. "South Africa is a good place," he told me. "Don't worry about apartheid, mate. It's finished. It's over."

As I walked back to The Pads later that evening, I was thinking that South Africa wasn't so bad, that it didn't feel much different than San Francisco. The scene at the border—the three white guards excluding the black—maybe I'd been projecting; maybe a truly unbiased person would have seen it in a different light.

But back at The Pads I sat down with the crowd in the lounge to watch the nightly news. A white anchorman read a report of an incident that had happened just that afternoon in the all-white Johannesburg suburb of Mayfair West. An Indian family had tried to move in, but a mob of screaming whites, armed with bats, bricks, and guns, had surrounded the house. A mob member threw a rope noose over the house's high front wall, and several others spray-painted swastikas on it and then clambered over it to deface the house as well. The Indians had fled. Now, amid a huge outcry from Indian groups, authorities were promising an investigation.

The group in the lounge watched the report in silence, and when it ended they remained that way. Several stole glances at me, but no one said anything. I felt my face burning. While the results of a cricket match were being broadcast, I rose from my chair and climbed to my room.

I awoke the next morning feeling agitated. What *was* I doing in Johannesburg, in a hotel room in a newly "gray" area? Memories of television clips showing slogan-chanting college students, of newspaper stories detailing the horrors of apartheid, haunted me. Several people had urged me not to come here, had said that my visit would support racism, and while I had seen their point, I had nonetheless decided to have a first-hand look. As Takesure in Harare had said, "It is better to see a place than to hear about it." But as I left the hotel that morning, I felt overwhelmed by the notion that I had no business here, that I was in the wrong place, doing the wrong thing, at exactly the wrong time.

As I stepped onto the street, I was spotted by a group of hookers doing what most people do on Monday—working.

"Hey, Sweetie!" called one seated on a low wall, legs splayed open. "Come sit with me."

Another: "Look at these tits, darling." Through her sheer black top I saw long, thin breasts drooping almost to her red belt.

On the next corner another woman, dressed in an all-black body stocking and black high heels, was fastening a golden butterfly pin at her crotch.

A man slipped me a flier for an escort agency named Romance. Another handed me one for a pawnshop, Midas Holdings, brazenly suggesting: "Help your neighbor by selling his old jewelry for him, and earn big money!"

Several blocks from The Pads, at an elegant outdoor cafe at the corner of Claim and Kotze streets, I saw a black man standing over the table of a white couple, who were eating croissants and sipping coffee. Braided hair flopped down around the black man's face, his muscular arms were folded resolutely over his broad bare chest, and he wore nothing but a kind of fur skirt. He struck me as crazed—like someone who had wandered away from a psych ward, or perhaps in from the bush for the first time. When the cafe's proprietor came to shoo him away, the man glared at him, grumbled, but then padded away on bare feet. Sixty seconds later I saw him sprinting back up the street, furiously chasing another black man—this one also shirtless and barefoot, but wearing tattered trousers and a Salvation Army sport coat. A white woman walking down the sidewalk with a bag full of groceries did not slow down or step aside, and barely glanced at the two men as they ripped past and disappeared around a corner.

I looked around the street, bewildered, but no one else seemed to find the small event notable. The white couple already seemed oblivious to anything but their breakfast and newspaper. The cafe owner, standing behind his cash register, smiled and made change for a customer. I headed downtown, crossing Joubert Park, where the green lawns were strewn with sleeping blacks, like corpses on the Gettysburg battlefield. In the park's center a black man and a white man were squared off across a giant chess board, contemplating three-foot tall pawns, kings, and queens.

The Indian woman working the American Express counter said she was sorry, but there was no mail for me. I cashed my third-to-last $100 traveler's check, and observed with a wave of concern that my once-bloated money belt was now limp as a popped balloon. On the sidewalk a black man asked for money and I gave him some coins, an act that triggered a memory, a memory that gave me a brief and welcome distraction from Johannesburg.

One sunny September afternoon in Boulder, Colorado—not long after my return from Afghanistan—I bought a banana, a cinnamon roll, and a carton of milk at a convenience store. Outside the door a fellow hippie spare-changed me and I gave him everything. Everything in my case was exactly thirty-nine cents; I knew, because I'd counted it as I'd stepped away from the cash register. I had no more money anywhere in the world: no meager bank account, no hidden coin jar, no loans to call in, no credit card (hah!), and no job. Still recovering from hepatitis, I'd hitchhiked to Boulder, arrived a few days earlier with nine dollars in my pocket, and—in the style and vernacular of the times—was "crashing with a friend." I estimated my welcome had a couple of weeks yet to run.

I ate my last lunch in the shade of an oak tree on the University of Colorado campus. My pennilessness was unnerving but, I assured myself, there was no need to panic. I was only twenty-three and my big earning years were supposedly dead ahead. Something would turn up. I napped under the oak and when I awoke, it was still a beautiful afternoon in Boulder, Colorado. Enjoy the day, I told myself. Things will work out. I walked back to my friend's house and found a party breaking out—or rather, in the style of the times, continuing.

The next morning I grabbed the want ads and began my long steady decline into respectability. I found work driving a Head Start school bus in the mornings ($2.10 *an hour) and washing dishes in a dope dealers' hangout at night ($2.50). Six months later I found full time work in the molybdenum mine ($4.90).*

And I'd been right—things *had* worked out. Now here I was in Johannesburg, a full-fledged credit-card-carrying adult who could charge my way home, if needed. And surely, I hoped, things would somehow work out again.

I wandered for a while along streets packed with cars and buses. A Benetton store, a Wimpy's, boutiques full of Rambo posters. Architectural wonders of steel and glass towered over colonial-era customs houses and government office buildings. The people walking the sidewalks were mainly black, and many wore sharp business outfits.

In San Francisco I had seen the South African movie *The Gods Must Be Crazy*, which included a scene showing whites and blacks working together, quite casually, in a newspaper office. Later I read a movie review that called the scene blatant propaganda: that sort of thing, said the reviewer, does not happen in racist South Africa.

But now, through the window of a bank office on the second floor of Johannesburg's Carlton Center, I saw blacks and whites and Indians staring at green computer screens. A black man in a white shirt and tie leaned over the desk of a white man as he pointed out something in a document. They brushed shoulders. They laughed. They smiled at each other. I watched for several minutes, recalling offices I'd known in Washington, D.C., Dallas, New York, San Francisco, and concluded that this office appeared to be at least as relaxed, if not more so.

I ate breakfast in a cafe named The Bakers Dozen, while, over the stereo system, James Taylor advised me to shower the people I loved with love. Seated at the next table was a black woman wearing a red bandana, cradling a baby, and reading a newspaper article: MOTHER SLAIN, CHILDREN BEATEN TO DEATH. I bought my own newspaper and read about the Dayals, the Indian family who had been run out of Mayfair West yesterday. Encouraged by the "graying" phenomenon, they had hoped to meet little or no resistance. But the mob, the noose, and the swastikas revealed a serious miscalculation, and before spending even one night in their new home, the Dayals had run to safety at the home of relatives.

My map showed that Mayfair West lay only three or four miles from where I sat. After breakfast, I walked west, out of the city center, cut across the growth rings surrounding Johannesburg, away from the high-rises, past the parking lots on the downtown fringe where commuting office workers parked their new Mercedes, BMWs, Fords, and Toyotas, past the tangle of freeways and railroad lines converging on Johannesburg from all over the country, through a warehouse district, and along a strip of aged stores and service stations. A white father and son maneuvered a long, rectangular cardboard box out the front door of a store named Field and Stream, where a huge sign in the window said ARMS AND AMMUNITION. I wondered what sort of reception Field and Stream might give a black father and son. Or the Dayal family.

Passing the Grosvenor train station, I saw the words FIRST AND SECOND CLASS ONLY painted above a tunnel leading to the platform. But the paint was new and not so thick, and the Afrikaans words NET BLANKES showed clearly through. A translation was supplied in parentheses: WHITES ONLY.

After an hour of walking, I asked an Indian man I met on the street if we were near Mayfair West. "Yes," he said, and pointed to a hill beyond a set of railroad tracks. "It is over there, but if you are Indian you do not go in."

Feeling none too confident myself, I crossed into Mayfair West— an old but immaculate suburb of modest homes with small, fenced off yards and deserted streets. Every hedge was neatly trimmed, and not a stray clipping, child's toy, or speck of litter marred the yards and sidewalks. At the top of the hill a black man knelt beside a Mayfair municipal truck, repairing a section of concrete curbing. He looked up and said, "Good morning, sah." In the distance loomed Johannesburg's skyscrapers and the white mine dumps streaked with orange and gold.

In the deadly suburban stillness I imagined I heard hair rising on the backs of guard dogs behind every wall and chain-link fence. A white woman cruised past in a car, windows rolled all the way up, white-knuckled hands gripping the steering wheel; her eyes never wavered from the road to meet my gaze. I tried to visualize the mob of angry whites from the day before, with guns and spray paint and twisted faces, but it made no sense.

A fiftyish black woman carrying a bucket full of cleaning brushes walked toward me on the sidewalk, her eyes averted. "Excuse me," I said. "Do you know number eleven Saint Gothard Street?"

She glanced up and down the empty street, then murmured, "Oh yes, number eleven." She pointed up a hill. "Three blocks. You go. You will see it. But they have cleaned everything up now." Behind a nearby wall a big dog, alerted by our voices, began barking and snarling; the woman and I separated like escaped cons caught in the glare of a searchlight.

The masonry wall surrounding number eleven St. Gothard Street was the tallest in the neighborhood; maybe the Dayals had hoped to go unnoticed behind it. Now it had several pale spots where the swastikas had been scrubbed or sandblasted away. Everything else was back to normal. Today the letter carrier, perhaps unaware of yesterday's drama, had crammed the slot in the wall with junk mail.

A middle-aged man with a head as bald as the tip of a rocket sat on the porch of a house directly across the street, and scowled at an open newspaper.

I crossed over, and from the sidewalk called, "Excuse me..."

A pit bull, previously unseen, shot from beside the porch and hurled himself, yelping and snorting, at the chain-link fence protecting the meat of my thigh from his jaws. Other dogs down the street rooted him on.

The man didn't move his head, but raised one hairless eyebrow and fixed an eyeball on me. "*Yes!*" he screamed.

I had envisioned an innocent chat about the riot but, instead, I held up my arm and pointed at my wrist. "Can you tell me the time?"

"Noon..." His eyebrow snapped back down; the paper shot up to cover his face. "Exactly."

So *that*, I thought, is a small peek at what the Dayals saw—the bald-headed, bald-browed face of apartheid. No wonder they fled. I hurried down the street and out of Mayfair West, feeling eyes on the back of my neck, gauging it for a noose, perhaps.

52

Tembisa

Other religions pointed to the sky and while we were looking at the sky,
they dug up all the gold and diamonds and went away with them.

—JIMMY CLIFF

A cold front moved through on my second day in Johannesburg. I awoke in the morning—"Apartheid, apartheid," ringing in my head—and looked out the window to see raindrops falling through the air shaft. I crawled back under the covers, made notes for a while, and then read Anne Tyler's *Dinner at the Homesick Restaurant* (a diversion I'd found in a local used book store) until noon, when hunger drove me and my umbrella to the streets.

The prostitutes had found something better, something drier, to do today. I headed downtown, past the deserted chess board and empty lawns of Joubert Park. During breakfast-and-a-newspaper at The Bakers Dozen I noticed *A Fish Called Wanda* and *Bull Durham* among the half dozen movies being advertised at a nearby theater. I'd missed both movies when they'd been current, and had always been on the lookout for them. Show time for *Fish* was imminent, and moments later I was walking through the front door of the Kine Entertainment Complex. Inside, people of all colors were eating at integrated snack bars and restaurants and rubbing shoulders at rows of video games. An adventure traveler parachuting into this happy world would never guess it was NET BLANKES South Africa. An Indian teenager took my money, a black teenager tore the stub, and a white one opened the the-

322

ater door for me. I was drawn right in by the movie, a John Cleese farce involving British bankrobbers, and Jamie Lee Curtis wearing various tight outfits; several times I heard my own belly laugh bouncing off the screen back at me, and for once in my life thought: *Thank God for Hollywood.*

At the film's conclusion, biographical follow-ups for several characters appeared on the screen. A character named Otto had proved to be a hard-hearted sadist, and now the last words to scroll up were: "Otto emigrated to South Africa and became Minister of Justice." The snicker of recognition from the audience, and the fact that this line had been permitted past the censors said, I thought, *something* good about the country.

I had enjoyed the escape immensely, and was in no rush to go back out to the real world. Instead I played video games until showtime for *Bull Durham*, and then for two hours watched Kevin Costner swat fastballs over minor league fences. When it was over, night had come to the wet streets of Johannesburg. I took a sandwich back to my room and ate it while finishing *Dinner at the Homesick Restaurant*. As I fell off to sleep that night, I thought: *O.K. Now I'm ready for a township.*

During the late 1800s, with the rush for gold consuming Johannesburg's citizenry, the city developed in a hurried, makeshift fashion. Tailings from the mines were dumped wherever an open space could be found and people lived wherever they could manage, with, relatively speaking, little attention paid to how close the races lived to each other. But in 1904, following an outbreak of bubonic plague, Johannesburg's whites relocated Johannesburg's blacks to a series of black-only townships ten miles outside the city proper.

On my last afternoon in Johannesburg I boarded a third-class train car full of black workers pouring out of downtown. I was going to meet Ian Pearson, whose brother I had met at my hotel in Harare. When I'd phoned Ian the previous night, he said he was planning to visit the black township of Tembisa and invited me along.

At the Kempton Park station I immediately spotted the old blue Peugeot station wagon Ian had described over the phone—and, beside it, Ian himself. He was in his early thirties, tall, with glasses, sandy brown hair, medium build, and had the calm, thoughtful demeanor of a clergyman. As we drove, he explained tonight's mission.

"I am a member of a Methodist church in Kempton Park. Over the years the church has provided monthly care packages of food and essential provisions to seventeen elderly pensioners and thirty-two disabled members of a Methodist church in Tembisa. For the recipients, these packages mean the difference between getting by or living a life of deprivation.

"Recently there have been some problems. We used to deliver the packages to the reverend in Tembisa, and he would distribute them. But a couple of months ago he left on a trip to the States, and the next day his house was firebombed. Now the recipients tell us that the reverend was always asking them for money, and if they didn't give it to him he would delay the packages. He would say we hadn't delivered them yet, when, in fact, we had. When he finally did deliver the packages, the residents said they'd often been pilfered. Whatever the case, when the reverend came back from the States, he was assigned to another church.

"So the purpose of tonight's visit is to meet the new reverend and see if things can't be smoothed over. And if this meeting doesn't run too late, I'd like to drop by the home of some friends of mine who live in Tembisa and see if we can't spend a few minutes with them."

One of the uncanny aspects of South Africa is how much like America it looks: suburbs ringed with shopping malls and car dealerships; parks where uniformed Little League teams play baseball under banks of bright lights; restaurants with names like the Kansas Ranch Steakhouse.

But I've seen nothing in America to compare to Tembisa. There was no sign announcing the township limits, nor was one needed. The suburbs petered out, and moments later we entered a sprawling flat area, which I first mistook for a huge industrial park—or industrial wasteland. Powerful floodlights were mounted on high towers and spaced every couple of hundred feet. We arrived in the early evening, but when dark fell, these lights would illuminate the entire district.

Most of the homes we passed were flimsy collections of scrap wood and cardboard. In a few neighborhoods many of the houses were built of brick, but tin shacks sprouted everywhere among them, apparently at random. These neighborhoods stretched for mile after numbing mile. Layers of coal smoke hung low and thick, giving the air a coppery look and the township a post-nuclear-holocaust feel.

Some of Tembisa's roads were paved, some were dirt, nearly all were potholed. A group of boys kicked a soccer ball across a flat area covered with so much broken glass that, even in the fading light, it sparkled like a field of diamonds. We drove past one impossibly littered hillside—patches of dirt showing through a blanket of paper wrappers and scraps of plastic, like prairie grasses poking through a dusting of late spring snow—the single illusion of greenery I would see here. The township was almost devoid of grass, trees, and shrubs, and the yards around most houses were nothing but trampled earth. Nearly a million people lived here—more than the population of San Francisco. What effect, I wondered, would such surroundings have on one's imagination? No wonder blacks swarmed to the highrises and tree-lined streets of Hillbrow-Berea the moment the door was left ajar.

From afar it is tempting, even easy, to romanticize or trivialize a country's problems. Surely, thinks the optimist, goodness will prevail. Over time, hearts will change, equitable systems will develop. Things will work out. But a quick dash of Tembisa will sober up the most bubbly optimist. Can hope exist, I wondered, in a place awash in trash, a place whose population keeps increasing exponentially? As we rolled through Tembisa's depressing scenery, saying little to each other, I imagined Ian must be thinking a version of my own thought: *Thank God I don't live here!*

We parked in front of a trailer house next to a small church building. "I think this is the place," Ian said. Reverend Archie Dumela, wearing a white oxford shirt and a look of surprise, answered our knock. He'd never met Ian before, and, as he had no telephone, was not expecting our visit. But when Ian identified himself as being from the Kempton Park church, the door swung wide open. "Come in, brothers, come in."

Dumela's wife and several children, gathered around a television in the living room, watched American cops chase Mafioso hoodlums through the streets of New York City. Dumela introduced Ian and me, and then the three of us retreated to the dining room table. Over the blare of the television, Ian diplomatically explained the troubles with the previous reverend. Yes, Dumela said, he'd heard stories. He was glad that Ian had come, because people had been asking when their care packages would be arriving.

One of Dumela's sons appeared with tea for us; another jumped up every few minutes to make sure no one was bothering Ian's car.

Ian offered to facilitate a meeting between Dumela and the package recipients, to reassure them that Dumela had had nothing to do with the old reverend. Dumela said he was glad for the offer, but he felt confident of the congregation's trust, and worried that such a meeting might only raise doubts where none had previously existed. Fair enough, said Ian: a shipment of packages would arrive the next week. And that was that. We exchanged a few pleasantries and waved goodbye to the crowd in the living room. On-screen a white couple kissed while an announcer extolled the virtues of a line of feminine hygiene products.

Night had fully arrived, but the tall lights gave a murky orange glow to Tembisa. Shadowy figures walked the streets, half-obscured by the sooty air. Ian let out a relieved sigh when the Peugeot's engine turned over and caught. "Once someone stole my battery while I was visiting Tembisa," he said.

Every day since my arrival, I had read newspaper reports of murders and disturbances in the townships, but Ian hadn't expressed any qualms about coming here. "Are the townships really as dangerous as the newspapers make them out?" I asked Ian.

"I've been here many times," he said, "and so far losing my battery is the worst thing that's happened. But still, I pray a lot each time I come."

Ian steered us through Tembisa's curving maze of streets, toward the home of his friends. "I am a member of a group named *Koinonia* (*Koy-KNOWN-ya*)," he told me. "It means 'fellowship' in Afrikaans. One of the things we do is a home-exchange program: once a month my wife and I either have a black family from Tembisa over to dinner at our house, or we go to dinner at a Tembisa household. This way I have met two good friends, Linda and Victor, and I'm hoping you can meet them."

We came to a neighborhood with the feel of a modern subdivision still under construction: wide, paved streets with fresh-poured curbs; small houses that looked half-finished; yards seemingly awaiting the arrival of the landscapers. Ian saw a woman locking a driveway gate, and said, "Ah, there's Linda."

Linda watched with a frown as we pulled to the curb, and I thought she might bolt for the house. But when Ian leaned his head out the window and called a greeting, she clapped her hands.

"Oh, Ian!"

She unlocked the gate and hurried toward us. She hugged Ian, and in response to his question, said, "Of course it's not too late. Victor will be thrilled."

Linda wore red lipstick, had straightened her shoulder-length hair, and shook my hand with the enthusiasm of a cheerleader. She led us through a gate in the low iron fence surrounding the house, and past a red compact car parked on the cement driveway. "Victor," Linda called as she opened the door, "you'll never guess who is here!"

The house was tiny—it was actually one modest-sized room walled off into four compartments (kitchen, bedroom, dining room, and a bathroom/storage room). Victor, a tall man with a trim beard, emerged from the darkened bedroom wearing a red and blue rugby shirt. When he saw Ian, a smile spread over his face. "Oh, wonderful," he said. There were handshakes all round. Victor stepped to the bedroom (a double bed took up almost every inch of floor space), turned down the sound on the television (the same cop show the Dumela kids had been watching), and scooped a baby girl off the bed. "Look, Angela," he said. "It's Ian." When Angela's eyes found Ian's, her cheeks swelled into a chubby smile.

We crowded around a department store dining room table that occupied most of the front room; a tall china cabinet and our chairs filled the remainder. Victor pulled gauzy curtains across the window. Linda stepped the few feet to the kitchen, put a teapot on the electric stove, then sat beside me, holding Angela in her arms. Angela's tiny fist clutched my little finger.

Victor and Linda, both thirty-one years old, had moved to Tembisa from another township eight years earlier. "Back then," said Linda, "the Tembisa City Council had a list of people waiting for housing. The list was five years long. We added our names to it and shared a room with some members of my family. I have six brothers and sisters, and the house was not much bigger than this one. So it was difficult."

"But we noticed," said Victor, "that many houses in this area were empty, and people told us they'd been empty for some years. This house once was a workers' hostel where sixteen people slept, and when they moved out, other people came and took the doors, windows, window frames, roofing—everything. It was just a shell—four walls and nothing else. So Linda and I moved in and started to make it livable. And other people moved into the other houses nearby. We started to make this a neighborhood. But the council got scared; this was beyond their control. They told us that before we could live here, we had to wait for them to fix up the houses. We asked how long that would take. They said, 'Oh, not long—maybe five years.' So we stayed right here. They sent the police, but every time they came, we ran away. If they had caught us, we would have gone to jail. And to get out of jail, we would have had to pay 500 rand. Finally it was too dangerous for us. But we could not leave the place empty—it would be stripped again the day we left—so Linda's young brother slept here and every time the police came, he would leap out the window and run away. He was never caught.

"Finally we decided we must become political. I joined a committee, and we asked advice from the South African Council of Churches, and also from a lawyer. The lawyer became our go-between with the Tembisa council. After a year, they agreed to let us keep the houses we'd been fixing up. Now we own the titles outright—we pay only for the monthly utilities."

Linda put a hand on Victor's shoulder. "It seems not long ago that we were sleeping on the ground, wondering if the police would come. But soon we will have owned this house for three years."

While Linda poured tea, Victor told the story of the house's construction; how with the help of their families they'd strengthened walls, fixed the plumbing, put on a roof, installed windows. "Now this house is airtight," said Victor.

I said that when people in the West thought of life in South Africa's townships, they did not imagine people like Linda and Victor sitting at their dining room table, drinking tea from fine china cups with late night visitors while the blue light of a television flickered from the bedroom. Out back was a car they used for running errands or taking weekend trips. They had one child, and were planning to stop at two. In the West, I said, people might call them yuppies.

They laughed. "Yes," said Victor, "sometimes our friends call us that. But we don't want to give you a wrong impression. We still have many problems. There are seven children in Linda's family, and five in mine, and they need lots of looking after. We both have jobs, but you never know what will happen. We are just happy for everything that has happened in the last five years."

It was after ten o'clock when Victor and Linda saw us to the car. We pulled away, waving good-byes, but had driven not more than fifty feet when a siren whooped once behind us and a small blue sedan shot up alongside. A man in the back seat reached out and held a small flashing blue police light to the rooftop. The driver extended a white arm out his window, motioning us to the curb, and then cut over in front of us. Ian stopped the car. Four white men, wearing civilian clothing, climbed slowly out of the sedan. Our headlights showed that each was sporting a dark, droopy moustache and, jammed into his belt, a pistol. One appeared to be a teenager.

"South African security forces," Ian said, quietly. "This will be interesting."

The four men surrounded our car and shone flashlights in on us. The oldest and the beefiest of the four leaned down to Ian's window and asked him to step out of the car. I glanced over my shoulder toward Victor's and Linda's house: they had surely seen us being pulled over, but now they had disappeared.

I caught snatches of Ian's explanation: "Kempton Park...Reverend Archie...Koinonia." The leader asked him to go around back and open the Peugeot's storage compartment. He gave several satisfied grunts as Ian rummaged its contents—a jack, a spare tire, an oil can, some rags. He came around to my window. "What hev you gawt in yaw beg?" he asked me.

"Clothes, books," I said. "Want to see?"

"Yiss, plizz."

I opened my daypack. My thick sweater and my copy of *Africa on a Shoestring* were on top. The man felt them and said, "Right you ah." Had he reached any farther he'd have found my notebook, camera, tape recorder.

"What were they looking for?" I asked Ian when we were again on our way.

"Drugs," he said. "Or arms. There are a lot of people not going to school these days, and the security forces are afraid of outsiders coming in and encouraging them."

"Did you tell them I was a foreigner?"

"Heavens, no," he said. "And all they need to hear is the word 'journalist'..."

"Does one ever get to relax in South Africa?" I asked. Each morning I'd been here, I'd awakened with the same alarm ringing in my head: Apartheid! And it rang straight through each day. What would that do to someone who lived here?

"My brother Bryan and his wife went to live in Australia for several years," Ian said.

"When they came back, although South Africa was their home, they said they were really uncomfortable here. They'd gotten used to Australia, to being able just to *live*, and not having to deal constantly with the guilt. They felt free, they said. Sometimes," Ian said, "I wonder what that's like."

53

To Get Lost

The world is built on discrimination...The South Africans admit it.
They don't say, like the French, "Algerians have a legal right to live in
the sixteenth arrondissement, but they can't afford to." They don't say,
like the Israelis, "Arabs have a legal right to live in West Jerusalem, but
they're afraid to." They don't say, like the Americans, "Indians have a
legal right to live in Ohio, but, oops, we killed them all."

— P. J. O'ROURKE, "In Whitest Africa"

Around noon of day ninety-four I checked out of The Pads and walked the few blocks to my local grocery store. From the trash receptacle out front I salvaged a square of cardboard, and inside I bought some yogurt and bananas, a box of crackers, and a fat blue marking pen. Following my guidebook's instructions, I walked downtown and boarded the number 55 bus for the five-mile ride to Ridgeway. Along the way I inked the letters C-A-P-E onto my square of cardboard.

I walked the leafy streets of Ridgeway, past an elementary school where white children in soccer uniforms kicked a ball around a green pitch, and climbed down an embankment to the busy six-lane highway, heading south out of Johannesburg. Almost immediately an ancient, rust-red Volkswagen bug, with its back seat missing, pulled over to the shoulder. The driver was a young Indian man named Hilton. He was not going far, he said, but knew a good place to drop me off.

Hilton's great-great-grandfather had come from Bombay around the turn of the century and, according to family lore, was jailed with Gandhi during the Mahatma's days in South Africa. Gandhi—a London-educated lawyer, unable to find work in India—had come to South Africa in 1893 on a one-year contract to do legal work. But after being thrown out of a first-class railway compartment, after being beaten up by a stagecoach driver for refusing to surrender his seat to a white man, and after being barred from hotels reserved for "Europeans only," Gandhi became enmeshed in the struggle for equal rights for South Africa's Indians and wound up staying for twenty years. His efforts were, for the most part, unsuccessful, but the philosophies and tactics he devised along the way eventually freed India.

Hilton drove past a truck stop marking Johannesburg's extreme southern periphery and let me off at a highway junction a couple of miles into the countryside. When the noise of the car's motor died away, I heard nothing but snickering insects. N1, the four-lane divided highway running southwest from Johannesburg 900 miles to Cape Town, cut across a landscape of rolling, forested hills that stretched as far as I could see. Traffic was light, a car or truck passing every minute or two, but I was in no hurry. The sun was warm on my face, my flight back to America didn't leave Cape Town for another six mornings, and if I were to spend a night or even two nights right here beside the road, I would be O.K. I had my air mattress, sleeping bag, and mosquito screen, and if I got hungry, I could always hike back to the truck stop for a meal.

It felt good to be out of the city and alone again. My four days in Johannesburg, trying to make sense of apartheid, had been like a night's sleep on a lumpy mattress—constant tossing and turning in search of a comfortable position. Now I propped my CAPE sign up against my backpack, sat down on the pavement and filled several pages in my notebook.

The previous evening I had made a gut decision to not consider inviting Linda and Victor to America. I had *liked* them—no problem there. The problem was, well...their china. Their china *and* the car out back.

Their township lives already seemed semi-Western. The street outside their house was newly paved, and inside they watched American television shows. They had regular work and took weekend getaways. By god, they even had a *lawyer!* Inviting them to visit San Francisco would seem not much different than inviting someone from, oh, maybe a tough section of Baltimore. It wouldn't be such a big deal to them. And I wanted my visitor to be just a little bit in awe of the West—I wanted him to help me see it newly, through fresh wide eyes.

So was this whole thing, as usual, all about *me?* Of course it was. Is a truly unselfish act an actual impossibility? Falling on a hand grenade in a crowded foxhole—now *that*, I thought, might be a genuine act of unselfishness. But maybe the unselfish act can be performed only on impulse. Maybe the act of considering or planning one—as I certainly had—automatically contaminates it.

I was touchy about the "playing God" criticisms. But who among us hasn't pulled out a few coins or bills from their pocket when the person ahead at the checkout counter—usually a kid buying candy—comes up a little short? Is *that* playing God? In my conscious mind I wasn't aware of any sinister personal motives, was aware only that I had chosen to give to someone else the sort of gift I wouldn't mind falling into my own lap. Strangers have often helped me out—goodness has rained down on me. I was heading off to my last year of college, short of my tuition, when my Aunt Cathy, who could not have known of my need, unexpectedly handed me an envelope containing a $300 check that exactly covered my shortfall. Did I resent this, suspect her motives? Not ever.

It seems unquestionable to me that every act a person performs tips the balance of the world. Do something nice and the world is immediately a nicer place. Do something mean and the world darkens a shade. Share your blessings and the world is instantly more generous, more friendly, easier, happier. And I want to live in a happier, easier world. What better way to bring that about than by giving away the thing that, so far in life, had meant the most to me—the chance to travel. At the end of my life, I told myself, I would not regret this act. And if I got my own trip around the world out of it, if I managed to write a publishable book about it, so much the better. If it made me happy, wonderful. If someone else had a problem with that, it was their own problem.

On the side of a South African highway I decided I was overthinking. All I was really trying to do on this trip was have a little fun—or even a lot. There was no point trying to justify my life. My mission really hadn't changed since Boulder. Enjoy the day. Let it all work out.

After half an hour, I was picked up by a young white man with sun-bleached brown hair. He said his name was Nico Viljoen and that he was South Africa's long distance canoeing champ; currently he was in training for a four-day, 256-kilometer race scheduled for July. I mentioned that I had once lived near the Arkansas River in Colorado, site of the U.S. national kayak championships. Nico said he'd read about the Arkansas, and hoped someday to compete in the States. There were more opportunities in the States. The total drainage of all South African rivers was, he said, equaled by that of the Delaware River.

Thirty miles later Nico let me off under an overpass near Parys—a small, distant ship of a town afloat on a sea of cornfields. The sky had filled with jostling clouds that now sprinkled rain. But I was dry under my overpass, and I was there not more than fifteen minutes before I was picked up by Alan, a young white man driving a brand new, jade-green BMW. A husky blond in his late twenties, Alan had the aura of a recent lottery winner—and a story to match. Two years and three months ago he'd taken a job with a construction company. After a year passed, he went to his boss and said that if he, Alan, were made fore-man, their jobs would get done much cheaper. "My boss said, 'O.K., let's see what you can do,' and he started giving me some small jobs. I started with two blacks just to carry my tools. A month later a big job came along, and my boss put me in charge of it. I finished it faster and cheaper than anyone could have guessed.

"When I saw how easy it was, and how good I was at it, I started my own company." He handed me a card from his wallet: *Engineering— Steel Construction. Alan Piet, Director.* "Within months I got some backing and bought big cranes and heavy equipment. Now I have two hundred and forty men working for me," he said proudly, adding almost as an afterthought, "and three hundred blacks. I am making money like I never dreamed possible. There is so much opportunity in this country. I love being a South African. A few months ago I bought a lovely farm for 1.1 million rand." (Roughly half a million dollars.) "And paid cash."

We came to the turnoff for Alan's spread, but he drove past it to a toll booth in the countryside—ten kilometers out of his way—dropped me off, and turned around.

Within minutes I was picked up by Willi Jonker, a man in his early thirties. Willi was coming from Johannesburg, where he'd just purchased a Mercedes second-hand, and this afternoon was driving it as far as his sister's house in Bloemfontein, 150 miles down the road. I told Willi about Alan Piet—the construction company, the BMW, the farm. His story had seemed so fantastic. "Do you think it's true?" I asked Willi.

"Oh, I do not doubt it," Willi said. "There *is* a lot of opportunity in this country. A man who is willing to work can make a go of it just about anywhere. Several years ago I was an educator, but now I've changed fields, and just recently I've been made a partner in my investment firm."

"Does becoming a partner mean you have to own a Mercedes?" I asked—playfully, I hoped.

"No," he said, chuckling. And a moment later: "Well, maybe."

Willi wore glasses, had a slight build, and a measured, even voice. Compared to Alan he had the humility of a Zen monk. When I began to ask about his life, he said, "I have a very ordinary life and I'll tell you anything you care to know about it, but it is not every day that I pick up an American by the side of the road, and first I want to hear about your travels, please."

I hadn't babbled at anyone in quite some time, and now I told Willi about my plan to surprise someone with an invitation to America, about all the places I'd seen during the last three months and the people I had met.

"You're living a fantastic dream," Willi said, sighing, and I didn't dispute it. We fell into a comfortable silence, cruising down a four-lane highway through wheat fields turning golden. Every few miles we passed a farmhouse, usually perched on a knoll and surrounded by a copse of trees. Sunk back into leather seats I watched all this through the Mercedes' spotless windshield, classical music lilting from the four speakers.

I liked this ride, appreciated Willi's flattery. I also liked his music, his air conditioning, the apparent comfort of his life. I started to fantasize what sort of life I might have had if I'd focused more on money. At the time, I had never earned $20,000 in a single year, but I always told myself that I could have earned a lot—if only I'd wanted to. I'd had at least one chance. In 1981 in Tucson, Arizona, I became friends with a man who owned a string of successful automobile body shops. I liked him and coveted his wealth, and he apparently saw something in me. One night after we'd known each other for several months, he said he'd been waiting for the right person to appear and now he asked me to become his general manager. My salary would be $35,000, but I would earn commissions based on the volume of business. Plugging in numbers from his previous years, it seemed that I could not earn less than $80,000 a year. He wanted an answer in two days.

I mulled it over for forty-eight insanity-inducing hours. In the end I told him that I *really* appreciated the offer. It had forced me to look at what was important to me, and I'd concluded that what was really important to me was travel. (I didn't tell him I'd also realized that I didn't want any part of automobile repair at any price—well, certainly not a mere $80,000 a year.) Three months later I was on my way to India for the first time.

After an hour in the car with Willi, it occurred to me that I had not seen a black person since Johannesburg. Out in the countryside one might forget all about apartheid.

"What," I asked Willi, "do you think of the political situation?"

He said, "I would prefer to hear your thoughts."

I told him I found South Africa confusing and thought-provoking—sometimes almost overwhelmingly so. On the one hand there were the squalid townships, on the other the impressive economy. Coming from America it was hard, I said, to have any sympathy for a system that subjugated one people to another. But it was also hard to imagine turning over such a fragile and rich economy to any group not prepared to operate it. Americans would never do it. I had just come from Zimbabwe and before that Kenya, and I would not like to see South Africa be sucked down by the kinds of problems plaguing those places; but I would not want to see it stay the same either.

"We are changing," Willi said. "The vast majority of white South Africans know that there is no choice—to survive we must change. And in the last ten or fifteen years we have probably changed as much as any country in the world. It is a very unjust thing that has happened to the black man here, and I want to see him liberated as soon as possible. But, it's a terribly difficult thing logistically. Most blacks, due to reasons quite beyond their control, are not educated or trained to run a modern economy. There is the very real fear that if we change too quickly, the whole situation might unravel. I would hate to see South Africa fall apart. Personally, I am optimistic. I have to be. This is my country. Where else would I go?"

For every white person in southern Africa who struck me as overtly racist, there were perhaps five or ten who seemed as thoughtful, as even, as Willi. I found myself sympathizing not just with them, but with *everyone* in the troubled land. All of America's many problems seemed absolutely inconsequential when considered from the vantage point of South Africa.

Late in the afternoon the wheat fields gave way to a countryside of prairie grasses and cactus and distant hills. Willi dropped me at a gas station/convenience mart in the bush a few kilometers outside Bloemfontein and wished me well. I bought two chicken-mayo sandwiches, a bag of chips, and a Stoney Ginger Beer, consumed them at an outdoor picnic table, and then walked back to the highway. The sun was setting and the western sky had the look of a huge canvas onto which a gleeful artist had hurled a fat, overripe tomato, and then, one by one, a dozen eggs. Cars were rare, so before the light faded away completely, I scouted the immediate area and found a level spot beneath a tree, where I might camp if need be.

And then it was night. I stood and listened to the crickets chirp, threw rocks at a nearby power pole until my arm ached, and recalled other days on the road. I was eighteen when I bit off my first big hitch—from St. Louis to Dallas. My third lift came from two scruffy-looking men who asked me: "Do you have a driver's license? Do you have any money?" I had been with them less than five minutes when a Missouri state trooper pulled the car over, confiscated a long knife from under the front seat, and arrested the two men for armed robbery in a nearby town. He checked my driver's license, and said, "I was tailing these fellows before they picked you up, son. There's no telling what they were planning to do with you."

I sat by that Missouri highway for a while and contemplated my hitchhiking career. If I'd had enough money, I might have walked to the next town and bought a bus ticket. But I didn't, and it was hot, and I had a heavy pack, and before long I stuck out my thumb again. Five minutes later someone picked me up and drove me right to my destination in Dallas, 500 miles away, and hitchhiking seemed like a grand adventure. By the time I was twenty-two, I'd hitchhiked more than 10,000 miles around the United States; by twenty-five, I'd lost count.

Now, on the shoulder outside Bloemfontein, stars were coming out. My mind wandered to my family, my girlfriend. I wondered what sort of future lay ahead of me, and sometime during the evening I pulled out my notebook and scribbled: "The definition of infinity: the number of things I don't know, divided by the number of things I do." And: "Having once hitchhiked to find myself, I do it now to get lost."

Around 10 o'clock I vowed to call it a night after the next thirty cars passed. When thirty zipped past, I renewed the pledge, and after thirty more renewed it again. But after the hundredth car, I lifted my pack, flicked on my flashlight, and started through the grass toward my campsite, worrying now about snakes. I had taken just a few steps when—in strict accordance with the Hitchhiker's Law of Surrender— a car braked to a halt, tires crunching the gravel on the shoulder behind me. A man leaned his head out the window. In the thick heavy accent of the Afrikaner, he called, "Are you looking for a ride, mate?"

54

O'Boyle and the *Abakwetas*

*The test of an adventure is that when you're in the middle of it, you
say to yourself, "Oh, now I've got myself into an awful mess; I wish
I were sitting quietly at home." And the sign that something's wrong
with you is when you sit quietly at home wishing you were out having
lots of adventure.*

—THORNTON WILDER, *The Matchmaker, Act IV*

Jake O'Boyle said I was welcome to ride along if I would promise to
keep him awake. He had departed Johannesburg in mid-afternoon
and had stopped along the way to visit a friend. It was now 11 o'clock,
and he was headed for the town of Colesburg—still two and a half
hours down the highway. He was pudgy, balding, wore glasses, and had
the air of a headmaster who had chosen to stay on to earn his pension
after having long ago wearied of teenagers. And as we rolled up, down,
and around the low, arid hills of the Orange Free State, his sad story
rumbled out of the driver's side's darkness.

O'Boyle's parents, too poor to care for him, had placed him in an
orphanage when he was five years old. They visited once a year until he
was fifteen. His mother came alone that year and told O'Boyle that his
father had died, and then she never came again. O'Boyle had no idea
what became of her.

At nineteen he left the orphanage. He met his first wife on a blind
date and had three kids with her—now 31, 29, and 19 years old. One
night when the youngest, Michael, was only 8, O'Boyle came home and

found his wife in bed with two policemen. "The two older kids were away at the time," he said, "but Mikie was in the living room. I walked into the bedroom, surveyed the situation, and said, 'What's Mikie doing here?' I picked him up and walked out of the house—for good. I've never tried to stop the kids from seeing her, but that was the last time I ever saw my wife."

I said, "That must have hurt."

"Ah, but it's ancient history," he said. "Life is what you make it. I've got a good wife now and a nice home in Port E."

O'Boyle was the general manager of a Port Elizabeth furniture chain, and had just this morning, in Johannesburg, arranged the purchase of two truckloads of sofabeds. We would, he said, probably see his drivers along the route.

"Do you like your work?" I asked.

"The work is not bad. Work is work, I feel. I could probably be happy doing just about anything. But I am not getting paid what I'm worth. After the last review period, during which I saved the division from disaster—single-handedly mind you—I received a piddling raise. When I complained, my boss said I was free to look for another job if I didn't like it. This from a man who wouldn't even have a job if it weren't for me. I turned his division around, brought it from deep in the red and into the black, and *that*'s the kind of thanks he gives me. But I'm not about to quit. Life is what you make it, and I'll do an even better job this next year. I'll bet you I outlast this boss. He's a 'rummy' and it wouldn't surprise me if he drank himself to death before long."

Apparently, in the short time I'd been with him—priming him with *Oh, reallys* and *Hmmn, interestings*—O'Boyle had decided I was O.K. "Tell you what," he said. "I'm just spending the night in Colesburg. There's a hotel there with rooms for only twenty-nine rand. I want to be on the road by seven A.M., and, if you want to get your own room, and if you don't mind getting up early, you can ride on with me tomorrow. And when we reach Port Elizabeth, you're welcome to spend a night or two with my wife and me."

The ride offer came as a relief. Several people had recommended that at Colesburg I should veer off the main Johannesburg-to-Cape Town route onto a small road winding south through the Drakensburg mountains to Port Elizabeth. From Port Elizabeth I could take the fabled "Garden Route" along the Indian Ocean coast to Cape Town. The one catch was that the Colesburg-Port Elizabeth stretch was dry, windy, dusty, and so lightly-traveled that it was sometimes a hard hitch.

I thanked O'Boyle and accepted his ride and hotel room suggestions, but said I would wait until tomorrow to see how I felt about staying in Port Elizabeth. I had only five days left.

"Suit yourself," he said.

We were quiet a while, staring out at the occasional cactus and cartwheeling sagebrush illuminated by our headlights. O'Boyle pointed out a huge lake trapped behind the Hendrik Verwoerd Dam—a black hole under the starry sky...

Some time later I felt the car decelerate, and realized that I had drifted off. O'Boyle had slowed to look at a tractor-trailer stopped at a turnout. The truck driver was standing in the roadside weeds, his back to the road, taking a leak; when he turned toward our headlights, we saw the face of a white man. "Oh," said O'Boyle, stepping on the gas pedal, "I thought he might be one of our drivers, but all of ours are blacks."

Trying to cover my sleepiness, I now blurted the first thing that came to mind: "Are there black managers in your business?"

"South Africa has the most sophisticated and educated blacks in all of Africa," O'Boyle said. "Probably nowhere else in the world are blacks as well taken care of as they are here. But do they appreciate this? No! So many of them leave the country to carry on about how terribly they've been treated..."

"I didn't mean anything," I said. "I just wondered..."

But I'd set him off. "If South Africa is treating these people so badly," he said, his voice gathering strength, "why do they keep coming—from Zambia, Zimbabwe, Namibia, Botswana, Mozambique? Just last week we had people from Tanzania and Kenya show up, looking for work at the warehouse. Now would they come all that way unless they'd been told that they'd get a better deal here? There is a black man, Jackson, who is a janitor at the warehouse." O'Boyle's pronunciation of black always hit my ear as "*bleck*," and each time I cringed. "Last year when he was sick, we got him to a doctor in Port E who said he needed a heart operation. We flew him to Cape Town and a specialist did the operation. Could a janitor in America afford a heart operation? For the whole thing Jackson paid twenny cents. Me? It would have cost me eighteen thousand rand—and I'd have had to pay every last cent. But do you think these people appreciate that? No, they expect it. These people pay two rand a month for rent, and always they are in arrears. They don't know anything about turning off a lightbulb, and they talk on the phone for hours at a time. Last week one of my men says to me, 'Your telephone bill is fifty-three rand and mine is two hundred and nineteen. I think I am being cheated.'"

I stole a peek over at O'Boyle. The dim light of the dash panel made his round face and set jaw look like an angry mask. I thought: *I will not be staying in Port Elizabeth.*

But O'Boyle wasn't finished. "Let me ask you this," he said. "What are your beaches like in America? Do you have some standards? I don't think it's asking too much that when you go to the beach with your family that there be a few standards. For years we've had separate beaches. The white beaches have minimal standards. Women wear bikinis, small ones like in the West. They may undo their tops as they lay down so they won't get a tan line, but they don't bare their boobs, if you will. But you go to one of the beaches we've opened up recently and here's what you'll see: blacks completely naked, or the women will be topless, or maybe wearing bra and panties, or just wearing panties shot with holes, or with no elastic, so they have to hold them up. In America, would you permit this?"

I thought this would not be a good time to mention my favorite beach, the nude beach at the base of the Golden Gate Bridge. Nor the clothing-optional hot springs where I'd met Rhonda. I said, "Well, I'm sure that's not very much fun for you."

"No," he said. "No fun et ull."

It was one-thirty and I was wide awake when we reached Colesburg. We parked inside a walled compound behind the hotel, where two black men huddled by a campfire, guarding cars. The hotel had immaculate rooms with firm mattresses and clean towels. I slept solidly, but not for long; breakfast trays were left outside our rooms at six-thirty. O'Boyle rapped on my door a few minutes later. He seemed like a different man in the morning: his hair was still wet and slicked back from his shower, and the smile with which he greeted me seemed boyish. He asked how I'd slept. By seven o'clock we were on the road again.

It was a calm, clear morning, with a soft apricot glow coming from behind the mountains to the east. We drove along a two-lane road through a wide, arid valley. "Nude cactus" (no thorns) was planted in rows to collect moisture and serve as sheep fodder. "This area used to be a big farming and ranching center," O'Boyle said, "but it's been through a drought for the last eleven years, and now it's turning into a desert. Hardly anything will grow here. Those spiky green plants are sisal. The spindly trees—those are aloe. They bind the soil. Without them and these cactus all this land would blow away." We passed windmill after windmill, all still. "Boreholes," O'Boyle said. "Dried up now. No more water. All these small dams we've been passing are only storing dust." I hoped that drought-prone California would never come to this.

From time to time the mountains closed in, squeezing the road up over tight, twisting passes or curling it around the edges of table-topped mesas. O'Boyle pointed out a particular cactus with a large white blossom. "We are lucky," he said. "That one blooms for only one day every year. And there are other species that bloom only at night." When we came to a sign that said KUDU CROSSING, he said, "We will see no kudus in the day time." And indeed we didn't see any of these antelope with their long corkscrew horns. But in the roadside scrub we saw ostriches, gophers, eagles, goats, and springbok—the small, jumpy gazelle that are South Africa's national symbol.

"Do you see the golf course?" O'Boyle asked me.

Out the window I saw only brown scrub and miles of cactus. Then: two white men wearing knickerbockers and pulling golf carts along a strip of earth that had been scraped with a blade. "That is the fairway they are walking on," O'Boyle said. "Hard as a parking lot. It'll add fifty yards to any man's drive. Up ahead, see the green?" A pin was planted in a circle of dirt that had been poured with a red oil. "They are red here, but we still call them greens."

In the small town of Graffen we passed some one hundred black men and women standing outside what looked like a warehouse.

"That's an unemployment center," O'Boyle said. "They come in from the bush to learn little skills that might get them a job someday. Sewing—so they might become maids. How to serve tea—so they might work in restaurants. They are paid two-rand-forty a day, but the program lasts only two weeks and they can only come once a year. Otherwise they'd be here forever."

In mid-morning, at the top of a mountain pass, we saw a tractor-trailer stopped in a turnout. "At last," said O'Boyle. "One of my men." The driver was out checking the rear tires. O'Boyle drove right up beside him and rolled down his window. I watched the truck driver's face as he turned toward us, and was surprised to see no flicker of displeasure, no trace of the hate I expected. Recognizing O'Boyle, the driver's brow lifted, his mouth spread into a smile, and a happy little yelp escaped him. Through the open window he and O'Boyle shook hands like victorious teammates and shared a jocular exchange in Afrikaans.

Back on the road O'Boyle told me, "It's better here between blacks and whites than in the States. We hear so much about how we should treat our blacks the way American blacks are treated." *Blecks, blecks, blecks.* "But I spent two months visiting one of my sons when he was living in Detroit, and it's no different there. We say 'bloody kaffirs,' you say 'fookin' niggers.' The only difference is that we've got our prejudice written into our laws."

I was not unsympathetic to this part of O'Boyle's argument. It is certainly easier to insist on fairness for the oppressed in a distant country rather than in one's own. And from South Africa the rest of the world did, indeed, appear to be hypocritical. ("I could name a couple of countries where the whites simply slaughtered the native peoples," a man in Cape Town would point out to me.) But I was starting to hate O'Boyle and now I said nothing, hoping that he would just shut up.

"This is a good country, South Africa," he continued. "It's a rich country. America is a poor country. Everything is plastic money in America. An American will charge $200 a month and when the bill comes he pays the $15 minimum. Now the balance is $185. The next month he charges $40. Now the balance is $225, plus interest, $230 maybe—but again he pays only $15. And your government does the same thing."

"It's true," I said, and that quieted him for a brief while.

On the downside of the pass we saw a black boy sitting atop a high fence, picking something off his arm. O'Boyle said, "Did you see that baboon back there?"

I said, "That was not a baboon."

"How you expect us to give this country over to these people is beyond me," he said, snorting. "You talk about how we are all equal and they need their rights. But these people are not like you and me. It's not just a joke that the most confusing day in a township is Father's Day. One of these blacks will see a woman on the other side of the street, and he will call out, 'Hey, sis,' and then they will go fook in the grahz. I have seen this."

It seemed that something had snapped inside O'Boyle, as though his facade of intelligence had crumbled and now his nasty side was gushing out. "What do you get when you cross a kaffir and a baboon?" he asked.

I said nothing.

"A retarded baboon," he said. "Why did God give blacks rhythm? Because he buggered up their hair."

I said, "I don't appreciate these jokes."

He laughed. "Why did God give flies wings? So they could beat the blacks to all the shit."

"Please!" I said, and I must have said it loudly, because finally he stopped.

To excuse O'Boyle's behavior, to write it off to ignorance or to his atrocious childhood, would be like saying: Poor Hitler. I thought: *A real man would say, "Stop! Let me out right here."* In San Francisco, telling an ethnic joke means almost automatic expulsion from my cab. But that was on my own turf, and now, in South Africa, O'Boyle and I were already several miles deep into an immense, inhospitable cactus forest—big tangled fields of it, two stories high. We were approaching the coast at sixty miles an hour, and before long I would, I rationalized, be rid of him.

We began seeing black people with buckets of small red cactus apples sitting at the roadside, and waving for us to stop and buy them. O'Boyle, now his calmer self again, asked, "Ev you evva eaten prickly pear?"

"No."

"Oh, then you must."

He stopped the car and began chatting and joking with the sellers who came to his window, speaking Afrikaans in the same amiable tone he'd used with the truck driver. The sellers responded with hoots of laughter. O'Boyle bought us each a prickly pear. They were bland, but wet. I thought: *If I jump out of the car here, I'll survive until I get my next ride.*

But I stayed, and before long we emerged from the mountains onto a four-lane divided highway that cut across a scrub plain on the edge of Port Elizabeth. Vast slums and dreary housing projects spread across the distant hillsides. After a week in South Africa, I didn't need to ask (and with O'Boyle, I dared not): these were the townships (black) that lay outside every city (white) and supplied cheap labor.

I spotted a young black man standing in the roadside bush. His face and body were painted white, and he wore a tattered tunic. His head turned to follow the motion of our car.

"What's he up to?" I asked O'Boyle.

"He's what they call an *abakwetas* (ah-bah-KWAY-tuss). He has just recently been circumcised. In the old days an *abakwetas* would smear himself with this white paste and go out and live in the bush for a month, wearing nothing. He would have to kill his own food and was not permitted to talk to anyone. But these days there is not so much bush, and since he's near a town, he has to wear some clothes. And since there is no more game to kill, he stands next to the road and hopes that people like us will stop and give him fifty cents, so that a friend can buy him some chips at the local store."

"I'd love to talk to him," I said.

"He won't speak English," O'Boyle said, "but if you want, I can translate."

When we turned around and pulled off the road, the man walked over to us. He wore red tennis shoes and carried a walking stick. His tunic was made of a coarse brown wool with vertical white stripes. He leaned down to my window and he and O'Boyle spoke past me in Afrikaans. But when O'Boyle said the word "America," the *abakwetas* turned his face toward mine. "America," he murmured, quizzically.

"What do you want me to ask him?" O'Boyle said.

"What's his name?"

O'Boyle asked my question in Afrikaans.

The *abakwetas* said, "Lennox Mevana."

O'Boyle translated: "Lennox Mevana."

"When was he circumcised?"

O'Boyle interpreted my question, and then Lennox's answer: "Back in December."

"Was it painful?"

I don't know what translation O'Boyle gave my question, but Lennox startled me by pulling up his tunic to reveal a Polish-sausage-sized penis. Near its knobby end a thin strip of gauze was tied around the circumcision wound.

"Thanks," I said, and Lennox lowered his tunic.

"What will he do when this is over?" I asked O'Boyle.

O'Boyle didn't bother asking Lennox the question, but started in on his own answer: "When his time is completed, in another couple of weeks maybe, he will paint himself red and put on pants and a cap like those men behind him..."

Since we had stopped, several other men—some wearing the same white face and tunics as Lennox, and some wearing pants and shirts and having red-painted faces—had been gathering in the nearby bush. For a couple of hundred yards in each direction the landscape was litter-strewn: snack wrappers, scraps of plastic, bits of cardboard stuck on every bush. Behind Lennox was a patchwork hut made of hunks of cloth and cardboard.

As I looked past him, I heard him say softly, so softly that only I could hear, "Find a wife."

Find a wife! Lennox spoke English! I looked up at him, and before he glanced away, I saw an unmistakable pride in his eye. On the other side of the car O'Boyle was rattling on: "...and after two more weeks, he will be a man, and can return to his home and begin looking for a wife."

This was incredible: O'Boyle stuffed behind the wheel of his car, pontificating about the circumcision rites of the dumb savages—unaware that this dumb savage spoke English. Was this what South Africa's problem came down to? The proverbial failure to communicate?

"How old are you?" I said directly to Lennox.

"Twenty-five," he said.

O'Boyle said, "They're all twenty-five when they go to be circumcised."

I turned to O'Boyle. "Lennox speaks English," I said.

"They all know a few words," he said.

I said, "Just a minute ago he said, 'Find a wife.'"

"Oh?" said O'Boyle, smirking.

I turned back to Lennox. "Do you speak English?"

"Yes," he said.

I glanced back at O'Boyle. *See?*

"Keep going," O'Boyle said.

"Do you have an address for mail?" I asked Lennox.

"Yes."

"Then I'd like to take your picture and send it to you."

"Yes," he said.

Lennox —Twenty-five years old and quite newly circumcised. His ambition: "Find a wife."

I pulled out my notebook. "What is your address?"

"Yes," he said, and broke my heart.

I looked past him toward his hut. "How long did it take you to build your house?"

"Yes," he said.

I showed him my camera.

"Fo-to," he said. He smiled, stepped back, and posed for me.

I opened my notebook and showed Lennox the list of addresses I'd collected on this trip. "If-you-have-an-address," I said, speaking very slowly, my pen poised over the paper, "I-will-mail-you-a-photo."

He stared, expectantly, as though I might write him out a check.

"You won't get an address," O'Boyle said. But he sounded sad, the gloating gone from his voice. "These fellows don't get mail."

"Would you ask him anyway?" I said.

They rattled away in Afrikaans.

"Well, how about that," O'Boyle said. "He does have an address." And using a mixture of English and Afrikaans the two of them hammered out Lennox's address; O'Boyle jotted it into my notebook.

"In-one-month," I said, raising an index finger toward Lennox, "I-send-you-a-photo." But again he seemed not to understand.

O'Boyle translated, and Lennox's face brightened when he understood. It brightened even more when I gave him two rand.

Back on the highway O'Boyle said, "Now you tell me...How do you change *that*? How do we integrate *that*? How long does America think it should take us? It's not like we've got Bill Cosby wanting to live next door."

I did not respond. Perhaps the travel writer James Morris gave the best answer possible. After spending several months in South Africa in 1957 (and before sex- and name-change procedures changed him into the better-known woman, Jan Morris), he wrote: "We can hope for a change of heart among the rigid Afrikaner zealots, the shock troops of racialism; we can wish for the emergence of some moderate African leaders of genius; we can keep our fingers crossed for compromise rather than revolution; but if we feel like praying about it all, we must be frank with the Almighty, and ask for a miracle."

55

Emergency?

*Having had so many rude things said about their country for so long,
South Africans find themselves clinging to the one thing no one can
argue about—its physical beauty.*

*The cliche most commonly used: "Ah, but this land is beautiful."
The "Ah" is essential, the pregnant pause that means, "so, the whites
are oppressing the blacks and the blacks are rioting, the economy's going
down the drain, it is the most hated country in the world...." but this
land is beautiful.*

—GRAHAM BOYNTON,
"South Africa: Yes or No?" *Conde Nast Traveler*

O'Boyle dropped me off at a turnout designated as a pickup point
for South African soldiers. Andrew, a nineteen-year-old wearing
a pea green uniform, was there ahead of me. He had scored a weekend
pass and was now headed to his family's summer home in Plettenburg
Bay, two hours away. I told Andrew I would stand back from the road
and give him first shot at the passing cars, and he said that if anyone
stopped he would put in a good word for me.

Ten minutes later we were both riding—Andrew in the front seat,
me and my pack in the back—in a new Ford with the air conditioner
going full blast. On the tape deck a song extolled the virtues of "Ja-
maica, Key Largo..." Neal, the driver, was also going to Plettenburg
Bay—"Plett," he called it—to spend the weekend at his vacation home.
Upon hearing that I was a foreigner, he immediately said, "Then you

must stay the weekend with me. I'm having a party tomorrow night—lots of beer, lots of girls. And you won't find a prettier place than Plett in all South Africa, maybe in all the world. It's fantastic. People come from all over to see Plett. The permanent population is only 3,000, but in December it hits 85,000."

"How do 3,000 residents handle so many visitors?" I asked.

"Many hotels, many restaurants," Neal said.

"But who works in them?"

"Six thousand blacks," he said, "live in the townships."

Neal had a droopy brown moustache and an Afrikaans accent. His Plett came out "Plitt," his fantastic "fuh-TUSS-tic." He was twenty-nine years old and managed a United Dairies Creamery. "People say it's time for me to get married," he told Andrew and me, "but why should I? I'm too young. I've got my salary all to myself. I have a company car and a place in Plitt for weekends. I'm having a fantastic time. Beer, anyone?"

It had been scorching outside, and Andrew and I welcomed the cans Neal pulled from his ice chest.

"Is drinking and driving legal here?" I asked.

Neal said, "Oh, yes."

Andrew disagreed. "Technically," he said, "it's illegal, but if you can handle your car, no one will ever say anything."

"I could du-reenk tu-wanny of these," Neal said.

Andrew said, "It *is* hot today."

"Bleddy hawt," said Neal.

Driving along the coast we were entertained by views of a royal blue ocean dumping foam breakers onto one wide, white horseshoe-shaped beach after another. "They go on like this for hundreds of klicks," said Neal. "Best surfing in the world. Did you ever see the surfer movie 'Endless Summer?' The best parts were shot right here on this coast."

As we entered the shade of a eucalyptus forest, I thought it remarkable how the area so resembled California: light blue sky, dark blue ocean; piney green hills sloping down to bluffs above sandy beaches; bark peeling in strips from the trunks of towering eucalyptus; white people in cars crammed with beach gear, getting an early start on the weekend. But there were small reminders that this wasn't the Golden State: a sign pointing down a dirt road, TOWNSHIP—1K; two bare-foot black boys crawling over a barbed wire fence; raggedly-dressed groups of black men and women walking along the shoulder. The trees cleared suddenly, yielding a quick view of a hillside crawling with shacks, and then closed as suddenly, leaving us back in the dense leafy forest.

The morning newspaper had reported on a hunger strike at Johan-nesburg's Deipkloof Prison. Some prisoners arrested under the provi-sions of South Africa's declared state of emergency (many of them detained as long as twenty-eight months so far without being charged) had refused food and water for the past eighteen days. Now 105 pris-oners at St. Albans Prison in Port Elizabeth had joined in, and author-ities were worried that the strike would spread to other prisons or become a cause in the townships.

"Do you folks ever wonder what South Africa will be like in five years?" I asked from the back seat.

"Oh, we'll get on," said Neal. "You've been here a week now—does it seem to you like there is any emergency?"

He did have a point. I had hitchhiked 500 miles without seeing a roadblock or an armed soldier or noticing any need for such.

"No, of course not," Neal said. "We never think about it."

But Andrew was not so sure. "Even if we aren't always consciously aware of the situation, we're always thinking about it," he said. "In the army we're always asking each other: 'Will you shoot if told to?' 'If you were black, would you be rioting?' Everyone knows that if we don't all get together and work out our problems amicably, we are going to lose our country."

"Yes," said Neal. "But we won't let that happen. It's too fantastic a country."

South Africa indeed seemed like America during the heyday of hitch-hiking—the 1960s and 1970s. Between Johannesburg and Cape Town I would be offered free lodging no fewer than five times. All the whites I met appeared successful; business opportunities seemed as numerous and natural to them as the sunshine and balmy air.

Neal was right: there was no sense of emergency here. Like a painting on a wall, the emergency had blended into South African daily life, and the only white people required to give it much thought were the politicians, news media, security forces, and soldiers, like Andrew, who were confronted with it every day. But for the country's 20 million blacks, coloureds, and Indians, it was a different story.

As we entered Plettenburg Bay, I noticed a small car with a blue police light on top, much like the car that had stopped Ian Pearson and me in Tembisa. Two white men with hand guns jammed into their belts stood outside the car questioning a group of five blacks picnicking in a park; one of the whites was emptying a liquor bottle into the grass. Andrew and Neal didn't even look. Maybe, I thought, South Africans were blind to such an event; maybe only someone who came to South Africa looking for trouble would find it noteworthy. A taxi fare, a man from Germany, had once asked me why there was so much trouble between Asians and whites in San Francisco.

But, I said, perplexed, there was hardly any such friction.

Oh, no, he told me. He'd just ridden a bus and seen a white woman passenger arguing with the Asian bus driver, so he knew better.

Neal regretfully accepted my decision not to stay with him, and dropped me off at Plettenburg Bay's one stoplight. The town was set on a bluff above a perfect curve of beach laced by white breakers. Beneath a famously blue sky, a gentle breeze nudged the salty air around. Designer cactus and palm trees grew in planters along the business district sidewalks. Retirees hobbled toward their Mercedes. Towheaded teenagers cruised the main street in VW bugs with racing stripes and big fat tires. Blond women in shorts pushed baby strollers past trendy boutiques, trickling *isn't-that-cute*s in their wakes. I thought: *Change the highway signs pointing toward HUMANSDORP and MOSSELBAI to read SAN CLEMENTE and LA JOLLA, and any parachuting adventure travelers dropped here would guess it was Laguna Beach, California.* Still, the illusion only went so far: while I ate a pineapple, ham, and mushroom pizza at a pizza parlor, a flatbed truck with thirty black laborers standing in back lumbered past. In Laguna Beach they all would have been Latinos.

In late afternoon I walked to the edge of town and tried hitching; no one stopped, but the view and the air were so intoxicating that I didn't mind. Around dusk I climbed to a motel atop a nearby hill. At about US$25 this was by far the costliest lodging of my trip, but it was worth it. From my deck I had a view of the semicircular bay, a line of windbent pines, and eucalyptus groves. I watched the sun set and stars appear over the Indian Ocean, and for the second night in a row I slept in a double bed under crisp, ironed sheets.

No bushes for this hitchhiker.

There are days in San Francisco, most often in September, when the air is so exceptionally clear that it seems each ray of light has been strained through crystals, and the next morning in Plett was such a day. From my deck I looked out at the navy blue water, cobalt sky, and forested green mountains, and felt the cool air tickle my bare arms and legs. Cape Town could wait a few hours.

I walked through Plett's seaside villas down to the public beach. A row of catamarans sat on the sand, above the tide marks. A teenager at a kiosk rented out umbrellas and sold cold drinks. Offshore a young man hummed across the water on a jetski. Along the water's edge a man with an office worker's paunch and skin as white as typing paper poked at a beached, three-foot sand shark, and ordered his young son, "Get yaw finguz from its mouth."

I stopped at the ten-story Big Island Hotel, Plett's first-class resort, to use the bathroom. The Big Island was built on a rocky point jutting out into the sea, and this morning large waves were smashing the rocks and sending fountains of spray twenty feet into the air. A black valet stood at the hotel's entrance, and in the lounge chairs around the swimming pool white guests struggled from prone positions to reclining ones in order to accept drinks served by black waiters.

Back on the beach, I looked for signs designating this beach as either open to all or closed to some, but saw none. White families ringed their coolers with beach towels, like pioneers circling their wagons. Bikinied blondes read glossy magazines, and two men with skin the color of chocolate milk—"blacks" in America, "coloureds" here—had built themselves sand backrests to facilitate girl watching. Their surfer trunks, dark glasses, and washboard stomach muscles would have fit right in on any Southern California beach. But I saw no sign of the crazed, naked blacks from O'Boyle's diatribe, and I wondered if he'd actually seen the sights he'd described or merely feared them.

56
Under Budget

Each of us is given some seventy years, a decent amount of time...
In that time you shouldn't be afraid to take out a year or two or even
more to do something not in the straight path you originally chose...
to watch the slow turning of the stars and clouds and strange peoples.

—TED KERASOTE, *Navigations*

In 1984, seeking distance from a failing marriage, I flew from San Francisco across the rounded blue Pacific, took a leisurely bike tour through the quiet Japanese Alps, and later rode slow boats and slower buses through a dreamy Chinese landscape of tombstone-shaped mountains and wide, meandering rivers.

In Beijing I boarded the Trans-Siberian railroad and spent the warm heart of July traversing the great blooming grasslands of Mongolia and Siberia. More trains, more boats, and my thumb transported me from Moscow across Europe to London, and an airplane put me back in the States. I drove a car across the green Appalachians and rolling amber waves of the Great Plains, over the high passes and dry deserts of the American West, and finally, on a warm evening in late August, approached San Francisco.

Speeding across the Bay Bridge with my window down, I saw the most remarkable panorama of the entire trip. A spectacular golden sunset had turned the Bay Area into a pop-up fantasy from a children's book, with the pyramid-shaped Transamerica Building jutting among the city's highrises, and the whitewashed homes on Telegraph Hill standing brightly against the royal blue waters of the bay. In the distance, the graceful span across the Golden Gate looked like the drawbridge to a magic kingdom, and beneath it a huge cargo ship trailed a V-shaped wake as it steamed toward the open Pacific. The clouds turned pink, then orange, then crimson, and I wound my way back to the Haight-Ashbury a happy man, secure in the knowledge that mine was the prettiest city in the world.

Now, years later, to my surprise and grudging delight, I met Cape Town. Perhaps I should not have been surprised: four hundred years ago Sir Frances Drake wrote, "This Cape is the most stately thing, and the Fairest in the whole circumference of the earth."

Cape Town had constant reminders for me of San Francisco: tongues of fog licking the landscape in the evening; ships sailing in and out of the busy port; and, just offshore, Robben Island Prison —Cape Town's answer to Alcatraz, and the recent home of Nelson Mandela.

The city's architecture was quaint and interesting, and small blocks of colonial-era buildings surrounded its cobblestone center, Greenmarket Square. A tunnel of tall oaks formed Government Avenue —a half-mile pedestrian promenade lined with park benches and carpeted with fallen yellow leaves. Its sides were flanked by botanical gardens, and by a colonial Parliament building now converted into an art museum.

But Cape Town's most incomparable and unforgettable feature is Table Mountain, a gray marble plateau rising 3,000 feet right up out of the city. By day it is a constant noble presence; at night spotlights cast a dramatic glow on its sheer face. Each time I saw it I half-expected to see it rise like a theater curtain.

Late in the afternoon on the day of my arrival, I hiked up a trail etched into Table Mountain's face. The summit afforded a stunning view of the Indian and Atlantic oceans, of fog rolling in from Cape Point, the tip of Africa, thirty kilometers to the south, and of the green hills of Africa stretching away to the north. A display map showed distances from the other cities of the world; at 10,239 miles I was about as far as I could get from San Francisco without leaving the planet. But the clean ocean air had a familiar taste and caress, and when I closed my eyes and inhaled, I might as well have been standing outside the Cliff House in San Francisco.

I rented a room in a Victorian guest house occupied mostly by elderly pensioners. One evening I went out for pizza with the guest house's only other "youngster," a lighthearted English backpacker named Angela. When she left the next morning to catch a boat to St. Helena Island—a speck of British territory in the mid-Atlantic—I realized how little time I'd spent in the company of women since leaving home, and just how much I'd missed that.

Sometimes in Cape Town, I found myself missing hitchhiking. Conversation, so easy to come by on the road, was sporadic here. Cities that want to attract visitors should, I thought, place booths staffed by ordinary citizens every few blocks. A cab driver, say, or a househusband, a beauty queen, a homeless person (give him or her something to do), a teenager, a school teacher, a doctor, a lawyer, a butcher, a baker... Sometimes a stranger just wants someone to talk to, someone to ask, "Hey, what's it like to live here?" Or: "What's the best thing that ever happened to you?" Maybe I would inaugurate such a system back in San Francisco. On the other hand, I thought, maybe cab drivers and bartenders already perform that service.

By day I took long, invigorating walks around Cape Town or out to the beach at Camp's Bay for the afternoon. I spent one evening at the Stuttaford Cinema watching another old movie I'd missed, *The Milagro Bean Field Wars*, and another in my room, where I leafed through the nine small notebooks I'd filled during the last fourteen weeks.

Like all my trips, this one had been the best. And it had certainly been my healthiest. I'd suffered the brief, almost predictable bout of Indian dysentery, but had dodged malaria, bilharzia, lions, and the rest of Africa's perils. Along the way my back pain had diminished to the point that I could once in a while skip a day of stretching. I wondered how much credit to assign to Brother Casuga, how much to exercise, and how much to the cosmos.

Somehow I had finished my trip slightly under budget. Hotels, food, books, newspapers, taxis, buses, trains, bicycles, phone calls to America, and money given to beggars had cost me $2,460—or $24.60 a day. I still had my $300 splurge/emergency fund, plus an extra $40.

And I felt that I was coming home with a head of steam. In New York I would see, for the first time, a copy of my first book. In a few short weeks it would be in bookstores everywhere. If it made me wealthy (anything is possible, I kept telling myself), I would not pick just one person to invite to America—I'd invite everyone I'd connected with and we would tour the country in an old school bus.

On the last day of my trip I rode the train from Cape Town toward Cape Point—passing through suburbs of ranch style homes, and skirting the shore of False Bay. Clean ocean air poured through my open window. At the Steenberg station a white conductor came through the car checking tickets; he took the elbow of a black boy, who apparently had been riding without a ticket and without money, and led him away. It occurred to me that if this were my first morning in South Africa I might have thought to intervene, to pay the boy's fare. But in only ten days I'd already made some accommodations to the system. It was big. I was small. I was going home tomorrow. He was going to have to learn this lesson by himself.

At Muizenberg waves splashed onto bayside boulders barely twenty feet from my seat. A shirtless man, reading a fat book, lay in the sand with his head propped on a rock. At Kalk Bay, boats were drydocked for spray cleaning—and possibly, I thought, for caulking.

In Fish Hoek I rented a bicycle. My map showed that Cape Point was roughly 35 kilometers away—a round trip of 70 kilometers (44 miles). It was now eleven-thirty in the morning, and the bike had to be returned by five that afternoon. Five hours at 9 miles an hour would leave me half an hour at Cape Point. No problem, I thought: *I'm in shape*.

But two minutes out of Fish Hoek I rounded a curve and slammed into an impossible headwind. Even in first gear, the most imperceptible upgrade forced me to stand on my pedals and grind away. Before long the skin on my face and legs was buffed raw, and my right knee had developed a painful click. It took nearly an hour to ride the 6 kilometers to the village of Simon's Town, and another hour to cover the 6 to Miller's Point. Beyond Miller's Point the landscape was gorgeous—whitecapped ocean on the left, windswept cliffs to the right—but the gale was maddening. All I could hear was the rabble of wind in my ears.

Shortly after two o'clock I saw a sign that read CAPE POINT—21K. I immediately dismounted and stuck out my thumb. The first vehicle to pass was an orange pickup truck, driven by a man named Gerald. I thanked him profusely when he put my bike inside his camper shell.

Gerald was a draftsman from Johannesburg, but recently he'd been working on a new industrial complex being installed at Mossel Bay. The project was paying him twice his regular monthly salary, so he'd gotten into the habit of working two weeks and taking two off—"to see some of this country of mine." He was thirty-nine years old, and this was his first trip to Cape Town.

The road soon tilted sharply upward, validating my decision to abandon the ride. We passed a DO NOT FEED THE BABOONS sign, and then the baboons themselves—reddish brown beasts chasing one another across the road, or standing on hind legs to accept potato chips from the carload of tourists stopped in front of us.

At the entrance to Cape Point Nature Preserve, Gerald insisted on paying my two-rand admission. A wind ripped at the bills as he passed them to the ranger, a black man. We crossed a windswept stretch of scrubland and passed a deserted restaurant and several rock outcroppings. The road ended at a parking lot occupied by three other cars. Gerald said, "Congratulations, mate," and pulled two cold beers from his cooler.

When we had drunk them, we got out and began climbing the last hill. "Three months ago I couldn't have done this," Gerald said, screaming to be heard above the wind. He stopped, leaned down, and pointed out a small red scar on his right knee. "Cartilage operation. It used to lock up on me. I'd be walking with someone and they'd say, 'Do you hear a grinding noise?' A hundred years ago I'd have just been stuck with it, but now it's good as new. Like magic."

A series of stone steps brought us to the Cape Point summit. Wind sang through the girders of a truncated steel tower whose top section appeared to have blown off into the sea. As wide as the Mediterranean in the north and as the Sahara in the middle, Africa tapers to a rocky tail in the south. Cliffs fell dramatically away all around us. Below, to the left, waves from the Indian Ocean crashed onto the coast of Africa; and, to the right, waves from the Atlantic.

The only other person at the top was an American panning a video camera across the horizon. His name was Ted. He wore a GOLD's GYM t-shirt, and was the first American I could recall talking to since Linda at Victoria Falls. Forty years ago, Ted's relatives had fled Russia; half had gone to Miami, half to South Africa, and this, Ted's trip, was the first contact between them. The South African clan was a wild bunch, he said. The grandmother, a woman in her eighties, had told him a ribald joke at the dinner table last night, and now, laughing uproariously, Ted repeated it for Gerald and me. But the wind was so loud that I missed most of it, and by the time I got back to my notebook I could only remember the punch line: "He's not pissing in the refrigerator again, is he?"

Ted was on the fourth day of a two-week vacation, and said he was ecstatic about how far his dollars went in South Africa.

"It's awful," Gerald said. "None of us can travel. Did you hear that our Prime Minister and our Minister of Finance once shared the Nobel Prize for chemistry?"

"No!" I said.

"Yes," Gerald said, "it seems they were the chaps who discovered a way to turn the rand to shit."

Ted asked me, "When did you leave home?"

"I'm on a one-hundred-day trip," I told him. "This is day ninety-nine. Tomorrow morning I have a plane to catch."

"A hundred days!" he said. "I begged my boss for a month off, but the most he would go was two weeks. I would kill for a month, but a hundred days off..." He squinted and looked out at the thin white clouds that the wind had banished to the southern horizon, down toward Antarctica. "Where all have you been?" he asked me.

I told him.

"Oh, man," he said, almost moaning. "I hope you realize how lucky you are."

"I do," I said. "I certainly do."

57

The Choice

Namwa asked me if I had been to Abidjan.

I said that I had.

"Then you have seen the ocean. The ocean sounds like this," she said quietly and began to imitate perfectly the soft swishing sound of surf breaking on shore...

"Then you've been to Abidjan, too, Namwa!..."

"No," she said sadly. "I have never seen the ocean. But my second husband went and he came back and told me how it sounds." And she made the sound again, so perfectly, of one wave after another breaking, foaming, and subsiding on a shore she would never see.

—CAROL SPINDEL, *In the Shadow of the Sacred Grove*

Within a few months of returning home I had learned firsthand one of the primary truths of authorship: few authors survive on the proceeds of their books. It quickly became apparent that there would be no royalty-financed school bus to load up with visitors and jockey around the country. And no early retirement. To keep food on my table and to save up the money to provide just one of my new friends a trip to America I needed to *work*, brother. Fortunately my back had improved enough so that I could return to cab driving, and I began driving part-time, and writing this book.

And one recent morning—with my manuscript sitting on the edge of my desk, complete but for this epilogue—it was time to choose.

I had tried my best to keep in touch with all the people I'd met. I had sent each of them several letters (always including copies of the photographs I'd taken of him and, as a memory jog, one of myself), but I'm not sure how many got through. None were ever returned as undeliverable, but for some reason I heard back from only four.

Takesure, the restless, color-television-hungry office worker from Zimbabwe, was the first to respond. He wrote a short note in which he said he was interested in hotel managing and catering. Could I please secure for him a scholarship at one of the colleges in America? I responded that securing scholarships was, unfortunately, beyond my abilities, but that I would very much like for us to keep in touch. I never heard from him again.

Tony, my Filipino mountain guide, wrote that his wife had borne their fourth child, and that he had given up his wood-carving shop. He was now hoping to make his living as a full-time guide, and would appreciate any customers I could steer his way. I wrote letters recommending his services and mailed them to guidebook and travel section editors, and sent some money for a birthday party. We exchanged several letters. In one he told me that the land his house sat on was owned by a man who wanted Tony's house moved to someone else's land, or for Tony to buy the land from him for $1,400. I sent Tony $100 and later he wrote that he'd been able to raise the rest and buy the land.

Mahmoud, the donkey-riding Egyptian teenager, who invited me to tea at his home near the Valley of the Kings, finally responded to my fourth letter. He said he had been surprised at not hearing from me earlier, because I had promised to write and send photos. Now he was overjoyed that my letter had arrived. He said he was in good health, but he did have "some needs." Would I please send a shirt, jeans, sun glasses, a pair of sport shoes? He invited me to spend a week in Luxor with his family.

The last person to respond was Honest George, the young Tanzanian with a small store on the slopes of Kilimanjaro. Like Mahmoud, George said that the fourth letter I'd mailed to him was the first to reach him. He asked me to convey his greetings to Dave Stone, the *mzungu* with the Land Rover who drove us to the waterfalls (Dave and Julie now live in Montana with their two young children). George said he was glad to hear I was healthy. He, too, was healthy, and his store was still going well—although it did seem that in Tanzania life got harder and harder every day.

I stood at the window of my study and looked over the tops of the jasmine bushes, past the rows of Victorians in the valley below, toward the bay and the hills—emerald green after the rainy winter. I imagined each of these four coming to America. Wasn't it a shame that I could only afford to invite one? I thought of what my life would have been like had I never gone traveling, had I not wandered into Afghanistan in my early twenties, if I did not have the option, no, the *luxury*, of taking trips. And now I had the gift of travel to pass on to one other person. But whom?

I ruminated through the afternoon and late into the night. Who would most benefit? Whose family could best afford his absence for a month? Whose life might be the least disrupted, the most affected? Around one o'clock in the morning, after having made and changed my decision countless times, I decided to see what Chance had to say about this. I wrote the names Takesure, Tony, Mahmoud, and George on four slips of paper, crumpled each into a ball, and dropped them in a hat. I stirred them around, pulled one out, smiled, and sat down to compose a letter that began *Dear Tony*...

Postscript

"I'm better when I move."
—*The Sundance Kid*

Late on the night of June 7, 2001, Tony emerged from customs at San Francisco International Airport with just two small carry-on bags, one of them filled with exquisite wood carvings and tapestries—gifts for me and my family. We greeted with a solid hug—whiskers brushing whiskers—and I heard Tony chuckling softly, while my own delirious voice squeaked, "Am I dreaming? Am I dreaming?"

We passed a short night at my house, sleeping very poorly, and by seven o'clock the next morning were up walking in the nearby cemetery. Eight years had passed since Tony had received my invitation, twelve since we'd first met. We had traded dozens of letters over the years and knew the general shape of each other's lives. Rhonda and I were an old married couple now, with a four-year-old daughter, Sarah, and had moved to the other side of the bay, to a two-bedroom, one-bath house (Tony found it "huge") in Oakland. Tony and Rita now owned five rice terraces and had five children, the youngest seven. The rice terraces provided basic sustenance, but their oldest child, eighteen, was studying in college in Baguio, and Tony and Rita worried about how to afford schooling for the others.

All along I'd kept Tony posted on the financial quagmire that had kept me from following through sooner on my invitation. I'd dug a $16,000 credit card hole while writing this book, and it wasn't until

1999, just as I'd pulled clear of debt, that I sold the manuscript—for $8,000—and I'd put that aside to pay for his trip.

It took us another year and a half to secure Tony's American visa. He made the nine-hour bus trip from Banaue to Manila six times with nothing to show for it—the high-water mark of his achievement was a conversation with a U.S. Embassy security guard. Finally I contacted the office of Mr. Thomas Pickering, who had lived seven doors up the street when I was a boy—I had delivered Mr. Pickering's newspaper and shoveled snow off his driveway. Now, forty years later, Mr. Pickering was the Undersecretary of State for Political Affairs, the number two man in the U.S. State Department. "It's always nice to hear from someone from the old neighborhood," Mr. Pickering responded, ever the diplomat. The letter he wrote on Tony's behalf made an immediate, high-octane difference.

Now Tony and I sat atop the cemetery's most prominent hill, on the gravestones of Oakland's founding families, looked out across the bay at distant San Francisco, and laughed off our frustrations. All of our worries could wait for one month, while this long-running story of ours finally got a new chapter. I outlined the road trip I had planned for us—San Francisco to Washington, D.C., in a borrowed taxicab. Tony said he was game for whatever I had in mind. Midway across the Pacific he had felt the irrevocable sense that his life would never again be the same—and, at age forty-one, he was open to the idea of change.

We spent the next few days riding cable cars, listening to the urping sea lions at Fisherman's Wharf, and cruising around San Francisco in my taxicab, picking up fares. Tony had expected to see "just mostly whites, plus some few blacks" in America, and was surprised by the all-you-can-imagine soup-and-salad bar that is the Bay Area's populace.

Early one morning, as we walked toward the Powell Street cable car turnaround, I pointed toward a pile of cardboard boxes on the sidewalk.

"What?" Tony said.

"There . . ." I pointed toward what he had not noticed: an almost hidden pair of tennis shoes and a knit-capped head protruding from opposite ends of the pile.

Tony jerked backwards, and a quick *"Sheet!"* escaped him. He reached for his new camera. "I can take picture? At home no one believe. This ... *in America."*

One morning we went walking at Muir Woods National Monument, among 1,000-year-old redwood trees as big around as houses, as tall as rocket ships. On each of the several occasions that we entered forests, Tony seemed to transform, to relax into a natural connection with our surroundings. I like to think that—for a city guy, anyway—I spend a fair amount of time outdoors, but seeing Tony snap into his woodsman trance made me realize that he understood the language of trees and plants and animals in a way I barely knew existed.

Yet he was also at ease socially. In the weeks before his arrival I had come down with a case of world-class jitters—and who can imagine *his*? Would we still like each other? I wondered. Would he miss his quiet mountain home? Would he be comfortable on my turf, with me the guide? But my fears didn't last long. On his third day with us, Rhonda and Sarah and I threw an almost surreal party in our tiny backyard, where Tony had a kind word and a gracious smile for each of our 150 friends and neighbors who came to see him. "Tony can dance with people," he acknowledged, when I remarked on his charm. He was the same intelligent, considerate, straightforward, good-hearted, amusing and unassuming character who had once led me off into the mountains above Banaue for a three-day trek.

The only thing different about Tony—and it was an obvious difference—was his eye. As the wounds from his mugging (Tony referred to the 1988 attack that had put out his eye as "the accident") had healed, and as Tony had aged, the shape of his eye socket had altered. His prosthesis, the plastic eye fashioned in the government hospital in Manila, no longer fit, and seemed to float around in its socket, drifting to the side and pointing upward. The plastic itself was worn: thin layers were peeling away from the larger shell, and the original brown color had yellowed. During those first few days he almost always wore dark glasses or a baseball hat with the brim tugged low.

The first edition of this book was published nine months prior to Tony's arrival, and to promote it I had appeared on National Public Radio. Afterward, people from across the United States telephoned

NPR with offers of free places for Tony and me to stay or to eat, offers of river rafting trips, kayak excursions, amusement park admissions, baseball and festival tickets—more offers than we possibly could have accepted.

But I jumped on the free eye exam offered by Trudy Marin, office manager for a Bay Area eye doctor. On the morning of day four, Dr. John McNamara removed Tony's false eye to have a look.

Tony turned both his healthy eye and his red, raw socket in my direction. "Does it scare you?" he asked.

"No," I said. He was like family now—and what's an eye between brothers?

Dr. McNamara opined that Tony's good eye was plenty strong and that his missing eye seemed to pose no health problems. "But," he said, "you could sure get a better looking prosthesis."

I'd expected a vision test, an infection scan, perhaps some heavy duty cleaning, but *a new eye*! The idea had simply never entered my imagination. Now, with the examination all but finished, I began to ask a few questions.

Dr. McNamara did not make prosthetics, but Trudy dialed Dr. Steven Young, a renowned ocularist and faculty member at Stanford University, and told him our story. Dr. Young was booked full for the next six months, but said he would try to squeeze Tony in. To craft a new, snug-fitting, state-of-the-art prosthesis to match Tony's good eye would require three office visits during the next week. "Does your schedule allow for that?" Trudy asked me.

My plan had us leaving the Bay Area the very next morning, loading up our taxicab to head for the beaches, valleys, mountains, and the great beckoning plains that stretched toward the Atlantic. But what dimwit could ignore the eclipsing importance of a new eye? I gave a single nod toward Trudy, and whispered, "What'll it cost?" Already, half of my book advance was spent or spoken for.

"Seventeen hundred dollars," she said. "No credit cards."

Anyone who thinks in terms of life-as-story, who fantasizes that he can wander like his own legend across the earth, cannot for a moment tolerate the possibility of, years later, reminiscing: "Yeah, we saw the Grand Canyon and Las Vegas and New York City—but, geez, if we'd only had an extra $1,700 we might have *really* made a difference in Tony's life."

I nodded at Trudy a second time. At my side, Tony gasped.

Half an hour later, as we ate lunch in a nearby Filipino deli, Tony broke a long silence. "Brad," he said, clearly troubled, "I must tell you. For myself, you know I would love this new eye. But, really, for my family, it will be better . . . The amount . . . Seventeen hundred. I have to tell you. This is same amount for trike."

A trike—a 155cc Honda motorcycle with sidecar—the basic form of transport in steep, rugged Banaue. Tony's rice terraces and his house were two and a half miles from Banaue, a half-dollar fare with a trike driver, and none of the ten Tocdaan siblings had ever owned a trike. Acquiring one would mean not just transportation for Tony, but also financial security for Rita and the kids. With a trike, Tony would become able—like me—to earn a living hauling fare-paying customers around the area. With a trike, he would have better access to prospective trekkers, plus the means to shuttle them to the trailhead.

"For my family," Tony said. "I would rather. Is better."

We fell quiet again. "We're getting the eye," I announced, several well-chewed bites later. "And I'll figure some way to get the trike, too."

That afternoon, in a raw emotional state—*A new eye . . . a new trike . . . $3,400!*—we drove to Novato, half an hour north of San Francisco, to accept another generous offer: a ride in a private plane. We climbed into pilot Scott Sims' rattly little four-seater, a Beechcraft Bonanza built in 1949, and bobbed up to 3,500 feet to clear the pine-coated hump of Mt. Tamalpais. We soared out over the Pacific, made a left turn, south, along the coastal cliffs, with all my favorite Pt. Reyes hiking trails traced like spiderwebs in the woods beneath us. Nearing San Francisco we made another left turn and buzzed through the towers of the Golden Gate Bridge—lower than the towertops, just above the deck of traffic. Below I could easily distinguish the faces of individual drivers, tilting upward to glimpse our plane.

"Is this legal?" I asked Scott.

"It's only illegal to fly *under* the bridge," Scott said. "But this is fine."

Fine, indeed!

We sailed over Alcatraz, puttered across the Bay to peer down on my Oakland neighborhood, and then spent the next hour cruising clear across the state of California to touch down at Lake Tahoe. The snow streaking the Sierras was the first snow Tony had ever seen.

On the return flight Scott said, "Tony, want to fly?"

And while I gaped from the back seat, Tony—smooth and unawed, and following Scott's instructions—gripped the auxiliary controls, began experimenting with the steering wheel and then massaging the foot pedals.

Moments later, curious, I called out, "Scott—who's flying?"

Scott lifted his idled hands away from his lap and his feet up off the floor. Four days after the first airplane flight of his life, Tony was now in control of his second. Scott coached him through a descent from 5,000 feet down to 800, and for more than fifteen minutes Tony skimmed us at 200 miles an hour over the small towns, the two-lane roads, the power lines and windmills, the green and yellow quilt of crops in California's Central Valley.

To keep our appointments with Dr. Young, Tony and I stuck close to the Bay Area for another week. We spent a day hiking at Pt. Reyes and made a two-night trip to Harbin Hot Springs, the backwoods, clothing-optional community where Rhonda and I originally met. Tony quickly became comfortable with, and appreciative of, the sight of so many casually naked men and women bathing together. Later, when friends of mine would ask what had most impressed him about America, Tony would invariably reply, "Muir Woods." A pause, a smile: "And Harbin Hot Springs."

It was a privilege for me to be present when Dr. Young installed the work of art that is Tony's new eye, a near-identical twin to his natural eye, and to then observe the gradual recharging of Tony's pride and self-esteem. His sunglasses began to make fewer and fewer appearances, and Tony began to routinely meet strangers face-to-face. Before long the baseball cap gave way to a Clint Eastwood–style leather cowboy hat. And when I learned that Tony fancied leather motorcycle jackets, I took him shopping in the secondhand stores in San Francisco's gayest neighborhood, the Castro. His sense of style was as finely calibrated as his sense of the outdoors, and we inspected many dozens of jackets—to me, all pretty much the same—before he found one that was just right.

As we were driving back to Oakland, Tony said, "The nice man, older, the one who give us the discount, you think he is gay?" I told him that everyone in the store was almost certainly gay, most of the people we saw in the neighborhood were almost certainly gay, and, for the record, anyone who had observed us—a tallish white guy a few months from turning fifty and a shortish Filipino shopping in a leather store—could quite fairly have assumed that I was a gay man dressing up my imported Asian lover. Tony turned to read my face—was I putting him on?—and then he laughed and laughed and laughed the laughter of enlightenment.

Before we left the Bay Area, my cell phone rang. A cab driver friend, Patrick Shannon, had just finished reading my book. "Tony must need some dental work," Patrick intuited. "Take him to my cousin in Red Bluff. He's a dentist. He'll do whatever needs to be done."

So we drove two and a half hours north to Red Bluff. Over the course of two days, Tony spent seven hours tipped back in a dental chair, while Dr. Skiffington Peters did who-knows-how-many thousands of dollars' worth of dental wizardry, including three root canals, and never once mentioned money. The mugging had left three of Tony's teeth loosened, blackened, and with massive infections, but by the time we left Dr. Peters' office those teeth were no longer wobbly, but anchored—and they were white and perfectly shaped.

We were eating chicken and rice in a Chinese restaurant in Red Bluff when my cell phone rang again. The Philippine ambassador to the United States had seen a front-page story in the *Christian Science Monitor* about our impending cross-country taxicab ride. Now he was inviting Tony and me to an embassy reception in our honor when we reached Washington.

I soon took to answering my cell phone: "Surprise me!" And after the BBC called from London to request an interview with the two of us, surprising me became difficult. Several other media outlets sought us out, and after each encounter Tony would criticize his performance, pointing out things he wished he'd said. "This all new to me," he apologized.

"Hey," I said. "This isn't my normal life, either."

We spent the first night of our cross-country trip at an inn atop a seaside cliff along the Big Sur Coast, south of San Francisco. We sat on our private deck and watched the dome of evening sky seemingly drip with splashings from successively hurled buckets of tangerine and crimson and burgundy paint. That night we slept with open windows, the sounds of crashing surf and barking seals enlivening our dreams. Dawn found us hiking a spongy trail to a waterfall in a hushed and glistening redwood canyon, all our own that morning.

We spent that night with Tony's dumbfounded cousin, Leo, in a hardscrabble section of Los Angeles. Leo had recently heard a rumor that Tony might be coming to America—to visit a cab driver or something—but when we showed up, the look on Leo's face said that he had not believed it. Leo's wife and three children were still in the Philippines, and the year he'd passed in America without them had been a lonely one. Leo and ten other Filipinos shared a cramped, ramshackle apartment, and I was glad that Tony got a chance to see and hear stories—in his own language—about the hard lives many immigrants lead in America. The group consensus, Tony said, was that all of them would prefer to live in the Philippines, but with the sort of opportunities for income they could find only in America.

Two evenings later we passed four dreamy hours watching the light fade from the sky over the Grand Canyon, then drove through a moonless night across Arizona's vast Navajo reservation, to be in position for dawn at Monument Valley. Already on this trip we'd discussed an encyclopedia of topics: skin color, racism, our kids, religion, our wives, sex, birth control, our favorite old girlfriends, our biggest mistakes, how much money each of us earned. That night, after singing along to a tape of cowboy songs—"Red River Valley," "Home on the Range"—

we talked about our futures. How might this trip change our lives? Would we ever see each other again? Tony said Rhonda and Sarah and I would be welcomed anytime in Banaue. He and Rita would love to cook for us—he thought that some of Rita's dishes were as good as any in Banaue. I asked if they had ever considered becoming lodgekeepers. He said that sometimes he and Rita mused about their house being ideally situated for a guesthouse. Visitors who step out the front door invariably gasp: ancient, silent rice terraces descend hundreds of feet to the river and rise in stacks up the nearby mountains. "Rice terraces are my television," Tony said.

Since leaving San Francisco, I'd occasionally noticed him studying his face in the sun visor mirror. Now, as our headlights swept across the empty two-lane Arizona highway, we talked about what his family might make of his new appearance. Tony said he was eager to find out. We revisited the story of his mugging, and my gut lurched when Tony told me that he'd initially been left for dead at the side of the road. For maybe fifteen minutes he had lain in a bloody, leaking heap while a group gathered nearby, smoking, talking, until someone noticed, "Hey, he's breathing!"

For twenty-four hours Tony was shuttled, unconscious, between clinics around Banaue, where almost nothing was done for him. The clinicians simply filibustered, waiting for the fundless rice farmer to die. Finally Rita located the American missionary, Marc, whose family had once gone trekking with Tony. Marc and Rita laid Tony on a mattress in the back of Marc's pickup truck and the three of them drove to Manila, saving Tony's life.

So many factors had had to line up to put Tony and me in the front seat of this taxi. Over the next few days—as we rolled out of Arizona, through the Colorado Rockies, and onto the plains of Kansas ("Is just *flat!*" Tony said, sounding swindled, seventy-eight miles east of Denver)—I found myself wondering more and more about Marc. Was he out on another mission, or back in America? Might our route bring us near his home?

But Tony had completely lost track of Marc and his family after they left the Philippines in 1992—and he remembered only first names. In Kansas City I posted a plea on my Web site: "Does anyone know a Seventh Day Adventist missionary named Marc who was married to Aunie, and who was in the Philippines in 1988?"

Trudy Marin, the woman who had arranged Tony's eye exam, called almost immediately with another cell phone surprise. "I was raised Seventh Day Adventist," she said. "I know the grapevine. I'll find him." Twelve hours later, as we sped toward St. Louis at seventy miles per hour, Tony had a twenty-minute cell phone conversation with Marc Scalzi, who now lived in Idaho. They chatted about their kids and their wives, about mutual acquaintances in Banaue, about this improbable trip of Tony's, and toward the end Tony said, "Marc, I must thank you for what you did. I owe you for my life."

When they were finished, I took the phone: "Marc, if I can arrange free airplane tickets and a free hotel room, can you and Aunie come to San Francisco next Saturday night? It will be Tony's last night in America, and we'll be having a bonfire on Ocean Beach."

Marc and Aunie had just scheduled a vacation for the following week, to go camping near home. But San Francisco . . . Tony . . . Yes, he said. Yes!

In St. Louis we rode to the top of the Arch, and three days later, in New York City, rode to the top of the Empire State Building. Tony seemed magnetically drawn to the streets of New York—"You can walk everywhere here!"—and on the Staten Island Ferry he used up nearly a whole roll of film on the fabled New York skyline. One night while we were flying down a freeway toward Queens, he made a cell phone call to an aunt in the Philippines. Warm air rushed through the open windows. Bridges and tall, yellow-lit office buildings loomed on all sides. In Tony's excited Ifugao I heard the phrases *cell phone*, *taxicab*, *New York City*, and *Statue of Liberty*.

As we had crossed the country, Tony had expressed trepidation about our date at the Philippine Embassy. He worried about what he might find in common with a swarm of diplomats, and suggested we cancel. "You have seen my life at home," he told me, accusingly. "Very simple."

I recommended that we not renege: "If you go back to Banaue and tell people the Ambassador invited you to the Embassy and you said no, they'll chase you right out of town—maybe right out of the Philippines!"

He recognized the truth in my ribbing, but remained uneasy right up to the moment our taxi rolled past the Washington Monument and the White House, swung onto Massachusetts Avenue and pulled through the embassy gates. Embassy staffers crowded the windows to get a look at the mismatched pair inside and to bear incredulous witness to the $20,644.90 showing on the meter.

Tony was immediately disarmed by the Ambassador, Mr. Ariel Abadilla. "I ask what to call him," Tony told me later, "and he says, 'Please! Don't call me Sir. Don't call me Ambassador. Use my name—Ariel.'" Toward evening's end Tony took the stage, alone, unprodded, and danced his own tribal dance. "I think they should see real Ifugao dance," he told me.

"I have been here two years and have seen many receptions," a high-ranking woman diplomat told me. "Politicians, judges, scholars, celebrities. But this is the best yet. A rice farmer and a cab driver—we have never had so much fun."

We flew back to San Francisco—another cab driver flew to Washington to retrieve the taxi—and on Tony's last night in America a hundred people came to his going-away bonfire. Marc and Aunie were there, beaming. One enthused reader flew all the way from Wisconsin to meet Tony and me. A former Peace Corps volunteer in the Philippines drove 500 miles from Los Angeles to present Tony with a gift both he and Tony knew would come in handy back in Banaue: a brand new circular saw. Toward midnight someone pulled out a guitar and Tony played and sang a haunting Ifugao song, while the fire's embers lit up his face, and the Pacific swished behind him.

As I write these words, almost seven weeks have passed since Tony disappeared into the San Francisco International Terminal with a last wave of his cowboy hat. Inside his sock were twenty-one $100 bills—the trike money, plus a little. We've spoken by phone several times since then, and Tony says he's doing just fine—he and Rita and the kids recently completed their rice harvest, he's looking forward to the winter tourist season—but he reflects constantly on our trip. "It is hard to appreciate while I am there," he told me. "Now I know how special it is."

Sometimes I consider the images—chatting with the ambassador, soaking at Harbin Hot Springs, or floating 5,000 feet above the Central Valley—that might parade through Tony's mind while he's up to his calves in paddy muck or while he's hanging out near the viewpoint, wondering if any tourists will happen by. I hope our rich one-month diet didn't spoil his appetite for his old life, but I shouldn't count on that—the downshift back into my own has often been jarring. Last night, as I dutifully maneuvered my taxicab along San Bruno Avenue, an inebriated passenger pounded on the seatback and screamed, "San *Bruno* Avenue! I said take me to *San Bruno Avenue*! Where do you think you're taking me, pal!"

I think it will be months, maybe years, before Tony and I fully understand the impact of our trip. I trust that we will look back as old men and see it as a blessing, and not as the disruption to Tony's life that some had warned me about. There was deceptive power in what we did, trusting in each other and in the idea of his visit. Many times I sensed that what we were experiencing was close to outright magic— and an emphatic validation of the "Travel is the best thing that could ever happen to anyone" mantra I'd chanted as a young man.

I did help Tony get his ticket and his visa, but for a month he *was* my passport to a whole new universe where people with lit up faces were constantly opening their hearts and wallets and saying, "Here, take what you need." Each time we visited friends, or started telling our story to reporters or inquisitive strangers, we saw eyes and cheeks and mouths blossoming into grins. *"Oh, man . . . You guys . . . This is so cool!"* In Washington, D.C., a police officer swaggered over to our illegally parked cab, and—*Surprise me!*—said, "Welcome to America, Tony." He offered his hand through the passenger side window. "I heard you fellows on NPR last night."

My publisher is waiting for this final section, and I know there is a last sentence lurking just up ahead somewhere, but I'm not looking forward to writing it. This project has percolated in my consciousness for twenty-seven years, has dominated it for the past fourteen, and part of me fears that if it ever ends I will simply cease to exist. Maybe that is one factor in my recent decision—after much brainstorming with Tony—to help fund the transformation of his and Rita's home into a four-room guest lodge: once the lodge idea surfaced, it began generating its own momentum. Tony's new circular saw will soon be buzzing madly, and before long his trekking operation will be full-service—a trike, a lodge, a trailhead leading to centuries past. I've never gazed down at the terraces on a full moon night when the shoots are low and the paddies brim with water, but people who have seen this spectacle say it is a heart-stopper. Tony has asked me to invite all the world to come and visit him. If you get there before I do, please, give him my warmest regards.

Brad Newsham
1 September 2001
Oakland, California

To read Brad's dispatches during Tony's visit, visit the author's website at www.bradnewsham.com

Acknowledgments

My wife, Rhonda Gillenwaters, was the first reader/editor of most of this book's manuscript, and her unflinching feedback has spared me much embarrassment.

My pal Blake Rodman, until recently the deft editor of *Teacher Magazine*, has for nearly twenty years been the first professional I send my work to—and his advice has always been perfect.

Beginning in her workshop, in 1986, the novelist Donna Levin helped me learn some of the tools of the writing craft. Literary agent Robert Stricker, sadly an unreformed Dodger fan, has also been in my corner for a long time now.

My friends and writing group colleagues, Donal Brown, Margaret Cuthbert, Marilyn Day, Bruce Hartford, Kristi Hein, Bob Hunt, Donna Gillespie, Waimea Williams, John Winch, and Leigh Anne Varney all gave important input to the manuscript.

The laughter I've shared with my mother, Margaret Newsham, and my siblings, Nancy Orcutt, Scott Newsham, and Grant Newsham, has meant the world to me. Also, Gloria Gillenwaters, Randy Gillenwaters, and Ellen Grady have supplied kinship laced with a valued and raucous friendship.

Steve Van Vleck, my first international travel partner, helped me wet my feet in 1973. And while I like to think the indomitable Bird Nietmann wouldn't have made it to Afghanistan without me, I *know* I wouldn't have made it there without him.

From my friendships with Diana, Jon, Drew, and Mason Bradley Van Vleck; David, Nancy, Stefan, and Maggie Ruenzel; Mark and Shawn Rosenmoss; Frank DeWitt; Charlie Piot; Bob and Nancy Whittlesey; and many others, I have drawn vital personal sustenance.

*   *   *

I consider it my tremendous good fortune to have had this book originally published by Travelers' Tales, the creative offspring of James O'Reilly, Sean O'Reilly, Tim O'Reilly, and Larry Habegger. I particularly salute James O'Reilly and Larry Habegger, the day-to-day nurturers of the series; I am but one of several hundred writers who are the happy beneficiaries of their remarkable quarter-century friendship.

Lisa Bach deserves special mention, as she was the manuscript's first Travelers' Tales reader, and the one whose enthusiasm lit the fire.

Also, at Travelers' Tales, I have had the warm pleasure of being assisted by Susan Brady, Deborah Greco, Krista Holmstrom, Jennifer Leo, Christine Nielsen, Wenda O'Reilly, Tanya Pearlman, and Tara Weaver. Several others, including Melanie Haage, Trigg Robinson McCloud, Elizabeth Oakley, and Michele Wetherbee, also made much-appreciated contributions to the book.

Kathy Meengs of Travelers' Tales flung herself into the promotion of this book as though she had written it herself; Debi Echlin, Helen Talley, and Carolyn J. Johnson of 2nd Edition Books in Oakland, pressed copies into the hands of more than five hundred of their customers; and the independent booksellers of America voted it onto their Booksense '76 list, which is where Anika Streitfeld of Ballantine first noticed it, and took it under her enthusiastic wing. For these unrepayable acts I will be forever indebted.

Countless thousands in foreign countries have extended aid and hospitality to me during my years of travel, and I was ecstatic at the way people from all over America did the same for Tony. Friends and complete strangers alike fell all over themselves to add something special and personal to his (and my) experience.

Scott Sims' airplane excursion took our trip to a whole new level. Our ride from sea to shining sea was made luxurious and extraordinary by Jamie Maddox of Service! Taxis in San Francisco. When Jamie heard about our trip he called me and said, "I'm buying a new cab, and while Tony's here you can drive it as far as you want."

Trudy Marin could have only been a godsend—her eye exam offer and her detective work resulted in what were, to me, miracles. Dr. John

McNamara gave us expert steering, and Rene and Dr. Steven Young cleared their busy schedule to make Tony's beautiful new prosthesis. Patrick Shannon, Denise Peters, Dr. Skiffington Peters and Sherry Smith teamed up to give Tony the incomparable gift of dental work. My gallant brother Grant sprang for domestic airplane tickets for me and Tony, and for Marc and Aunie Scalzi to fly down from Idaho. Michael Pace, general manager of the cozy Monticello Inn in San Francisco, graciously donated a slew of hotel rooms. Greg and Susan Cockcroft and Peter Nicholson at Pt. Reyes Seashore Lodge mistook Tony and me for royalty. In Las Vegas, the divine singer Dina Emerson of Cirque du Soleil gave Tony and me VIP treatment. At their homes in Washington, D.C., and Denver, my mother, Margy, and sister Nancy threw warm welcoming parties. David and Marilee Muchow bought running shoes or hiking boots for Tony's entire family—and they all fit perfectly! Daryt and Mina Frank motored up from Los Angeles to present Tony with a circular saw. James O'Reilly gave a new camera to Tony, and my pals Anne Marshall, Jennifer Evans, and Lori Jo Smith bought one for Tony's wife. When Jacques and Julie LaBelle learned that Tony's old Seiko wristwatch had been stolen in the Philippines, they replaced it with a gleaming new one. Bob Whittlesey, whose rave reviews of the rice terraces propelled me to Banaue in 1988, made a batch of stunning calling cards for Tony. Lenny Brandreit and Mark Giorgi provided invaluable technical and Web support. Robb and Peggy Moretti and Mike Ayer pitched in San Francisco Giants baseball tickets. Along our route we enjoyed the warm hearths of Leo Candelaria; Bird Nietmann; Tim, Karen, and Emily Jennings; Margie, Hank, and Jennifer Hamlin; Jim Pona; Lark Rodman; and George Wright. Tony asked me to give special thanks to the Honorable Thomas R. Pickering, of course, and to Rona Marech, Brad Knickerbocker, Robert Harbison, Lisa Simeone, Tracy Wahl, Abdullah Rufus, Alex Cota, and, again, Jamie Maddox of Service! Taxi.

There is no equitable way to thank Ambassador Ariel Abadilla and the many others, including Patricia Paez, Bing Cardenas-Branigin, Jennie Ilustre, and Mercedes Andrei, who made our visit to the Philippine Embassy so phenomenal. Nor to thank my mother-in-law, Gloria

Gillenwaters, and my wife, Rhonda, for lavishing love on Sarah while I was off with Tony.

Carl Lennertz, Peter Handel, Amy Orcutt, Steve Zeppelin, Ashley Orcutt, Charles and Doris Bohrer, Susie Whittlesey, Carl McMurdo, Bette McNeil, Juliette Sarmiento, Shellie Hatfield, Martin Buchbender, Ross Graham, Alan Cohen, Raphael Stricker, Janet Jensen, Donna Roberts, Laurie Armstrong of the San Francisco Visitors and Convention Bureau, and Sadie Mayne of Transworld Publishers in the U.K. all boosted us along our way. Also, I would especially like to thank Diane Meacham for creating this edition's stunning, transcendent cover. I must beg the pardon of the hundreds of others whose names I simply haven't the space to mention here, but please know that Tony and I both appreciate your generosity.

My deepest gratitude and very best wishes go to Tony's wife, Rita Tocdaan, and to their children Lori, Lyn, Franz, Gladys, and Rowel, and to Tony's parents, Pedro and Flora. Thank you for sharing your husband and father and son with me and so many others, and for understanding. He represented you and your country with complete dignity and a memorable flair.

And finally, thank you, Tony, for your warmth and level-headedness and good humor and willingness. You were absolutely perfect.

Mabuhay, kaibigan. Live long, my friend.

KITE STRINGS OF THE SOUTHERN CROSS:
Tales from the South Pacific
by Laurie Gough

'A travelogue tracing a life-changing journey across the globe
. . . Gough's experiences are never less than inspirational and
should encourage the would-be traveller to finally throw off
the shackles of the sofa and take flight around the world'
Wallpaper

Drinking the hallucinogen kava around a campfire, sleeping
in a California redwood or rolled up in a rug, hitchhiking
with an Austrian goatherd, fighting off a cab driver in Kuala
Lumpur, living in a Hare Krishna temple, taking an illicit
dip in Sylvester Stallone's pool . . . From a remote beach in
the South Pacific, Laurie Gough recalls her award-winning
journey across the globe.

On the Fijian island of Taveuni, she falls in love,
but discovers that even paradise has a darker side. In the
Moroccan walled city of Fez, she takes a trip on a magic
carpet of a different kind, on the back of a fanatical souvenir
hunter's motorbike she races across America and in Malaysia
she is pursued by the devil himself.

Lauded by *Time* magazine as one of the new generation of
intrepid young female travel writers, Laurie never shrinks
from the lessons of the open road. Funny, insightful and
inspiring, *Kite Strings of the Southern Cross* will appeal to
free spirits and armchair travellers alike – and to anyone who
has ever dreamt of trying to find heaven on earth.

'Gough is an enchanting guide . . . Passionate and poetic'
San Francisco Examiner

A Bantam paperback
0553 81424 9

Travel books by Peter Moore in Bantam paperback

'Moore has a parched dry wit, the solid *brass cojones* of a true traveller and rare eye for the madness of the wider world'
John Birmingham

NO SHITTING IN THE TOILET
The Travel Guide for When You've Really Lost It

Taking its title from a sign on the loo door of a dodgy café in remotest China and based on his award-winning website, Peter Moore's *NSITT* is not really a *normal* travel guide. Instead of practical hints, it gives you impractical ones; rather than tell you the best place to stay, it singles out the worst, and instead of celebrating transcendental travel experiences, it rejoices in the most demeaning.

0553 81451

THE FULL MONTEZUMA
Peter Moore recently invited the new love of his life, a.k.a. the girl next door, to join him on a romantic sojourn through Central America. The trip would take them into an area of the world emerging from decades of civil war, an area racked with poverty, disease and natural disasters. Naturally, she jumped at the chance.

Written with Moore's eye for the bizarre, and punctuated by a roll call of annoying habits – map-hogging, over packing, bite-scratching and over-zealous haggling – *The Full Montezuma* is a cautionary tale for anyone planning to cross a continent with their significant other.

0553 81335 8

THE WRONG WAY HOME
When Peter Moore announced he was going to travel home from London to Sydney without stepping on to an aeroplane he was met with a resounding Why? The answer was a severe case of hippie envy: hippies had the best music, the best drugs, the best sex. But most of all, they had the best trips.

The Wrong Way Home will strike a chord with anyone who has ventured on such a life-enhancing Grand Tour. It will also entertain (and perhaps alarm) all of those who love to read about such adventures but would never be fool enough to grab their rucksack and go.

0553 81238 6

A SELECTED LIST OF TRAVEL WRITING
AVAILABLE FROM TRANSWORLD

THE PRICES SHOWN BELOW WERE CORRECT AT THE TIME OF GOING TO PRESS. HOWEVER TRANSWORLD PUBLISHERS RESERVE THE RIGHT TO SHOW NEW RETAIL PRICES ON COVERS WHICH MAY DIFFER FROM THOSE PREVIOUSLY ADVERTISED IN THE TEXT OR ELSEWHERE.

81341	2	LIFE IN A POSTCARD	Rosemary Bailey	£7.99
99600	9	NOTES FROM A SMALL ISLAND	Bill Bryson	£7.99
99786	2	NOTES FROM A BIG COUNTRY	Bill Bryson	£7.99
99702	1	A WALK IN THE WOODS	Bill Bryson	£7.99
99808	7	THE LOST CONTINENT	Bill Bryson	£7.99
99805	2	MADE IN AMERICA	Bill Bryson	£7.99
99806	0	NEITHER HERE NOR THERE	Bill Bryson	£7.99
99703	X	DOWN UNDER	Bill Bryson	£7.99
99858	3	PERFUME FROM PROVENCE	Lady Fortescue	£7.99
81424	9	KITE STRINGS OF THE SOUTHERN CROSS		
			Laurie Gough	£6.99
14681	1	CASTAWAY	Lucy Irvine	£6.99
14680	3	FARAWAY	Lucy Irvine	£7.99
14595	5	BETWEEN EXTREMES		
			Brian Keenan & John McCarthy	£7.99
99841	9	NOTES FROM AN ITALIAN GARDEN	John Marble	£7.99
50667	6	UNDER THE TUSCAN SUN	Frances Mayes	£6.99
81250	5	BELLA TUSCANY	Frances Mayes	£6.99
81238	6	THE WRONG WAY HOME	Peter Moore	£7.99
81335	8	THE FULL MONTEZUMA	Peter Moore	£6.99
81451	6	NO SHITTING IN THE TOILET	Peter Moore	£6.99
99852	4	THE ELUSIVE TRUFFLE: Travels in Search of the Legendary Food of France	Mirabel Osler	£6.99

All Transworld titles are available by post from:
Bookpost, PO Box 29, Douglas, Isle of Man IM99 1BQ
Credit cards accepted. Please telephone 01624 836000,
fax 01624 837033, Internet http://www.bookpost.co.uk or
e-mail: bookshop@enterprise.net for details.
Free postage and packing in the UK.
Overseas customers allow £1 per book.